EVERYMAN, I will go with thee, and be thy guide,
In thy most need to go by thy side

EVERYMAN CLASSICS

GEORGE BERKELEY

Philosophical Works
including the works on vision

Introduction and notes by
M. R. Ayers
Wadham College, Oxford

J. M. Dent & Sons Ltd: London
EVERYMAN'S LIBRARY

Made in Great Britain by
Guernsey Press Co. Ltd, Guernsey, C.I. for
J. M. Dent & Sons Ltd
91 Clapham High Street, London SW4 7TA

This work was first published in Everyman's Library under the title
A New Theory of Vision and Other Writings in 1910
New edition, revised and enlarged, 1975
First published in paperback, 1980
Reprinted with minor revisions, 1983
Reprinted 1985
Last reprinted, with revisions and additions, 1989

This book is set in 8 on 9 pt Times New Roman

No 483 Hardback ISBN 0 460 10483 7
No 1483 Paperback ISBN 0 460 11483 2

Contents

Acknowledgments

Texts of the works reproduced in this volume are taken from the complete *Works* of George Berkeley, edited by Professor A. A. Luce and Professor T. E. Jessop, by permission of Thomas Nelson and Sons Ltd. © Thomas Nelson and Sons Ltd, 1948–57.

The text of the Correspondence between Berkeley and Johnson was first published in *Samuel Johnson, His Career and Writings* edited by H. and C. Schneider (New York, 1929), and is included with the permission of Columbia University Press.

Abbreviations

NTV   *New Theory of Vision*
PHK   *Principles of Human Knowledge*
DHP   *Three Dialogues between Hylas and Philonous*
DM   *De Motu*
TVV   *Theory of Vision Vindicated*
PC   *Philosophical Commentaries*
CBJ   *Correspondence between Berkeley and Johnson*
Works   *The Works of George Berkeley*, ed. A. A. Luce and T. E. Jessop

Introduction

George Berkeley, Bishop of Cloyne, was born in Kilkenny, Ireland, in 1685. In 1704 he graduated at Trinity College, Dublin, becoming a Fellow of the college in 1707. Within a very few years he had published his major works on metaphysics, but continued writing on broadly philosophical topics throughout his active life, always from a point of view consonant with his earlier doctrines, and often explicitly in order to explain them, defend them and extend their application. Despite these efforts his thought has often been poorly understood.

1 *The philosophical background*

Descartes' proof of the existence of Matter runs as follows:

> Although no one needs convincing that material objects exist . . . our present task is to examine the rational basis of our certainty. First, our sensations evidently come to us from something which is distinct from our own mind. For we cannot arbitrarily choose to have one sensation rather than another—the outcome plainly depends on the particular thing which is affecting our senses. It is true that we can ask whether that thing is God, or something other than God. Yet we have sensations—or rather we are stimulated by sensation to form a clear and distinct idea—of a certain stuff which is extended in three dimensions, which has various parts with various shapes moving in various ways, and which gives us sensations of colour, odour, pain etc. If God brought [*exhiberet*] the idea of this stuff before our mind immediately and through his own agency, or even if he arranged for it to be brought by the agency of some other thing in which there was no extension, shape or movement, then there would be no rational way of avoiding the conclusion that he is a deceiver. For we have a clear understanding of this stuff as a thing absolutely distinct from God and from ourself or, at least, from our mind. Moreover we have the impression of seeing clearly that our idea of it comes from objects outside us to which it entirely conforms. Now it is plainly contrary to the nature of God that he should be a deceiver. It therefore follows absolutely that there exists a certain substance extended in three dimensions and having all those properties which we clearly perceive must belong to an extended substance. It is this extended substance which we call Body or Matter. (*Principles of Philosophy* II.i).

This argument helped to set the scene for Berkeley's radical, theologically motivated reaction to the mechanic 'New Philosophy' of the seventeenth century. For Descartes, God has given us an innate scientific understanding of the physical world as a vast machine composed of homogeneous Matter but affecting our senses in a variety of ways. The essence of Matter consists in its purely geometrical attribute of extension, which is necessarily connected with its mobility and other general properties. Sensible qualities such as colours and smells (later known as 'secondary qualities') are not intrinsic attributes, but exist only in relation to observers. From the essence of Matter the laws which govern its motions (assuming that they are immutably upheld by God) can be demonstrated *a priori*. Here Descartes was under the influence of the model which dominated the New Philosophy. Particular changes were thought to be in principle intelligible as the motions of clockwork seem to be intelligible: by observing the particular rigid shapes involved and how they fit together, we can conclude how and with what consequences they *must* by their very construction interact. Physical change which appears to be purely qualitative, or otherwise unlike the workings of a clock, does so only because the mechanism involved lies beyond our powers of observation.

Berkeley's response is a fierce denial that we can achieve any sort of clear understanding of 'Matter'. On the contrary, the very idea of an independent material substance is self-contradictory and absurd. He accordingly seized on the other horn of Descartes' dilemma. God does 'immediately and through his direct agency' give us the sensations we have. Not that God thereby deceives us, for these 'ideas of sense' *constitute* the sensible world. Only through philosophical confusion do we take them to point beyond themselves to something other than an intelligent and benevolent agent. Berkeley was not the first to attribute our sensations to God rather than to Matter. Nicolas Malebranche had earlier argued that in sense perception two things happen. The subjective sensations of secondary qualities are produced in us by God in the presence of material things, and at the same time He reveals to our intellect his own ideas of the geometrical or mechanical attributes of these things. This view is part of an extraordinary account of knowledge as direct apprehension of the contents of God's mind, and of omnipotency as the sole true agency in the universe. There are echoes of this doctrine in Berkeley's thought, but, unlike Berkeley, Malebranche questions neither the status of Matter as a substance nor the adequacy of our understanding of its essence and its necessary laws. His concern is to deny it an independent active role in sense-perception and in physical change generally, and to ascribe that role to God. In many respects—even, to some extent, in these—Malebranche remains close to Descartes. Although he rejects the doctrine of innate ideas in favour of the notion that God exhibits his ideas to us immediately, he very much accepts Descartes' distinction between the pure intellect on the one hand and sense and imagination on the other. Knowledge and understanding consist in an intellectual union with God, and our scientific idea of Matter is an object of pure intellect. For all these reasons Berkeley distances himself from Malebranche, and his notion of an 'idea of sense' owes more to John Locke, a philosopher whose doctrinal roots lie largely outside the Cartesian school.

Locke differs from Descartes in several profound respects. Like Descartes he is inclined to accept a dualism of Spirit and Matter, taking thoughts and sensations to be modifications of an immaterial substance. Yet against Descartes the argues that the essence of Spirit or Mind is not consciousness or thought itself, but is something unknown to us. We are aware that we think and have experiences, but have no direct conception of the underlying processes of thought or of the nature of that which thinks. Hence even the presumption of a distinct 'immaterial' substance is open to question, for human thought might be, as Hobbes had asserted, an ultimately material process. How a material mechanism should be capable of thought is beyond our present comprehension, but then so is the alternative hypothesis that Spirit and Matter interact.

Such agnosticism is typical of Locke's position, and it extends to Matter or Body itself. Although he is a mechanist, he denies that we know the ultimate essence of Body. The best available hypothesis he takes to be the theory of minute particles and the void expounded by his teacher and colleague in the Royal Society, Robert Boyle. Matter, on this view, is solid as well as extended. Yet he saw many gaps in Boyle's theory. He finds difficulties, for example, in the communication of motion by impulse, the coherence of atoms and the infinite divisibility of extension. In such passages he concludes that we have as obscure an idea of the determinable essence or, as he puts it, of the 'substance' or '*substratum*' of Matter as we do of the 'substance' of Spirit.

This peculiar use of the terms 'substance' and '*substratum*' is something of a variation upon the Cartesian understanding of the originally Aristotelian concepts of substance and essence. For both Descartes and Locke, the distinction between a substance and its essence is only a distinction of reason, and to know and comprehend the essence *is* to know and comprehend the substance. But Locke holds that the very term 'substance' is a reflection of the limitations of human cognitive faculties. According to him, we use the term to denote an unknown, *whatever it may be* that underlies or 'supports' the properties that we do experience and know: 'the supposed, but unknown support of those qualities we find existing, which we imagine cannot subsist *sine re substante*'.[1] From observation and experiment we can usefully discover a certain significant order at the phenomenal level, which we can understand only as dependable associations among the powers and sensible qualities (the latter understood as powers to affect observers) that things possess. Such powers must be supposed to have a basis in an unperceived reality which falls under a comprehensive system of law and which would be wholly intelligible to beings with adequate faculties.

Thus it is his rationalist belief that there must be a comprehensive

[1] *Essay Concerning Human Understanding* 2.23.2.

explanation of the phenomena, not available to us, that supplies Locke's peculiar explanation of the category of 'substance'. For he tells us that the idea or definition of a specific or determinate substance, such as *gold* or *man*, or of a general or determinable substance, such as *Spirit* or *Matter*, includes not only ideas of the phenomenal properties by which we distinguish instances of the substance, the so-called 'nominal' as opposed to the 'real' essence, but also the idea of a *something* which is unknown. Locke describes it as the 'unknown cause of the union' and as the 'support' of the observable properties or 'accidents'; as the 'common subject' in which they 'co-exist' or 'inhere', and from the 'internal constitution or unknown essence' of which they necessarily 'flow'. In an allusion to the Aristotelian view of substances as logical subjects, he appeals to the verbal form of our definitions of substances: '. . . when we speak of any sort of substance, we say it is a *thing* having such or such qualities: as body is a *thing* that is extended, figured and capable of motion; a spirit, a *thing* capable of thinking . . . These and the like fashions of speaking intimate that the substance is supposed always *something* besides the extension, figure, solidity, motion, thinking or other observable ideas, though we know not what it is.' Thus by a re-interpretation of traditional terminology and theory Locke tries to show that we all have inescapable intuitions which have been wrongly interpreted by earlier philosophers, but which, when clarified, point to his own firmly rationalist, tentatively dualist, but at the same time agnostic account of science and nature.

Locke rejects the Cartesian notion of intellect. 'Ideas' are the constituents of consciousness which represent or symbolize what is being thought about. They are images or distinguishable aspects of images. Reason is never pure, but always operates on sensory data. That such representatives can always be identified Locke assumes even in the case of 'ideas of reflection', when the object of thought is thought itself. It can help us to understand this model for consciousness if we remember his special interest in 'scientific', necessary knowledge, of which geometry was the accepted paradigm. Locke believed that diagrams, whether seen or visualized, play an essential role in geometrical thinking. Without them nothing can really be 'perceived' or grasped. For he takes to an extreme the analogy between sense-perception and the 'seeing' or 'intuition' of conceptual connections. 'Ideas', the representatives of what our knowledge is about, constitute the 'immediate' objects of this rational intuition. Such a visual model for reasoning finds natural expression in the otherwise odd doctrine that knowledge *is* perception, 'consisting in the view the mind has of its own ideas'.[1] For Locke the most important function of 'ideas' is to serve in this way as 'the materials of reason and knowledge'.

Locke was interested in the nature of knowledge because he was interested in its extent and limits. His conception of these limits is

[1]id. 4.2.1.

expressed in the principle that all our ideas are ultimately derived from experience. As we have seen, his agnostic epistemology hinges on the distinction between the sensible or experimentally detectable properties of things on the one hand—their powers to affect us and other things— and the unknown structural properties that explain these powers on the other. There is never, for Locke, any interesting or disturbing general problem about how we get from the ideas given in sensation to knowledge of the existence of their external causes. Scepticism of the senses is given short shrift. Yet our knowledge of external objects is always *mediated* by sense, and so is relative to us and to our sensibility: we do not from sense experience know 'that particular constitution, which everything has within itself, without any relation to anything without it'. Every suggestion in the *Essay* that our knowledge or thought is restricted to our ideas must be understood in this way, i.e. as directed, first, towards emphasizing and explaining the epistemic gap, not between sensations and external objects, but between powers attributed on the basis of their observed exercise on the one hand and intrinsic properties on the other: a gap that exists with respect as much to Mind as to Matter. Locke would allow that, in a sense, this gap can or could be bridged, but, for human beings, by speculation rather than knowledge. His thesis here is that the ideas or concepts employed in such speculation are necessarily restricted to ideas acquired in experience. The mechanist hypothesis itself, of course, is taken to illustrate this thesis.

2   *Ideas and sensible qualities:* esse *is* percipi

Berkeley's logically first move is a paradox: the rejection of any distinction between sensations on the one hand and sensible things or qualities on the other. But it is a paradox that will receive cumulative support from a network of considerations gradually drawn into the argument. In *Principles I* it is first insinuated in an opening paragraph with a pronounced Lockean flavour, in which Berkeley deliberately exploits Locke's frequent, consciously loose use of 'idea' for the *quality* in the object which causes an idea in the perceiver,[1] as well as his occasional, equally loose account of specific substances as 'collections of ideas'.[2] Thus, from the start, Berkeley can allow himself to use the expressions 'ideas', 'sensations', 'sensible qualities', 'sensible things' and 'sensible objects' more or less indiscriminately.

The first proper argument for this usage is his famous appeal to the principle that the *esse* of 'sensible things' is *percipi*. He claims that, if we reflect on the appropriate meaning of 'exists', it is intuitively as unintelligible that sensible qualities and objects should exist unperceived as

[1] Cf. id. 2.8.8.
[2] See id. 2.26.1; cf. PC 179.

that ideas of the imagination should do so: 'There was a sound, that is to say, it was heard.'[1]

This peculiar doctrine, upon which Berkeley was prepared to rest his whole case,[2] deserves careful consideration. First, even if it were 'impossible for me to conceive in my thoughts any sensible thing or object distinct from the sensation or perception of it',[3] it is not clear why the impossibility should be taken to derive from the meaning of the word 'exists'. But a more pressing difficulty arises because the strong claim identifying the existence of a sensible object with the perception of an idea seems to be entangled with a weaker, rather more plausible claim, namely that a sensible object exists only if it is perceived or *would in appropriate circumstances* be perceived: '. . . if I were out of my study I should say (the table) existed, meaning thereby that if I was in my study I might perceive it.'[4] This latter thesis might be taken to imply that 'sensible things' have a kind of being, relative to perception perhaps, but different from that of 'ideas', which cannot exist unless actually before the mind. In other words, Berkeley might seem here to anticipate those modern empiricists who identify sensible objects with 'possibilities of sensation' rather than with sensations themselves.

In the discussion of this question, we should recognize that for these more recent phenomenalists the notion of 'possibilities of sensation' provides an ultimate explanation of the ontological implications of statements about the physical world: for them, there is nothing *behind* such possibilities. But there is no evidence that Berkeley ever even conceived of discarding that fundamental principle of contemporary anti-scholastic rationalism (and common sense), that the potential exists only in virtue of the actual. On Berkeley's theory, God is the direct cause of our sensations, which he produces in us according to his laws of nature. Consequently any 'possibility of sensation' is dependent upon actuality in the form of a divine fixed purpose or thought. The question remains, however, whether Berkeley is inconsistently trying *both* to account for sensible things and qualities by divine dispositions to cause ideas in us, *and* to identify them with the ideas caused: both allowing that my table exists when out of sight, and asserting that it is a collection of ideas. There are early passages in the *Commentaries* in which he forthrightly treats physical substances as 'collections of powers' in God's mind, and he is temporarily prepared even to share Locke's general account of bodies, 'by them meaning combinations of powers in an unknown substratum'.[5] But a decisive objection from Berkeley's general point of view is that, unlike 'sensible objects',

[1] PHK I § 3.
[2] id. § 22; DHP 1 *200*.
[3] PHK I § 5.
[4] id. § 3.
[5] PC 80, cf. id. 112. The 'substratum' is God for Berkeley, Matter for Locke. cp. DHP III *239*.

these 'powers' would not, strictly speaking, be themselves perceptible.[1] As he says in the course of the very argument that we are considering, '... what are (sensible) objects but the things we perceive by sense, and what do we perceive besides our own ideas or sensations?'[2] Should we then see the hypothetical, 'if I was in my study I might perceive it', as an echo of an early hypothesis which is retained only as part of a muddled or dishonest attempt to make the stronger theory appear less paradoxical?

We need not accuse Berkeley of holding both views at once if we pay attention to the interpretation of 'unperceived existence' which he arrived at later in the *Commentaries*. On this account the assertion that my table exists when not perceived may be true if it is understood as the *hypothetical* ascription of existence to a 'sensible thing', rather than as the *categorical* ascription of existence to a 'potentiality for sensation': or, rather, the latter explanation is loosely permissible provided that it is taken to be wholly reducible to the former: 'Bodies taken for Powers do exist when not perceived *but this existence is not actual.* When I say a power exists no more is meant than that if in the light I open my eyes and look that way I shall see *it, i.e. the body,* etc.'[3] Crudely, he held that in such circumstances 'My table exists' is short for 'My table *would* exist (i.e. be perceived), if someone were looking at it'. Unperceived, my table does not actually exist.

It should, however, be said that the *Principles* also contains suggestions that unperceived objects may be unperceived only by men; and in the *Dialogues* they are explicitly placed once again in God, not as powers, but as actual ideas. Perhaps Berkeley saw the two accounts as compatible, if he felt that from the ordinary man's point of view the existence of such objects is hypothetical, even if founded upon actual existence in God's mind.

If we can see the '*esse* is *percipi*' argument as reasonably coherent, can we also see it as plausible? It will help if we define more precisely what Berkeley is trying to deny. He is not here more than incidentally interested in whether it is *true* that my table exists when I am out of my room. The real question is whether such existence is conceivable, and whether conceiving of it is conceiving of a physical object absolutely, as it is in itself. Berkeley's claim, roughly speaking, is that to think and talk of the table in an unoccupied room is still to think and talk of the potential perception of it, of how it would look, feel and so on. For if I 'imagine trees ... in a park or books existing in a closet, and nobody by to perceive them',[4] I merely imagine how it would be to perceive them myself. I do not conceive of Locke's 'particular constitution which everything has within itself, without any relation to anything without it'. The strength of this

---

[1] cf. TVV § 11–12, DHP I *passim*.
[2] PHK I § 4. For Berkeley's treatment of 'indirect' perception see, e.g. DHP I *203*.
[3] PC 293a, my italics. cf. id. 52 and 185.
[4] PHK I § 23.

argument should be obvious to anyone who has felt the temptations of phenomenalism.

Nevertheless it suffers from an unjust notoriety due to a feature that is inessential to it, if a natural consequence of its historical context. Both Locke and Berkeley explained imagining or conceiving of a sensible quality as *perceiving* a recalled idea or image no different from an idea of sense except in its immediate origin, context and vivacity. Thus Berkeley can say that in order to conceive of a sensible object unperceived 'it is necessary that you conceive of it unconceived or unthought of',[1] a dialectical move that has unfortunately led some to feel that the whole argument rests on a mere muddle between *per*ception and *con*ception. The move may be open to objection, in that Locke, while making no relevant distinction between imagining and perceiving blue, would not treat imagining a tree as perceiving a tree but as perceiving an idea of a tree, a distinction which Berkeley himself elsewhere recognizes.[2] But the important thing is to see that this issue does not affect the main contention that neither imagining a tree nor anything else can count as conceiving of a tree 'as it is in itself'.

Berkeley's Lockean opponent is not, of course, out of the fight. Yet the only case of conceiving of a thing's intrinsic properties that Locke can suggest (and his advocacy is not always wholehearted) is conceiving of its 'primary qualities', the ideas of which, as he himself holds, are acquired through sense. Thus the real issue between them is whether we get, or could possibly get, a *sensory* concept through which we could conceive of physical reality in a *sense-independent* way.

For Locke, our idea of extension is such an idea, which not only 'represents' but 'resembles' independent reality; and since it is acquired through both sight and touch, it must be supposed capable of being abstracted from either sense modality. But Berkeley attacks such notions with a battery of arguments: for example, that an idea cannot conceivably resemble anything except another idea;[3] that no idea of shape can be abstracted from admittedly sense-dependent qualities such as colour;[4]

---

[1] ibid.

[2] See id. §§ 34, 89–90, 41 etc. cp. PC 473, which considers the objection, roughly, that, if to exist is to be perceived and to imagine is to perceive, it follows, absurdly, that the chimera that I imagine exists. Berkeley replies that in a sense it does exist (as we might now say, 'intentionally'), but not in the vulgar sense. In the published works no such distinction is drawn between senses of 'exist'. Berkeley avoided in print another, more serious fault. For in PC 472 he seems to have hopes of dealing with the ordinary belief in the continued existence of unobserved objects by postulating that when I imagine (i.e. believe) that my books exist in my study, I 'perceive' the books themselves, and so they exist. Belief in continued existence, however irrational, would thus be self-verifying. No such quaint argument for the *truth* of any supposition of continued existence occurs elsewhere, and it is appropriately quashed in 474a.

[3] PHK I § 8, etc.

[4] id. § 10, etc.

that there is no idea common to sight and touch;[1] and that no conception of absolute size is possible since determinations of size are relative to perception.[2] If, therefore, as Berkeley himself suggests, his whole case is dependent upon the principle that an unperceived sensible object is inconceivable, it is so as an arch is dependent upon its keystone: if the keystone can be dislodged, the arch will fall but it is the supporting pressure of the rest of the arch that makes the keystone difficult to dislodge.

3 *Spiritual* versus *unthinking substance*

The next step in Berkeley's argument is so radical (and, it must be admitted, so peculiar) that very few commentators have been capable even of taking it seriously, while none, perhaps, has accorded it the central, structural role in his thought that it certainly possesses. The argument runs as follows.[3]

Colour, figure, motion, etc., the sensible qualities, have been shown to be ideas. An idea obviously cannot 'exist in', or be had by anything but a perceiving thing. It is thus self-contradictory to say that an unperceiving thing 'has' any sensible quality, and the philosophical theory that sensible qualities are inherent in and supported by a non-spiritual substance is necessarily false. Therefore Spirit is the only kind of substance, for a 'substance' is that in which qualities inhere, and all qualities inhere in Spirit.

Berkeley takes it that Mind-Body dualism postulates four kinds of being: *ideas* which are dependent upon and exist in *Spirits*, and *sensible qualities* which exist in *Matter*. His own view is that sensible qualities do indeed have a dependent status and logically require a 'support'. They must, as Locke and our intuitions tell us, 'inhere in' something. Since they are not distinct from ideas, what they depend upon is spiritual substance itself. The postulation of material substance is as unnecessary as it is self-contradictory.

An important and revealing feature of Berkeley's position is his diagnosis of the route by which philosophers arrive at the doctrine of material substance, a route allegedly comprising two stages, or three if we include an initial mistake committed by the ordinary man. The vulgar, Berkeley believes, do not make the distinction between ideas and qualities, but rightly assume that they immediately perceive physical objects. Yet, because ideas of sense are involuntary, they mistakenly believe that these have an entirely independent or 'absolute' existence.[4] Thus the ordinary conception of the physical world is self-contradictory. Some philosophers realize this obscurely, but cannot free themselves from the vulgar belief that sensible objects are independent of Spirit. They attempt to reconcile their contrary inclinations by drawing the distinction between mind-dependent ideas and mind-independent qualities, thus arriving at the representative

[1] NTV and TVV *passim*, etc.
[2] PHK I § 11, DHP I *passim*, etc.
[3] PHK I § 7.
[4] See, e.g., id. § 56.

theory of perception.[1] Another philosophical remedy for the conflict, however, is to accept the ordinary view that sensible qualities or ideas of sense are independent of Spirit, but to satisfy the intuition of dependence by postulating another, non-mental substance for them to depend upon.[2] Both remedies can be combined to produce the fourfold ontology of Spirits, ideas, sensible qualities, and Matter.

In order to appreciate the importance for Berkeley of the principle that 'there is no other substance in a strict sense, than *spirit*',[3] we must first understand it. Berkeley did not mean that physical objects do not exist, nor that they are really spiritual as Leibniz thought, but that they are not 'substantial': they are not *things* or *substances* in the sense in which spirits are. What does this mean?

Berkeley's concept of a 'substance' may be idiosyncratic, but his general method of arriving at it is not. He does so by presenting his metaphysics as the only way of making sense of an intuitive or traditional notion. His interpretation differs from other interpretations of that notion as Locke's differs from Descartes', and Descartes' from that of the Scholastics. Yet there is a continuity such that we can also speak of a single, shared concept of substance. Roughly, substances are the ultimate constituents of the universe upon which the phenomena depend. In order to understand the workings of the universe we must know the natures or essences of the substances within it. We might illustrate the concept by arguing that a *disease* is not a substance because it must be understood in terms of the nature of an organism. Moreover organisms are, intuitively, 'things' as diseases are not. Such an illustration must, however, be taken as provisional: e.g., for Spinoza only the universe itself could be a self-intelligible substance.

Disputes about the category of substance still go on. It has traditionally been thought possible to characterize 'substances', as distinct from events, acts, states, qualities etc., by means of a variety of principles. For example, substances can undergo and survive change, a logical fact that seems linked to the possibility of explaining their transitory behaviour in terms of an enduring nature. Or it may be said that individual substances, unlike processes, exist all at once. Then there is the difficult view that substances have some sort of priority as ultimate logical 'subjects'. All such principles may be controversial and ambiguous, at best needing detailed justification and elucidation. And if the category can be successfully characterized, there remains the question whether it is necessary for thought.

If interest in such problems has recently revived, it has become normal to treat them as narrowly logical, even linguistic. Yet it may be a mistake to assume the possibility of separating logical or linguistic issues from a central strand in the traditional debate, wholly predominant in the time of Berkeley, which concerns rather the requirements of a conceptual

[1] ibid.
[2] id. § 73.
[3] DHP III *261*.

apparatus adequate for *science* or, indeed (since there is no logical gulf between them), for the intuitive, pre-scientific but rational interpretation of experienced causality.

Philosophers of that time seldom engaged in the philosophy of science, as we might understand it today, purely and simply. Nature was hardly to be thought of without reference to its Creator, who seemed, for obvious reasons, to be the substance *par excellence*. Theology and philosophy of science were intertwined, spectacularly in the theories of Spinoza and Malebranche, less obtrusively, but still firmly, in the doctrines of Locke. Yet it was the interest in the nature of scientific explanation, and changing conceptions of natural causality, that decisively shaped philosophical conceptions of substance. Certainly, 'logical' considerations were always subordinate. Locke, as we have seen, does take some theoretical notice of what may be called the logical properties of substance-terms; but only in order to interpret these properties as intimations of the causal dependence of the phenomena upon underlying structures. There is, for Locke, no sort of logical or ontological priority to be understood otherwise than as causal priority.

Where, against this background, does Berkeley stand? There is no doubt that he thinks entirely within the traditional terms of priority and dependence. In a late work he aptly presents his theory in the context of an ancient debate: 'Proclus, in his *Commentary on the Theology of Plato* observes there are two sorts of philosophers. The one placed Body first in the order of beings, and made the faculty of thinking depend thereupon, supposing that the principles of all things are corporeal; that Body most really or principally exists, and all other things in a secondary sense, and by virtue of that. Others, making all corporeal things to be dependent upon Soul or Mind, think this to exist in the first place and primary sense, and the being of bodies to be altogether derived from and presuppose that of Mind.'[1] But Berkeley's argument is unusual in falling into two halves, since he attributes two sorts of dependence to bodies, corresponding to the 'supporting' and the 'causing' functions that in his system together constitute the ontological priority of Spirit. The former function is exercised in perception: as we have seen, sensible objects exist or 'inhere' in the spirit that perceives them. The causal function is exercised in acts of will, our own in the case of 'ideas of imagination', the creative acts of God in the case of 'real' bodies. This division between sorts of dependence is a philosophical novelty, but there is a balance and an interplay between the two lines of argument that contribute to the unity and elegance of the whole theory. It is important for Berkeley that percipience and agency, understanding and will, are intimately related and, in a way, inseparable aspects of Spirit, although separable to the extent that a particular spirit can perceive ideas that it does not will.

---

[1] *Siris* § 263. Here is a clue as to why Berkeley takes the *esse* is *percipi* principle as identifying a sense or meaning of 'exist'. cf. PHK I § 89, PC 412-13.

'Substance', then, is Spirit; 'supporting' is immediate perception,[1] 'accidents' are ideas.[2] Other conceptions of substance are contradictory or empty. Doctrines associated with the subject-predicate relationship are 'groundless and unintelligible',[3] while talk of 'supporting' has previously been an unexplained metaphor concerning which we can be certain only that it is not meant literally.[4] It should be said that Locke is here treated very unsympathetically, indeed unjustly: for, as we have seen, he does offer an interpretation of 'supporting' in terms of his rationalist conception of causality. In the end, however, the injustice hardly matters, for Berkeley's later critique of that conception has proved, for good or ill, one of the most influential elements in his thought.

4 *Spiritual* versus *material causality*

Like the notion of an unthinking support, that of an unthinking cause or agent is held by Berkeley to be obscure and self-contradictory. Every idea or sensible quality is self-evidently inactive, and yet self-evidently dependent upon a cause. The only possible cause of ideas is therefore a substance, i.e. Spirit, which is essentially active, possessing a will. The very notion of causality is founded solely upon the experience of volition, from which it cannot be abstracted. Those ideas that we do not ourselves cause by willing them must be caused by some other spirit. Ideas of sense, which constitute the natural, 'real' world, bear the marks of an author with divine attributes. Indeed, the wisdom and goodness of God are evident in the very institution of Laws of Nature, which make it possible for us to predict consequences and adopt means to ends, and thus to be moral agents.

This argument may today seem merely odd and unconvincing; but, when Berkeley wrote, it was, to say the least, a living problem how to reconcile natural, mechanical causality with the causality of God the Creator. Clocks, however vast, achieve independence of clockmakers.[5] In the Cartesian universe, God retains a role in conserving the quantity both of Matter and of motion, and, it seems, is also responsible for the transference of motion from one body to another. Malebranche, as we have seen, goes even further, making God the one true agent. Locke is more sceptical as to God's continuous role, yet he does suggest that our idea of active power, involving 'the beginning of motion', cannot be obtained

[1] PHK I §§ 135-7.
[2] id. § 73.
[3] id. § 49, cf. § 27. Interestingly, in both passages Berkeley has Locke's peculiar interpretation of the thing-property distinction in mind, although not exclusively in § 49.
[4] id. §§ 16–17, DHP I *197*ff. It is partly because these passages have been misread as attacks on talk of 'substance' and 'supporting' *per se* that commentators have had such difficulty in digesting, or even noticing, the importance of the concepts to Berkeley himself. cp. DHP III *233*f.
[5] cf. CBJ II § 3.

from the communication of motion from body to body, but only from our own voluntary actions. Thus Berkeley's denial of physical causality might have seemed bold, but not unprecedented or bizarre. It constitutes, moreover, an essential ingredient of the thesis that Matter is not a substance.

Berkeley's aim was the subordination of natural science to theology and ethics. He pursued it, in effect, by denying the distinction upon which Locke's philosophy hinges, between descriptive 'natural history' and explanatory physical theory: consequently when Locke complains of the lack of an adequate, intelligible theory he is requiring the impossible. Whatever scientists discover, it will be more of the same thing, useful knowledge of the arbitrary order and regularity of God's activity. Real understanding of the natural world will come, not with penetration into atomic essences, but with a proper appreciation of God's purposes and their attainment. Thus natural science both has the immediate object ascribed by Locke to natural history (i.e. the useful, if not logically certain, knowledge of means to ends) and also serves as a preliminary and part of a higher science, natural theology, through which we may 'enlarge our notions of the grandeur, wisdom and beneficence of the Creator', the divine substance underlying the phenomena.

If this spells out Berkeley's motives, modern philosophers are likely to be most interested in his rejection of Locke's ideal of an 'intelligible', deductive physics of which the basic concepts are given in sense perception; and in his positive conception of the kind of explanation that the scientist can achieve by drawing analogies between observable processes. For Berkeley, analogy is the essence of natural explanation, as it is the foundation of natural inference. Analogy constitutes the function of theoretical terms such as 'gravity', 'attraction' or 'impulse', which do not stand for incompletely understood, unperceived processes, as Locke and Newton thought, but mark similarities between perceived processes.

Here Berkeley may seem to be striding (or sliding) towards Hume, but it would be unjust to both to assimilate their views too closely. It is essential to Hume's position, for example, that the rationality (such as he allows) of causal or inductive inference be independent of any presumption of universal causality: rather, he holds that a reasonable belief in the latter can be based, and can only be based, on induction.[1] Berkeley, however, holds that inductive inference depends upon a metaphysical 'supposition that the Author of Nature always operates uniformly'. Another difference concerns the status of the terms of 'Laws of Nature'.

---

[1] It is difficult to see how Hume could be right, for (a) it is impossible to conceive of any causal relationships except as part of a comprehensive system of causality, and (b) it is impossible to conceive of acausal chaos, since even chaos must have elements, and it is impossible to make sense of what they would be. Probability is not a function of repetition but of explanatory force, a criterion that presupposes that reality is intelligible and not chaotic.

Berkeley sees no difficulty in taking laws as constant conjunctions hold-ing between ideas of sense, the actual elements in our experience with which he identifies 'sensible objects'. Hume may at first seem to follow Berkeley in this assumption, but only in order eventually to argue that in fact there are no given exceptionless conjunctions between our 'impres-sions': it is only by supposing that the immediate objects of our percep-tion continue to exist when not perceived that we can maintain a belief in universal conjunctions between them. Hume's unperceived perceptions are unattractive entities, but he has shrewdly seen the flaws in the theory that there are universal connections between sensations or anything like Berkeley's mind-dependent 'ideas'. The realist, of course, faces no such problem in the natural and easy contrast between the relatively irregular course of subjective experience, and the perfectly lawful order of the physical world that gives rise to that experience.

We need not dwell on less appealing aspects of Berkeley's treatment of causality. The experience of the voluntary creation of ideas in imagina-tion is implausibly supposed to render intelligible God's creation of ideas in minds other than his own. Moreover, no explanation is offered of the difference between voluntarily imagining one's leg moving and volun-tarily moving a leg. Worse, no coherent explanation could be offered, since in the latter case the ideas that constitute the leg-movement would have to be both voluntary and, being 'real', involuntary. Such objections to do with human action raise difficulties that no phenomenalist has ever satisfactorily met; which is a consideration that may mitigate any tend-ency to regard Berkeley's theory as foolish as well as untenable.

5 *The arguments for God's existence*

The conception of sensible things as inert dependent beings whose *esse* is *percipi*, together with the conception of spirit as the substance which both supports and causes them, supplies the material for the two arguments for God's existence for which Berkeley is famous. They have been called the 'Continuity Argument' and the 'Passivity Argument', but better names would be the 'Distinctness Argument' and the 'Causal Argument'. In the *Principles* the former appears without the latter, but in the *Dialogues* both arguments are elegantly intertwined and counter-balanced, correspondent as they are to the two sides of God's spiritual nature, understanding and will.

The Causal Argument has been set out at the beginning of Section 4, above. The Distinctness Argument starts in effect from the same pre-mise: my ideas of sense, or sensible things, arise involuntarily; perception is passive. But where the Causal Argument concludes that ideas of sense are caused by an external spirit, the Distinctness Argument proceeds as follows. Since sensible things 'depend not on my thought', they 'have an existence distinct from being perceived by me'. That is, although they are perceived by me and exist in my mind, their existence does not consist in their being perceived by me. Yet their *esse* is *percipi*: therefore 'there must be some other mind wherein they exist'. [1]

The crucial move in the argument is the deduction of the proposition that sensible things are *ontologically* independent of my mind, from the premise that they are *causally* independent of it (i.e., of my will). This move may seem less arbitrary if we recognize its affinity with a realist argument employed by Locke. Locke had started from the premise that the words I write, although voluntarily produced, are such that I cannot 'choose afterward but see them as they are'. Because 'they are not barely the sport and play of my own imagination', it follows that they 'do really exist without me'.[2] Of course, Locke's contrast was not only between voluntary images and involuntary sensations, but at the same time between the plasticity of imaginary objects and the obduracy of real ones. Yet Berkeley, despite his own principles, found it possible to mirror even this duality of sensation and object, taking his argument to be that my ideas of sense, 'either themselves or their archetypes', have a distinct existence in the mind of God. He differed from the realist, however, not only in stressing the mind-dependence of any archetypes, but in treating it as unimportant whether the distinctly existing sensible thing is taken to be the *archetype* of my idea, or to be *identical* with it. Even under very friendly pressure from Johnson, he said only that he had 'no objection' to calling God's ideas 'archetypes' of ours. The reason for this studied neutrality, it seems, was that he took the question, like the closely related question whether two people can see the same thing, to be a merely verbal one. The answer depends on how we choose to use the word 'same'.[3]

The distinctness argument has commonly been misread as if its premise were the proposition that sensible things continue to exist when not perceived by me (hence the misnomer, 'Continuity Argument'). This proposition, however, is not stated until a recapitulation of the Distinctness Argument in the Third Dialogue in response to a particular objection by Hylas that immaterialism cannot deal with continuity. Here it appears, not as a premise of the argument, but as a gloss on the conclusion: 'There is therefore some other mind wherein they exist, during the intervals between the times of my perceiving them.' Distinctness entails continuity. No doubt Berkeley would have agreed with Hume that continuity also entails distinctness, but that is not the direction of his argument.

6 *Primary and secondary qualities, ideas of two senses and abstract ideas*

By concentrating on the main structural features of his argument, I have tried to bring out the unity of Berkeley's metaphysics, as well as to

[1] DHP 166–9. It is immediately followed by the Causal Argument.
[2] *Essay* 4.11.7.
[3] cf. CBJ III and DHP III *247*f.

suggest that his role is more complex and interesting than that once commonly ascribed to him of an empiricist critic of Locke who did not go far enough. This unaccustomed emphasis has left little space for the discussion of some of Berkeley's best known arguments, such as add muscle to the bones of his strange ontology.

Here again distorted conceptions of his meaning and achievement are prevalent. On the topic of primary and secondary qualities, it is widely supposed that Berkeley merely extends to the former Locke's arguments against the objectivity of the latter. Yet it is difficult to say how much or how little of Berkeley's philosophy constitutes criticism of the distinction. As he himself suggests,[1] the whole of the *New Theory of Vision* could be regarded in this light. On the other hand, even in the *First Dialogue* he relies upon difficulties associated with the independent and ancient problems of the relativity of size and infinite divisibility, so that the comparison drawn between Locke's treatment of secondary qualities and his own attack on extension could be regarded as little more than a debating point.[2]

In his books on vision, Berkeley raises a number of problems of immense and continuing importance in the philosophy of perception, all related to the question of 'ideas of two senses'. Locke had assumed that we can get the concept of squareness from the experience of square objects just because the objects cause in us 'ideas' or sense-data which instantiate squareness, i.e. are themselves square. Thus if we can get the same concept from both sight and touch, then whatever their qualitative differences the visual and tactual sense-data must have at least one abstractible property, squareness, in common. Berkeley's arguments against such a common property are extremely powerful, so that many have thought that we must admit two concepts of squareness, visual and tactual. The initial assumption is itself questionable, but a clear and acceptable alternative is not easy to find.

The polemic against abstract ideas, despite Hume's famous compliment, does to an extent miss its target. Yet it goes less astray than those modern attempts to defend Locke's theory which have proposed that abstract ideas, on a properly sympathetic understanding, are not sensory images but modes of thought of a more refined type: i.e. that Locke is not a consistent imagist. On a better-grounded interpretation, Lockean abstract ideas do consist in images, but are not fully separate in the way that Berkeley's criticisms assume. An abstract idea of white is a determinate but 'partially considered' image, all but its whiteness being selectively ignored. To put the point differently, it is an aspect of an image. The general idea of *being*, or of *unity*, is any idea whatsoever considered barely as existent, or as one thing. Consequently the best defence of Locke (as far as it goes) is that his doctrine is little different from

[1] TVV § 15.
[2] cf. PHK I §§ 14–15 where it occurs almost as an afterthought.

Berkeley's own. Nevertheless Locke's concrete language of 'retaining' and (despite a disclaimer) 'separating' the abstract idea, of 'leaving out' its concomitants and so forth, does blur the edges of his doctrine, supplying excuse, if not justification, for Berkeley's line of argument.

Another criticism of Berkeley, of more recent origin, is that his rejection of abstract ideas is logically irrelevant to his metaphysics, since it does not entail immaterialism. Such an allegation of incoherence, however, betrays a perversely narrow understanding of what constitutes a connection in argument. In attacking a theory about universal thought and knowledge and proposing another in its stead, Berkeley is trying to discredit the assumption that, if we can talk and reason about something in isolation, then that thing can be conceived of as existing in isolation. Of course, from a general warning against treating inseparables as separable, nothing follows deductively about the possibility of this or that separation. The relationship is that of methodological principle to substantive belief. No substantive conclusion follows deductively from the comparable principle, even more famous than Berkeley's, that entities should not be multiplied beyond necessity. It would obviously be wrong to conclude that either is a mere excrescence.

The fact that Berkeley's polemic on methodology occurs in an introduction is one indication that we are dealing with a man who knows what he is doing. There are many more in the skilful dialectical structure of his works, and in the subtle cross-references and allusions with which they abound. It is more true of Berkeley than of most philosophers that every word counts. This is not to claim that his system is uniquely free from logical discords and logical gaps, but we need not invent them where none exists.

7 *The Philosophical Commentaries*

It may seem perverse to include in a popular edition the series of philosophical remarks called by A. A. Luce the *Philosophical Commentaries*. Berkeley evidently wrote them while revising and refining his theory, some apparently stimulated by his reading at the time, and some, perhaps, written as comments on earlier manuscripts of his own. They were obviously not intended for publication. Often terse and allusive, sometimes even cryptic, they are best approached after some acquaintance with the published works and knowledge of the contemporary philosophical scene.

Worse still, he wrote them together with a number of other notes, memoranda and the like in two notebooks since bound together. The suggestion first made in 1905 that the notebooks were bound in the wrong order has long been generally accepted. Since the first printing of the present edition, however, this hypothesis has been questioned, and it has been proposed that Berkeley might have used both notebooks concurrently.[1] Yet, even if none of the available evidence rules out this new hypothesis absolutely, the relation between the contents of the two books gives strong support for the orthodox ordering. There is, for example, an apparent development of Berkeley's thought about existence from Notebook B to Notebook A, while the principle that all significant words stand for ideas, rejected in the course of A, appears throughout B, where it is qualified only in later *verso* entries.

Another problem concerns the significance of the entries: do they all record Berkeley's beliefs at the time of writing, or do at least some of them represent the deliberately experimental formulation of queries, proposals and arguments concurrently pursued so that each should illuminate, test and correct the others? If the latter, then in itself an entry can indicate no more than that Berkeley had envisaged this possibility or explored that avenue, perhaps merely in order to clarify an issue.

Nevertheless, for all the obscurities and uncertainties, the *Commentaries* have perhaps a unique claim to be the full and self-contained record of a crucial period in the development of one of the classic systems of philosophy. They invite the attempt to reconstruct that development, and readers who accept the challenge will find themselves engaged on a fascinating and intellectually rewarding task which in itself constitutes an education in philosophy and its history. Certainly the notebooks shed a special light on almost every theme of the later works. To take but one example, it was once generally, if ignorantly, supposed that Berkeley's treatment of Spirit was *ad hoc* and careless: even that spiritual substance survived in his system only because he had left it to Hume to subject it to the criticisms that he himself levels against material substance. Consideration of passages in the *Commentaries* has contributed to the overthrow of such an interpretation. Not only had Berkeley himself conceived of the possibility that 'Mind is a congeries of Perceptions',[2] but he did so only in the course of prolonged, complex and somewhat agonized reflections, from a generally Cartesian viewpoint, on the essence, unity and activity of Spirit. It was from these reflections that he distilled the carefully wrought but easily overlooked account in the *Principles*: 'A spirit is one simple, undivided, active being: as it perceives ideas, it is called the *understanding*, and as it produces or otherwise operates about them, it is called the *will*.'

Berkeley's very useful marginal signs need to be treated with some caution. His own key to the letters is given for convenience at the beginning of the text, but it stands in the original at the start of the second notebook. There is some reason to think that he may have used slightly different principles of classification in each book. He certainly changed

---

[1] By B. Belfrage, *Revue Internationale de Philosophie* 1985. A review of the arguments for placing B before A, including persuasive stylistic considerations of his own, are given in the edition of G. H. Thomas (Alliance, Ohio 1976).
[2] PC 580; cf. DHP III *233*.

his mind in many individual cases, erasing signs and replacing them. The symbol '×' comprehends topics relating to mathematics and extension, including optics, such as were dealt with (presumably later) in the *New Theory of Vision*. The appended numbers 1, 2 and 3 mark off specific topics in that work, respectively distance, magnitude and the heterogeneity of sight and touch. '3a' indicates the problem of the inverted image. The meaning of the symbol '+' is controversial, but it is difficult to believe that it does not in general indicate entries for which Berkeley at some time felt that he would have (or had had) no further use, whether because they expressed falsehood (as with entry 378), or because they adopted the wrong tone (as with entry 372), or for some other reason.[1]

8 Relations between the works

It is still disputed whether Berkeley's doctrines are modified from one work to another. In my own view, if we except the *Commentaries*, he unfolds, but does not change or modify his metaphysics.

The *Essay on Vision* is a special case, since in it Berkeley deliberately suppressed a part of his metaphysics, treating the objects of touch as independent and in external space. Its conclusions are nevertheless essential or conducive to the whole theory. The best indication of its intimate relation to the later works (which has been doubted) is given in *The Theory of Vision Vindicated*, sections 9–29.

The other works in the present volume are more clearly expressions of a single philosophy. The doctrine that God perceives the ideas constitutive of the real world when we do not is not definitely asserted in the *Principles*, but figures prominently in the *Dialogues* as part of the argument for God's existence. Yet it would be rash to attribute great significance to the fact, for the *Principles* was unfinished and contains elaborate, very probably premonitory hints that unperceived objects *may* 'subsist in the mind of some eternal spirit'. *De Motu* is an expansion of aspects of Berkeley's philosophy of Science. The *Correspondence* with Johnson illuminates especially the topics of divine ideas, identity and the essence of spirit. It is not less valuable for Johnson's shrewd comments from a Lockean and Newtonian standpoint, than for Berkeley's sometimes evasive replies.

Finally, a word about some works not included. *The Analyst* is an extended attack on the infinitesimals of the Newtonian Calculus, and ranks as a significant contribution to the philosophy of mathematics. *Alciphron or the Minute Philosopher* is a polemic against 'free-thinking' in morals and religion, involving only so much of the metaphysics as is relevant to Berkeley's anti-mechanistic natural theology. Yet it contains an interesting discussion of theoretical terms in theology as well as in

---

[1] Based on the edition of Luce (London 1944) and G. H. Thomas. Debate on the meaning of the signs has continued in *Hermathena* and *The Berkeley Newsletter*.

science, in which the flavour of pragmatism is pronounced. The engaging *Siris*, notorious for its commendation of tar-water as a panacea, should be read as a different sort of exercise in natural theology, although again backed by the immaterialist metaphysics. The supposed special importance of aether in the physical world is taken for a divine analogy—as the sun was to Plato—for a more profound, metaphysical primacy: that of Spirit over the physical world generally. The atomism of his physical speculations and the affinity that Berkeley discerns between himself and Plato, have been taken to indicate a change of mind. On the contrary, the flirtation with Neoplatonism gives rise to a clear statement of the ontological implications of his own theory which can help us to perceive its true nature.[1]

9 *The texts*

The texts used throughout are the excellent, partially modernized texts of the standard *Works of George Berkeley, Bishop of Cloyne* edited by A. A. Luce and T. E. Jessop (London 1948–51), to which I have made some minor modifications and improvements.

1   Except in the *Commentaries* I have modernized certain forms and spellings, e.g.: 'ourselves', 'anything', etc. for 'our selves', 'any thing', etc.; 'entire' for 'intire'; 'plane' for 'plain'; etc.

2   I have sometimes, for emphasis etc., returned to Berkeley's italics and capitals, e.g.: Berkeley's *'phenomenon -a'* (e.g., PHK I §§ 50, 62, 104) may emphasize etymology (cp, 'phenomenon -a' at id. §§ 50, 60, 62); 'the terms *upper* and *lower*' for 'the terms upper and lower'; 'Eternal, Invisible Mind' for 'eternal, invisible Mind' (italicized as well in original); etc.

3   Following Jessop, I have dropped capitals after colons, as retained by Luce.

4   I have corrected presumed misprints, e.g. returning to Berkeley's 'cause all the motions' for 'choose all the motions' (PHK I § 62); 'show of reason' for 'show or reason' (id. § 74); etc.

5   I have occasionally preferred a First Edition reading to the Second adopted in the *Works,* e.g.: 'whole system of beings' for 'whole system of being' (PHK I § 151, supported by 'beings' in § 153); 'can never equal' for 'can ever equal' (id. § 130, demanded by the sense); etc.

6   I have omitted the Latin original of the passage from Barrow, NTV § 29.

7   I have incorporated the improvements to the *Commentaries* adopted by Luce in *Hermathena* 1971. But I have generally omitted the asterisk from the marginal signs, when recto and verso entries are sufficiently related by the numbering.

[1] See above, p. xvi.

Footnotes in the text signalled by non-numerical symbols are the author's; those in square brackets and signalled by superior numerals are editorial. When texts are based on editions later than the first, I have indicated significant changes.

The translation of *De Motu* is that of A. A. Luce: the Latin original is not included.

To facilitate a standard method of reference to the *Three Dialogues,* the corresponding page number from the *Works* is placed in the outer margin.

1974   M. R. AYERS

Editor's Note to the 1989 Printing

As in 1983, I have taken the opportunity of a further reprinting of the present edition to make some minor revisions to the Introduction. I am grateful to David Berman for some corrections. In particular, a new Section 5 has been added, on Berkeley's proofs of God's existence, and the remarks about the *Philosophical Commentaries* have been brought into line with some recent scholarship. A large number of changes have been made to the text of the *Commentaries* following the more significant, or potentially more significant, amendments to Luce's readings published in the edition of George H. Thomas, some of which were due to Bertil Belfrage. I am extremely grateful to Professor Thomas for his help.

M. R. AYERS

Chronology

1685 (12th March) Born in Co. Kilkenny, Ireland. (Grew up in Dysert Castle, Kilkenny.)
1696 Entered the Duke of Ormond School, Kilkenny.
1700 Entered Trinity College, Dublin.
1704 B.A.
1707 Elected Junior Fellow of Trinity College.
1709 Ordained.
1713 In London.
1713–14 In Italy as chaplain to the Earl of Peterborough.
1716–20 On the Continent as tutor to George Ashe.
1721 Returned to Trinity College as Senior Fellow.
1724 Made Dean of Derry.
1724–28 In London, advancing his project to found a college in Bermuda.
1728 Married Anne Forster.
1728–31 In America, chiefly at Newport, Rhode Island.
1734 Made Bishop of Cloyne in Ireland.
1752 Left Cloyne for Oxford.
1753 (14th January) Died at Oxford.

Select Bibliography

Works by Berkeley (For a full list see *Works* Vol. IX)

1707 *Arithmetica* and *Miscellanea Mathematica*. London.
1709 (1709, 1732, 1732) *An Essay towards a New Theory of Vision*. Dublin.
1710 (1734) *A Treatise concerning the Principles of Human Knowledge*. Dublin.
1712 *Passive Obedience*. Dublin and London.
1713 (1725, 1734) *Three Dialogues between Hylas and Philonous*. London.
1715 *Advice to the Tories who have taken the Oaths*. London.
1721 (1752) *De Motu*. London.
1721 *An Essay towards preventing the Ruin of Great Britain*. London.
1725 *A Proposal for the better Supplying of Churches in our Foreign Plantations*, etc. London.
1732 *Alciphron: or the Minute Philosopher*. London.
1733 *The Theory of Vision, Vindicated and Explained*. London.
1734 *The Analyst*. Dublin and London.
1735 *A Defence of Free-thinking in Mathematics*. Dublin and London.
1735–37 *The Querist*. Dublin.

1738   *A Discourse addressed to Magistrates*, etc. Dublin.
1744   *Siris: a Chain of Philosophical Reflections and Enquiries con-
        cerning the Virtues of Tar-water*, etc. Dublin and London.
1744–47   *Letters on Tar-water*, to Thomas Prior and Dr Hales.
1752   *A Miscellany*. Dublin and London.

Collected Works
The best is *The Works of George Berkeley, Bishop of Cloyne* edited by
A. A. Luce and T. E. Jessop (1948–51). Others are the editions of
J. Stock (1784), G. N. Wright (1843), A. C. Fraser (1871 and 1901) and
G. Sampson (1897–98).

Biography
The Life of George Berkeley, Bishop of Cloyne by A. A. Luce (1949) is
the standard biography. The earliest is J. Stock's *Life of Bishop Berkeley*
(1776).

Criticism, etc.
The following works represent a very wide variety of approaches to
Berkeley.

ARMSTRONG, D. M. *Berkeley's Theory of Vision* (1960).
BRACKEN, H. M. *The Early Reception of Berkeley's Immaterialism* (1959).
DANCY, J. *Berkeley: An Introduction* (1987).
FOSTER, J. and ROBINSON, H. (eds.) *Essays on Berkeley* (1985).
GRAYLING, A. C. *Berkeley: The Central Arguments* (1986).
JESSOP, T. E. and LUCE, A. A. *Bibliography of George Berkeley* (revised
    edition 1973).
LUCE, A. A. (1) *Berkeley and Malebranche* (1934).
            (2) *Berkeley's Immaterialism* (1945).
            (3) *The Dialectic of Immaterialism* (1963. A discussion of PC).
MARTIN, C. B. and ARMSTRONG, D. M. (eds.) *Locke and Berkeley* (1968).
PITCHER, G. *Berkeley* (1977).
SILLEM, F. A. *George Berkeley and the Proofs for the Existence of God*
    (1957).
SOSA, E. (ed.) *Essays on the Philosophy of George Berkeley* (1987).
STEINKRAUS, W. E. (ed.) *New Studies in Berkeley's Philosophy* (1966).
TIPTON, I. C. *Berkeley: The Philosophy of Immaterialism* (1974).
TURBAYNE, C. (ed.) *Berkeley: Critical and Interpretive Essays* (1983).
URMSON, J. O. *Berkeley* (1982).
WARNOCK, G. J. *Berkeley* (1953; enlarged edition 1982).
WINKLER, K. P. *Berkeley: An Interpretation* (1989).

An Essay towards a New Theory of Vision

Text based on the Fourth Edition of 1732
First printed in 1709

The Contents

An Essay towards a New Theory of Vision

1 My design is to shew the manner wherein we perceive by sight the distance, magnitude, and situation of objects. Also to consider the difference there is betwixt the ideas of sight and touch, and whether there be any idea common to both senses.

2 It is, I think, agreed by all that distance, of itself and immediately, cannot be seen. For distance being a line directed end-wise to the eye, it projects only one point in the fund of the eye, which point remains invariably the same, whether the distance be longer or shorter.

3 I find it also acknowledged that the estimate we make of the distance of objects considerably remote is rather an act of judgment grounded on experience than of sense. For example, when I perceive a great number of intermediate objects, such as houses, fields, rivers, and the like, which I have experienced to take up a considerable space, I thence form a judgment or conclusion that the object I see beyond them is at a great distance. Again, when an object appears faint and small, which at a near distance I have experienced to make a vigorous and large appearance, I instantly conclude it to be far off: And this, 'tis evident, is the result of experience; without which, from the faintness and littleness I should not have inferred anything concerning the distance of objects.

4 But when an object is placed at so near a distance as that the interval between the eyes bears any sensible proportion to it, the opinion of speculative men is that the two optic axes (the fancy that we see only with one eye at once being exploded) concurring at the object do there make an angle, by means of which, according as it is greater or lesser, the object is perceived to be nearer or farther off.*

5 Betwixt which and the foregoing manner of estimating distance there is this remarkable difference: that whereas there was no apparent, necessary connexion between small distance and a large and strong appearance, or between great distance and a little and faint appearance, there appears a very necessary connexion between an obtuse angle and near distance, and an acute angle and farther distance. It does not in the least depend upon experience, but may be evidently known by anyone before he had experienced it, that the nearer the concurrence of the optic axes, the greater the angle, and the remoter their concurrence is, the lesser will be the angle comprehended by them.

* See what Descartes and others have written on this subject.

6 There is another way mentioned by optic writers, whereby they will have us judge of those distances, in respect of which the breadth of the pupil hath any sensible bigness: And that is the greater or lesser divergency of the rays, which issuing from the visible point do fall on the pupil, that point being judged nearest which is seen by most diverging rays, and that remoter which is seen by less diverging rays: and so on, the apparent distance still increasing, as the divergency of the rays decreases, till at length it becomes infinite, when the rays that fall on the pupil are to sense parallel. And after this manner it is said we perceive distance when we look only with one eye.

7 In this case also it is plain we are not beholding to experience: it being a certain, necessary truth that the nearer the direct rays falling on the eye approach to a parallelism, the farther off is the point of their intersection, or the visible point from whence they flow.

8 Now though the accounts here given of perceiving near distance by sight are received for true, and accordingly made use of in determining the apparent places of objects, they do nevertheless seem very unsatisfactory: and that for these following reasons.

9 It is evident that when the mind perceives any idea, not immediately and of itself, it must be by the means of some other idea. Thus, for instance, the passions which are in the mind of another are of themselves to me invisible. I may nevertheless perceive them by sight, though not immediately, yet by means of the colours they produce in the countenance. We often see shame or fear in the looks of a man, by perceiving the changes of his countenance to red or pale.

10 Moreover it is evident that no idea which is not itself perceived can be the means of perceiving any other idea. If I do not perceive the redness or paleness of a man's face themselves, it is impossible I should perceive by them the passions which are in his mind.

11 Now from sect. 2 it is plain that distance is in its own nature imperceptible, and yet it is perceived by sight. It remains, therefore, that it be brought into view by means of some other idea that is itself immediately perceived in the act of vision.

12 But those lines and angles, by means whereof some men pretend to explain the perception of distance, are themselves not at all perceived, nor are they in truth ever thought of by those unskilful in optics. I appeal to anyone's experience whether upon sight of an object he computes its distance by the bigness of the angle made by the meeting of the two optic axes? Or whether he ever thinks of the greater or lesser divergency of the rays, which arrive from any point to his pupil? Everyone is himself the best judge of what he perceives, and what not. In vain shall any man tell me that I perceive certain lines and angles which introduce into my mind the various ideas of distance, so long as I myself am conscious of no such thing.

13 Since, therefore, those angles and lines are not themselves perceived by sight, it follows from sect. 10 that the mind doth not by them judge of the distance of objects.

14 The truth of this assertion will be yet farther evident to anyone that

considers those lines and angles have no real existence in nature, being only an hypothesis framed by the mathematicians, and by them introduced into optics, that they might treat of that science in a geometrical way.

15 The last reason I shall give for rejecting that doctrine is, that though we should grant the real existence of those optic angles, etc., and that it was possible for the mind to perceive them, yet these principles would not be found sufficient to explain the *phenomena* of distance, as shall be shewn hereafter.

16 Now, it being already shewn that distance is suggested to the mind by the mediation of some other idea which is itself perceived in the act of seeing, it remains that we inquire what ideas or sensations there be that attend vision, unto which we may suppose the ideas of distance are connected, and by which they are introduced into the mind. And *first*, it is certain by experience that when we look at a near object with both eyes, according as it approaches or recedes from us, we alter the disposition of our eyes, by lessening or widening the interval between the pupils. This disposition or turn of the eyes is attended with a sensation, which seems to me to be that which in this case brings the idea of greater or lesser distance into the mind.

17 Not that there is any natural or necessary connexion between the sensation we perceive by the turn of the eyes and greater or lesser distance, but because the mind has by constant experience found the different sensations corresponding to the different dispositions of the eyes to be attended each with a different degree of distance in the object, there has grown an habitual or customary connexion between those two sorts of ideas, so that the mind no sooner perceives the sensation arising from the different turn it gives the eyes, in order to bring the pupils nearer or farther asunder, but it withal perceives the different idea of distance which was wont to be connected with that sensation; just as upon hearing a certain sound, the idea is immediately suggested to the understanding which custom had united with it.

18 Nor do I see how I can easily be mistaken in this matter. I know evidently that distance is not perceived of itself. That by consequence it must be perceived by means of some other idea which is immediately perceived, and varies with the different degrees of distance. I know also that the sensation arising from the turn of the eyes is of itself immediately perceived, and various degrees thereof are connected with different distances, which never fail to accompany them into my mind, when I view an object distinctly with both eyes, whose distance is so small that in respect of it the interval between the eyes has any considerable magnitude.

19 I know it is a received opinion that by altering the disposition of the eyes the mind perceives whether the angle of the optic axes or the lateral angles comprehended between the interval of the eyes and the optic axes are made greater or lesser; and that accordingly by a kind of natural geometry it judges the point of their intersection to be nearer or farther off. But that this is not true I am convinced by my own experience, since I am not conscious that I make any such use of the perception I have by

the turn of my eyes. And for me to make those judgments, and draw those conclusions from it, without knowing that I do so, seems altogether incomprehensible.

20 From all which it follows that the judgment we make of the distance of an object, viewed with both eyes, is entirely the result of experience. If we had not constantly found certain sensations arising from the various disposition of the eyes, attended with certain degrees of distance, we should never make those sudden judgments from them concerning the distance of objects; no more than we would pretend to judge of a man's thoughts by his pronouncing words we had never heard before.

21 *Secondly*, an object placed at a certain distance from the eye, to which the breadth of the pupil bears a considerable proportion, being made to approach, is seen more confusedly: and the nearer it is brought the more confused appearance it makes. And this being found constantly to be so, there ariseth in the mind an habitual connexion between the several degrees of confusion and distance; the greater confusion still implying the lesser distance, and the lesser confusion the greater distance of the object.

22 This confused appearance of the object doth therefore seem to be the medium whereby the mind judgeth of distance in those cases wherein the most approved writers of optics will have it judge by the different divergency with which the rays flowing from the radiating point fall on the pupil. No man, I believe, will pretend to see or feel those imaginary angles that the rays are supposed to form according to their various inclinations on his eye. But he cannot choose seeing whether the object appear more or less confused. It is therefore a manifest consequence from what hath been demonstrated, that instead of the greater or lesser divergency of the rays, the mind makes use of the greater or lesser confusedness of the appearance, thereby to determine the apparent place of an object.

23 Nor doth it avail to say there is not any necessary connexion between confused vision and distance, great or small. For I ask any man what necessary connexion he sees between the redness of a blush and shame? And yet no sooner shall he behold that colour to arise in the face of another, but it brings into his mind the idea of that passion which hath been observed to accompany it.

24 What seems to have misled the writers of optics in this matter is that they imagine men judge of distance as they do of a conclusion in mathematics, betwixt which and the premises it is indeed absolutely requisite there be an apparent, necessary connexion: but it is far otherwise in the sudden judgments men make of distance. We are not to think that brutes and children, or even grown reasonable men, whenever they perceive an object to approach, or depart from them, do it by virtue of geometry and demonstration.

25 That one idea may suggest another to the mind it will suffice that they have been observed to go together, without any demonstration of the necessity of their coexistence, or without so much as knowing what it is that makes them so to coexist. Of this there are innumerable instances of which no one can be ignorant.

26 Thus, greater confusion having been constantly attended with nearer distance, no sooner is the former idea perceived, but it suggests the latter to our thoughts. And if it had been the ordinary course of Nature that the farther off an object were placed, the more confused it should appear, it is certain the very same perception that now makes us think an object approaches would then have made us to imagine it went farther off. That perception, abstracting from custom and experience, being equally fitted to produce the idea of great distance, or small distance, or no distance at all.

27 *Thirdly*, an object being placed at the distance above specified, and brought nearer to the eye, we may nevertheless prevent, at least for some time, the appearances growing more confused, by straining the eye. In which case that sensation supplies the place of confused vision in aiding the mind to judge of the distance of the object; it being esteemed so much the nearer by how much the effort or straining of the eye in order to distinct vision is greater.

28 I have here set down those sensations or ideas that seem to be the constant and general occasions of introducing into the mind the different ideas of near distance. It is true in most cases that divers other circumstances contribute to frame our idea of distance, to wit, the particular number, size, kind, etc., of the things seen. Concerning which, as well as all other the forementioned occasions which suggest distance, I shall only observe they have none of them, in their own nature, any relation or connexion with it: nor is it possible they should ever signify the various degrees thereof, otherwise than as by experience they have been found to be connected with them.

29 I shall proceed upon these principles to account for a phenomenon which has hitherto strangely puzzled the writers of optics, and is so far from being accounted for by any of their theories of vision that it is, by their own confession, plainly repugnant to them; and of consequence, if nothing else could be objected, were alone sufficient to bring their credit in question. The whole difficulty I shall lay before you in the words of the learned Dr. Barrow, with which he concludes his optic lectures.

'I have here delivered what my thoughts have suggested to me concerning that part of optics which is more properly mathematical. As for the other parts of that science (which being rather physical, do consequently abound with plausible conjectures instead of certain principles), there has in them scarce anything occur'd to my observation different from what has been already said by Kepler, Scheinerus, Descartes, and others. And methinks, I had better say nothing at all, than repeat that which has been so often said by others. I think it therefore high time to take my leave of this subject: but before I quit it for good and all, the fair and ingenuous dealing that I owe both to you and to truth obligeth me to acquaint you with a certain untoward difficulty, which seems directly opposite to the doctrine I have been hitherto inculcating, at least, admits of no solution from it. In short it is this. Before the double convex glass or concave speculum EBF, let the point A be placed at such a distance that the rays proceeding from A, after refraction or reflexion, be brought to unite somewhere in the Ax AB. And suppose the point of union (i.e. the image of the point A, as hath been already set forth) to be Z; between which and B, the vertex of the glass or speculum, conceive the eye to be anywhere placed. The question now is, where the point A ought to appear? Experience shews that it doth not appear behind at the point Z, and it were

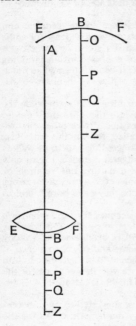

contrary to nature that it should, since all the impression which affects the sense comes from towards A. But from our tenets it should seem to follow that it would appear before the eye at a vast distance off, so great as should in some sort surpass all sensible distance. For since if we exclude all anticipations and prejudices, every object appears by so much the farther off, by how much the rays it sends to the eye are less diverging. And that object is thought to be most remote from which parallel rays proceed unto the eye. Reason would make one think that object should appear at yet a greater distance which is seen by converging rays. Moreover it may in general be asked concerning this case what it is that determines the apparent place of the point A, and maketh it to appear after a constant manner sometimes nearer, at other times farther off? To which doubt I see nothing that can be answered agreeable to the principles we have laid down except only that the point A ought always to appear extremely remote. But on the contrary we are assured by experience that the point A appears variously distant, according to the different situations of the eye between the points B and Z. And that it doth [almost] never (if at all) seem farther off, than it would if it were beheld by the naked eye, but on the contrary it doth sometimes appear much nearer. Nay, it is even certain that by how much the rays falling on the eye do more converge by so much the nearer doth the object seem to approach. For the eye being placed close to the point B, the object A appears nearly in its own natural place, if the point B is taken in the glass, or at the same distance, if in the speculum. The eye being brought back to O, the object seems to draw near: and being come to P it beholds it still nearer. And so on by little and little, till at length the eye being placed somewhere, suppose at Q, the object appearing extremely near, begins to vanish into mere confusion. All which doth seem repugnant to our principles, at least not rightly to agree with them. Nor is our tenet alone struck at by this experiment, but likewise all others that ever came to my knowledge are, every whit as much, endangered by it. The ancient one especially (which is most commonly received, and comes nearest to mine) seems to be so effectually overthrown thereby that the most learned Tacquet has been forced to reject that principle, as false and uncertain, on which alone he had built almost his whole *Catoptrics*; and consequently by taking away the foundation, hath himself pulled down the superstructure he had raised on it. Which, nevertheless, I do not believe he would have done had he but considered the whole matter more thoroughly, and examined the difficulty to the bottom. But as for me, neither this nor any other difficulty shall have so great an influence on me as to make me renounce what I know to be manifestly agreeable to reason: especially when, as it here falls out, the difficulty is founded in the peculiar nature of a certain odd and particular case. For in the present case something peculiar lies hid, which being involved in the subtilty of nature will, perhaps, hardly be discovered till such time as the manner of vision is more perfectly made known. Concerning which, I must own, I have hitherto been able to find out nothing that has the least shew of probability, not to mention certainty. I shall, therefore, leave this knot to be untied by you, wishing you may have better success in it than I have had.'

30 The ancient and received principle, which Dr. Barrow here mentions as the main foundation of Tacquet's *Catoptrics*, is that *every visible point seen by reflexion from a speculum shall appear placed at the intersection of the reflected ray, and the perpendicular of incidence*. Which intersection in the present case, happening to be behind the eye, it greatly shakes the authority of that principle, whereon the aforementioned author proceeds throughout his whole *Catoptrics* in determining the apparent place of objects seen by reflexion from any kind of speculum.

31 Let us now see how this phenomenon agrees with our tenets. The eye the nearer it is placed to the point B in the foregoing figures, the more distinct is the appearance of the object; but as it recedes to O the appearance grows more confused; and at P it sees the object yet more confused; and so on till the eye being brought back to Z sees the object in the greatest confusion of all. Wherefore by sect. 21 the object should seem to approach the eye gradually as it recedes from the point B, that is, at O it should (in consequence of the principle I have laid down in the aforesaid section) seem nearer than it did at B, and at P nearer than at O, and at Q nearer than at P; and so on, till it quite vanishes at Z. Which is the very matter of fact, as anyone that pleases may easily satisfy himself by experiment.

32 This case is much the same as if we should suppose an Englishman to meet a foreigner who used the same words with the English, but in a direct contrary signification. The Englishman would not fail to make a wrong judgment of the ideas annexed to those sounds in the mind of him that used them. Just so, in the present case the object speaks (if I may so say) with words that the eye is well acquainted with, that is, confusions

of appearance; but whereas heretofore the greater confusions were always wont to signify nearer distances, they have in this case a direct, contrary signification, being connected with the greater distances. Whence it follows that the eye must unavoidably be mistaken, since it will take the confusions in the sense it has been used to, which is directly opposed to the true.

33 This phenomenon as it entirely subverts the opinion of those who will have us judge of distance by lines and angles, on which supposition it is altogether inexplicable, so it seems to me no small confirmation of the truth of that principle whereby it is explained. But in order to a more full explication of this point, and to shew how far the hypothesis of the mind's judging by the various divergency of rays may be of use in determining the apparent place of an object, it will be necessary to premise some few things, which are already well known to those who have any skill in dioptrics.

34 *First*, any radiating point is then distinctly seen when the rays proceeding from it are, by the refractive power of the crystalline, accurately reunited in the retina or fund of the eye: but if they are reunited, either before they arrive at the retina, or after they have passed it, then there is confused vision.

35 *Secondly*, suppose in the adjacent figures NP represent an eye duly framed and retaining its natural figure. In Fig. 1 the rays falling nearly parallel on the eye, are by the crystalline AB refracted, so as their focus or point of union F falls exactly on the retina: but if the rays fall sensibly diverging on the eye, as in Fig. 2, then their focus falls beyond the retina: or if the rays are made to converge by the lens QS before they come at the eye, as in Fig. 3, their focus F will fall before the retina. In which two last cases it is evident from the foregoing section that the appearance of the point Z is confused. And by how much the greater is the convergency, or divergency, of the rays falling on the pupil, by so much the farther will the point of their reunion be from the retina, either before or behind it, and consequently the point Z will appear by so much the more confused. And this, by the bye, may shew us the difference between confused and faint vision. Confused vision is when the rays proceeding from each distinct point of the object are not accurately recollected in one corresponding point on the retina, but take up some space thereon, so that rays from different points become mixed and confused together. This is opposed to a distinct vision, and attends near objects. Faint vision is when by reason of the distance of the object or grossness of the interjacent medium few rays arrive from the object to the eye. This is opposed to vigorous or clear vision, and attends remote objects. But to return.

36 The eye, or (to speak truly) the mind, perceiving only the confusion itself, without ever considering the cause from which it proceeds, doth constantly annex the same degree of distance to the same degree of confusion. Whether that confusion be occasioned by converging or by diverging rays, it matters not. Whence it follows that the eye viewing the object Z through the glass QS (which by refraction causeth the rays ZQ, ZS, etc., to converge) should judge it to be at such a nearness at which if it were

placed, it would radiate on the eye with rays diverging to that degree as would produce the same confusion which is now produced by converging rays, *i.e.* would cover a portion of the retina equal to DC (*vid.* Fig. 3 *supra*). But then this must be understood (to use Dr. Barrow's phrase) *seclusis prænotionibus et præjudiciis*, in case we abstract from all other circumstances of vision, such as the figure, size, faintness, etc. of the visible objects; all which do ordinarily concur to form our idea of distance, the mind having by frequent experience observed their several sorts or degrees to be connected with various distances.

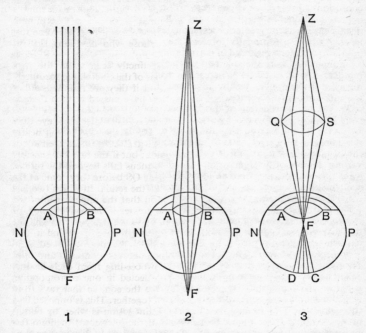

37 It plainly follows from what hath been said that a person perfectly purblind (*i.e.* that could not see an object distinctly but when placed close to his eye) would not make the same wrong judgment that others do in the forementioned case. For to him greater confusions constantly suggesting greater distances, he must, as he recedes from the glass and the object grows more confused, judge it to be at a farther distance, contrary to what they do who have had the perception of the objects growing more confused connected with the idea of approach.

38 Hence also it doth appear there may be good use of computation by lines and angles in optics; not that the mind judgeth of distance immediately by them, but because it judgeth by somewhat which is connected with them, and to the determination whereof they may be subservient. Thus the mind judging of the distance of an object by the confusedness of its appearance, and this confusedness being greater or lesser to the naked eye, according as the object is seen by rays more or less diverging, it follows that a man may make use of the divergency of the rays in computing the apparent distance, though not for its own sake, yet on account of the confusion with which it is connected. But, so it is, the confusion itself is entirely neglected by mathematicians as having no necessary relation with distance, such as the greater or lesser angles of divergency are conceived to have. And these (especially for that they fall under mathematical computation) are alone regarded in determining the apparent places of objects, as though they were the sole and immediate cause of the judgments the mind makes of distance. Whereas, in truth, they should not at all be regarded in themselves, or any otherwise, than as they are supposed to be the cause of confused vision.

39 The not considering of this has been a fundamental and perplexing oversight. For proof whereof we need go no farther than the case before us. It having been observed that the most diverging rays brought into the mind the idea of nearest distance, and that still, as the divergency decreased, the distance increased: and it being thought the connexion between the various degrees of divergency and distance was immediate; this naturally leads one to conclude, from an ill-grounded analogy, that converging rays shall make an object appear at an immense distance: and that, as the convergency increases, the distance (if it were possible) should do so likewise. That this was the cause of Dr. Barrow's mistake is evident from his own words which we have quoted. Whereas had the learned doctor observed that diverging and converging rays, how opposite soever they may seem, do nevertheless agree in producing the same effect, to wit, confusedness of vision, greater degrees whereof are produced indifferently, either as the divergency or convergency of the rays increaseth. And that it is by this effect, which is the same in both, that either the divergency or convergency is perceived by the eye; I say, had he but considered this, it is certain he would have made a quite contrary judgment, and rightly concluded that those rays which fall on the eye with greater degrees of convergency should make the object from whence they proceed appear by so much the nearer. But it is plain it was impossible for any man to attain to a right notion of this matter so long as he had regard only to lines and angles, and did not apprehend the true nature of vision, and how far it was of mathematical consideration.

40 Before we dismiss this subject, it is fit we take notice of a query relating thereto, proposed by the ingenious Mr. Molyneux, in his *Treatise of Dioptrics*,* where speaking of this difficulty, he has these words: 'And

* Par. I. Prop. 31, Sect. 9.

so he (*i.e.* Dr. Barrow) leaves this difficulty to the solution of others, which I (after so great an example) shall do likewise; but with the resolution of the same admirable author of not quitting the evident doctrine which we have before laid down, for determining the *locus objecti*, on account of being pressed by one difficulty which seems inexplicable till a more intimate knowledge of the visive faculty be obtained by mortals. In the meantime, I propose it to the consideration of the ingenious, whether the *locus apparens* of an object placed as in this 9th section be not as much before the eye as the distinct base is behind the eye?' To which query we may venture to answer in the negative. For in the present case the rule for determining the distance of the distinct base, or respective focus from the glass, is this: *As the difference between the distance of the object and focus is to the focus or focal length, so the distance of the object from the glass is to the distance of the respective focus or distinct base from the glass.** Let us now suppose the object to be placed at the distance of the focal length, and one half of the focal length from the glass, and the eye close to the glass, hence it will follow by the rule that the distance of the distinct base behind the eye is double the true distance of the object before the eye. If therefore Mr. Molyneux's conjecture held good, it would follow that the eye should see the object twice as far off as it really is; and in other cases at three or four times its due distance, or more. But this manifestly contradicts experience, the object never appearing, at farthest, beyond its due distance. Whatever, therefore, is built on this supposition (*vid. Corol.* 1. *Prop.* 57, *ibid.*) comes to the ground along with it.

41 From what hath been premised it is a manifest consequence that a man born blind, being made to see, would, at first, have no idea of distance by sight; the sun and stars, the remotest objects as well as the nearer, would all seem to be in his eye, or rather in his mind. The objects intromitted by sight would seem to him (as in truth they are) no other than a new set of thoughts or sensations, each whereof is as near to him as the perceptions of pain or pleasure, or the most inward passions of his soul. For our judging objects perceived by sight to be at any distance, or without the mind, is (*vid.* sect. 28) entirely the effect of experience, which one in those circumstances could not yet have attained to.

42 It is indeed otherwise upon the common supposition that men judge of distance by the angle of the optic axes, just as one in the dark, or a blind-man by the angle comprehended by two sticks, one whereof he held in each hand. For if this were true, it would follow that one blind from his birth being made to see, should stand in need of no new-experience in order to perceive distance by sight. But that this is false has, I think, been sufficiently demonstrated.

43 And perhaps upon a strict inquiry we shall not find that even those who from their birth have grown up in a continued habit of seeing are irrecoverably prejudiced on the other side, to wit, in thinking what they see to be at a distance from them. For at this time it seems agreed on all

* Molyneux Dioptr., Par. I. Prop. 5.

hands, by those who have had any thoughts of that matter, that colours, which are the proper and immediate object of sight, are not without the mind. But then it will be said, by sight we have also the ideas of extension, and figure, and motion; all which may well be thought without, and at some distance from the mind, though colour should not. In answer to this I appeal to any man's experience, whether the visible extension of any object doth not appear as near to him as the colour of that object; nay, whether they do not both seem to be in the very same place. Is not the extension we see coloured, and is it possible for us, so much as in thought, to separate and abstract colour from extension? Now, where the extension is there surely is the figure, and there the motion too. I speak of those which are perceived by sight.

44 But for a fuller explication of this point, and to shew that the immediate objects of sight are not so much as the ideas or resemblances of things placed at a distance, it is requisite that we look nearer into the matter and carefully observe what is meant in common discourse, when one says that which he sees is at a distance from him. Suppose, for example, that looking at the moon I should say it were fifty or sixty semidiameters of the earth distant from me. Let us see what moon this is spoken of: it is plain it cannot be the visible moon, or anything like the visible moon, or that which I see, which is only a round, luminous plane of about thirty visible points in diameter. For in case I am carried from the place where I stand directly towards the moon, it is manifest the object varies, still as I go on; and by the time that I am advanced fifty or sixty semidiameters of the earth, I shall be so far from being near a small, round, luminous flat that I shall perceive nothing like it; this object having long since disappeared, and if I would recover it, it must be by going back to the earth from whence I set out. Again, suppose I perceive by sight the faint and obscure idea of something which I doubt whether it be a man, or a tree, or a tower, but judge it to be at the distance of about a mile. It is plain I cannot mean that what I see is a mile off, or that it is the image or likeness of anything which is a mile off, since that every step I take towards it the appearance alters, and from being obscure, small, and faint, grows clear, large, and vigorous. And when I come to the mile's end, that which I saw first is quite lost, neither do I find anything in the likeness of it.

45 In these and the like instances the truth of the matter stands thus: having of a long time experienced certain ideas, perceivable by touch, as distance, tangible figure, and solidity, to have been connected with certain ideas of sight, I do upon perceiving these ideas of sight forthwith conclude what tangible ideas are, by the wonted ordinary course of Nature like to follow. Looking at an object I perceive a certain visible figure and colour, with some degree of faintness and other circumstances, which from what I have formerly observed, determine me to think that if I advance forward so many paces or miles, I shall be affected with such and such ideas of touch: so that in truth and strictness of speech I neither see distance itself, nor anything that I take to be at a distance. I say, neither distance nor

things placed at a distance are themselves, or their ideas, truly perceived by sight. This I am persuaded of, as to what concerns myself: and I believe whoever will look narrowly into his own thoughts and examine what he means by saying he sees this or that thing at a distance, will agree with me that what he sees only suggests to his understanding that after having passed a certain distance, to be measured by the motion of his body, which is perceivable by touch, he shall come to perceive such and such tangible ideas which have been usually connected with such and such visible ideas. But that one might be deceived by these suggestions of sense, and that there is no necessary connexion between visible and tangible ideas suggested by them, we need go no farther than the next looking-glass or pictures to be convinced. Note that when I speak of tangible ideas, I take the word idea for any the immediate object of sense or understanding, in which large signification it is commonly used by the moderns.

46 From what we have shewn it is a manifest consequence that the ideas of space, outness, and things placed at a distance are not, strictly speaking, the object of sight; they are not otherwise perceived by the eye than by the ear. Sitting in my study I hear a coach drive along the street; I look through the casement and see it; I walk out and enter into it; thus, common speech would incline one to think I heard, saw, and touched the same thing, to wit, the coach. It is nevertheless certain, the ideas intromitted by each sense are widely different and distinct from each other; but having been observed constantly to go together, they are spoken of as one and the same thing. By the variation of the noise I perceive the different distances of the coach, and know that it approaches before I look out. Thus by the ear I perceive distance, just after the same manner as I do by the eye.

47 I do not nevertheless say I hear distance in like manner as I say that I see it, the ideas perceived by hearing not being so apt to be confounded with the ideas of touch as those of sight are. So likewise a man is easily convinced that bodies and external things are not properly the object of hearing; but only sounds, by the mediation whereof the idea of this or that body or distance is suggested to his thoughts. But then one is with more difficulty brought to discern the difference there is betwixt the ideas of sight and touch: though it be certain a man no more sees and feels the same thing than he hears and feels the same thing.

48 One reason of which seems to be this. It is thought a great absurdity to imagine that one and the same thing should have any more than one extension, and one figure. But the extension and figure of a body, being let into the mind two ways, and that indifferently either by sight or touch, it seems to follow that we see the same extension and the same figure which we feel.

49 But if we take a close and accurate view of things, it must be acknowledged that we never see and feel one and the same object. That which is seen is one thing, and that which is felt is another. If the visible figure and extension be not the same with the tangible figure and extension, we are not to infer that one and the same thing has divers extensions. The true

consequence is that the objects of sight and touch are two distinct things. It may perhaps require some thought rightly to conceive this distinction. And the difficulty seems not a little increased, because the combination of visible ideas hath constantly the same name as the combination of tangible ideas wherewith it is connected: which doth of necessity arise from the use and end of language.

50 In order therefore to treat accurately and unconfusedly of vision, we must bear in mind that there are two sorts of objects apprehended by the eye, the one primarily and immediately, the other secondarily and by intervention of the former. Those of the first sort neither are, nor appear to be, without the mind, or at any distance off; they may indeed grow greater or smaller, more confused, or more clear, or more faint, but they do not, cannot approach or recede from us. Whenever we say an object is at a distance, whenever we say it draws near, or goes farther off, we must always mean it of the latter sort, which properly belong to the touch, and are not so truly perceived as suggested by the eye in like manner as thoughts by the ear.

51 No sooner do we hear the words of a familiar language pronounced in our ears, but the ideas corresponding thereto present themselves to our minds: in the very same instant the sound and the meaning enter the understanding: so closely are they united that it is not in our power to keep out the one, except we exclude the other also. We even act in all respects as if we heard the very thoughts themselves. So likewise the secondary objects, or those which are only suggested by sight, do often more strongly affect us, and are more regarded than the proper objects of that sense; along with which they enter into the mind, and with which they have a far more strict connexion, than ideas have with words. Hence it is we find it so difficult to discriminate between the immediate and mediate objects of sight, and are so prone to attribute to the former what belongs only to the latter. They are, as it were, most closely twisted, blended, and incorporated together. And the prejudice is confirmed and riveted in our thoughts by a long tract of time, by the use of language, and want of reflexion. However, I believe anyone that shall attentively consider what we have already said, and shall say, upon this subject before we have done (especially if he pursue it in his own thoughts) may be able to deliver himself from that prejudice. Sure I am it is worth some attention, to whoever would understand the true nature of vision.

52 I have now done with distance, and proceed to shew how it is that we perceive by sight the magnitude of objects. It is the opinion of some that we do it by angles, or by angles in conjunction with distance: but neither angles nor distance being perceivable by sight, and the things we see being in truth at no distance from us, it follows that as we have shewn lines and angles not to be the medium the mind makes use of in apprehending the apparent place, so neither are they the medium whereby it apprehends the apparent magnitude of objects.

53 It is well known that the same extension at a near distance shall subtend a greater angle, and at a farther distance a lesser angle. And by

this principle (we are told) the mind estimates the magnitude of an object, comparing the angle under which it is seen with its distance, and thence inferring the magnitude thereof. What inclines men to this mistake (beside the humour of making one see by geometry) is that the same perceptions or ideas which suggest distance do also suggest magnitude. But if we examine it we shall find they suggest the latter as immediately as the former. I say, they do not first suggest distance, and then leave it to the judgment to use that as a medium whereby to collect the magnitude; but they have as close and immediate a connexion with the magnitude as with the distance; and suggest magnitude as independently of distance as they do distance independently of magnitude. All which will be evident to whoever considers what hath been already said, and what follows.

54 It hath been shewn there are two sorts of objects apprehended by sight; each whereof hath its distinct magnitude, or extension. The one, properly tangible, *i.e.* to be perceived and measured by touch, and not immediately falling under the sense of seeing: the other, properly and immediately visible, by mediation of which the former is brought in view. Each of these magnitudes are greater or lesser, according as they contain in them more or fewer points, they being made up of points or minimums. For, whatever may be said of extension in abstract, it is certain sensible extension is not infinitely divisible. There is a *Minimum Tangibile* and a *Minimum Visibile*, beyond which sense cannot perceive. This everyone's experience will inform him.

55 The magnitude of the object which exists without the mind, and is at a distance, continues always invariably the same: but the visible object still changing as you approach to, or recede from, the tangible object, it hath no fixed and determinate greatness. Whenever, therefore, we speak of the magnitude of anything, for instance a tree or a house, we must mean the tangible magnitude, otherwise there can be nothing steady and free from ambiguity spoken of it. But though the tangible and visible magnitude in truth belong to two distinct objects: I shall nevertheless (especially since those objects are called by the same name, and are observed to coexist), to avoid tediousness and singularity of speech, sometimes speak of them as belonging to one and the same thing.

56 Now in order to discover by what means the magnitude of tangible objects is perceived by sight, I need only reflect on what passes in my own mind, and observe what those things be which introduce the ideas of greater or lesser into my thoughts, when I look on any object. And these I find to be, *first*, the magnitude or extension of the visible object, which being immediately perceived by sight, is connected with that other which is tangible and placed at a distance. *Secondly*, the confusion or distinctness. And *thirdly*, the vigorousness or faintness of the aforesaid visible appearance. *Ceteris paribus*, by how much the greater or lesser the visible object is, by so much the greater or lesser do I conclude the tangible object to be. But, be the idea immediately perceived by sight never so large, yet if it be withal confused, I judge the magnitude of the thing to be but small. If it be distinct and clear, I judge it greater. And if it be faint, I apprehend it

to be yet greater. What is here meant by confusion and faintness hath been explained in sect. 35.

57 Moreover the judgments we make of greatness do, in like manner as those of distance, depend on the disposition of the eye, also on the figure, number, and situation of objects and other circumstances that have been observed to attend great or small tangible magnitudes. Thus, for instance, the very same quantity of visible extension, which in the figure of a tower doth suggest the idea of great magnitude, shall in the figure of a man suggest the idea of much smaller magnitude. That this is owing to the experience we have had of the usual bigness of a tower and a man no one, I suppose, need be told.

58 It is also evident that confusion or faintness have no more a necessary connexion with little or great magnitude than they have with little or great distance. As they suggest the latter, so they suggest the former to our minds. And by consequence, if it were not for experience, we should no more judge a faint or confused appearance to be connected with great or little magnitude, than we should that it was connected with great or little distance.

59 Nor will it be found that great or small visible magnitude hath any necessary relation to great or small tangible magnitude: so that the one may certainly be inferred from the other. But before we come to the proof of this, it is fit we consider the difference there is betwixt the extension and figure which is the proper object of touch, and that other which is termed visible; and how the former is principally, though not immediately taken notice of, when we look at any object. This has been before mentioned, but we shall here inquire into the cause thereof. We regard the objects that environ us in proportion as they are adapted to benefit or injure our own bodies, and thereby produce in our minds the sensations of pleasure or pain. Now bodies operating on our organs, by an immediate application, and the hurt or advantage arising therefrom, depending altogether on the tangible, and not at all on the visible, qualities of any object: this is a plain reason why those should be regarded by us much more than these: and for this end the visive sense seems to have been bestowed on animals, to wit, that by the perception of visible ideas (which in themselves are not capable of affecting or any wise altering the frame of their bodies) they may be able to foresee (from the experience they have had what tangible ideas are connected with such and such visible ideas) and damage or benefit which is like to ensue, upon the application of their own bodies to this or that body which is at a distance. Which foresight, how necessary it is to the preservation of an animal, everyone's experience can inform him. Hence it is that when we look at an object, the tangible figure and extension thereof are principally attended to; whilst there is small heed taken of the visible figure and magnitude, which, though more immediately perceived, do less concern us, and are not fitted to produce any alteration in our bodies.

60 That the matter of fact is true will be evident to anyone who considers that a man placed at ten foot distance is thought as great as if he were

placed at a distance only of five foot: which is true not with relation to the visible, but tangible greatness of the object: the visible magnitude being far greater at one station than it is at the other.

61 Inches, feet, etc., are settled stated lengths whereby we measure objects and estimate their magnitude: we say, for example, an object appears to be six inches or six foot long. Now, that this cannot be meant of visible inches, etc., is evident, because a visible inch is itself no constant, determinate magnitude, and cannot therefore serve to mark out and determine the magnitude of any other thing. Take an inch marked upon a ruler: view it, successively, at the distance of half a foot, a foot, a foot and a half, etc., from the eye: at each of which, and at all the intermediate distances, the inch shall have a different visible extension, *i.e.* there shall be more or fewer points discerned in it. Now I ask which of all these various extensions is that stated, determinate one that is agreed on for a common measure of other magnitudes? No reason can be assigned why we should pitch on one more than another: and except there be some invariable, determinate extension fixed on to be marked by the word inch, it is plain it can be used to little purpose; and to say a thing contains this or that number of inches shall imply no more than that it is extended, without bringing any particular idea of that extension into the mind. Farther, an inch and a foot, from different distances, shall both exhibit the same visible magnitude, and yet at the same time you shall say that one seems several times greater than the other. From all which it is manifest that the judgments we make of the magnitude of objects by sight are altogether in reference to their tangible extension. Whenever we say an object is great, or small, of this or that determinate measure, I say it must be meant of the tangible, and not the visible extension, which, though immediately perceived, is nevertheless little taken notice of.

62 Now, that there is no necessary connexion between these two distinct extensions is evident from hence: because our eyes might have been framed in such a manner as to be able to see nothing but what were less than the *minimum tangibile*. In which case it is not impossible we might have perceived all the immediate objects of sight, the very same that we do now: but unto those visible appearances there would not be connected those different tangible magnitudes that are now. Which shews the judgments we make of the magnitude of things placed at a distance from the various greatness of the immediate objects of sight do not arise from any essential or necessary but only a customary tie, which has been observed between them.

63 Moreover, it is not only certain that any idea of sight might not have been connected with this or that idea of touch, which we now observe to accompany it: but also that the greater visible magnitudes might have been connected with, and introduced into our minds lesser tangible magnitudes, and the lesser visible magnitudes greater tangible magnitudes. Nay, that it actually is so we have daily experience; that object which makes a strong and large appearance, not seeming near so great as another, the visible magnitude whereof is much less, but more faint, and the

appearance [1] upper, or which is the same thing painted lower on the *retina*, which faintness and situation suggest both greater magnitude and greater distance.

64 From which, and from sect. 57 and 58, it is manifest that as we do not perceive the magnitudes of objects immediately by sight, so neither do we perceive them by the mediation of anything which has a necessary connexion with them. Those ideas that now suggest unto us the various magnitudes of external objects before we touch them, might possibly have suggested no such thing: or they might have signified them in a direct contrary manner: so that the very same ideas, on the perception whereof we judge an object to be small, might as well have served to make us conclude it great. Those ideas being in their own nature equally fitted to bring into our minds the idea of small or great, or no size at all of outward objects; just as the words of any language are in their own nature indifferent to signify this or that thing or nothing at all.

65 As we see distance, so we see magnitude. And we see both in the same way that we see shame or anger in the looks of a man. Those passions are themselves invisible, they are nevertheless let in by the eye along with colours and alterations of countenance, which are the immediate object of vision: and which signify them for no other reason than barely because they have been observed to accompany them. Without which experience we should no more have taken blushing for a sign of shame than of gladness.

66 We are nevertheless exceeding prone to imagine those things which are perceived only by the mediation of others to be themselves the immediate objects of sight; or, at least, to have in their own nature a fitness to be suggested by them, before ever they had been experienced to coexist with them. From which prejudice everyone, perhaps, will not find it easy to emancipate himself, by any [but] the clearest convictions of reason. And there are some grounds to think that if there was one only invariable and universal language in the world, and that men were born with the faculty of speaking it, it would be the opinion of many that the ideas of other men's minds were properly perceived by the ear, or had at least a necessary and inseparable tie with the sounds that were affixed to them. All which seems to arise from want of a due application of our discerning faculty, thereby to discriminate between the ideas that are in our understandings, and consider them apart from each other; which would preserve us from confounding those that are different, and make us see what ideas do, and what do not include or imply this or that other idea.

67 There is a celebrated phenomenon, the solution whereof I shall attempt to give by the principles that have been laid down, in reference to the manner wherein we apprehend by sight the magnitude of objects. The apparent magnitude of the moon when placed in the horizon is much greater than when it is in the meridian, though the angle under which the diameter of the moon is seen be not observed greater in the former case

---

[1] [*and the appearance . . . greater distance.* Added in 1732 edition.]

than in the latter: and the horizontal moon doth not constantly appear of the same bigness, but at some times seemeth far greater than at others.

68 Now in order to explain the reason of the moon's appearing greater than ordinary in the horizon, it must be observed that the particles which compose our atmosphere intercept the rays of light proceeding from any object to the eye; and by how much the greater is the portion of atmosphere interjacent between the object and the eye, by so much the more are the rays intercepted; and by consequence the appearance of the object rendered more faint, every object appearing more vigorous or more faint in proportion as it sendeth more or fewer rays into the eye. Now between the eye and the moon, when situated in the horizon, there lies a far greater quantity of atmosphere than there does when the moon is in the meridian. Whence it comes to pass that the appearance of the horizontal moon is fainter, and therefore by sect. 56 it should be thought bigger in that situation than in the meridian, or in any other elevation above the horizon.

69 Farther, the air being variously impregnated, sometimes more and sometimes less, with vapours and exhalations fitted to retund and intercept the rays of light, it follows that the appearance of the horizontal moon hath not always an equal faintness, and by consequence that luminary, though in the very same situation, is at one time judged greater than at another.

70 That we have here given the true account of the phenomena of the horizontal moon will, I suppose, be farther evident to anyone from the following considerations. *First*, it is plain that which in this case suggests the idea of greater magnitude must be something which is itself perceived; for that which is unperceived cannot suggest to our perception any other thing. *Secondly*, it must be something that does not constantly remain the same, but is subject to some change or variation, since the appearance of the horizontal moon varies, being at one time greater than at another. And yet, *thirdly*,[1] it cannot be the visible figure or magnitude, since that remains the same, or is rather lesser, by how much the moon is nearer to the horizon. It remains therefore that the true cause is that affection or alteration of the visible appearance which proceeds from the greater paucity of rays arriving at the eye, and which I term faintness: since this answers all the forementioned conditions, and I am not conscious of any other perception that doth.

71 Add to this that in misty weather it is a common observation that the appearance of the horizontal moon is far larger than usual, which greatly conspires with and strengthens our opinion. Neither would it prove in the least irreconcilable with what we have said, if the horizontal moon should chance sometimes to seem enlarged beyond its usual extent, even in more serene weather. For we must not only have regard to the mist which happens

---

[1] [First edition: Thirdly, *it must not lie in the external circumjacent or intermediate objects but be an affection of the very visible moon itself; since by looking thro' a tube, when all other objects are excluded from sight, the appearance is as great as ever. And yet,* Fourthly,]

to be in the place where we stand; we ought also to take into our thoughts the whole sum of vapours and exhalations which lie betwixt the eye and the moon: all which cooperating to render the appearance of the moon more faint, and thereby increase its magnitude, it may chance to appear greater than it usually does, even in the horizontal position, at a time when, though there be no extraordinary fog or haziness, just in the place where we stand, yet the air between the eye and the moon, taken all together, may be loaded with a greater quantity of interspersed vapours and exhalations that at other times.

72 It may be objected that in consequence of our principles the interposition of a body in some degree opaque, which may intercept a great part of the rays of light, should render the appearance of the moon in the meridian as large as when it is viewed in the horizon. To which I answer, it is not faintness anyhow applied that suggests greater magnitude, there being no necessary but only an experimental connexion between those two things. It follows that the faintness which enlarges the appearance must be applied in such sort, and with such circumstances, as have been observed to attend the vision of great magnitudes. When from a distance we behold great objects, the particles of the intermediate air and vapours, which are themselves unperceivable, do interrupt the rays of light, and thereby render the appearance less strong and vivid: now, faintness of appearance caused in this sort hath been experienced to coexist with great magnitude. But when it is caused by the interposition of an opaque sensible body, this circumstance alters the case, so that a faint appearance this way caused doth not suggest greater magnitude, because it hath not been experienced to coexist with it.

73 Faintness, as well as all other ideas or perceptions which suggest magnitude or distance, doth it in the same way that words suggest the notions to which they are annexed. Now, it is known a word pronounced with certain circumstances, or in a certain context with other words, hath not always the same import and signification that it hath when pronounced in some other circumstances or different context of words. The very same [1] visible appearance as to faintness and all other respects, if placed on high, shall not suggest the same magnitude that it would if it were seen at an equal distance on a level with the eye. The reason whereof is that we are rarely accustomed to view objects at a great height; our concerns lie among things situated rather before than above us, and accordingly our eyes are not placed on the top of our heads, but in such a position as is most convenient for us to see distant objects standing in our way. And this situation of them being a circumstance which usually attends the vision of distant objects, we may from hence account for (what is commonly observed) an object's appearing of different magnitude, even with respect to its horizontal extension, on the top of a steeple, for example, an hundred feet high to one standing below, from what it would if placed at an hundred feet distance on a level with his eye. For it hath been shewn that the judg-

---

[1] [*The very same* ... (to end of section) not in first edition.]

ment we make on the magnitude of a thing depends not on the visible appearance alone, but also on divers other circumstances, any one of which being omitted or varied may suffice to make some alteration in our judgment. Hence, the circumstance of viewing a distant object in such a situation as is usual, and suits with the ordinary posture of the head and eyes being omitted, and instead thereof a different situation of the object, which requires a different posture of the head taking place, it is not to be wondered at if the magnitude be judged different: but it will be demanded why an high object should constantly appear less than an equidistant low object of the same dimensions, for so it is observed to be: it may indeed be granted that the variation of some circumstances may vary the judgment made on the magnitude of high objects, which we are less used to look at: but it does not hence appear why they should be judged less rather than greater? I answer that in case the magnitude of distant objects was suggested by the extent of their visible appearance alone, and thought proportional thereto, it is certain they would then be judged much less than now they seem to be (*vide* sect. 79). But several circumstances concurring to form the judgment we make on the magnitude of distant objects, by means of which they appear far larger than others, whose visible appearance hath an equal or even greater extension; it follows that upon the change or omission of any of those circumstances which are wont to attend the vision of distant objects, and so come to influence the judgments made on their magnitude, they shall proportionably appear less than otherwise they would. For any of those things that caused an object to be thought greater than in proportion to its visible extension being either omitted or applied without the usual circumstances, the judgment depends more entirely on the visible extension, and consequently the object must be judged less. Thus in the present case the situation of the thing seen being different from what it usually is in those objects we have occasion to view, and whose magnitude we observe, it follows that the very same object, being an hundred feet high, should seem less than if it was an hundred feet off on (or nearly on) a level with the eye. What has been here set forth seems to me to have no small share in contributing to magnify the appearance of the horizontal moon, and deserves not to be passed over in the explication of it.

74 If we attentively consider the phenomenon before us, we shall find the not discerning between the mediate and immediate objects of sight to be the chief cause of the difficulty that occurs in the explication of it. The magnitude of the visible moon, or that which is the proper and immediate object of vision, is no greater when the moon is in the horizon than when it is in the meridian. How comes it, therefore, to seem greater in one situation than the other? What is it can put this cheat on the understanding? It has no other perception of the moon than what it gets by sight: and that which is seen is of the same extent, I say, the visible appearance hath the same, or rather a less, magnitude when the moon is viewed in the horizontal than when in the meridional position: and yet it is esteemed greater in the former than in the latter. Herein consists the difficulty, which doth vanish

and admit of a most easy solution, if we consider that as the visible moon is not greater in the horizon than in the meridian, so neither is it thought to be so. It hath been already shewn that in any act of vision the visible object absolutely, or in itself, is little taken notice of, the mind still carrying its view from that to some tangible ideas which have been observed to be connected with it, and by that means come to be suggested by it. So that when a thing is said to appear great or small, or whatever estimate be made of the magnitude of any thing, this is meant not of the visible but of the tangible object. This duly considered, it will be no hard matter to reconcile the seeming contradiction there is, that the moon should appear of a different bigness, the visible magnitude thereof remaining still the same. For by sect. 56 the very same visible extension, with a different faintness, shall suggest a different tangible extension. When therefore the horizontal moon is said to appear greater than the meridional moon, this must be understood not of a greater visible extension, but a of greater tangible or real extension, which by reason of the more than ordinary faintness of the visible appearance, is suggested to the mind along with it.

75 Many attempts have been made by learned men to account for this appearance. Gassendus, Descartes, Hobbes, and several others have employed their thoughts on that subject; but how fruitless and unsatisfactory their endeavours have been is sufficiently shewn in *The Philosophical Transactions,** where you may see their several opinions at large set forth and confuted, not without some surprize at the gross blunders that ingenious men have been forced into by endeavouring to reconcile this appearance with the ordinary Principles of optics. Since the writing of which there hath been published in the *Transactions*† another paper relating to the same affair by the celebrated Dr. Wallis, wherein he attempts to account for that phenomenon which, though it seems not to contain anything new or different from what had been said before by others, I shall nevertheless consider in this place.

76 His opinion, in short, is this; we judge not of the magnitude of an object by the visual angle alone, but by the visual angle in conjunction with the distance. Hence, though the angle remain the same, or even become less, yet if withal the distance seem to have been increased, the object shall appear greater. Now, one way whereby we estimate the distance of any-thing is by the number and extent of the intermediate objects: when therefore the moon is seen in the horizon, the variety of fields, houses, etc., together with the large prospect of the wide extended land or sea that lies between the eye and the utmost limb of the horizon, suggest unto the mind the idea of greater distance, and consequently magnify the appearance. And this, according to Dr. Wallis, is the true account of the extraordinary largeness attributed by the mind to the horizontal moon at a time when the angle subtended by its diameter is not one jot greater than it used to be.

77 With reference to this opinion, not to repeat what hath been already

* Phil. Trans. Num. 187. p. 314.
† Numb. 187. p. 323.

said concerning distance, I shall only observe, *first*, that if the prospect of interjacent objects be that which suggests the idea of farther distance, and this idea of farther distance be the cause that brings into the mind the idea of greater magnitude, it should hence follow that if one looked at the horizontal moon from behind a wall, it would appear no bigger than ordinary. For in that case the wall interposing cuts off all that prospect of sea and land, etc. which might otherwise increase the apparent distance, and thereby the apparent magnitude of the moon. Nor will it suffice to say the memory doth even then suggest all that extent of land, etc., which lies within the horizon; which suggestion occasions a sudden judgment of sense that the moon is farther off and larger than usual. For ask any man who, from such a station beholding the horizontal moon, shall think her greater than usual, whether he hath at that time in his mind any idea of the intermediate objects, or long tract of land that lies between his eye and the extreme edge of the horizon? And whether it be that idea which is the cause of his making the aforementioned judgment? He will, I suppose, reply in the negative, and declare the horizontal moon shall appear greater than the meridional, though he never thinks of all or any of those things that lie between him and it. *Secondly*, it seems impossible by this hypothesis to account for the moon's appearing in the very same situation at one time greater than at another; which nevertheless has been shewn to be very agreeable to the principles we have laid down, and receives a most easy and natural explication from them. For the further clearing [1] up of this point it is to be observed that what we immediately and properly see are only lights and colours in sundry situations and shades and degrees of faintness and clearness, confusion and distinctness. All which visible objects are only in the mind, nor do they suggest ought external, whether distance or magnitude, otherwise than by habitual connexion as words do things. We are also to remark that, beside the straining of the eyes, and beside the vivid and faint, the distinct and confused appearances (which, bearing some proportion to lines and angles, have been substituted instead of them in the foregoing part of this treatise), there are other means which suggest both distance and magnitude; particularly the situation of visible points or objects, as upper or lower; the one suggesting a farther distance and greater magnitude, the other a nearer distance and lesser magnitude: all which is an effect only of custom and experience; there being really nothing intermediate in the line of distance between the uppermost and lowermost, which are both equidistant, or rather at no distance from the eye, as there is also nothing in upper or lower, which by necessary connexion should suggest greater or lesser magnitude. Now, as these customary, experimental means of suggesting distance do likewise suggest magnitude, so they suggest the one as immediately as the other. I say they do not (*vide* sect. 53) first suggest distance, and then leave the mind from thence to infer or compute magnitude, but suggest magnitude as immediately and directly as they suggest distance.

[1] [*For the further clearing* . . . (to the end of section). Added in 1732 edition.]

78 This phenomenon of the horizontal moon is a clear instance of the insufficiency of lines and angles for explaining the way wherein the mind perceives and estimates the magnitude of outward objects. There is nevertheless a use of computation by them in order to determine the apparent magnitude of things, so far as they have a connexion with, and are proportional to, those other ideas or perceptions which are the true and immediate occasions that suggest to the mind the apparent magnitude of things. But this in general may, I think, be observed concerning mathematical computation in optics: that it can never be very precise and exact, since the judgments we make of the magnitude of external things do often depend on several circumstances, which are not proportionable to, or capable of being defined by, lines and angles.

79 From what has been said we may safely deduce this consequence; to wit, that a man born blind and made to see would, at first opening of his eyes, make a very different judgment of the magnitude of objects intromitted by them from what others do. He would not consider the ideas of sight with reference to, or as having any connexion with, the ideas of touch: his view of them being entirely terminated within themselves, he can no otherwise judge them great or small than as they contain a greater or lesser number of visible points. Now, it being certain that any visible point can cover or exclude from view only one other visible point, it follows that whatever object intercepts the view of another hath an equal number of visible points with it; and consequently they shall both be thought by him to have the same magnitude. Hence it is evident one in those circumstances would judge his thumb, with which he might hide a tower or hinder its being seen, equal to that tower, or his hand, the interposition whereof might conceal the firmament from his view, equal to the firmament: how great an inequality soever there may in our apprehensions seem to be betwixt those two things, because of the customary and close connexion that has grown up in our minds between the objects of sight and touch; whereby the very different and distinct ideas of those two senses are so blended and confounded together as to be mistaken for one and the same thing; out of which prejudice we cannot easily extricate ourselves.

80 For the better explaining the nature of vision, and setting the manner wherein we perceive magnitudes in a due light, I shall proceed to make some observations concerning matters relating thereto, whereof the want of reflexion, and duly separating between tangible and visible ideas, is apt to create in us mistaken and confused notions. And *first*, I shall observe that the *minimum visibile* is exactly equal in all beings whatsoever that are endowed with the visive faculty. No exquisite formation of the eye, no peculiar sharpness of sight, can make it less in one creature than in another; for it not being distinguishable into parts, nor in any wise consisting of them, it must necessarily be the same to all. For suppose it otherwise, and that the *minimum visibile* of a mite, for instance, be less than the *minimum visibile* of a man: the latter therefore may by detraction of some part be made equal to the former: it doth therefore consist of parts, which is inconsistent with the notion of a *minimum visibile* or point.

81 It will perhaps be objected that the *minimum visibile* of a man doth really and in itself contain parts whereby it surpasses that of a mite, though they are not perceivable by the man. To which I answer, the *minimum visibile* having (in like manner as all other the proper and immediate objects of sight) been shewn not to have any existence without the mind of him who sees it, it follows there cannot be any part of it that is not actually perceived, and therefore visible. Now for any object to contain several distinct visible parts, and at the same time to be a *minimum visibile*, is a manifest contradiction.

82 Of these visible points we see at all times an equal number. It is every whit as great when our view is contracted and bounded by near objects as when it is extended to larger and remoter. For it being impossible that one *minimum visibile* should obscure or keep out of sight more than one other, it is a plain consequence that when my view is on all sides bounded by the walls of my study, I see just as many visible points as I could, in case that by the removal of the study-walls and all other obstructions, I had a full prospect of the circumjacent fields, mountains, sea, and open firmament: for so long as I am shut up within the walls, by their interposition every point of the external objects is covered from my view: but each point that is seen being able to cover or exclude from sight one only other corresponding point, it follows that whilst my sight is confined to those narrow walls I see as many points, or *minima visibilia*, as I should were those walls away, by looking on all the external objects whose prospect is intercepted by them. Whenever therefore we are said to have a greater prospect at one time than another, this must be understood with relation, not to the proper and immediate, but the secondary and mediate objects of vision, which, as hath been shewn, properly belong to the touch.

83 The visive faculty considered with reference to its immediate objects may be found to labour of two defects. *First*, in respect of the extent or number of visible points that are at once perceivable by it, which is narrow and limited to a certain degree. It can take in at one view but a certain determinate number of *minima visibilia*, beyond which it cannot extend its prospect. *Secondly*, our sight is defective in that its view is not only narrow, but also for the most part confused: of those things that we take in at one prospect we can see but a few at once clearly and unconfusedly: and the more we fix our sight on any one object, by so much the darker and more indistinct shall the rest appear.

84 Corresponding to these two defects of sight, we may imagine as many perfections, to wit, 1*st*, that of comprehending in one view a greater number of visible points. 2*dly*, of being able to view them all equally and at once with the utmost clearness and distinction. That those perfections are not actually in some intelligences of a different order and capacity from ours it is impossible for us to know.

85 In neither of those two ways do microscopes contribute to the improvement of sight; for when we look through a microscope we neither see more visible points, nor are the collateral points more distinct than when we look with the naked eye at objects placed in a due distance. A

microscope brings us, as it were, into a new world: it presents us with a new scene of visible objects quite different from what we behold with the naked eye. But herein consists the most remarkable difference, to wit, that whereas the objects perceived by the eye alone have a certain connexion with tangible objects, whereby we are taught to foresee what will ensue upon the approach or application of distant objects to the parts of our own body, which much conduceth to its preservation, there is not the like connexion between things tangible and those visible objects that are perceived by help of a fine microscope.

86 Hence it is evident that were our eyes turned into the nature of microscopes, we should not be much benefited by the change; we should be deprived of the forementioned advantage we at present receive by the visive faculty, and have left us only the empty amusement of seeing, without any other benefit arising from it. But in that case, it will perhaps be said, our sight would be endued with a far greater sharpness and penetration than it now hath. But it is certain from what we have already shewn that the *minimum visibile* is never greater or lesser, but in all cases constantly the same: and in the case of microscopical eyes I see only this difference, to wit, that upon the ceasing of a certain observable connexion betwixt the divers perceptions of sight and touch, which before enabled us to regulate our actions by the eye, it would now be rendered utterly unserviceable to that purpose.

87 Upon the whole it seems that if we consider the use and end of sight, together with the present state and circumstances of our being, we shall not find any great cause to complain of any defect or imperfection in it, or easily conceive how it could be mended. With such admirable wisdom is that faculty contrived, both for the pleasure and convenience of life.

88 Having finished what I intended to say concerning the distance and magnitude of objects, I come now to treat of the manner wherein the mind perceives by sight their situation. Among the discoveries of the last age, it is reputed none of the least that the manner of vision hath been more clearly explained than ever it had been before. There is at this day no one ignorant that the pictures of external objects are painted on the *retina*, or fund of the eye: that we can see nothing which is not so painted: and that, according as the picture is more distinct or confused, so also is the perception we have of the object: but then in this explication of vision there occurs one mighty difficulty. The objects are painted in an inverted order on the bottom of the eye: the upper part of any object being painted on the lower part of the eye, and the lower part of the object on the upper part of the eye: and so also as to right and left. Since therefore the pictures are thus inverted, it is demanded how it comes to pass that we see the objects erect and in their natural posture?

89 In answer to this difficulty we are told that the mind, perceiving an impulse of a ray of light on the upper part of the eye, considers this ray as coming in a direct line from the lower part of the object; and in like manner tracing the ray that strikes on the lower part of the eye, it is directed to the upper part of the object. Thus in the adjacent figure, C, the lower point of

the object ABC, is projected on *c* the upper part of the eye. So likewise the highest point A is projected on *a* the lowest part of the eye, which makes the representation *cba* inverted: but the mind considering the stroke that is made on *c* as coming in the straight line C*c* from the lower end of the object; and the stroke or impulse on *a* as coming in the line A*a* from the upper end of the object, is directed to make a right judgment of the situation of the object ABC, notwithstanding the picture of it is inverted. This is illustrated by conceiving a blind man who, holding in his hands two sticks that cross each other, doth with them touch the extremities of an object, placed in a perpendicular situation. It is certain this man will judge that to be the upper part of the object which he touches with the stick held in the

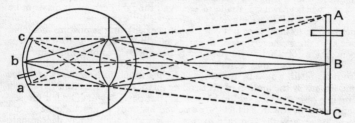

undermost hand, and that to be the lower part of the object which he touches with the stick in his uppermost hand. This is the common explication of the erect appearance of objects, which is generally received and acquiesced in, being (as Mr. Molyneux tells us*) 'allowed by all men as satisfactory'.

90 But this account to me does not seem in any degree true. Did I perceive those impulses, decussations, and directions of the rays of light in like manner as hath been set forth, then indeed it would not be altogether void of probability. And there might be some pretence for the comparison of the blind man and his cross sticks. But the case is far otherwise. I know very well that I perceive no such thing. And of consequence I cannot thereby make an estimate of the situation of objects. I appeal to anyone's experience, whether he be conscious to himself that he thinks on the intersection made by the radious pencils, or pursues the impulses they give in right lines, whenever he perceives by sight the position of any object? To me it seems evident that crossing and tracing of the rays is never thought on by children, idiots, or in truth by any other, save only those who have applied themselves to the study of optics. And for the mind to judge of the situation of objects by those things without perceiving them, or to perceive them without knowing it, is equally beyond my comprehension. Add to this that the explaining the manner of vision by the example of cross sticks and hunting for the object along the axes of the radious pencils, doth

* Diopt. par. 2. c. 7. p. 289.

suppose the proper objects of sight to be perceived at a distance from us, contrary to what hath been demonstrated.

91 It remains, therefore, that we look for some other explication of this difficulty: and I believe it not impossible to find one, provided we examine it to the bottom, and carefully distinguish between the ideas of sight and touch; which cannot be too oft inculcated in treating of vision: but more especially throughout the consideration of this affair we ought to carry that distinction in our thoughts: for that from want of a right understanding thereof the difficulty of explaining erect vision seems chiefly to arise.

92 In order to disentangle our minds from whatever prejudices we may entertain with relation to the subject in hand, nothing seems more apposite than the taking into our thoughts the case of one born blind, and afterwards, when grown up, made to see. And though, perhaps, it may not be an easy task to divest ourselves entirely of the experience received from sight, so as to be able to put our thoughts exactly in the posture of such a one's, we must, nevertheless, as far as possible, endeavour to frame true conceptions of what might reasonably be supposed to pass in his mind.

93 It is certain that a man actually blind, and who had continued so from his birth, would by the sense of feeling attain to have ideas of upper and lower. By the motion of his hand he might discern the situation of any tangible object placed within his reach. That part on which he felt himself supported, or towards which he perceived his body to gravitate, he would term lower, and the contrary to this upper; and accordingly denominate whatsoever objects he touched.

94 But then, whatever judgments he makes concerning the situation of objects are confined to those only that are perceivable by touch. All those things that are intangible and of a spiritual nature, his thoughts and desires, his passions, and in general all the modifications of the soul, to these he would never apply the terms *upper* and *lower*, except only in a metaphorical sense. He may, perhaps, by way of allusion, speak of high or low thoughts: but those terms in their proper signification would never be applied to anything that was not conceived to exist without the mind. For a man born blind, and remaining in the same state, could mean nothing else by the words *higher* and *lower* than a greater or lesser distance from the earth: which distance he would measure by the motion or application of his hand or some other part of his body. It is therefore evident that all those things which, in respect of each other, would by him be thought higher or lower, must be such as were conceived to exist without his mind, in the ambient space.

95 Whence it plainly follows that such a one, if we suppose him made to see, would not at first sight think that anything he saw was high or low, erect or inverted; for it hath been already demonstrated in sect. 41 that he would not think the things he perceived by sight to be at any distance from him, or without his mind. The objects to which he had hitherto been used to apply the terms *up* and *down*, *high* and *low*, were such only as affected or were some way perceived by his touch: but the proper objects of vision make a new set of ideas, perfectly distinct and different

from the former, and which can in no sort make themselves perceived by touch. There is, therefore, nothing at all that could induce him to think those terms applicable to them: nor would he ever think it till such time as he had observed their connexion with tangible objects, and the same prejudice began to insinuate itself into his understanding, which from their infancy had grown up in the understandings of other men.

96 To set this matter in a clearer light I shall make use of an example. Suppose the above-mentioned blind person by his touch perceives a man to stand erect. Let us inquire into the manner of this. By the application of his hand to the several parts of a human body he had perceived different tangible ideas, which being collected into sundry complex ones, have distinct names annexed to them. Thus one combination of a certain tangible figure, bulk, and consistency of parts is called the head, another the hand, a third the foot, and so of the rest: all which complex ideas could, in his understanding, be made up only of ideas perceivable by touch. He had also by his touch obtained an idea of earth or ground, towards which he perceives the parts of his body to have a natural tendency. Now, by *erect* nothing more being meant than that perpendicular position of a man wherein his feet are nearest to the earth, if the blind person by moving his hand over the parts of the man who stands before him perceives the tangible ideas that compose the head to be farthest from, and those that compose the feet to be nearest to, that other combination of tangible ideas which he calls earth, he will denominate that man erect. But if we suppose him on a sudden to receive his sight, and that he behold a man standing before him, it is evident in that case he would neither judge the man he sees to be erect nor inverted; for he never having known those terms applied to any other save tangible things, or which existed in the space without him, and what he sees neither being tangible nor perceived as existing without, he could not know that in propriety of language they were applicable to it.

97 Afterwards, when upon turning his head or eyes up and down to the right and left he shall observe the visible objects to change, and shall also attain to know that they are called by the same names, and connected with the objects perceived by touch; then indeed he will come to speak of them and their situation, in the same terms that he has been used to apply to tangible things; and those that he perceives by turning up his eyes he will call upper, and those that by turning down his eyes he will call lower.

98 And this seems to me the true reason why he should think those objects uppermost that are painted on the lower part of his eye: for by turning the eye up they shall be distinctly seen; as likewise those that are painted on the highest part of the eye shall be distinctly seen by turning the eye down, and are for that reason esteemed lowest; for we have shewn that to the immediate objects of sight considered in themselves, he would not attribute the terms *high* and *low*. It must therefore be on account of some circumstances which are observed to attend them: and these, it is plain, are the actions of turning the eye up and down, which suggest a very obvious reason why the mind should denominate the objects of sight accordingly high or low. And without this motion of the eye, this turning

it up and down in order to discern different objects, doubtless *erect*, *inverse*, and other the like terms relating to the position of tangible objects, would never have been transferred, or in any degree apprehended to belong to the ideas of sight: the mere act of seeing including nothing in it to that purpose; whereas the different situations of the eye naturally direct the mind to make a suitable judgment of the situation of objects intromitted by it.

99 Farther, when he has by experience learned the connexion there is between the several ideas of sight and touch, he will be able, by the perception he has of the situation of visible things in respect of one another, to make a sudden and true estimate of the situation of outward, tangible things corresponding to them. And thus it is he shall perceive by sight the situation of external objects which do not properly fall under that sense.

100 I know we are very prone to think that, if just made to see, we should judge of the situation of visible things as we do now: but we are also as prone to think that, at first sight, we should in the same way apprehend the distance and magnitude of objects as we do now: which hath been shewn to be a false and groundless persuasion. And for the like reasons the same censure may be passed on the positive assurance that most men, before they have thought sufficiently of the matter, might have of their being able to determine by the eye at first view, whether objects were erect or inverse.

101 It will, perhaps, be objected to our opinion that a man, for instance, being thought erect when his feet are next the earth, and inverted when his head is next the earth, it doth hence follow that by the mere act of vision, without any experience or altering the situation of the eye, we should have determined whether he were erect or inverted: for both the earth itself, and the limbs of the man who stands thereon, being equally perceived by sight, one cannot choose seeing what part of the man is nearest the earth, and what part farthest from it, *i.e.* whether he be erect or inverted.

102 To which I answer, the ideas which constitute the tangible earth and man are entirely different from those which constitute the visible earth and man. Nor was it possible, by virtue of the visive faculty alone, without superadding any experience of touch, or altering the position of the eye, ever to have known, or so much as suspected, there had been any relation or connexion between them. Hence a man at first view would not denominate anything he saw earth, or head, or foot; and consequently he could not tell by the mere act of vision whether the head or feet were nearest the earth: nor, indeed, would we have thereby any thought of earth or man, erect or inverse, at all: which will be made yet more evident if we nicely observe, and make a particular comparison between, the ideas of both senses.

103 That which I see is only variety of light and colours. That which I feel is hard or soft, hot or cold, rough or smooth. What similitude, what connexion have those ideas with these? Or how is it possible that anyone should see reason to give one and the same name to combinations of ideas

so very different before he had experienced their coexistence? We do not find there is any necessary connexion betwixt this or that tangible quality and any colour whatsoever. And we may sometimes perceive colours where there is nothing to be felt. All which doth make it manifest that no man, at first receiving of his sight, would know there was any agreement between this or that particular object of his sight and any object of touch he had been already acquainted with: the colours, therefore, of the head would to him no more suggest the idea of head than they would the idea of foot.

104 Farther, we have at large shewn (*vid*. sect. 63 and 64) there is no discoverable necessary connexion between any given visible magnitude and any one particular tangible magnitude; but that it is entirely the result of custom and experience, and depends on foreign and accidental circumstances that we can by the perception of visible extension inform ourselves what may be the extension of any tangible object connected with it. Hence it is certain that neither the visible magnitude of head or foot would bring along with them into the mind, at first opening of the eyes, the respective tangible magnitudes of those parts.

105 By the foregoing section it is plain the visible figure of any part of the body hath no necessary connexion with the tangible figure thereof, so as at first sight to suggest it to the mind. For figure is the termination of magnitude; whence it follows that no visible magnitude having in its own nature an aptness to suggest any one particular tangible magnitude, so neither can any visible figure be inseparably connected with its corresponding tangible figure: so as of itself and in a way prior to experience, it might suggest it to the understanding. This will be farther evident if we consider that what seems smooth and round to the touch may to sight, if viewed through a microscope, seem quite otherwise.

106 From all which laid together and duly considered, we may clearly deduce this inference. In the first act of vision no idea entering by the eye would have a perceivable connexion with the ideas to which the names *earth, man, head, foot*, etc., were annexed in the understanding of a person blind from his birth; so as in any sort to introduce them into his mind, or make themselves be called by the same names, and reputed the same things with them, as afterwards they come to be.

107 There doth, nevertheless, remain one difficulty, which perhaps may seem to press hard on our opinion, and deserve not to be passed over: for though it be granted that neither the colour, size, nor figure of the visible feet have any necessary connexion with the ideas that compose the tangible feet, so as to bring them at first sight into my mind, or make me in danger of confounding them before I had been used to, and for some time experienced their connexion: yet thus much seems undeniable, namely, that the number of the visible feet being the same with that of the tangible feet, I may from hence without any experience of sight reasonably conclude that they represent or are connected with the feet rather than the head. I say, it seems the idea of two visible feet will sooner suggest to the mind the idea of two tangible feet than of one head; so that the blind man upon

first reception of the visive faculty might know which were the feet or two, and which the head or one.

108 In order to get clear of this seeming difficulty we need only observe that diversity of visible objects doth not necessarily infer diversity of tangible objects corresponding to them. A picture painted with great variety of colours affects the touch in one uniform manner; it is therefore evident that I do not by any necessary consecution, independent of experience, judge of the number of things tangible from the number of things visible. I should not, therefore, at first opening my eyes conclude that because I see two I shall feel two. How, therefore, can I, before experience teaches me, know that the visible legs, because two, are connected with the tangible legs, or the visible head, because one, is connected with the tangible head? The truth is, the things I see are so very different and heterogeneous from the things I feel that the perception of the one would never have suggested the other to my thoughts, or enabled me to pass the least judgment thereon, until I had experienced their connexion.

109 But for a fuller illustration of this matter it ought to be considered that number (however some may reckon it amongst the primary qualities) is nothing fixed and settled, really existing in things themselves. It is entirely the creature of the mind, considering either an idea by itself, or any combination of ideas to which it gives one name, and so makes it pass for an unit. According as the mind variously combines its ideas the unit varies: and as the unit, so the number, which is only a collection of units, doth also vary. We call a window one, a chimney one, and yet a house in which there are many windows and many chimneys hath an equal right to be called one, and many houses go to the making of one city. In these and the like instances it is evident the unit constantly relates to the particular draughts the mind makes of its ideas, to which it affixes names, and wherein it includes more or less as best suits its own ends and purposes. Whatever, therefore, the mind considers as one, that is an unit. Every combination of ideas is considered as one thing by the mind, and in token thereof is marked by one name. Now, this naming and combining together of ideas is perfectly arbitrary, and done by the mind in such sort as experience shews it to be most convenient: without which our ideas had never been collected into such sundry distinct combinations as they now are.

110 Hence it follows that a man born blind and afterwards, when grown up, made to see, would not in the first act of vision parcel out the ideas of sight into the same distinct collections that others do, who have experienced which do regularly coexist and are proper to be bundled up together under one name. He would not, for example, make into one complex idea, and thereby esteem an unit, all those particular ideas which constitute the visible head or foot. For there can be no reason assigned why he should do so, barely upon his seeing a man stand upright before him. There crowd into his mind the ideas which compose the visible man, in company with all the other ideas of sight perceived at the same time: but all these ideas offered at once to his view, he would not distribute into sundry

distinct combinations till such time as by observing the motion of the parts of the man and other experiences he comes to know which are to be separated and which to be collected together.

111 From what hath been premised it is plain the objects of sight and touch make, if I may so say, two sets of ideas which are widely different from each other. To objects of either kind we indifferently attribute the terms high and low, right and left, and suchlike, denoting the position or situation of things: but then we must well observe that the position of any object is determined with respect only to objects of the same sense. We say any object of touch is high or low, according as it is more or less distant from the tangible earth: and in like manner we denominate any object of sight high or low in proportion as it is more or less distant from the visible earth: but to define the situation of visible things with relation to the distance they bear from any tangible thing, or *vice versa*, this were absurd and perfectly unintelligible. For all visible things are equally in the mind, and take up no part of the external space: and consequently are equidistant from any tangible thing which exists without the mind.

112 Or rather, to speak truly, the proper objects of sight are at no distance, neither near nor far, from any tangible thing. For if we inquire narrowly into the matter we shall find that those things only are compared together in respect of distance which exist after the same manner, or appertain unto the same sense. For by the distance between any two points nothing more is meant than the number of intermediate points: if the given points are visible the distance between them is marked out by the number of the interjacent visible points: if they are tangible, the distance between them is a line consisting of tangible points; but if they are one tangible and the other visible, the distance between them doth neither consist of points perceivable by sight nor by touch, *i.e.* it is utterly inconceivable. This, perhaps, will not find an easy admission into all men's understanding: however, I should gladly be informed whether it be not true by anyone who will be at the pains to reflect a little and apply it home to his thoughts.

113 The not observing what has been delivered in the two last sections seems to have occasioned no small part of the difficulty that occurs in the business of erect appearances. The head, which is painted nearest the earth, seems to be farthest from it: and on the other hand the feet, which are painted farthest from the earth, are thought nearest to it. Herein lies the difficulty, which vanishes if we express the thing more clearly and free from ambiguity, thus: how comes it that to the eye the visible head which is nearest the tangible earth seems farthest from the earth, and the visible feet, which are farthest from the tangible earth, seem nearest the earth? The question being thus proposed, who sees not the difficulty is founded on a supposition that the eye, or visive faculty, or rather the soul by means thereof, should judge of the situation of visible objects with reference to their distance from the tangible earth? Whereas it is evident the tangible earth is not perceived by sight: and it hath been shewn in the two last preceding sections that the location of visible objects is determined only

by the distance they bear from one another; and that it is nonsense to talk of distance, far or near, between a visible and tangible thing.

114 If we confine our thoughts to the proper objects of sight, the whole is plain and easy. The head is painted farthest from, and the feet nearest to, the visible earth; and so they appear to be. What is there strange or unaccountable in this? Let us suppose the pictures in the fund of the eye to be the immediate objects of the sight. The consequence is that things should appear in the same posture they are painted in; and is it not so? The head which is seen seems farthest from the earth which is seen; and the feet which are seen seem nearest to the earth, which is seen; and just so they are painted.

115 But, say you, the picture of the man is inverted, and yet the appearance is erect: I ask, what mean you by the picture of the man, or, which is the same thing, the visible man's being inverted? You tell me it is inverted, because the heels are uppermost and the head undermost? Explain me this. You say that by the head's being undermost you mean that it is nearest to the earth; and by the heels being uppermost that they are farthest from the earth. I ask again what earth you mean? You cannot mean the earth that is painted on the eye, or the visible earth: for the picture of the head is farthest from the picture of the earth, and the picture of the feet nearest to the picture of the earth; and accordingly the visible head is farthest from the visible earth, and the visible feet nearest to it. It remains, therefore, that you mean the tangible earth, and so determine the situation of visible things with respect to tangible things; contrary to what hath been demonstrated in sect. 111 and 112. The two distinct provinces of sight and touch should be considered apart, and as if their objects had no intercourse, no manner of relation one to another, in point of distance or position.

116 Farther, what greatly contributes to make us mistake in this matter is that when we think of the pictures in the fund of the eye, we imagine ourselves looking on the fund of another's eye, or another looking on the fund of our own eye, and beholding the pictures painted thereon. Suppose two eyes A and B: A from some distance looking on the pictures in B sees them inverted, and for that reason concludes they are inverted in B: but this is wrong. There are projected in little on the bottom of A the images of the pictures of, suppose, man, earth, etc., which are painted on B. And besides these the eye B itself, and the objects which environ it, together with another earth, are projected in a larger size on A. Now, by the eye A these larger images are deemed the true objects, and the lesser only pictures in miniature. And it is with respect to those greater images that it determines the situation of the smaller images: so that comparing the little man with the great earth, A judges him inverted, or that the feet are farthest from and the head nearest to the great earth. Whereas, if A compare the little man with the little earth, then he will appear erect, *i.e.* his head shall seem farthest from, and his feet nearest to, the little earth. But we must consider that B does not see two earths as A does: it sees only what is represented by the little pictures in A, and consequently shall judge the man erect. For, in truth, the man in B is not inverted, for

there the feet are next the earth; but it is the representation of it in A which is inverted, for there the head of the representation of the picture of the man in B is next the earth, and the feet farthest from the earth, meaning the earth which is without the representation of the pictures in B. For if you take the little images of the pictures in B, and consider them by themselves, and with respect only to one another, they are all erect and in their natural posture.

117 Farther, there lies a mistake in our imagining that the pictures of external objects are painted on the bottom of the eye. It hath been shewn there is no resemblance between the ideas of sight and things tangible. It hath likewise been demonstrated that the proper objects of sight do not exist without the mind. Whence it clearly follows that the pictures painted on the bottom of the eye are not the pictures of external objects. Let anyone consult his own thoughts, and then say what affinity, what likeness there is between that certain variety and disposition of colours which constitute the visible man, or picture of a man, and that other combination of far different ideas, sensible by touch, which compose the tangible man. But if this be the case, how come they to be accounted pictures or images, since that supposes them to copy or represent some originals or other?

118 To which I answer: in the forementioned instance the eye A takes the little images, included within the representation of the other eye B, to be pictures or copies, whereof the archetypes are not things existing without, but the larger pictures projected on its own fund: and which by A are not thought pictures, but the originals, or true things themselves. Though if we suppose a third eye C from a due distance to behold the fund of A, then indeed the things projected thereon shall, to C, seem pictures or images in the same sense that those projected on B do to A.

119 Rightly to conceive this point we must carefully distinguish between the ideas of sight and touch, between the visible and tangible eye; for certainly on the tangible eye nothing either is or seems to be painted. Again, the visible eye, as well as all other visible objects, hath been shewn to exist only in the mind, which perceiving its own ideas, and comparing them together, calls some *pictures* in respect of others. What hath been said, being rightly comprehended and laid together, doth, I think, afford a full and genuine explication of the erect appearance of objects; which phenomenon, I must confess, I do not see how it can be explained by any theories of vision hitherto made public.

120 In treating of these things the use of language is apt to occasion some obscurity and confusion, and create in us wrong ideas: for language being accommodated to the common notions and prejudices of men, it is scarce possible to deliver the naked and precise truth without great circumlocution, impropriety, and (to an unwary reader) seeming contradictions; I do therefore once for all desire whoever shall think it worth his while to understand what I have written concerning vision, that he would not stick in this or that phrase, or manner of expression, but candidly collect my meaning from the whole sum and tenor of my discourse, and laying aside the words as much as possible, consider the bare notions themselves, and

then judge whether they are agreeable to truth and his own experience, or no.

121 We have shewn the way wherein the mind by mediation of visible ideas doth perceive or apprehend the distance, magnitude, and situation of tangible objects. We come now to inquire more particularly concerning the difference between the ideas of sight and touch, which are called by the same names, and see whether there be any idea common to both senses. From what we have at large set forth and demonstrated in the foregoing parts of this treatise, it is plain there is no one selfsame numerical extension perceived both by sight and touch; but that the particular figures and extensions perceived by sight, however they may be called by the same names and reputed the same things with those perceived by touch, are nevertheless different, and have an existence distinct and separate from them: so that the question is not now concerning the same numerical ideas, but whether there be any one and the same sort or species of ideas equally perceivable to both senses; or, in other words, whether extension, figure, and motion perceived by sight are not specifically distinct from extension, figure, and motion perceived by touch.

122 But before I come more particularly to discuss this matter, I find it proper to consider extension in abstract: for of this there is much talk, and I am apt to think that when men speak of extension as being an idea common to two senses, it is with a secret supposition that we can single out extension from all other tangible and visible qualities, and form thereof an abstract idea, which idea they will have common both to sight and touch. We are therefore to understand by extension in abstract an idea of extension, for instance, a line or surface entirely stripped of all other sensible qualities and circumstances that might determine it to any particular existence; it is neither black nor white, nor red, nor hath it any colour at all, or any tangible quality whatsoever, and consequently it is of no finite determinate magnitude: for that which bounds or distinguishes one extension from another is some quality or circumstance wherein they disagree.

123 Now I do not find that I can perceive, imagine, or any wise frame in my mind such an abstract idea as is here spoken of. A line or surface which is neither black, nor white, nor blue, nor yellow, etc., nor long, nor short, nor rough, nor smooth, nor square, nor round, etc., is perfectly incomprehensible. This I am sure of as to myself: how far the faculties of other men may reach they best can tell.

124 It is commonly said that the object of geometry is abstract extension: but geometry contemplates figures: now, figure is the termination of magnitude: but we have shewn that extension in abstract hath no finite determinate magnitude. Whence it clearly follows that it can have no figure, and consequently is not the object of geometry. It is indeed a tenet as well of the modern as of the ancient philosophers that all general truths are concerning universal abstract ideas; without which, we are told, there could be no science, no demonstration of any general proposition in geometry. But it were no hard matter, did I think it necessary to my present purpose, to shew that propositions and demonstrations in geometry might

be universal, though they who make them never think of abstract general ideas of triangles or circles.

125 After reiterated endeavours to apprehend the general idea of a triangle, I have found it altogether incomprehensible. And surely if any-one were able to introduce that idea into my mind, it must be the author of the *Essay concerning Human Understanding*; he who has so far distinguished himself from the generality of writers by the clearness and significancy of what he says. Let us therefore see how this celebrated author describes the general or abstract idea of a triangle. 'It must be (says he) neither oblique nor rectangular, neither equilateral, equicrural, nor scalenum; but all and none of these at once. In effect, it is somewhat imperfect that cannot exist; an idea, wherein some parts of several different and inconsistent ideas are put together' *Essay on Hum. Understand. B.* iv. C. 7. S. 9. This is the idea which he thinks needful for the enlargement of knowledge, which is the subject of mathematical demonstration, and without which we could never come to know any general proposition concerning triangles. That author acknowledges it doth 'require some pains and skill to form this general idea of a triangle.' *ibid.* But had he called to mind what he says in another place, to wit, 'That ideas of mixed modes wherein any inconsistent ideas are put together cannot so much as exist in the mind, *i.e.* be conceived.' *vid. B.* iii. C. 10. S. 33. *ibid.* I say, had this occurred to his thoughts, it is not improbable he would have owned it above all the pains and skill he was master of to form the above-mentioned idea of a triangle, which is made up of manifest, staring contradictions. That a man who laid so great a stress on clear and determinate ideas should nevertheless talk at this rate seems very surprising. But the wonder will lessen if it be considered that the source whence this opinion flows is the prolific womb which has brought forth innumerable errors and difficulties in all parts of philosophy and in all the sciences: but this matter, taken in its full extent, were a subject too comprehensive to be insisted on in this place. And so much for extension in abstract.

126 Some, perhaps, may think pure space, *vacuum*, or trine dimension to be equally the object of sight and touch: but though we have a very great propension to think the ideas of outness and space to be the im-mediate object of sight, yet, if I mistake not, in the foregoing parts of this essay that hath been clearly demonstrated to be a mere delusion, arising from the quick and sudden suggestion of fancy, which so closely connects the idea of distance with those of sight, that we are apt to think it is itself a proper and immediate object of that sense till reason corrects the mistake.

127 It having been shewn that there are no abstract ideas of figure, and that it is impossible for us by any precision of thought to frame an idea of extension separate from all other visible and tangible qualities which shall be common both to sight and touch: the question now remaining is, whether the particular extensions, figures, and motions perceived by sight be of the same kind with the particular extensions, figures, and motions perceived by touch? In answer to which I shall venture to lay down the

following proposition: *The extension, figures, and motions perceived by sight are specifically distinct from the ideas of touch called by the same names, nor is there any such thing as one idea or kind of idea common to both senses.* This proposition may without much difficulty be collected from what hath been said in several places of this essay. But because it seems so remote from, and contrary to, the received notions and settled opinion of mankind, I shall attempt to demonstrate it more particularly and at large by the following arguments.

128 When upon perception of an idea I range it under this or that sort, it is because it is perceived after the same manner, or because it has a likeness or conformity with, or affects me in the same way as, the ideas of the sort I rank it under. In short, it must not be entirely new, but have something in it old and already perceived by me. It must, I say, have so much at least in common with the ideas I have before known and named as to make me give it the same name with them. But it has been, if I mistake not, clearly made out that a man born blind would not at first reception of his sight think the things he saw were of the same nature with the objects of touch, or had anything in common with them; but that they were a new set of ideas, perceived in a new manner, and entirely different from all he had ever perceived before: so that he would not call them by the same name, nor repute them to be of the same sort with anything he had hitherto known.[1]

129 *Secondly,* light and colours are allowed by all to constitute a sort or species entirely different from the ideas of touch: nor will any man, I presume, say they can make themselves perceived by that sense: but there is no other immediate object of sight besides light and colours. It is therefore a direct consequence that there is no idea common to both senses.

130 It is a prevailing opinion, even amongst those who have thought and writ most accurately concerning our ideas and the ways whereby they enter into the understanding, that something more is perceived by sight than barely light and colours with their variations. Mr. Locke termeth sight, 'The most comprehensive of all our senses, conveying to our minds the ideas of light and colours, which are peculiar only to that sense; and also the far different ideas of space, figure, and motion.' *Essay on Human Understand. B.* ii. C. 9. S. 9. Space or distance, we have shewn, is not otherwise the object of sight than of hearing. *vid.* sect. 46. And as for figure and extension, I leave it to anyone that shall calmly attend to his own clear and distinct ideas to decide whether he has any idea intromitted immediately and properly by sight save only light and colours: or whether it be possible for him to frame in his mind a distinct abstract idea of visible extension or figure exclusive of all colour: and on the other hand, whether he can conceive colour without visible extension? For my own part, I

---

[1] [First edition: *And surely, the judgment of such an unprejudiced person is more to be relied on in this case, than the sentiments of the generality of men: who in this, as in almost everything else, suffer themselves to be guided by custom, and the erroneous suggestions of prejudice, rather than reason and sedate reflexion.*]

must confess I am not able to attain so great a nicety of abstraction: in a strict sense, I see nothing but light and colours, with their several shades and variations. He who beside these doth also perceive by sight ideas far different and distinct from them hath that faculty in a degree more perfect and comprehensive than I can pretend to. It must be owned that by the mediation of light and colours other far different ideas are suggested to my mind: but so they are by hearing, which beside sounds which are peculiar to that sense, doth by their mediation suggest not only space, figure, and motion, but also all other ideas whatsoever that can be signified by words.

131 *Thirdly*, it is, I think, an axiom universally received that quantities of the same kind may be added together and make one entire sum. Mathematicians add lines together: but they do not add a line to a solid, or conceive it as making one sum with a surface: these three kinds of quantity being thought incapable of any such mutual addition, and consequently of being compared together in the several ways of proportion, are by then esteemed entirely disparate and heterogeneous. Now let anyone try in his thoughts to add a visible line or surface to a tangible line or surface, so as to conceive them making one continued sum or whole. He that can do this may think them homogeneous: but he that cannot, must by the foregoing axiom think them heterogeneous. A blue and a red line I can conceive added together into one sum and making one continued line: but to make in my thoughts one continued line of a visible and tangible line added together is, I find, a task far more difficult, and even insurmountable: and I leave it to the reflexion and experience of every particular person to determine for himself.

132 A farther confirmation of our tenet may be drawn from the solution of Mr. Molyneux's problem, published by Mr. Locke in his *Essay*: which I shall set down as it there lies, together with Mr. Locke's opinion of it, ' "Suppose a man born blind, and now adult, and taught by his touch to distinguish between a cube and a sphere of the same metal, and nighly of the same bigness, so as to tell, when he felt one and t'other, which is the cube and which the sphere. Suppose then the cube and sphere placed on a table, and the blind man to be made to see: *quaere*, whether by his sight, before he touched them, he could now distinguish and tell which is the globe, which the cube?" To which the acute and judicious proposer answers: "Not. For though he has obtained the experience of how a globe, how a cube, affects his touch, yet he has not yet attained the experience that what affects his touch so or so must affect his sight so or so: or that a protuberant angle in the cube that pressed his hand unequally shall appear to his eye as it doth in the cube." I agree with this thinking gentleman, whom I am proud to call my friend, in his answer to this his problem; and am of opinion that the blind man at first sight would not be able with certainty to say which was the globe, which the cube, whilst he only saw them.' (*Essay on Human Understanding*, B. ii. C. 9. S. 8.)

133 Now, if a square surface perceived by touch be of the same sort with a square surface perceived by sight, it is certain the blind man here mentioned might know a square surface as soon as he saw it: it is no more

but introducing into his mind by a new inlet an idea he has been already well acquainted with. Since, therefore, he is supposed to have known by his touch that a cube is a body terminated by square surfaces, and that a sphere is not terminated by square surfaces: upon the supposition that a visible and tangible square differ only *in numero* it follows that he might know, by the unerring mark of the square surfaces, which was the cube, and which not, while he only saw them. We must therefore allow either that visible extension and figures are specifically distinct from tangible extension and figures, or else that the solution of this problem given by those two thoughtful and ingenious men is wrong.

134 Much more might be laid together in proof of the proposition I have advanced: but what has been said is, if I mistake not, sufficient to convince anyone that shall yield a reasonable attention: and as for those that will not be at the pains of a little thought, no multiplication of words will ever suffice to make them understand the truth, or rightly conceive my meaning.

135 I cannot let go the above-mentioned problem without some reflexion on it. It hath been made evident that a man blind from his birth would not, at first sight, denominate anything he saw by the names he had been used to appropriate to ideas of touch, *vid*. sect. 106. Cube, sphere, table are words he has known applied to things perceivable by touch, but to things perfectly intangible he never knew them applied. Those words in their wonted application always marked out to his mind bodies or solid things which were perceived by the resistance they gave: but there is no solidity, no resistance or protrusion, perceived by sight. In short, the ideas of sight are all new perceptions, to which there be no names annexed in his mind: he cannot therefore understand what is said to him concerning them: and to ask of the two bodies he saw placed on the table, which was the sphere, which the cube? were to him a question downright bantering and unintelligible; nothing he sees being able to suggest to his thoughts the idea of body, distance, or in general of anything he had already known.

136 It is a mistake to think the same thing affects both sight and touch. If the same angle or square which is the object of touch be also the object of vision, what should hinder the blind man at first sight from knowing it? For though the manner wherein it affects the sight be different from that wherein it affected his touch, yet, there being beside this manner or circumstance, which is new and unknown, the angle or figure, which is old and known, he cannot choose but discern it.

137 Visible figure and extension having been demonstrated to be of a nature entirely different and heterogeneous from tangible figure and extension, it remains that we inquire concerning motion. Now that visible motion is not of the same sort with tangible motion seems to need no farther proof, it being an evident corollary from what we have shewn concerning the difference there is between visible and tangible extension: but for a more full and express proof hereof we need only observe that one who had not yet experienced vision would not at first sight know motion. Whence it clearly follows that motion perceivable by sight is of a

sort distinct from motion perceivable by touch. The antecedent I prove thus: by touch he could not perceive any motion but what was up or down, to the right or left, nearer or farther from him; besides these and their several varieties or complications, it is impossible he should have any idea of motion. He would not therefore think anything to be motion, or give the name motion to any idea which he could not range under some or other of those particular kinds thereof. But from sect. 95 it is plain that by the mere act of vision he could not know motion upwards or downwards, to the right or left, or in any other possible direction. From which I conclude he would not know motion at all at first sight. As for the idea of motion in abstract, I shall not waste paper about it, but leave it to my reader to make the best he can of it. To me it is perfectly unintelligible.

138 The consideration of motion may furnish a new field for inquiry: but since the manner wherein the mind apprehends by sight the motion of tangible objects, with the various degrees thereof, may be easily collected from what hath been said concerning the manner wherein that sense doth suggest their various distances, magnitudes, and situations, I shall not enlarge any farther on this subject, but proceed to consider what may be alleged, with greatest appearance of reason, against the proposition we have shewn to be true. For where there is so much prejudice to be encountered, a bare and naked demonstration of the truth will scarce suffice. We must also satisfy the scruples that men may raise in favour of their preconceived notions, shew whence the mistake arises, how it came to spread, and carefully disclose and root out those false persuasions that an early prejudice might have implanted in the mind.

139 *First*, therefore, it will be demanded how visible extension and figures come to be called by the same name with tangible extension and figures, if they are not of the same kind with them? It must be something more than humour or accident that could occasion a custom so constant and universal as this, which has obtained in all ages and nations of the world, and amongst all ranks of men, the learned as well as the illiterate.

140 To which I answer, we can no more argue a visible and tangible square to be of the same species from their being called by the same name, than we can that a tangible square and the monosyllable consisting of six letters whereby it is marked are of the same species because they are both called by the same name. It is customary to call written words and the things they signify by the same name: for words not being regarded in their own nature, or otherwise than as they are marks of things, it had been superfluous, and beside the design of language, to have given them names distinct from those of the things marked by them. The same reason holds here also. Visible figures are the marks of tangible figures, and from sect. 59 it is plain that in themselves they are little regarded, or upon any other score than for their connexion with tangible figures, which by nature they are ordained to signify. And because this language of nature doth not vary in different ages or nations, hence it is that in all times and places visible figures are called by the same names as the respective tangible figures suggested by them, and not because they are alike or of the same sort with them.

141 But, say you, surely a tangible square is liker to a visible square than to a visible circle: it has four angles and as many sides: so also has the visible square: but the visible circle has no such thing, being bounded by one uniform curve without right lines or angles, which makes it unfit to represent the tangible square but very fit to represent the tangible circle. Whence it clearly follows that visible figures are patterns of, or of the same species with, the respective tangible figures represented by them: that they are like unto them, and of their own nature fitted to represent them, as being of the same sort: and that they are in no respect arbitrary signs, as words.

142 I answer, it must be acknowledged the visible square is fitter than the visible circle to represent the tangible square, but then it is not because it is liker, or more of a species with it, but because the visible square contains in it several distinct parts, whereby to mark the several distinct corresponding parts of a tangible square, whereas the visible circle doth not. The square perceived by touch hath four distinct, equal sides, so also hath it four distinct equal angles. It is therefore necessary that the visible figure which shall be most proper to mark it contain four distinct equal parts corresponding to the four sides of the tangible square, as likewise four other distinct and equal parts whereby to denote the four equal angles of the tangible square. And accordingly we see the visible figures contain in them distinct visible parts, answering to the distinct tangible parts of the figures signified or suggested by them.

143 But it will not hence follow that any visible figure is like unto, or of the same species with, its corresponding tangible figure, unless it be also shewn that not only the number but also the kind of the parts be the same in both. To illustrate this, I observe that visible figures represent tangible figures much after the same manner that written words do sounds. Now, in this respect words are not arbitrary, it not being indifferent what written word stands for any sound: but it is requisite that each word contain in it so many distinct characters as there are variations in the sound it stands for. Thus the single letter *a* is proper to mark one simple uniform sound; and the word *adultery* is accommodated to represent the sound annexed to it, in the formation whereof there being eight different collisions or modifications of the air by the organs of speech, each of which produces a difference of sound, it was fit the word representing it should consist of as many distinct characters, thereby to mark each particular difference or part of the whole sound. And yet nobody, I presume, will say the single letter *a*, or the word *adultery*, are like unto, or of the same species with, the respective sounds by them represented. It is indeed arbitrary that, in general, letters of any language represent sounds at all: but when that is once agreed, it is not arbitrary what combination of letters shall represent this or that particular sound. I leave this with the reader to pursue, and apply it in his own thoughts.

144 It must be confessed that we are not so apt to confound other signs with the things signified, or to think them of the same species, as we are visible and tangible ideas. But a little consideration will shew us how this

may be without our supposing them of a like nature. These signs are constant and universal, their connexion with tangible ideas has been learnt at our first entrance into the world; and ever since, almost every moment of our lives, it has been occurring to our thoughts, and fastening and striking deeper on our minds. When we observe that signs are variable, and of human institution; when we remember there was a time they were not connected in our minds with those things they now so readily suggest; but that their signification was learned by the slow steps of experience: this preserves us from confounding them. But when we find the same signs suggest the same things all over the world; when we know they are not of human institution, and cannot remember that we ever learned their signification, but think that at first sight they would have suggested to us the same things they do now: all this persuades us they are of the same species as the things respectively represented by them, and that it is by a natural resemblance they suggest them to our minds.

145 Add to this that whenever we make a nice survey of any object, successively directing the optic axis to each point thereof, there are certain lines and figures described by the motion of the head or eye, which being in truth perceived by feeling, do nevertheless so mix themselves, as it were, with the ideas of sight, that we can scarce think but they appertain to that sense. Again, the ideas of sight enter into the mind several at once, more distinct and unmingled than is usual in the other senses beside the touch. Sounds, for example, perceived at the same instant, are apt to coalesce, if I may so say, into one sound: but we can perceive at the same time great variety of visible objects, very separate and distinct from each other. Now tangible extension being made up of several distinct coexistent parts, we may hence gather another reason that may dispose us to imagine a likeness or an analogy between the immediate objects of sight and touch. But nothing, certainly, doth more contribute to blend and confound them together than the strict and close connexion they have with each other. We cannot open our eyes but the ideas of distance, bodies, and tangible figures are suggested by them. So swift and sudden and unperceived is the transition from visible to tangible ideas that we can scarce forbear thinking them equally the immediate object of vision.

146 The prejudice which is grounded on these, and whatever other causes may be assigned thereof, sticks so fast that it is impossible without obstinate striving and labour of the mind to get entirely clear of it. But then the reluctancy we find in rejecting any opinion can be no argument of its truth to whoever considers what has been already shewn with regard to the prejudices we entertain concerning the distance, magnitude, and situation of objects; prejudices so familiar to our minds, so confirmed and inveterate, as they will hardly give way to the clearest demonstration.

147 Upon the whole, I think we may fairly conclude that the proper objects of vision constitute an universal language of the Author of Nature,[1] whereby we are instructed how to regulate our actions in order to attain

---

[1] [First edition: *the universal language of Nature.*]

those things that are necessary to the preservation and well-being of our bodies, as also to avoid whatever may be hurtful and destructive of them. It is by their information that we are principally guided in all the transactions and concerns of life. And the manner wherein they signify and mark unto us the objects which are at a distance is the same with that of languages and signs of human appointment, which do not suggest the things signified by any likeness or identity of nature, but only by an habitual connexion that experience has made us to observe between them.

148 Suppose one who had always continued blind be told by his guide that after he has advanced so many steps he shall come to the brink of a precipice, or by stopped by a wall; must not this to him seem very admirable and surprizing? He cannot conceive how it is possible for mortals to frame such predictions as these, which to him would seem as strange and unaccountable as prophesy doth to others. Even they who are blessed with the visive faculty may (though familiarity make it less observed) find therein sufficient cause of admiration. The wonderful art and contrivance wherewith it is adjusted to those ends and purposes for which it was apparently designed, the vast extent, number, and variety of objects that are at once with so much ease and quickness and pleasure suggested by it: all these afford subject for much and pleasing speculation, and may, if anything, give us some glimmering, analogous prænotion of things which are placed beyond the certain discovery and comprehension of our present state.

149 I do not design to trouble myself with drawing corollaries from the doctrine I have hitherto laid down. If it bears the test others may, so far as they shall think convenient, employ their thoughts in extending it farther, and applying it to whatever purposes it may be subservient to: only, I cannot forbear making some inquiry concerning the object of geometry, which the subject we have been upon doth naturally lead one to. We have shewn there is no such idea as that of extension in abstract, and that there are two kinds of sensible extension and figures which are entirely distinct and heterogeneous from each other. Now, it is natural to inquire which of these is the object of geometry.

150 Some things there are which at first sight incline one to think geometry conversant about visible extension. The constant use of the eyes, both in the practical and speculative parts of that science, doth very much induce us thereto. It would, without doubt, seem odd to a mathematician to go about to convince him the diagrams he saw upon paper were not the figures, or even the likeness of the figures, which make the subject of the demonstration. The contrary being held an unquestionable truth, not only by mathematicians, but also by those who apply themselves more particularly to the study of logic; I mean, who consider the nature of science, certainty, and demonstration: it being by them assigned as one reason of the extraordinary clearness and evidence of geometry that in this science the reasonings are free from those inconveniences which attend the use of arbitrary signs, the very ideas themselves being copied out and exposed to view upon paper. But, by the bye, how well this agrees with

what they likewise assert of abstract ideas being the object of geometrical demonstration I leave to be considered.

151 To come to a resolution in this point we need only observe what hath been said in sect. 59, 60, 61, where it is shewn that visible extensions in themselves are little regarded, and have no settled determinate greatness, and that men measure altogether, by the application of tangible extension to tangible extension. All which makes it evident that visible extension and figures are not the object of geometry.

152 It is therefore plain that visible figures are of the same use in geometry that words are: and the one may as well be accounted the object of that science as the other, neither of them being otherwise concerned therein than as they represent or suggest to the mind the particular tangible figures connected with them. There is indeed this difference between the signification of tangible figures by visible figures, and of ideas by words: that whereas the latter is variable and uncertain, depending altogether on the arbitrary appointment of men, the former is fixed and immutably the same in all times and places. A visible square, for instance, suggests to the mind the same tangible figure in Europe that it doth in America. Hence it is that the voice of the Author of [1] Nature, which speaks to our eyes, is not liable to that misinterpretation and ambiguity that languages of human contrivance are unavoidably subject to.

153 Though what has been said may suffice to shew what ought to be determined with relation to the object of geometry, I shall nevertheless, for the fuller illustration thereof, consider the case of an intelligence, or unbodied spirit, which is supposed to see perfectly well, *i.e.* to have a clear perception of the proper and immediate objects of sight, but to have no sense of touch. Whether there be any such being in Nature or no is beside my purpose to inquire. It sufficeth that the supposition contains no contradiction in it. Let us now examine what proficiency such a one may be able to make in geometry. Which speculation will lead us more clearly to see whether the ideas of sight can possibly be the object of that science.

154 *First,* then, it is certain the aforesaid intelligence could have no idea of a solid, or quantity of three dimensions, which followeth from its not having any idea of distance. We indeed are prone to think that we have by sight the ideas of space and solids, which ariseth from our imagining that we do, strictly speaking, see distance and some parts of an object at a greater distance than others; which hath been demonstrated to be the effect of the experience we have had, what ideas of touch are connected with such and such ideas attending vision: but the intelligence here spoken of is supposed to have no experience of touch. He would not, therefore, judge as we do, nor have any idea of distance, outness, or profundity, nor consequently of space or body, either immediately or by suggestion. Whence it is plain he can have no notion of those parts of geometry which relate to the mensuration of solids and their convex or concave surfaces, and contemplate the properties of lines generated by the section of a

[1] [*the Author of* not in first edition.]

solid. The conceiving of any part whereof is beyond the reach of his faculties.

155 Farther, he cannot comprehend the manner wherein geometers describe a right line or circle; the rule and compass with their use being things of which it is impossible he should have any notion: nor is it an easier matter for him to conceive the placing of one plane or angle on another, in order to prove their equality: since that supposeth some idea of distance or external space. All which makes it evident our pure intelligence could never attain to know so much as the first elements of plane geometry. And perhaps upon a nice inquiry it will be found he cannot even have an idea of plane figures any more than he can of solids; since some idea of distance is necessary to form the idea of a geometrical plane, as will appear to whoever shall reflect a little on it.

156 All that is properly perceived by the visive faculty amounts to no more than colours, with their variations and different proportions of light and shade. But the perpetual mutability and fleetingness of those immediate objects of sight render them incapable of being managed after the manner of geometrical figures; nor is it in any degree useful that they should. It is true there are divers of them perceived at once, and more of some and less of others: but accurately to compute their magnitude and assign precise determinate proportions between things so variable and inconstant, if we suppose it possible to be done, must yet be a very trifling and insignificant labour.

157 I must confess men are tempted to think that flat or plane figures are immediate objects of sight, though they acknowledge solids are not. And this opinion is grounded on what is observed in painting, wherein (it seems) the ideas immediately imprinted on the mind are only of planes variously coloured, which by a sudden act of the judgment are changed into solids. But with a little attention we shall find the planes here mentioned as the immediate objects of sight are not visible but tangible planes. For when we say that pictures are planes, we mean thereby that they appear to the touch smooth and uniform. But then this smoothness and uniformity, or, in other words, this planeness of the picture, is not perceived immediately by vision: for it appeareth to the eye various and multiform.

158 From all which we may conclude that planes are no more the immediate object of sight than solids. What we strictly see are not solids, nor yet planes variously coloured: they are only diversity of colours. And some of these suggest to the mind solids, and others plane figures, just as they have been experienced to be connected with the one or the other: so that we see planes in the same way that we see solids, both being equally suggested by the immediate objects of sight, which accordingly are themselves denominated planes and solids. But though they are called by the same names with the things marked by them, they are nevertheless of a nature entirely different, as hath been demonstrated.

159 What hath been said is, if I mistake not, sufficient to decide the question we proposed to examine, concerning the ability of a pure spirit, such as we have described, to know *geometry*. It is, indeed, no easy matter

for us to enter precisely into the thoughts of such an intelligence, because we cannot without great pains cleverly separate and disentangle in our thoughts the proper objects of sight from those of touch which are connected with them. This, indeed, in a complete degree seems scarce possible to be performed: which will not seem strange to us if we consider how hard it is for anyone to hear the words of his native language pronounced in his ears without understanding them. Though he endeavour to disunite the meaning from the sound, it will nevertheless intrude into his thoughts, and he shall find it extreme difficult, if not impossible, to put himself exactly in the posture of a foreigner that never learned the language, so as to be affected barely with the sounds themselves, and not perceive the signification annexed to them. By this time, I suppose, it is clear that neither abstract nor visible extension makes the object of geometry; the not discerning of which may perhaps have created some difficulty and useless labour in mathematics.

An Appendix [1]

The censures which, I am informed, have been made on the foregoing essay inclined me to think I had not been clear and express enough in some points, and to prevent being misunderstood for the future, I was willing to make any necessary alterations or additions in what I had

written. But that was impracticable, the present edition having been almost finished before I received this information. Wherefore I think it proper to consider in this place the principal objections that are come to my notice.

In the first place it's objected that in the beginning of the essay I argue

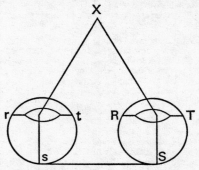

[1] [In the second edition (1709) only.]

56

either against all use of lines and angles in optics, and then what I say is false; or against those writers only who will have it that we can perceive by sense the optic axes, angles, etc., and then it's insignificant, this being an absurdity which no one ever held. To which I answer that I argue only against those who are of opinion that we perceive the distance of objects by lines and angles or, as they term it, by a kind of innate geometry. And to shew that this is not fighting with my own shadow, I shall here set down a passage from the celebrated Descartes.

Distantiam praeterea discimus, per mutuam quandam conspirationem oculorum. Ut enim caecus noster duo bacilla tenens AE et CE, de quorum longitudine incertus, solumque intervallum manuum A et C, cum magnitudine angulorum ACE, et CAE exploratum habens, inde, ut ex geometria quadam omnibus innata, scire potest ubi sit punctum E. Sic quum nostri oculi RST et *rst* ambo, vertuntur ad X, magnitudo lineae S*s*, et angulorum XS*s* et X*s*S, certos nos redunt ubi sit punctum X. Et idem opera alterutrius possumus indagare, loco illum movendo, ut si versus X illum semper dirigentes, primo sistamus in puncto S, et statim post in puncto *s*, hoc sufficiet ut magnitudo lineae S*s*, et duorum angulorum XS*s* et X*s*S nostrae imaginationi simul occurrant, et distantiam puncti X nos edoceant; idque per actionem mentis, quae licet simplex judicium esse videatur, ratiocinationem tamen quandam involutam habet; similem illi, qua geometrae per duas stationes diversas, loca inaccessa dimetiuntur.[1]

I might amass together citations from several authors to the same purpose, but this being so clear in the point, and from an author of so great note, I shall not trouble the reader with any more. What I have said on this head was not for the sake of finding fault with other men, but because I judged it necessary to demonstrate in the first place that we

[1] [We apprehend distance, moreover, through a sort of joint activity of the eyes For in the same way as our blind man, holding two sticks of indeterminate length, AE and CE, and knowing only the distance between his hands, A and C, together with the size of the angles ACE and CAE, can thence determine the position of E by a sort of innate geometrical knowledge shared by all men, so, when both our eyes, RST and *rst*, are focused on X, the length of the line S*s* and the size of the angles XS*s* and X*s*S let us know the position of the point X. We can also discover that position by means of either one of our eyes alone, by changing its location. If we keep the eye fixed on X and hold it first at point S and then immediately afterwards at point *s*, that will be enough for the length of the line S*s* and the size of the angles XS*s* and X*s*S to be present together in the imagination and thus to inform us of the distance of the point X. They do so in virtue of an act of the mind which, while it may seem to be a simple judgment, nevertheless involves a kind of complicated reasoning process like that by which geometers calculate inaccessible positions from two separate given points. (From Descartes' *Dioptrics*, VI 13.)]

neither see distance immediately, nor yet perceive it by the mediation of anything that hath (as lines and angles) a necessary connexion with it. For on the demonstration of this point the whole theory depends.

Secondly, it is objected that the explication I give of the appearance of the horizontal moon (which may also be applied to the sun) is the same that Gassendus had given before. I answer, there is indeed mention made of the grossness of the atmosphere in both, but then the methods wherein it is applied to solve the phenomenon are widely different, as will be evident to whoever shall compare what I have said on this subject with the following words of Gassendus.

> Heinc dici posse videtur: solem humilem oculo spectatum ideo apparere majorem, quam dum altius egreditur, quia dum vicinus est horizonti prolixa est series vaporum, atque adeo corpusculorum quae solis radios ita retundunt, ut oculus minus conniveat, et pupilla quasi umbrefacta longe magis amplificetur, quam dum sole multum elato rari vapores intercipiuntur, solque ipse ita splendescit, ut pupilla in ipsum spectans contractissima efficiatur. Nempe ex hoc esse videtur, cur visibilis species ex sole procedens, et per pupillam amplificatam intromissa in retinam, ampliorem in illa sedem occupet, majoremque proinde creet solis apparentiam, quam dum per contractam pupillam eodem intromissa contendit (vid. *Epist. I de apparente Magnitudine solis humilis et sublimis*, page 6).[1]

This solution of Gassendus proceeds on a false principle, *viz.*, that the pupil's being enlarged augments the species or image on the fund of the eye.

Thirdly, against what is said in sect. 80, it is objected that the same thing which is so small as scarce to be discerned by a man may appear like a mountain to some small insect; from which it follows that the *minimum visibile* is not equal in respect of all creatures. I answer, if this objection be sounded to the bottom it will be found no more than that the same particle of matter, which is marked to a man by one *minimum visibile*, exhibits to an insect a great number of *minima visibilia*. But this does not prove that one *minimum visibile* of the insect is not equal to one *minimum visibile* of the man. The not distinguishing between the mediate

[1] [The truth, then, seems to be as follows: the reason why the sun, when it is low, appears to the eye to be larger than when it has climbed higher is because, as long as it is near to the horizon, the [intervening] layer of vapour is deeper, and the atoms so dull the brightness of the sun's rays that the eye blinks less. For the pupil is as if shaded and is far more dilated than when the sun is high in the sky: then a thinner layer of vapour intervenes and the sun itself shines so brightly that, in looking towards it, the pupil closes up and becomes highly contracted. Doubtless this is the explanation why the visible *species* coming from the sun, when it reaches the retina through a dilated pupil, occupies a larger place on it and so creates the appearance of a larger sun than when it strikes the retina after entering by the same route but through a contracted pupil.]

and immediate objects of sight is, I suspect, a cause of misapprehension in this matter.

Some other misinterpretations and difficulties have been made, but in the points they refer to I have endeavoured to be so very plain that I know not how to express myself more clearly. All I shall add is that if they who are pleased to criticise on my essay would but read the whole over with some attention, they might be the better able to comprehend my meaning and consequently to judge of my mistakes.

I am informed that, soon after the first edition of this treatise a man somewhere near London was made to see, who had been born blind, and continued so for about twenty years. Such a one may be supposed a proper judge to decide how far some tenets laid down in several places of the foregoing essay are agreeable to truth, and if any curious person hath the opportunity of making proper interrogatories to him thereon, I should gladly see my notions either amended or confirmed by experience.

A Treatise Concerning the Principles
of Human Knowledge

wherein the Chief Causes of Error and Difficulty in the *Sciences*, with the Grounds of Scepticism, Atheism, and Irreligion, are inquired into.

Text based on the Second Edition of 1734
First Printed in 1710

The Preface [1]

What I here make public has, after a long and scrupulous inquiry, seem'd to me evidently true, and not unuseful to be known, particularly to those who are tainted with scepticism, or want a demonstration of the existence and immateriality of *God*, or the natural immortality of the soul. Whether it be so or no, I am content the reader should impartially examine. Since I do not think myself any farther concerned for the success of what I have written, than as it is agreeable to *truth*. But to the end *this* may not suffer, I make it my request that the reader suspend his judgment, till he has once, *at least*, read the whole through with that degree of attention and thought which the subject matter shall seem to deserve. For as there are some passages that, taken by themselves, are very liable (nor could it be remedied) to gross misinterpretation, and to be charged with most absurd consequences, which, nevertheless, upon an entire perusal will appear not to follow from them: so likewise, though the whole should be read over, yet, if this be done transiently, 'tis very probable my sense may be mistaken; but to a thinking reader, I flatter myself, it will be throughout clear and obvious. As for the characters of novelty and singularity, which some of the following notions may seem to bear, 'tis, I hope, needless to make any apology on that account. He must surely be either very weak, or very little acquainted with the sciences, who shall reject a truth, that is capable of demonstration, for no other reason but because it's newly known and contrary to the prejudices of mankind. Thus much I thought fit to premise, in order to prevent, if possible, the hasty censures of a sort of men, who are too apt to condemn an opinion before they rightly comprehend it.

[1] [Omitted from the second edition.]

Introduction

1 Philosophy being nothing else but the study of wisdom and truth, it may with reason be expected, that those who have spent most time and pains in it should enjoy a greater calm and serenity of mind, a greater clearness and evidence of knowledge, and be less disturbed with doubts and difficulties than other men. Yet so it is we see the illiterate bulk of mankind that walk the high-road of plain, common sense, and are governed by the dictates of nature, for the most part easy and undisturbed. To them nothing that's familiar appears unaccountable or difficult to comprehend. They complain not of any want of evidence in their senses, and are out of all danger of becoming *sceptics*. But no sooner do we depart from sense and instinct to follow the light of a superior principle, to reason, meditate, and reflect on the nature of things, but a thousand scruples spring up in our minds, concerning those things which before we seemed fully to comprehend. Prejudices and errors of sense do from all parts discover themselves to our view; and endeavouring to correct these by reason we are insensibly drawn into uncouth paradoxes, difficulties, and inconsistencies, which multiply and grow upon us as we advance in speculation; till at length, having wander'd through many intricate mazes, we find ourselves just where we were, or, which is worse, sit down in a forlorn scepticism.

2 The cause of this is thought to be the obscurity of things, or the natural weakness and imperfection of our understandings. It is said the faculties we have are few, and those designed by nature for the support and comfort of life, and not to penetrate into the inward essence and constitution of things. Besides, the mind of man being finite, when it treats of things which partake of infinity, it is not be wondered at, if it run into absurdities and contradictions; out of which it is impossible it should ever extricate itself, it being of the nature of infinite not to be comprehended by that which is finite.

3 But perhaps we may be too partial to ourselves in placing the fault originally in our faculties, and not rather in the wrong use we make of them. It is a hard thing to suppose, that right deductions from true principles should ever end in consequences which cannot be maintained or made consistent. We should believe that God has dealt more bountifully with the sons of men, than to give them a strong desire for that knowledge, which He had placed quite out of their reach. This were not agreeable

to the wonted, indulgent methods of Providence, which, whatever appetites it may have implanted in the creatures, doth usually furnish them with such means as, if rightly made use of, will not fail to satisfy them. Upon the whole, I am inclined to think that the far greater part, if not all, of those difficulties which have hitherto amused philosophers, and blocked up the way to knowledge, are entirely owing to ourselves. That we have first raised a dust, and then complain, we cannot see.

4 My purpose therefore is, to try if I can discover what those principles are, which have introduced all that doubtfulness and uncertainty, those absurdities and contradictions into the several sects of philosophy; insomuch that the wisest men have thought our ignorance incurable, conceiving it to arise from the natural dulness and limitation of our faculties. And surely it is a work well deserving our pains, to make a strict inquiry concerning the first principles of *human knowledge,* to sift and examine them on all sides: especially since there may be some grounds to suspect that those lets and difficulties, which stay and embarrass the mind in its search after truth, do not spring from any darkness and intricacy in the objects, or natural defect in the understanding, so much as from false principles which have been insisted on, and might have been avoided.

5 How difficult and discouraging soever this attempt may seem, when I consider how many great and extraordinary men have gone before me in the same designs: yet I am not without some hopes, upon the consideration that the largest views are not always the clearest, and that he who is short-sighted will be obliged to draw the object nearer, and may, perhaps, by a close and narrow survey discern that which had escaped far better eyes.

6 In order to prepare the mind of the reader for the easier conceiving what follows, it is proper to premise somewhat, by way of introduction, concerning the nature and abuse of language. But the unravelling this matter leads me in some measure to anticipate my design, by taking notice of what seems to have had a chief part in rendering speculation intricate and perplexed, and to have occasioned innumerable errors and difficulties in almost all parts of knowledge. And that is the opinion that the mind hath a power of framing *abstract ideas* or notions of things. He who is not a perfect stranger to the writings and disputes of philosophers, must needs acknowledge that no small part of them are spent about abstract ideas. These are in a more especial manner, thought to be the object of those sciences which go by the name of *Logic* and *Metaphysics,* and of all that which passes under the notion of the most abstracted and sublime learning, in all which one shall scarce find any question handled in such a manner, as does not suppose their existence in the mind, and that it is well acquainted with them.

7 It is agreed on all hands, that the qualities or modes of things do never really exist each of them apart by itself, and separated from all others, but are mixed, as it were, and blended together, several in the same object. But we are told, the mind being able to consider each quality singly, or

abstracted from those other qualities with which it is united, does by that means frame to itself abstract ideas. For example, there is perceived by sight an object extended, coloured, and moved: this mixed or compound idea the mind resolving into its simple, constituent parts, and viewing each by itself, exclusive of the rest, does frame the abstract ideas of extension, colour, and motion. Not that it is possible for colour or motion to exist without extension: but only that the mind can frame to itself by *abstraction* the idea of colour exclusive of extension, and of motion exclusive of both colour and extension.

8 Again, the mind having observed that in the particular extensions perceived by sense, there is something common and alike in all, and some other things peculiar, as this or that figure or magnitude, which distinguish them one from another; it considers apart or singles out by itself that which is common, making thereof a most abstract idea of extension, which is neither line, surface, nor solid, nor has any figure or magnitude but is an idea entirely prescinded from all these. So likewise the mind by leaving out of the particular colours perceived by sense, that which distinguishes them one from another, and retaining that only which is common to all, makes an idea of colour in abstract which is neither red, nor blue, nor white, nor any other determinate colour. And in like manner by considering motion abstractedly not only from the body moved, but likewise from the figure it describes, and all particular directions and velocities, the abstract idea of motion is framed; which equally corresponds to all particular motions whatsoever that may be perceived by sense.

9 And as the mind frames to itself abstract ideas of qualities or modes, so does it, by the same precision or mental separation, attain abstract ideas of the more compounded beings, which include several coexistent qualities. For example, the mind having observed that Peter, James, and John, resemble each other, in certain common agreements of shape and other qualities, leaves out of the complex or compounded idea it has of Peter, James, and any other particular man, that which is peculiar to each, retaining only what is common to all; and so makes an abstract idea wherein all the particulars equally partake, abstracting entirely from and cutting off all those circumstances and differences, which might determine it to any particular existence. And after this manner it is said we come by the abstract idea of *man* or, if you please, humanity or human nature; wherein it is true, there is included colour, because there is no man but has some colour, but then it can be neither white, nor black, nor any particular colour; because there is no one particular colour wherein all men partake. So likewise there is included stature, but then it is neither tall stature nor low stature, nor yet middle stature, but something abstracted from all these. And so of the rest. Moreover, there being a great variety of other creatures that partake in some parts, but not all, of the complex idea of *man*, the mind leaving out those parts which are peculiar to men, and retaining those only which are common to all the living creatures, frameth the idea of *animal*, which abstracts not only from all particular men, but also all birds, beasts, fishes, and insects. The constituent parts of the abstract idea

of animal are body, life, sense, and spontaneous motion. By *body* is meant, body without any particular shape or figure, there being no one shape or figure common to all animals, without covering, either of hair or feathers, or scales, &c. nor yet naked: hair, feathers, scales, and nakedness being the distinguishing properties of particular animals, and for that reason left out of the *abstract idea*. Upon the same account the spontaneous motion must be neither walking, nor flying, nor creeping, it is nevertheless a motion, but what that motion is, it is not easy to conceive.

10 Whether others have this wonderful faculty of *abstracting their ideas*, they best can tell: for myself I find indeed I have a faculty of imagining, or representing to myself the ideas of those particular things I have perceived and of variously compounding and dividing them. I can imagine a man with two heads or the upper parts of a man joined to the body of a horse. I can consider the hand, the eye, the nose, each by itself abstracted or separated from the rest of the body. But then whatever hand or eye I imagine, it must have some particular shape and colour. Likewise the idea of man that I frame to myself, must be either of a white, or a black, or a tawny, a straight, or a crooked, a tall, or a low, or a middle-sized man. I cannot by any effort of thought conceive the abstract idea above described. And it is equally impossible for me to form the abstract idea of motion distinct from the body moving, and which is neither swift nor slow, curvilinear nor rectilinear; and the like may be said of all other abstract general ideas whatsoever. To be plain, I own myself able to abstract in one sense, as when I consider some particular parts or qualities separated from others, with which though they are united in some object, yet, it is possible they may really exist without them. But I deny that I can abstract one from another, or conceive separately, those qualities which it is impossible should exist so separated; or that I can frame a general notion by abstracting from particulars in the manner aforesaid. Which two last are the proper acceptations of *abstraction*. And there are grounds to think most men will acknowledge themselves to be in my case. The generality of men which are simple and illiterate never pretend to *abstract notions*. It is said they are difficult and not to be attained without pains and study. We may therefore reasonably conclude that, if such there be, they are confined only to the learned.

11 I proceed to examine what can be alleged in defence of the doctrine of abstraction, and try if I can discover what it is that inclines the men of speculation to embrace an opinion, so remote from common sense as that seems to be. There has been a late deservedly esteemed philosopher,[1] who, no doubt, has given it very much countenance by seeming to think the having abstract general ideas is what puts the widest difference in point of understanding betwixt man and beast. 'The having of general ideas (*saith he*) is that which puts a perfect distinction betwixt man and brutes, and is an excellency which the faculties of brutes do by no means attain unto. For it is evident we observe no footsteps in them of making use of general

[1] [Locke.]

signs for universal ideas; from which we have reason to imagine that they have not the faculty of *abstracting* or making general ideas, since they have no use of words or any other general signs. *And a little after.* Therefore, I think, we may suppose that it is in this that the species of brutes are discriminated from men, and 'tis that proper difference wherein they are wholly separated, and which at last widens to so wide a distance. For if they have any ideas at all, and are not bare machines (as some would have them) we cannot deny them to have some reason. It seems as evident to me that they do some of them in certain instances reason as that they have sense, but it is only in particular ideas, just as they receive them from their senses. They are the best of them tied up within those narrow bounds, and have not (as I think) the faculty to enlarge them by any kind of *abstraction*.' *Essay on Hum. Underst.* B.2. C.11. Sect. 10 and 11. I readily agree with this learned author, that the faculties of brutes can by no means attain to *abstraction*. But then if this be made the distinguishing property of that sort of animals, I fear a great many of those that pass for men must be reckoned into their number. The reason that is here assigned why we have no grounds to think brutes have abstract general ideas, is that we observe in them no use of words or any other general signs; which is built on this supposition, to wit, that the making use of words, implies the having general ideas. From which it follows, that men who use language are able to abstract or generalize their ideas. That this is the sense and arguing of the author will further appear by his answering the question he in another place puts. 'Since all things that exist are only particulars, how come we by general terms?' *His answer is,* 'Words become general by being made the signs of general ideas.' *Essay on Hum. Underst.* B.3. C.3. Sect. 6. But it seems that a word becomes general by being made the sign, not of an abstract general idea but, of several particular ideas, any one of which it indifferently suggests to the mind. For example, when it is said *the change of motion is proportional to the impressed force*, or that *whatever has extension is divisible*; these propositions are to be understood of motion and extension in general, and nevertheless it will not follow that they suggest to my thoughts an idea of motion without a body moved, or any determinate direction and velocity, or that I must conceive an abstract general idea of extension, which is neither line, surface nor solid, neither great nor small, black, white, nor red, nor of any other determinate colour. It is only implied that whatever motion I consider, whether it be swift or slow, perpendicular, horizontal or oblique, or in whatever object, the axiom concerning it holds equally true. As does the other of every particular extension, it matters not whether line, surface or solid, whether of this or that magnitude or figure.

12 By observing how ideas become general, we may the better judge how words are made so. And here it is to be noted that I do not deny absolutely there are general ideas, but only that there are any *abstract general ideas*: for in the passages above quoted, wherein there is mention of general ideas, it is always supposed that they are formed by *abstraction*, after the manner set forth in Sect. 8 and 9. Now if we will annex a meaning

to our words, and speak only of what we can conceive, I believe we shall acknowledge, that an idea, which considered in itself is particular, becomes general, by being made to represent or stand for all other particular ideas of the same sort. To make this plain by an example, suppose a geometrician is demonstrating the method, of cutting a line in two equal parts. He draws, for instance, a black line of an inch in length, this which in itself is a particular line is nevertheless with regard to its signification general, since as it is there used, it represents all particular lines whatsoever; for that what is demonstrated of it, is demonstrated of all lines or, in other words, of a line in general. And as that particular line becomes general, by being made a sign, so the name *line* which taken absolutely is particular, by being a sign is made general. And as the former owes its generality, not to its being the sign of an abstract or general line, but of all particular right lines that may possibly exist, so the latter must be thought to derive its generality from the same cause, namely, the various particular lines which it indifferently denotes.

13 To give the reader a yet clearer view of the nature of abstract ideas, and the uses they are thought necessary to, I shall add one more passage out of the *Essay on Human Understanding*, which is as follows. '*Abstract ideas* are not so obvious or easy to children or the yet unexercised mind as particular ones. If they seem so to grown men, it is only because by constant and familiar use they are made so. For when we nicely reflect upon them, we shall find that general ideas are fictions and contrivances of the mind, that carry difficulty with them, and do not so easily offer themselves, as we are apt to imagine. For example, does it not require some pains and skill to form the general idea of a triangle (which is yet none of the most abstract comprehensive and difficult) for it must be neither oblique nor rectangle, neither equilateral, equicrural, nor scalenon, but *all and none* of these at once. In effect, it is something imperfect that cannot exist, an idea wherein some parts of several different and *inconsistent* ideas are put together. It is true the mind in this imperfect state has need of such ideas, and makes all the haste to them it can, for the conveniency of communication and enlargement of knowledge, to both which it is naturally very much inclined. But yet one has reason to suspect such ideas are marks of our imperfection. At least this is enough to shew that the most abstract and general ideas are not those that the mind is first and most easily acquainted with, nor such as its earliest knowledge is conversant about.' B.4. C.7. Sect. 9. If any man has the faculty of framing in his mind such an idea of a triangle as is here described, it is in vain to pretend to dispute him out of it, nor would I go about it. All I desire is, that the reader would fully and certainly inform himself whether he has such an idea or no. And this, methinks, can be no hard task for anyone to perform. What more easy than for anyone to look a little into his own thoughts, and there try whether he has, or can attain to have, an idea that shall correspond with the description that is here given of the general idea of a triangle, which is, *neither oblique, nor rectangle, equilateral, equicrural, nor scalenon, but all and none of these at once?*

14 Much is here said of the difficulty that abstract ideas carry with them, and the pains and skill requisite to the forming them. And it is on all hands agreed that there is need of great toil and labour of the mind, to emancipate our thoughts from particular objects, and raise them to those sublime speculations that are conversant about abstract ideas. From all which the natural consequence should seem to be, that so difficult a thing as the forming abstract ideas was not necessary for *communication*, which is so easy and familiar to all sorts of men. But we are told, if they seem obvious and easy to grown men, *it is only because by constant and familiar use they are made so*. Now I would fain know at what time it is, men are employed in surmounting that difficulty, and furnishing themselves with those necessary helps for discourse. It cannot be when they are grown up, for then it seems they are not conscious of any such pains-taking; it remains therefore to be the business of their childhood. And surely, the great and multiplied labour of framing abstract notions, will be found a hard task for that tender age. Is it not a hard thing to imagine, that a couple of children cannot prate together, of their sugar-plumbs and rattles and the rest of their little trinkets, till they have first tacked together numberless inconsistencies, and so framed in their minds *abstract general ideas,* and annexed them to every common name they make use of?

15 Nor do I think them a whit more needful for the *enlargement of knowledge* than for *communication*. It is I know a point much insisted on, that all knowledge and demonstration are about universal notions, to which I fully agree: but then it doth not appear to me that those notions are formed by *abstraction* in the manner premised; *universality,* so far as I can comprehend, not consisting in the absolute, positive nature or conception of anything, but in the relation it bears to the particulars signified or represented by it: by virtue whereof it is that things, names, or notions, being in their own nature *particular*, are rendered *universal*. Thus when I demonstrate any proposition concerning triangles, it is to be supposed that I have in view the universal idea of a triangle; which ought not to be understood as if I could frame an idea of a triangle which was neither equilateral nor scalenon nor equicrural. But only that the particular triangle I consider, whether of this or that sort it matters not, doth equally stand for and represent all rectilinear triangles whatsoever, and is in that sense *universal*. All which seems very plain and not to include any difficulty in it.

16 But here it will be demanded, how we can know any proposition to be true of all particular triangles, except we have first seen it demonstrated of the abstract idea of a triangle which equally agrees to all? For because a property may be demonstrated to agree to some one particular triangle, it will not thence follow that it equally belongs to any other triangle, which in all respects is not the same with it. For example, having demonstrated that the three angles of an isosceles rectangular triangle are equal to two right ones, I cannot therefore conclude this affection agrees to all other triangles, which have neither a right angle, nor two equal sides. It seems therefore that, to be certain this proposition is universally true, we must either make a particular demonstration for every particular triangle, which is impossible,

or once for all demonstrate it of the *abstract idea of a triangle*, in which all the particulars do indifferently partake, and by which they are all equally represented. To which I answer, that though the idea I have in view whilst I make the demonstration, be, for instance, that of an isosceles rectangular triangle, whose sides are of a determinate length, I may nevertheless be certain it extends to all other rectilinear triangles, of what sort or bigness soever. And that, because neither the right angle, nor the equality, nor determinate length of the sides, are at all concerned in the demonstration. It is true, the diagram I have in view includes all these particulars, but then there is not the least mention made of them in the proof of the proposition. It is not said, the three angles are equal to two right ones, because one of them is a right angle, or because the sides comprehending it are of the same length. Which sufficiently shews that the right angle might have been oblique, and the sides unequal, and for all that the demonstration have held good. And for this reason it is, that I conclude that to be true of any obliquangular or scalenon, which I had demonstrated of a particular right-angled, equicrural triangle; and not because I demonstrated the proposition of the abstract idea of a triangle. And here it must be acknowledged that a man may consider a figure merely as triangular, without attending to the particular qualities of the angles, or relations of the sides. So far he may abstract: but this will never prove, that he can frame an abstract general inconsistent idea of a triangle. In like manner we may consider Peter so far forth as man, or so far forth as animal, without framing the forementioned abstract idea, either of man or of animal, in as much as all that is perceived is not considered.[1]

17 It were an endless, as well as an useless thing, to trace the Schoolmen, those great masters of abstraction, through all the manifold inextricable labyrinths of error and dispute, which their doctrine of abstract natures and notions seems to have led them into. What bickerings and controversies, and what a learned dust have been raised about those matters, and what mighty advantage hath been from thence derived to mankind, are things at this day too clearly known to need being insisted on. And it had been well if the ill effects of that doctrine were confined to those only who make the most avowed profession of it. When men consider the great pains, industry and parts, that have for so many ages been laid out on the cultivation and advancement of the sciences, and that notwithstanding all this, the far greater part of them remain full of darkness and uncertainty, and disputes that are like never to have an end, and even those that are thought to be supported by the most clear and cogent demonstrations, contain in them paradoxes which are perfectly irreconcilable to the understandings of men, and that taking all together, a small portion of them doth supply any real benefit to mankind, otherwise than by being an innocent diversion and amusement. I say, the consideration of all this is apt to throw them into a despondency, and perfect contempt of all study. But this may perhaps cease, upon a view of the false principles that have obtained in the

[1] [Last three sentences of § 16 added in second edition.]

world, amongst all which there is none, methinks, hath a more wide influence over the thoughts of speculative men, than this of abstract general ideas.

18 I come now to consider the source of this prevailing notion, and that seems to me to be language. And surely nothing of less extent than reason itself could have been the source of an opinion so universally received. The truth of this appears as from other reasons, so also from the plain confession of the ablest patrons of abstract ideas, who acknowledge that they are made in order to naming; from which it is a clear consequence, that if there had been no such thing as speech or universal signs, there never had been any thought of abstraction. See B. 3 C. 6. Sect. 39 *and elsewhere of the Essay on Human Understanding*. Let us therefore examine the manner wherein words have contributed to the origin of that mistake. First then, 'tis thought that every name hath, or ought to have, one only precise and settled signification, which inclines men to think there are certain *abstract, determinate ideas*, which constitute the true and only immediate signification of each general name. And that it is by the mediation of these abstract ideas, that a general name comes to signify any particular thing. Whereas, in truth, there is no such thing as one precise and definite signification annexed to any general name, they all signifying indifferently a great number of particular ideas. All which doth evidently follow from what has been already said, and will clearly appear to anyone by a little reflexion. To this it will be objected, that every name that has a definition, is thereby restrained to one certain signification. For example, a *triangle* is defined to be a *plane surface comprehended by three right lines*; by which that name is limited to denote one certain idea and no other. To which I answer, that in the definition it is not said whether the surface be great or small, black or white, nor whether the sides are long or short, equal or unequal, nor with what angles they are inclined to each other; in all which there may be great variety, and consequently there is no one settled idea which limits the signification of the word *triangle*. 'Tis one thing for to keep a name constantly to the same definition, and another to make it stand everywhere for the same idea: the one is necessary, the other useless and impracticable.

19 But to give a farther account how words came to produce the doctrine of abstract ideas, it must be observed that it is a received opinion, that language has no other end but the communicating our ideas, and that every significant name stands for an idea. This being so, and it being withal certain, that names, which yet are not thought altogether insignificant, do not always mark out particular conceivable ideas, it is straightway concluded that they stand for abstract notions. That there are many names in use amongst speculative men, which do not always suggest to others determinate particular ideas, is what nobody will deny. And a little attention will discover, that it is not necessary (even in the strictest reasonings) significant names which stand for ideas should, every time they are used, excite in the understanding the ideas they are made to stand for: in reading and discoursing, names being for the most part used as letters are in

algebra, in which though a particular quantity be marked by each letter, yet to proceed right it is not requisite that in every step each letter suggest to your thoughts, that particular quantity it was appointed to stand for.

20 Besides, the communicating of ideas marked by words is not the chief and only end of language, as is commonly supposed. There are other ends, as the raising of some passion, the exciting to, or deterring from an action, the putting the mind in some particular disposition; to which the former is in many cases barely subservient, and sometimes entirely omitted, when these can be obtained without it, as I think doth not infrequently happen in the familiar use of language. I entreat the reader to reflect with himself, and see if it doth not often happen either in hearing or reading a discourse, that the passions of fear, love, hatred, admiration, disdain, and the like arise, immediately in his mind upon the perception of certain words, without any ideas coming between. At first, indeed, the words might have occasioned ideas that were fit to produce those emotions; but, if I mistake not, it will be found that when language is once grown familiar, the hearing of the sounds or sight of the characters is oft immediately attended with those passions, which at first were wont to be produced by the intervention of ideas, that are now quite omitted. May we not, for example, be affected with the promise of a *good thing*, though we have not an idea of what it is? Or is not the being threatened with danger sufficient to excite a dread, though we think not of any particular evil likely to befall us, nor yet frame to ourselves an idea of danger in abstract? If anyone shall join ever so little reflection of his own to what has been said, I believe it will evidently appear to him, that general names are often used in the propriety of language without the speaker's designing them for marks of ideas in his own, which he would have them raise in the mind of the hearer. Even proper names themselves do not seem always spoken, with a design to bring into our view the ideas of those individuals that are supposed to be marked by them. For example, when a Schoolman tells me *Aristotle hath said it*, all I conceive he means by it, is to dispose me to embrace his opinion with the deference and submission which custom has annexed to that name. And this effect may be so instantly produced in the minds of those who are accustomed to resign their judgment to the authority of that philosopher, as it is impossible any idea either of his person, writings, or reputation should go before. Innumerable examples of this kind may be given, but why should I insist on those things, which everyone's experience will, I doubt not, plentifully suggest unto him?

21 We have, I think, shewn the impossibility of *abstract ideas*. We have considered what has been said for them by their ablest patrons; and endeavoured to shew they are of no use for those ends, to which they are thought necessary. And lastly, we have traced them to the source from whence they flow, which appears to be language. It cannot be denied that words are of excellent use, in that by their means all that stock of knowledge which has been purchased by the joint labours of inquisitive men in all ages and nations, may be drawn into the view and made the possession of one single person. But at the same time it must be owned that most

parts of knowledge have been strangely perplexed and darkened by the abuse of words, and general ways of speech wherein they are delivered. Since therefore words are so apt to impose on the understanding, whatever ideas I consider, I shall endeavour to take them bare and naked into my view, keeping out of my thoughts, so far as I am able, those names which long and constant use hath so strictly united with them; from which I may expect to derive the following advantages.

22 First, I shall be sure to get clear of all controversies purely verbal; the springing up of which weeds in almost all the sciences has been a main hindrance to the growth of true and sound knowledge. Secondly, this seems to be a sure way to extricate myself out of that fine and subtle net of *abstract ideas*, which has so miserably perplexed and entangled the minds of men, and that with this peculiar circumstance, that by how much the finer and more curious was the wit of any man, by so much the deeper was he like to be ensnared, and faster held therein. Thirdly, so long as I confine my thoughts to my own ideas divested of words, I do not see how I can easily be mistaken. The objects I consider, I clearly and adequately know. I cannot be deceived in thinking I have an idea which I have not. It is not possible for me to imagine, that any of my own ideas are alike or unlike, that are not truly so. To discern the agreements or disagreements there are between my ideas, to see what ideas are included in any compound idea, and what not, there is nothing more requisite, than an attentive perception of what passes in my own understanding.

23 But the attainment of all these advantages doth presuppose an entire deliverance from the deception of words, which I dare hardly promise myself; so difficult a thing it is to dissolve an union so early begun, and confirmed by so long a habit as that betwixt words and ideas. Which difficulty seems to have been very much increased by the doctrine of *abstraction*. For so long as men thought abstract ideas were annexed to their words, it doth not seem strange that they should use words for ideas: it being found an impracticable thing to lay aside the word, and retain the abstract idea in the mind, which in itself was perfectly inconceivable. This seems to me the principal cause, why those men who have so emphatically recommended to others, the laying aside all use of words in their meditations, and contemplating their bare ideas, have yet failed to perform it themselves. Of late many have been very sensible of the absurd opinions and insignificant disputes, which grow out of the abuse of words. And in order to remedy these evils they advise well, that we attend to the ideas signified, and draw off our attention from the words which signify them. But how good soever this advice may be, they have given others, it is plain they could not have a due regard to it themselves, so long as they thought the only immediate use of words was to signify ideas, and that the immediate signification of every general name was a *determinate, abstract idea*.

24 But these being known to be mistakes, a man may with greater ease prevent his being imposed on by words. He that knows he has no other than particular ideas, will not puzzle himself in vain to find out and

conceive the abstract idea, annexed to any name. And he that knows names do not always stand for ideas, will spare himself the labour of looking for ideas, where there are none to be had. It were therefore to be wished that everyone would use his utmost endeavours, to obtain a clear view of the ideas he would consider, separating from them all that dress and encumbrance of words which so much contribute to blind the judgment and divide the attention. In vain do we extend our view into the heavens, and pry into the entrails of the earth, in vain do we consult the writings of learned men, and trace the dark footsteps of antiquity; we need only draw the curtain of words, to behold the fairest tree of knowledge, whose fruit is excellent, and within the reach of our hand.

25 Unless we take care to clear the first principles of knowledge, from the embarras and delusion of words, we may make infinite reasonings upon them to no purpose; we may draw consequences from consequences, and be never the wiser. The farther we go, we shall only lose ourselves the more irrecoverably, and be the deeper entangled in difficulties and mistakes. Whoever therefore designs to read the following sheets, I entreat him to make my words the occasion of his own thinking, and endeavour to attain the same train of thoughts in reading, that I had in writing them. By this means it will be easy for him to discover the truth or falsity of what I say. He will be out of all danger of being deceived by my words, and I do not see how he can be led into an error by considering his own naked, undisguised ideas.

Of the Principles of Human Knowledge

PART I

1 It is evident to anyone who takes a survey of the objects of human knowledge, that they are either ideas actually imprinted on the senses, or else such as are perceived by attending to the passions and operations of the mind,[1] or lastly ideas formed by help of memory and imagination, either compounding, dividing, or barely representing those originally perceived in the aforesaid ways. By sight I have the ideas of light and colours with their several degrees and variations. By touch I perceive, for example, hard and soft, heat and cold, motion and resistance, and of all these more and less either as to quantity or degree. Smelling furnishes me with odours; the palate with tastes, and hearing conveys sounds to the mind in all their variety of tone and composition. And as several of these are observed to accompany each other, they come to be marked by one name, and so to be reputed as one thing. Thus, for example, a certain colour, taste, smell, figure and consistence having been observed to go together, are accounted one distinct thing, signified by the name *apple*. Other collections of ideas constitute a stone, a tree, a book, and the like sensible things; which, as they are pleasing or disagreeable, excite the passions of love, hatred, joy, grief, and so forth.

2 But besides all that endless variety of ideas or objects of knowledge, there is likewise something which knows or perceives them, and exercises divers operations, as willing, imagining, remembering about them. This perceiving, active being is what I call *mind, spirit, soul* or *myself*. By which words I do not denote any one of my ideas, but a thing entirely distinct from them, wherein they exist, or, which is the same thing, whereby they are perceived; for the existence of an idea consists in being perceived.

3 That neither our thoughts, nor passions, nor ideas formed by the imagination, exist without the mind, is what everybody will allow. And it seems no less evident that the various sensations or ideas imprinted on the sense, however blended or combined together (that is, whatever objects

---

[1] [The rejection of 'ideas of reflection' is essential to Berkeley's published philosophy (see, e.g., PC 684, PHK I § 27, DHP III *233*; cp. PC 377). It seems impossible that an opening sentence should contain a careless survival. Jessop's suggestion that 'such' refers to 'objects' rather than 'ideas' might also seem improbable, but the clumsy ambiguity accords with Berkeley's evident intention that this paragraph should read like a statement of Lockean principles. See editor's Introduction p. x.]

they compose) cannot exist otherwise than in a mind perceiving them. I think an intuitive knowledge may be obtained of this, by anyone that shall attend to what is meant by the term *exist* when applied to sensible things. The table I write on, I say, exists, that is, I see and feel it; and if I were out of my study I should say it existed, meaning thereby that if I was in my study I might perceive it, or that some other spirit actually does perceive it. There was an odour, that is, it was smelled; there was a sound, that is to say, it was heard; a colour or figure, and it was perceived by sight or touch. This is all that I can understand by these and the like expressions. For as to what is said of the absolute existence of unthinking things without any relation to their being perceived, that seems perfectly unintelligible. Their *esse* is *percipi*, nor is it possible they should have any existence, out of the minds or thinking things which perceive them.

4 It is indeed an opinion strangely prevailing amongst men, that houses, mountains, rivers, and in a word all sensible objects have an existence natural or real, distinct from their being perceived by the understanding. But with how great an assurance and acquiescence soever this principle may be entertained in the world; yet whoever shall find in his heart to call it in question, may, if I mistake not, perceive it to involve a manifest contradiction. For what are the forementioned objects but the things we perceive by sense, and what do we perceive besides our own ideas or sensations; and is it not plainly repugnant that any one of these or any combination of them should exist unperceived?

5 If we thoroughly examine this tenet, it will, perhaps, be found at bottom to depend on the doctrine of *abstract ideas*. For can there be a nicer strain of abstraction than to distinguish the existence of sensible objects from their being perceived, so as to conceive them existing unperceived? Light and colours, heat and cold, extension and figures, in a word the things we see and feel, what are they but so many sensations, notions, ideas or impressions on the sense; and is it possible to separate, even in thought, any of these from perception? For my part I might as easily divide a thing from itself. I may indeed divide in my thoughts or conceive apart from each other those things which, perhaps, I never perceived by sense so divided. Thus I imagine the trunk of a human body without the limbs, or conceive the smell of a rose without thinking on the rose itself. So far I will not deny I can abstract, if that may properly be called *abstraction*, which extends only to the conceiving separately such objects, as it is possible may really exist or be actually perceived asunder. But my conceiving or imagining power does not extend beyond the possibility of real existence or perception. Hence as it is impossible for me to see or feel anything without an actual sensation of that thing, so is it impossible for me to conceive in my thoughts any sensible thing or object distinct from the sensation or perception of it.

6 Some truths there are so near and obvious to the mind, that a man need only open his eyes to see them. Such I take this important one to be, to wit, that all the choir of heaven and furniture of the earth, in a word all those bodies which compose the mighty frame of the world, have not any

subsistence without a mind, that their being is to be perceived or known; that consequently so long as they are not actually perceived by me, or do not exist in my mind or that of any other created spirit, they must either have no existence at all, or else subsist in the mind of some eternal spirit: it being perfectly unintelligible and involving all the absurdity of abstraction, to attribute to any single part of them an existence independent of a spirit. To be convinced of which, the reader need only reflect and try to separate in his own thoughts the being of a sensible thing from its being perceived.

7 From what has been said, it follows, there is not any other substance than *spirit*, or that which perceives. But for the fuller proof of this point, let it be considered, the sensible qualities are colour, figure, motion, smell, taste, and such like, that is, the ideas perceived by sense. Now for an idea to exist in an unperceiving thing, is a manifest contradiction; for to have an idea is all one as to perceive: that therefore wherein colour, figure, and the like qualities exist, must perceive them; hence it is clear there can be no unthinking substance or *substratum* of those ideas.

8 But say you, though the ideas themselves do not exist without the mind, yet there may be things like them whereof they are copies or resemblances, which things exist without the mind, in an unthinking substance. I answer, an idea can be like nothing but an idea; a colour or figure can be like nothing but another colour or figure. If we look but ever so little into our thoughts, we shall find it impossible for us to conceive a likeness except only between our ideas. Again, I ask whether those supposed originals or external things, of which our ideas are the pictures or representations, be themselves perceivable or no? If they are, then they are ideas, and we have gained our point; but if you say they are not, I appeal to anyone whether it be sense, to assert a colour is like something which is invisible; hard or soft, like something which is intangible; and so of the rest.

9 Some there are who make a distinction betwixt *primary* and *secondary* qualities: by the former, they mean extension, figure, motion, rest, solidity or impenetrability and number: by the latter they denote all other sensible qualities, as colours, sounds, tastes, and so forth. The ideas we have of these they acknowledge not to be the resemblances of anything existing without the mind or unperceived; but they will have our ideas of the primary qualities to be patterns or images of things which exist without the mind, in an unthinking substance which they call *matter*. By matter therefore we are to understand an inert, senseless substance, in which extension, figure, and motion, do actually subsist. But it is evident from what we have already shewn, that extension, figure and motion are only ideas existing in the mind, and that an idea can be like nothing but another idea, and that consequently neither they nor their archetypes can exist in an unperceiving substance. Hence it is plain, that the very notion of what is called *matter* or *corporeal substance*, involves a contradiction in it.

10 They who assert that figure, motion, and the rest of the primary or original qualities do exist without the mind, in unthinking substances, do at the same time acknowledge that colours, sounds, heat, cold, and such

like secondary qualities, do not, which they tell us are sensations existing in the mind alone, that depend on and are occasioned by the different size, texture and motion of the minute particles of matter. This they take for an undoubted truth, which they can demonstrate beyond all exception. Now if it be certain, that those original qualities are inseparably united with the other sensible qualities, and not, even in thought, capable of being abstracted from them, it plainly follows that they exist only in the mind. But I desire anyone to reflect and try, whether he can by any abstraction of thought, conceive the extension and motion of a body, without all other sensible qualities. For my own part, I see evidently that it is not in my power to frame an idea of a body extended and moved, but I must withal give it some colour or other sensible quality which is acknowledged to exist only in the mind. In short, extension, figure, and motion, abstracted from all other qualities, are inconceivable. Where therefore the other sensible qualities are, there must these be also, to wit, in the mind and nowhere else.

11 Again, *great* and *small*, *swift* and *slow*, are allowed to exist nowhere without the mind, being entirely relative, and changing as the frame or position of the organs of sense varies. The extension therefore which exists without the mind, is neither great nor small, the motion neither swift nor slow, that is, they are nothing at all. But say you, they are extension in general, and motion in general: thus we see how much the tenet of extended, moveable substances existing without the mind, depends on that strange doctrine of *abstract ideas*. And here I cannot but remark, how nearly the vague and indeterminate description of matter or corporeal substance, which the modern philosophers are run into by their own principles, resembles that antiquated and so much ridiculed notion of *materia prima*, to be met with in Aristotle and his followers. Without extension solidity cannot be conceived; since therefore it has been shewn that extension exists not in an unthinking substance, the same must also be true of solidity.

12 That number is entirely the creature of the mind, even though the other qualities be allowed to exist without, will be evident to whoever considers, that the same thing bears a different denomination of number, as the mind views it with different respects. Thus, the same extension is one or three or thirty-six, according as the mind considers it with reference to a yard, a foot, or an inch. Number is so visibly relative, and dependent on men's understanding, that it is strange to think how anyone should give it an absolute existence without the mind. We say one book, one page, one line; all these are equally units, though some contain several of the others. And in each instance it is plain, the unit relates to some particular combination of ideas arbitrarily put together by the mind.

13 Unity I know some will have to be a simple or uncompounded idea, accompanying all other ideas into the mind. That I have any such idea answering the word *unity*, I do not find; and if I had, methinks I could not miss finding it; on the contrary it should be the most familiar to my understanding, since it is said to accompany all other ideas, and to be

perceived by all the ways of sensation and reflexion. To say no more, it is an *abstract idea*.

14 I shall farther add, that after the same manner, as modern philosophers prove certain sensible qualities to have no existence in matter, or without the mind, the same thing may be likewise proved of all other sensible qualities whatsoever. Thus, for instance, it is said that heat and cold are affections only of the mind, and not at all patterns of real beings, existing in the corporeal substances which excite them, for that the same body which appears cold to one hand, seems warm to another. Now why may we not as well argue that figure and extension are not patterns or resemblances of qualities existing in matter, because to the same eye at different stations, or eyes of a different texture at the same station, they appear various, and cannot therefore be the images of anything settled and determinate without the mind? Again, it is proved that sweetness is not really in the sapid thing, because the thing remaining unaltered the sweetness is changed into bitter, as in case of a fever or otherwise vitiated palate. Is it not as reasonable to say, that motion is not without the mind, since if the succession of ideas in the mind become swifter, the motion, it is acknowledged, shall appear slower without any alteration in any external object.

15 In short, let anyone consider those arguments, which are thought manifestly to prove that colours and tastes exist only in the mind, and he shall find they may with equal force, be brought to prove the same thing of extension, figure, and motion. Though it must be confessed this method of arguing doth not so much prove that there is no extension or colour in an outward object, as that we do not know by sense which is the true extension or colour of the object. But the arguments foregoing plainly shew it to be impossible that any colour or extension at all, or other sensible quality whatsoever, should exist in an unthinking subject without the mind, or in truth, that there should be any such thing as an outward object.

16 But let us examine a little the received opinion. It is said extension is a mode or accident of matter, and that matter is the *substratum* that supports it. Now I desire that you would explain what is meant by matter's *supporting* extension: say you, I have no idea of matter, and therefore cannot explain it. I answer, though you have no positive, yet if you have any meaning at all, you must at least have a relative idea of matter; though you know not what it is, yet you must be supposed to know what relation it bears to accidents, and what is meant by its supporting them. It is evident *support* cannot here be taken in its usual or literal sense, as when we say that pillars support a building: in what sense therefore must it be taken?

17 If we inquire into what the most accurate philosophers declare themselves to mean by *material substance*; we shall find them acknowledge, they have no other meaning annexed to those sounds, but the idea of being in general, together with the relative notion of its supporting accidents. The general idea of being appeareth to me the most abstract and incompre-

hensible of all other; and as for its supporting accidents, this, as we have just now observed, cannot be understood in the common sense of those words; it must therefore be taken in some other sense, but what that is they do not explain. So that when I consider the two parts or branches which make the signification of the words *material substance*, I am convinced there is no distinct meaning annexed to them. But why should we trouble ourselves any farther, in discussing this material *substratum* or support of figure and motion, and other sensible qualities? Does it not suppose they have an existence without the mind? And is not this a direct repugnancy, and altogether inconceivable?

18 But though it were possible that solid, figured, moveable substances may exist without the mind, corresponding to the ideas we have of bodies, yet how is it possible for us to know this? Either we must know it by sense, or by reason. As for our senses, by them we have the knowledge only of our sensations, ideas, or those things that are immediately perceived by sense, call them what you will: but they do not inform us that things exist without the mind, or unperceived, like to those which are perceived. This the materialists themselves acknowledge. It remains therefore that if we have any knowledge at all of external things, it must be by reason, infer-ring their existence from what is immediately perceived by sense. But what reason can induce us to believe the existence of bodies without the mind, from what we perceive, since the very patrons of matter themselves do not pretend, there is any necessary connexion betwixt them and our ideas? I say it is granted on all hands (and what happens in dreams, phrensies, and the like, puts it beyond dispute) that it is possible we might be affected with all the ideas we have now, though no bodies existed without, resem-bling them. Hence it is evident the supposition of external bodies is not necessary for the producing our ideas: since it is granted they are produced sometimes, and might possibly be produced always in the same order we see them in at present, without their concurrence.

19 But though we might possibly have all our sensations without them, yet perhaps it may be thought easier to conceive and explain the manner of their production, by supposing external bodies in their likeness rather than otherwise; and so it might be at least probable there are such things as bodies that excite their ideas in our minds. But neither can this be said; for though we give the materialists their external bodies, they by their own confession are never the nearer knowing how our ideas are produced: since they own themselves unable to comprehend in what manner body can act upon spirit, or how it is possible it should imprint any idea in the mind. Hence it is evident the production of ideas or sensations in our minds, can be no reason why we should suppose matter or corporeal substances, since that is acknowledged to remain equally inexplicable with, or without this supposition. If therefore it were possible for bodies to exist without the mind, yet to hold they do so, must needs be a very precarious opinion; since it is to suppose, without any reason at all, that God has created innumerable beings that are entirely useless, and serve to no manner of purpose.

20 In short, if there were external bodies, it is impossible we should ever come to know it; and if there were not, we might have the very same reasons to think there were that we have now. Suppose, what no one can deny possible, an intelligence, without the help of external bodies, to be affected with the same train of sensations or ideas that you are, imprinted in the same order and with like vividness in his mind. I ask whether that intelligence hath not all the reason to believe the existence of corporeal substances, represented by his ideas, and exciting them in his mind, that you can possibly have for believing the same thing? Of this there can be no question; which one consideration is enough to make any reasonable person suspect the strength of whatever arguments he may think himself to have, for the existence of bodies without the mind.

21 Were it necessary to add any farther proof against the existence of matter, after what has been said, I could instance several of those errors and difficulties (not to mention impieties) which have sprung from that tenet. It has occasioned numberless controversies and disputes in philosophy, and not a few of far greater moment in religion. But I shall not enter into the detail of them in this place, as well because I think, arguments *a posteriori* are unnecessary for confirming what has been, if I mistake not, sufficiently demonstrated *a priori*, as because I shall hereafter find occasion to say somewhat of them.

22 I am afraid I have given cause to think me needlessly prolix in handling this subject. For to what purpose is it to dilate on that which may be demonstrated with the utmost evidence in a line or two, to anyone that is capable of the least reflexion? It is but looking into your own thoughts, and so trying whether you can conceive it possible for a sound, or figure, or motion, or colour, to exist without the mind, or unperceived. This easy trial may make you see, that what you contend for, is a downright contradiction. Insomuch that I am content to put the whole upon this issue; if you can but conceive it possible for one extended moveable substance, or in general, for any one idea or anything like an idea, to exist otherwise than in a mind perceiving it, I shall readily give up the cause: and as for all that *compages* of external bodies which you contend for, I shall grant you its existence, though you cannot either give me any reason why you believe it exists, or assign any use to it when it is supposed to exist. I say, the bare possibility of your opinion's being true, shall pass for an argument that it is so.

23 But say you, surely there is nothing easier than to imagine trees, for instance, in a park, or books existing in a closet, and nobody by to perceive them. I answer, you may so, there is no difficulty in it: but what is all this, I beseech you, more than framing in your mind certain ideas which you call *books* and *trees*, and at the same time omitting to frame the idea of anyone that may perceive them? But do not you yourself perceive or think of them all the while? This therefore is nothing to the purpose: it only shows you have the power of imagining or forming ideas in your mind; but it doth not shew that you can conceive it possible, the objects of your thought may exist without the mind: to make out this, it is necessary

that you conceive them existing unconceived or unthought of, which is a manifest repugnancy. When we do our utmost to conceive the existence of external bodies, we are all the while only contemplating our own ideas. But the mind taking no notice of itself, is deluded to think it can and doth conceive bodies existing unthought of or without the mind; though at the same time they are apprehended by or exist in itself. A little attention will discover to anyone the truth and evidence of what is here said, and make it unnecessary to insist on any other proofs against the existence of material substance.

24 It is very obvious, upon the least inquiry into our own thoughts, to know whether it be possible for us to understand what is meant, by the *absolute existence of sensible objects in themselves, or without the mind*. To me it is evident those words mark out either a direct contradiction, or else nothing at all. And to convince others of this, I know no readier or fairer way, than to entreat they would calmly attend to their own thoughts: and if by this attention, the emptiness or repugnancy of those expressions does appear, surely nothing more is requisite for their conviction. It is on this therefore that I insist, to wit, that the absolute existence of unthinking things are words without a meaning, or which include a contradiction. This is what I repeat and inculcate, and earnestly recommend to the attentive thoughts of the reader.

25 All our ideas, sensations, or the things which we perceive, by whatsoever names they may be distinguished, are visibly inactive, there is nothing of power or agency included in them. So that one idea or object of thought cannot produce, or make any alteration in another. To be satisfied of the truth of this, there is nothing else requisite but a bare observation of our ideas. For since they and every part of them exist only in the mind, it follows that there is nothing in them but what is perceived. But whoever shall attend to his ideas, whether of sense or reflexion, will not perceive in them any power or activity; there is therefore no such thing contained in them. A little attention will discover to us that the very being of an idea implies passiveness and inertness in it, insomuch that it is impossible for an idea to do anything, or, strictly speaking, to be the cause of anything: neither can it be the resemblance or pattern of any active being, as is evident from *Sect*. 8. Whence it plainly follows that extension, figure and motion, cannot be the cause of our sensations. To say therefore, that these are the effects of powers resulting from the configuration, number, motion, and size of corpuscles, must certainly be false.

26 We perceive a continual succession of ideas, some are anew excited, others are changed or totally disappear. There is therefore some cause of these ideas whereon they depend, and which produces and changes them. That this cause cannot be any quality or idea or combination of ideas, is clear from the preceding section. It must therefore be a substance; but it has been shewn that there is no corporeal or material substance: it remains therefore that the cause of ideas is an incorporeal active substance or spirit.

27 A spirit is one simple, undivided, active being: as it perceives ideas, it is called the *understanding*, and as it produces or otherwise operates about them, it is called the *will*. Hence there can be no idea formed of a soul or spirit: for all ideas whatever, being passive and inert, *vide Sect*. 25, they cannot represent unto us, by way of image or likeness, that which acts. A little attention will make it plain to anyone, that to have an idea which shall be like that active principle of motion and change of ideas, is absolutely impossible. Such is the nature of *spirit* or that which acts, that it cannot be of itself perceived, but only by the effects which it produceth. If any man shall doubt of the truth of what is here delivered, let him but reflect and try if he can frame the idea of any power or active being; and whether he hath ideas of two principal powers, marked by the names *will* and *understanding*, distinct from each other as well as from a third idea of substance or being in general, with a relative notion of its supporting or being the subject of the aforesaid powers, which is signified by the name *soul* or *spirit*. This is what some hold; but so far as I can see, the words *will, soul, spirit*, do not stand for different ideas, or in truth, for any idea at all, but for something which is very different from ideas, and which being an agent cannot be like unto, or represented by, any idea whatsoever. Though it must be owned at the same time, that we have some notion of soul, spirit, and the operations of the mind, such as willing, loving, hating, in as much as we know or understand the meaning of those words.[1]

28 I find I can excite ideas in my mind at pleasure, and vary and shift the scene as oft as I think fit. It is no more than willing, and straightway this or that idea arises in my fancy: and by the same power it is obliterated, and makes way for another. This making and unmaking of ideas doth very properly denominate the mind active. Thus much is certain, and grounded on experience: but when we talk of unthinking agents, or of exciting ideas exclusive of volition, we only amuse ourselves with words.

29 But whatever power I may have over my own thoughts, I find the ideas actually perceived by sense have not a like dependence on my will. When in broad day-light I open my eyes, it is not in my power to choose whether I shall see or no, or to determine what particular objects shall present themselves to my view; and so likewise as to the hearing and other senses, the ideas imprinted on them are not creatures of my will. There is therefore some other will or spirit that produces them.

30 The ideas of sense are more strong, lively, and distinct than those of the imagination; they have likewise a steadiness, order, and coherence, and are not excited at random, as those which are the effects of human wills often are, but in a regular train or series, the admirable connexion whereof sufficiently testifies the wisdom and benevolence of its Author. Now the set rules or established methods, wherein the mind we depend on excites in us the ideas of sense, are called the *Laws of Nature*: and these we learn by experience, which teaches us that such and such ideas are

---

[1] [Last sentence added in second edition. See note on § 140, below.]

attended with such and such other ideas, in the ordinary course of things.

31 This gives us a sort of foresight, which enables us to regulate our actions for the benefit of life. And without this we should be eternally at a loss: we could not know how to act anything that might procure us the least pleasure, or remove the least pain of sense. That food nourishes, sleep refreshes, and fire warms us; that to sow in the seed-time is the way to reap in the harvest, and, in general, that to obtain such or such ends, such or such means are conducive, all this we know, not by discovering any necessary connexion between our ideas, but only by the observation of the settled laws of Nature, without which we should be all in uncertainty and confusion, and a grown man no more know how to manage himself in the affairs of life, than an infant just born.

32 And yet this consistent uniform working, which so evidently displays the goodness and wisdom of that governing spirit whose will constitutes the Laws of Nature, is so far from leading our thoughts to him, that it rather sends them a wandering after second causes. For when we perceive certain ideas of sense constantly followed by other ideas, and we know this is not of our doing, we forthwith attribute power and agency to the ideas themselves, and make one the cause of another, than which nothing can be more absurd and unintelligible. Thus, for example, having observed that when we perceive by sight a certain round luminous figure, we at the same time perceive by touch the idea or sensation called *heat*, we do from thence conclude the sun to be the cause of heat. And in like manner perceiving the motion and collision of bodies to be attended with sound, we are inclined to think the latter an effect of the former.

33 The ideas imprinted on the senses by the Author of Nature are called *real things*: and those excited in the imagination being less regular, vivid and constant, are more properly termed *ideas*, or *images of things*, which they copy and represent. But then our sensations, be they never so vivid and distinct, are nevertheless *ideas*, that is, they exist in the mind, or are perceived by it, as truly as the ideas of its own framing. The ideas of sense are allowed to have more reality in them, that is, to be more strong, orderly, and coherent than the creatures of the mind; but this is no argument that they exist without the mind. They are also less dependent on the spirit, or thinking substance which perceives them, in that they are excited by the will of another and more powerful spirit: yet still they are *ideas*, and certainly no *idea*, whether faint or strong, can exist otherwise than in a mind perceiving it.

34 Before we proceed any farther, it is necessary to spend some time in answering objections which may probably be made against the principles hitherto laid down. In doing of which, if I seem too prolix to those of quick apprehensions, I hope it may be pardoned, since all men do not equally apprehend things of this nature; and I am willing to be understood by everyone. First then, it will be objected that by the foregoing principles, all that is real and substantial in Nature is banished out of the world: and instead thereof a chimerical scheme of ideas takes place. All things

that exist, exist only in the mind, that is, they are purely notional. What therefore becomes of the sun, moon, and stars? What must we think of houses, rivers, mountains, trees, stones; nay, even of our own bodies? Are all these but so many chimeras and illusions on the fancy? To all which, and whatever else of the same sort may be objected, I answer, that by the principles premised, we are not deprived of any one thing in Nature. Whatever we see, feel, hear, or any wise conceive or understand, remains as secure as ever, and is as real as ever. There is a *rerum natura*, and the distinction between realities and chimeras retains its full force. This is evident from *Sect*. 29, 30, and 33, where we have shewn what is meant by *real things* in opposition to *chimeras*, or ideas of our own framing; but then they both equally exist in the mind, and in that sense are alike *ideas*.

35 I do not argue against the existence of any one thing that we can apprehend, either by sense or reflexion. That the things I see with mine eyes and touch with my hands do exist, really exist, I make not the least question. The only thing whose existence we deny, is that which philosophers call matter or corporeal substance. And in doing of this, there is no damage done to the rest of mankind, who, I dare say, will never miss it. The atheist indeed will want the colour of an empty name to support his impiety; and the philosophers may possibly find, they have lost a great handle for trifling and disputation.

36 If any man thinks this detracts from the existence or reality of things, he is very far from understanding what hath been premised in the plainest terms I could think of. Take here an abstract of what has been said. There are spiritual substances, minds, or human souls, which will or excite ideas in themselves at pleasure: but these are faint, weak, and unsteady in respect of others they perceive by sense, which being impressed upon them according to certain rules or laws of Nature, speak themselves the effects of a mind more powerful and wise than human spirits. These latter are said to have more *reality* in them than the former: by which is meant that they are more affecting, orderly, and distinct, and that they are not fictions of the mind perceiving them. And in this sense, the sun that I see by day is the real sun, and that which I imagine by night is the idea of the former. In the sense here given of *reality*, it is evident that every vegetable, star, mineral, and in general each part of the mundane system, is as much a *real being* by our principles as by any other. Whether others mean any-thing by the term *reality* different from what I do, I entreat them to look into their own thoughts and see.

37 It will be urged that thus much at least is true, to wit, that we take away all corporeal substances. To this my answer is, that if the word *substance* be taken in the vulgar sense, for a combination of sensible qualities, such as extension, solidity, weight, and the like; this we cannot be accused of taking away. But if it be taken in a philosophic sense, for the support of accidents or qualities without the mind: then indeed I acknow-ledge that we take it away, if one may be said to take away that which never had any existence, not even in the imagination.

38 But, say you, it sounds very harsh to say we eat and drink ideas,

and are clothed with ideas. I acknowledge it does so, the word *idea* not being used in common discourse to signify the several combinations of sensible qualities, which are called *things*: and it is certain that any expression which varies from the familiar use of language, will seem harsh and ridiculous. But this doth not concern the truth of the proposition, which in other words is no more than to say, we are fed and clothed with those things which we perceive immediately by our senses. The hardness or softness, the colour, taste, warmth, figure, and such like qualities, which combined together constitute the several sorts of victuals and apparel, have been shewn to exist only in the mind that perceives them; and this is all that is meant by calling them *ideas*; which word, if it was as ordinarily used as *thing*, would sound no harsher nor more ridiculous than it. I am not for disputing about the propriety, but the truth of the expression. If therefore you agree with me that we eat and drink, and are clad with the immediate objects of sense which cannot exist unperceived or without the mind: I shall readily grant it is more proper or conformable to custom, that they should be called things rather than ideas.

39 If it be demanded why I make use of the word *idea*, and do not rather in compliance with custom call them things, I answer, I do it for two reasons: first, because the term *thing*, in contradistinction to *idea*, is generally supposed to denote somewhat existing without the mind: secondly, because *thing* hath a more comprehensive signification than *idea*, including spirits or thinking things as well as ideas. Since therefore the objects of sense exist only in the mind, and are withal thoughtless and inactive, I chose to mark them by the word *idea*, which implies those properties.

40 But say what we can, someone perhaps may be apt to reply, he will still believe his senses, and never suffer any arguments, how plausible soever, to prevail over the certainty of them. Be it so, assert the evidence of sense as high as you please, we are willing to do the same. That what I see, hear and feel doth exist, that is to say, is perceived by me, I no more doubt than I do of my own being. But I do not see how the testimony of sense can be alleged, as a proof for the existence of anything, which is not perceived by sense. We are not for having any man turn *sceptic*, and disbelieve his senses; on the contrary we give them all the stress and assurance imaginable; nor are there any principles more opposite to scepticism, than those we have laid down, as shall be hereafter clearly shewn.

41 Secondly, it will be objected that there is a great difference betwixt real fire, for instance, and the idea of fire, betwixt dreaming or imagining oneself burnt, and actually being so:[1] this and the like may be urged in opposition to our tenets. To all which the answer is evident from what hath been already said, and I shall only add in this place, that if real fire be very different from the idea of fire, so also is the real pain that it occasions, very different from the idea of the same pain: and yet nobody will pretend

---

[1] [First edition: *being so: if you suspect it to be only the idea of fire which you see, do but put your hand into it, and you'll be convinced with a witness. This* . . .]

that real pain either is, or can possibly be, in an unperceiving thing or without the mind, any more than its idea.

42 Thirdly, it will be objected that we see things actually without or at a distance from us, and which consequently do not exist in the mind, it being absurd that those things which are seen at the distance of several miles, should be as near to us as our own thoughts. In answer to this, I desire it may be considered, that in a dream we do oft perceive things as existing at a great distance off, and yet for all that, those things are acknowledged to have their existence only in the mind.

43 But for the fuller clearing of this point, it may be worth while to consider, how it is that we perceive distance and things placed at a distance by sight. For that we should in truth see external space, and bodies actually existing in it, some nearer, others farther off, seems to carry with it some opposition to what hath been said, of their existing nowhere without the mind. The consideration of this difficulty it was, that gave birth to my *Essay towards a new Theory of Vision*, which was published not long since. Wherein it is shewn that *distance* or outness is neither immediately of itself perceived by sight, nor yet apprehended or judged of by lines and angles, or anything that hath a necessary connexion with it: but that it is only suggested to our thoughts, by certain visible ideas and sensations attending vision, which in their own nature have no manner of similitude or relation, either with distance, or things placed at a distance. But by a connexion taught us by experience, they come to signify and suggest them to us, after the same manner that words of any language suggest the ideas they are made to stand for. Insomuch that a man born blind, and afterwards made to see, would not, at first sight, think the things he saw, to be without his mind, or at any distance from him. See *Sect.* 41 of the forementioned treatise.

44 The ideas of sight and touch make two species, entirely distinct and heterogeneous. The former are marks and prognostics of the latter. That the proper objects of sight neither exist without the mind, nor are the images of external things, was shewn even in that treatise. Though throughout the same, the contrary be supposed true of tangible objects: not that to suppose that vulgar error, was necessary for establishing the notion therein laid down; but because it was beside my purpose to examine and refute it in a discourse concerning *vision*. So that in strict truth the ideas of sight, when we apprehend by them distance and things placed at a distance, do not suggest or mark out to us things actually existing at a distance, but only admonish us that ideas of touch will be imprinted in our minds at such and such distances of time, and in consequence of such and such actions. It is, I say, evident from what has been said in the foregoing parts of this treatise, and in *Sect.* 147, and elsewhere of the essay concerning vision, that visible ideas are the language whereby the governing spirit, on whom we depend, informs us what tangible ideas he is about to imprint upon us, in case we excite this or that motion in our own bodies. But for a fuller information in this point, I refer to the essay itself.

45 Fourthly, it will be objected that from the foregoing principles it

follows, things are every moment annihilated and created anew. The objects of sense exist only when they are perceived: the trees therefore are in the garden, or the chairs in the parlour, no longer than while there is somebody by to perceive them. Upon shutting my eyes all the furniture in the room is reduced to nothing, and barely upon opening them it is again created. In answer to all which, I refer the reader to what has been said in *Sect.* 3, 4, &c. and desire he will consider whether he means anything by the actual existence of an idea, distinct from its being perceived. For my part, after the nicest inquiry I could make, I am not able to discover that anything else is meant by those words. And I once more entreat the reader to sound his own thoughts, and not suffer himself to be imposed on by words. If he can conceive it possible either for his ideas or their archetypes to exist without being perceived, then I give up the cause: but if he cannot, he will acknowledge it is unreasonable for him to stand up in defence of he knows not what, and pretend to charge on me as an absurdity, the not assenting to those propositions which at bottom have no meaning in them.

46 It will not be amiss to observe, how far the received principles of philosophy are themselves chargeable with those pretended absurdities. It is thought strangely absurd that upon closing my eyelids, all the visible objects round me should be reduced to nothing; and yet is not this what philosophers commonly acknowledge, when they agree on all hands, that light and colours, which alone are the proper and immediate objects of sight, are mere sensations that exist no longer than they are perceived? Again, it may to some perhaps seem very incredible, that things should be every moment creating, yet this very notion is commonly taught in the Schools. For the Schoolmen, though they acknowledge the existence of matter, and that the whole mundane fabric is framed out of it, are nevertheless of opinion that it cannot subsist without the divine conservation, which by them is expounded to be a continual creation.

47 Farther, a little thought will discover to us, that though we allow the existence of matter or corporeal substance, yet it will unavoidably follow from the principles which are now generally admitted, that the particular bodies of what kind soever, do none of them exist whilst they are not perceived. For it is evident from *Sect.* 11. and the following sections, that the matter philosophers contend for, is an incomprehensible somewhat which hath none of those particular qualities, whereby the bodies falling under our senses are distinguished one from another. But to make this more plain, it must be remarked, that the infinite divisibility of matter is now universally allowed, at least by the most approved and considerable philosophers, who on the received principles demonstrate it beyond all exception. Hence it follows, that there is an infinite number of parts in each particle of matter, which are not perceived by sense. The reason therefore, that any particular body seems to be of a finite magnitude, or exhibits only a finite number of parts to sense, is, not because it contains no more, since in itself it contains an infinite number of parts, but because the sense is not acute enough to discern them. In proportion therefore as the sense is rendered more acute, it perceives a greater number of parts in the object,

that is, the object appears greater, and its figure varies, those parts in its extremities which were before unperceivable, appearing now to bound it in very different lines and angles from those perceived by an obtuser sense. And at length, after various changes of size and shape, when the sense becomes infinitely acute, the body shall seem infinite. During all which there is no alteration in the body, but only in the sense. Each body therefore considered in itself, is infinitely extended, and consequently void of all shape or figure. From which it follows, that though we should grant the existence of matter to be ever so certain, yet it is withal as certain, the materialists themselves are by their own principles forced to acknowledge, that neither the particular bodies perceived by sense, nor anything like them exists without the mind. Matter, I say, and each particle thereof is according to them infinite and shapeless, and it is the mind that frames all that variety of bodies which compose the visible world, any one whereof does not exist longer than it is perceived.

48 If we consider it, the objection proposed in *Sect.* 45 will not be found reasonably charged on the principles we have premised, so as in truth to make any objection at all against our notions. For though we hold indeed the objects of sense to be nothing else but ideas which cannot exist unperceived; yet we may not hence conclude they have no existence except only while they are perceived by us, since there may be some other spirit that perceives them, though we do not. Wherever bodies are said to have no existence without the mind, I would not be understood to mean this or that particular mind, but all minds whatsoever. It does not therefore follow from the foregoing principles, that bodies are annihilated and created every moment, or exist not at all during the intervals between our perception of them.

49 Fifthly, it may perhaps be objected, that if extension and figure exist only in the mind, it follows that the mind is extended and figured; since extension is a mode or attribute, which (to speak with the Schools) is predicated of the subject in which it exists. I answer, those qualities are in the mind only as they are perceived by it, that is, not by way of *mode* or *attribute*, but only by way of *idea*; and it no more follows, that the soul or mind is extended because extension exists in it alone, than it does that it is red or blue, because those colours are on all hands acknowledged to exist in it, and nowhere else. As to what philosophers say of subject and mode, that seems very groundless and unintelligible. For instance, in this proposition, a die is hard, extended and square, they will have it that the word *die* denotes a subject or substance, distinct from the hardness, extension and figure, which are predicated of it, and in which they exist. This I cannot comprehend: to me a die seems to be nothing distinct from those things which are termed its modes or accidents. And to say a die is hard, extended and square, is not to attribute those qualities to a subject distinct from and supporting them, but only an explication of the meaning of the word *die*.

50 Sixthly, you will say there have been a great many things explained by matter and motion: take away these, and you destroy the whole corpuscular philosophy, and undermine those mechanical principles which

have been applied with so much success to account for the phenomena. In short, whatever advances have been made, either by ancient or modern philosophers, in the study of Nature, do all proceed on the supposition, that corporeal substance or matter doth really exist. To this I answer, that there is not any one *phenomenon* explained on that supposition, which may not as well be explained without it, as might easily be made to appear by an induction of particulars. To explain the *phenomena*, is all one as to shew, why upon such and such occasions we are affected with such and such ideas. But how matter should operate on a spirit, or produce any idea in it, is what no philosopher will pretend to explain. It is therefore evident, there can be no use of matter in natural philosophy. Besides, they who attempt to account for things, do it not by corporeal substance, but by figure, motion, and other qualities, which are in truth no more than mere ideas, and therefore cannot be the cause of anything, as hath been already shewn. See *Sect.* 25.

51 Seventhly, it will upon this be demanded whether it does not seem absurd to take away natural causes, and ascribe everything to the immediate operation of spirits? We must no longer say upon these principles that fire heats, or water cools, but that a spirit heats, and so forth. Would not a man be deservedly laughed at, who should talk after this manner? I answer, he would so; in such things we ought to *think with the learned, and speak with the vulgar*. They who to demonstration are convinced of the truth of the Copernican system, do nevertheless say the sun rises, the sun sets, or comes to the meridian: and if they affected a contrary style in common talk, it would without doubt appear very ridiculous. A little reflexion on what is here said will make it manifest, that the common use of language would receive no manner of alteration or disturbance from the admission of our tenets.

52 In the ordinary affairs of life, any phrases may be retained, so long as they excite in us proper sentiments, or dispositions to act in such a manner as is necessary for our well-being, how false soever they may be, if taken in a strict and speculative sense. Nay this is unavoidable, since propriety being regulated by custom, language is suited to the received opinions, which are not always the truest. Hence it is impossible, even in the most rigid philosophic reasonings, so far to alter the bent and genius of the tongue we speak, as never to give a handle for cavillers to pretend difficulties and inconsistencies. But a fair and ingenuous reader will collect the sense, from the scope and tenor and connexion of a discourse, making allowances for those inaccurate modes of speech, which use has made inevitable.

53 As to the opinion that there are no corporeal causes, this has been heretofore maintained by some of the Schoolmen, as it is of late by others among the modern philosophers, who though they allow matter to exist, yet will have God alone to be the immediate efficient cause of all things. These men saw, that amongst all the objects of sense, there was none which had any power or activity included in it, and that by consequence this was likewise true of whatever bodies they supposed to exist without the mind,

like unto the immediate objects of sense. But then, that they should suppose an innumerable multitude of created beings, which they acknowledge are not capable of producing any one effect in Nature, and which therefore are made to no manner of purpose, since God might have done everything as well without them; this I say, though we should allow it possible, must yet be a very unaccountable and extravagant supposition.

54 In the eighth place, the universal concurrent assent of mankind may be thought by some, an invincible argument in behalf of matter, or the existence of external things. Must we suppose the whole world to be mistaken? And if so, what cause can be assigned of so widespread and predominant an error? I answer, first, that upon a narrow inquiry, it will not perhaps be found, so many as is imagined do really believe the existence of matter or things without the mind. Strictly speaking, to believe that which involves a contradiction, or has no meaning in it, is impossible: and whether the foregoing expressions are not of that sort, I refer it to the impartial examination of the reader. In one sense indeed, men may be said to believe that matter exists, that is, they act as if the immediate cause of their sensations, which affects them every moment and is so nearly present to them, were some senseless unthinking being. But that they should clearly apprehend any meaning marked by those words, and form thereof a settled speculative opinion, is what I am not able to conceive. This is not the only instance wherein men impose upon themselves, by imagining they believe those propositions they have often heard, though at bottom they have no meaning in them.

55 But secondly, though we should grant a notion to be ever so universally and steadfastly adhered to, yet this is but a weak argument of its truth, to whoever considers what a vast number of prejudices and false opinions are everywhere embraced with the utmost tenaciousness, by the un-reflecting (which are the far greater) part of mankind. There was a time when the *antipodes* and motion of the earth were looked upon as monstrous absurdities, even by men of learning: and if it be considered what a small proportion they bear to the rest of mankind, we shall find that at this day, those notions have gained but a very inconsiderable footing in the world.

56 But it is demanded, that we assign a cause of this prejudice, and account for its obtaining in the world. To this I answer, that men knowing they perceived several ideas, whereof they themselves were not the authors, as not being excited from within, nor depending on the operation of their wills, this made them maintain, those ideas or objects of perception had an existence independent of, and without the mind, without ever dreaming that a contradiction was involved in those words. But philosophers having plainly seen, that the immediate objects of perception do not exist without the mind, they in some degree corrected the mistake of the vulgar, but at the same time run into another which seems no less absurd, to wit, that there are certain objects really existing without the mind, or having a subsistence distinct from being perceived, of which our ideas are only images or resemblances, imprinted by those objects on the mind. And this notion of the philosophers owes its origin to the same cause with the former,

namely, their being conscious that they were not the authors of their own sensations, which they evidently knew were imprinted from without, and which therefore must have some cause, distinct from the minds on which they are imprinted.

57 But why they should suppose the ideas of sense to be excited in us by things in their likeness, and not rather have recourse to *spirit* which alone can act, may be accounted for, first, because they were not aware of the repugnancy there is, as well in supposing things like unto our ideas existing without, as in attributing to them power or activity. Secondly, because the supreme spirit which excites those ideas in our minds, is not marked out and limited to our view by any particular finite collection of sensible ideas, as human agents are by their size, complexion, limbs, and motions. And thirdly, because his operations are regular and uniform. Whenever the course of Nature is interrupted by a miracle, men are ready to own the presence of a superior agent. But when we see things go on in the ordinary course, they do not excite in us any reflection; their order and concatenation, though it be an argument of the greatest wisdom, power, and goodness in their Creator, is yet so constant and familiar to us, that we do not think them the immediate effects of a *free spirit*: especially since inconstancy and mutability in acting, though it be an imperfection, is looked on as a mark of *freedom*.

58 Tenthly, it will be objected, that the notions we advance, are inconsistent with several sound truths in philosophy and mathematics. For example, the motion of the earth is now universally admitted by astronomers, as a truth grounded on the clearest and most convincing reasons; but on the foregoing principles, there can be no such thing. For motion being only an idea, it follows that if it be not perceived, it exists not; but the motion of the earth is not perceived by sense. I answer, that tenet, if rightly understood, will be found to agree with the principles we have premised: for the question, whether the earth moves or no, amounts in reality to no more than this, to wit, whether we have reason to conclude from what hath been observed by astronomers, that if we were placed in such and such circumstances, and such or such a position and distance, both from the earth and sun, we should perceive the former to move among the choir of the planets, and appearing in all respects like one of them: and this, by the established rules of Nature, which we have no reason to mistrust, is reasonably collected from the phenomena.

59 We may, from the experience we have had of the train and succession of ideas in our minds, often make, I will not say uncertain conjectures, but sure and well-grounded predictions, concerning the ideas we shall be affected with, pursuant to a great train of actions, and be enabled to pass a right judgment of what would have appeared to us, in case we were placed in circumstances very different from those we are in at present. Herein consists the knowledge of Nature, which may preserve its use and certainty very consistently with what hath been said. It will be easy to apply this to whatever objections of the like sort may be drawn from the magnitude of the stars, or any other discoveries in astronomy or Nature.

60 In the eleventh place, it will be demanded to what purpose serves that curious organization of plants, and the admirable mechanism in the parts of animals; might not vegetables grow, and shoot forth leaves and blossoms, and animals perform all their motions, as well without as with all that variety of internal parts so elegantly contrived and put together, which being ideas have nothing powerful or operative in them, nor have any necessary connexion with the effects ascribed to them? If it be a spirit that immediately produces every effect by a *fiat*, or act of his will, we must think all that is fine and artificial in the works, whether of man or Nature, to be made in vain. By this doctrine, though an artist hath made the spring and wheels, and every movement of a watch, and adjusted them in such a manner as he knew would produce the motions he designed; yet he must think all this done to no purpose, and that it is an intelligence which directs the index, and points to the hour of the day. If so, why may not the intelligence do it, without his being at the pains of making the movements, and putting them together? Why does not an empty case serve as well as another? And how comes it to pass, that whenever there is any fault in the going of a watch, there is some corresponding disorder to be found in the movements, which being mended by a skilful hand, all is right again? The like may be said of all the clockwork of Nature, great part whereof is so wonderfully fine and subtle, as scarce to be discerned by the best microscope. In short, it will be asked, how upon our principles any tolerable account can be given, or any final cause assigned of an innumerable multitude of bodies and machines framed with the most exquisite art, which in the common philosophy have very apposite uses assigned them, and serve to explain abundance of phenomena.

61 To all which I answer, first, that though there were some difficulties relating to the administration of providence, and the uses by it assigned to the several parts of Nature, which I could not solve by the foregoing principles, yet this objection could be of small weight against the truth and certainty of those things which may be proved *a priori*, with the utmost evidence. Secondly, but neither are the received principles free from the like difficulties; for it may still be demanded, to what end God should take those round-about methods of effecting things by instruments and machines, which no one can deny might have been effected by the mere command of his will, without all that *apparatus*: nay, if we narrowly consider it, we shall find the objection may be retorted with greater force on those who hold the existence of those machines without the mind; for it has been made evident, that solidity, bulk, figure, motion and the like, have no *activity* or *efficacy* in them, so as to be capable of producing any one effect in Nature. See *Sect*. 25. Whoever therefore supposes them to exist (allowing the supposition possible) when they are not perceived, does it manifestly to no purpose; since the only use that is assigned to them, as they exist unperceived, is that they produce those perceivable effects, which in truth cannot be ascribed to anything but spirit.

62 But to come nearer the difficulty, it must be observed, that though the fabrication of all those parts and organs be not absolutely necessary

to the producing any effect, yet it is necessary to the producing of things in a constant, regular way, according to the Laws of Nature. There are certain general laws that run through the whole chain of natural effects: these are learned by the observation and study of Nature, and are by men applied as well to the framing artificial things for the use and ornament of life, as to the explaining the various *phenomena*: which explication consists only in shewing the conformity any particular phenomenon hath to the general Laws of Nature, or, which is the same thing, in discovering the *uniformity* there is in the production of natural effects; as will be evident to whoever shall attend to the several instances, wherein philosophers pretend to account for appearances. That there is a great and conspicuous use in these regular constant methods of working observed by the Supreme Agent, hath been shewn in *Sect.* 31. And it is no less visible, that a particular size, figure, motion and disposition of parts are necessary, though not absolutely to the producing any effect, yet to the producing it according to the standing mechanical Laws of Nature. Thus, for instance, it cannot be denied that God, or the intelligence which sustains and rules the ordinary course of things might, if he were minded to produce a miracle, cause all the motions on the dial-plate of a watch, though nobody had ever made the movements, and put them in it: but yet if he will act agreeably to the rules of mechanism, by him for wise ends established and maintained in the Creation, it is necessary that those actions of the watchmaker, whereby he makes the movements and rightly adjusts them, precede the production of the aforesaid motions; as also that any disorder in them be attended with the perception of some corresponding disorder in the movements, which being once corrected all is right again.

63 It may indeed on some occasions be necessary, that the Author of Nature display his overruling power in producing some appearance out of the ordinary series of things. Such exceptions from the general rules of Nature are proper to surprise and awe men into an acknowledgement of the Divine Being: but then they are to be used but seldom, otherwise there is a plain reason why they should fail of that effect. Besides, God seems to choose the convincing our reason of his attributes by the works of Nature, which discover so much harmony and contrivance in their make, and are such plain indications of wisdom and beneficence in their Author, rather than to astonish us into a belief of his being by anomalous and surprising events.

64 To set this matter in a yet clearer light, I shall observe that what has been objected in *Sect.* 60 amounts in reality to no more than this: ideas are not anyhow and at random produced, there being a certain order and connexion between them, like to that of cause and effect: there are also several combinations of them, made in a very regular and artificial manner, which seem like so many instruments in the hand of Nature, that being hid as it were behind the scenes, have a secret operation in producing those appearances which are seen on the theatre of the world, being themselves discernible only to the curious eye of the philosopher. But since one

idea cannot be the cause of another, to what purpose is that connexion? And since those instruments, being barely *inefficacious perceptions* in the mind, are not subservient to the production of natural effects; it is demanded why they are made, or, in other words, what reason can be assigned why God should make us, upon a close inspection into his works, behold so great variety of ideas, so artfully laid together, and so much according to rule; it not being credible, that he would be at the expense (if one may so speak) of all that art and regularity to no purpose?

65 To all which my answer is, first, that the connexion of ideas does not imply the relation of *cause* and *effect*, but only of a mark or *sign* with the thing *signified*. The fire which I see is not the cause of the pain I suffer upon my approaching it, but the mark that forewarns me of it. In like manner, the noise that I hear is not the effect of this or that motion or collision of the ambient bodies, but the sign thereof. Secondly, the reason why ideas are formed into machines, that is, artificial and regular combinations, is the same with that for combining letters into words. That a few original ideas may be made to signify a great number of effects and actions, it is necessary they be variously combined together: and to the end their use be permanent and universal, these combinations must be made by *rule*, and with *wise contrivance*. By this means abundance of information is conveyed unto us, concerning what we are to expect from such and such actions, and what methods are proper to be taken, for the exciting such and such ideas: which in effect is all that I conceive to be distinctly meant, when it is said that by discerning the figure, texture, and mechanism of the inward parts of bodies, whether natural or artificial, we may attain to know the several uses and properties depending thereon, or the nature of the thing.

66 Hence it is evident, that those things which under the notion of a cause co-operating or concurring to the production of effects, are altogether inexplicable, and run us into great absurdities, may be very naturally explained, and have a proper and obvious use assigned them, when they are considered only as marks or signs for our information. And it is the searching after, and endeavouring to understand those signs instituted by the Author of Nature, that ought to be the employment of the natural philosopher, and not the pretending to explain things by corporeal causes; which doctrine seems to have too much estranged the minds of men from that active principle, that supreme and wise spirit, *in whom we live, move, and have our being*.

67 In the twelfth place, it may perhaps be objected, that though it be clear from what has been said, that there can be no such thing as an inert, senseless, extended, solid, figured, moveable substance, existing without the mind, such as philosophers describe matter: yet if any man shall leave out of his idea of *matter*, the positive ideas of extension, figure, solidity and motion, and say that he means only by that word, an inert senseless substance, that exists without the mind, or unperceived, which is the occasion of our ideas, or at the presence whereof God is pleased to excite ideas in us: it doth not appear, but that matter taken in this sense

may possibly exist. In answer to which I say, first, that it seems no less absurd to suppose a substance without accidents, than it is to suppose accidents without a substance. But secondly, though we should grant this unknown substance may possibly exist, yet where can it be supposed to be? That it exists not in the mind is agreed, and that it exists not in place is no less certain; since all extension exists only in the mind, as hath been already proved. It remains therefore that it exists nowhere at all.

68 Let us examine a little the description that is here given us of *matter*. It neither acts, nor perceives, nor is perceived: for this is all that is meant by saying it is an inert, senseless, unknown substance; which is a definition entirely made up of negatives, excepting only the relative notion of its standing under or supporting: but then it must be observed, that it *supports* nothing at all; and how nearly this comes to the description of a *non-entity*, I desire may be considered. But, say you, it is the *unknown occasion*, at the presence of which, ideas are excited in us by the will of God. Now I would fain know how anything can be present to us, which is neither perceivable by sense nor reflexion, nor capable of producing any idea in our minds, nor is at all extended, nor hath any form, nor exists in any place. The words *to be present*, when thus applied, must needs be taken in some abstract and strange meaning, and which I am not able to comprehend.

69 Again, let us examine what is meant by *occasion*: so far as I can gather from the common use of language, that word signifies, either the agent which produces any effect, or else something that is observed to accompany, or go before it, in the ordinary course of things. But when it is applied to matter as above described, it can be taken in neither of those senses. For matter is said to be passive and inert, and so cannot be an agent or efficient cause. It is also unperceivable, as being devoid of all sensible qualities, and so cannot be the occasion of our perceptions in the latter sense: as when the burning my finger is said to be the occasion of the pain that attends it. What therefore can be meant by calling matter an *occasion*? This term is either used in no sense at all, or else in some sense very distant from its received signification.

70 You will perhaps say that matter, though it be not perceived by us, is nevertheless perceived by God, to whom it is the occasion of exciting ideas in our minds. For, say you, since we observe our sensations to be imprinted in an orderly and constant manner, it is but reasonable to suppose there are certain constant and regular occasions of their being produced. That is to say, that there are certain permanent and distinct parcels of matter, corresponding to our ideas, which, though they do not excite them in our minds, or any ways immediately affect us, as being altogether passive and unperceivable to us, they are nevertheless to God, by whom they are perceived, as it were so many occasions to remind him when and what ideas to imprint on our minds: that so things may go on in a constant uniform manner.

71 In answer to this I observe, that as the notion of matter is here stated, the question is no longer concerning the existence of a thing distinct from

spirit and *idea*, from perceiving and being perceived: but whether there
are not certain ideas, of I know not what sort, in the mind of God, which
are so many marks or notes that direct him how to produce sensations in
our minds, in a constant and regular method: much after the same manner
as a musician is directed by the notes of music to produce that harmonious
train and composition of sound, which is called a *tune*; though they who
hear the music do not perceive the notes, and may be entirely ignorant of
them. But this notion of matter[1] seems too extravagant to deserve a con-
futation. Besides, it is in effect no objection against what we have advanced,
to wit, that there is no senseless, unperceived *substance*.

72 If we follow the light of reason, we shall, from the constant uniform
method of our sensations, collect the goodness and wisdom of the *spirit*
who excites them in our minds. But this is all that I can see reasonably
concluded from thence. To me, I say, it is evident that the being of a
spirit infinitely wise, good, and powerful is abundantly sufficient to explain
all the appearances of Nature. But as for *inert senseless matter*, nothing
that I perceive has any the least connexion with it, or leads to the thoughts
of it. And I would fain see anyone explain any the meanest phenomenon
in Nature by it, or shew any manner of reason, though in the lowest rank
of probability, that he can have for its existence; or even make any tolerable sense or meaning of that supposition. For as to its being an occasion,
we have, I think, evidently shewn that with regard to us it is no occasion:
it remains therefore that it must be, if at all, the occasion to God of exciting
ideas in us; and what this amounts to, we have just now seen.

73 It is worth while to reflect a little on the motives which induced men
to suppose the existence of material substance; that so having observed
the gradual ceasing, and expiration of those motives or reasons, we may
proportionably withdraw the assent that was grounded on them. First
therefore, it was thought that colour, figure, motion, and the rest of the
sensible qualities or accidents, did really exist without the mind; and for this
reason, it seemed needful to suppose some unthinking *substratum* or
substance wherein they did exist, since they could not be conceived to
exist by themselves. Afterwards, in process of time, men being convinced
that colours, sounds, and the rest of the sensible secondary qualities had no
existence without the mind, they stripped this *substratum* or material
substance of those qualities, leaving only the primary ones, figure, motion,
and such like, which they still conceived to exist without the mind, and
consequently to stand in need of a material support. But it having been
shewn, that none, even of these, can possibly exist otherwise than in a
spirit or mind which perceives them, it follows that we have no longer any
reason to suppose the being of *matter*. Nay, that it is utterly impossible

---

[1] [First edition: *matter (which after all is the only intelligible one that I can pick,
from what is said of unknown occasions)*. Berkeley is not here criticizing as
such the identification of physical objects with divine ideas, but their identification with divine ideas of a kind unknown to us which direct the activity of
'an all-sufficient spirit'.]

there should be any such thing, so long as that word is taken to denote an *unthinking substratum* of qualities or accidents, wherein they exist without the mind.

74 But though it be allowed by the *materialists* themselves, that matter was thought of only for the sake of supporting accidents; and the reason entirely ceasing, one might expect the mind should naturally, and without any reluctance at all, quit the belief of what was solely grounded thereon. Yet the prejudice is riveted so deeply in our thoughts, that we can scarce tell how to part with it, and are therefore inclined, since the *thing* itself is indefensible, at least to retain the *name*; which we apply to I know not what abstracted and indefinite notions of *being*, or *occasion*, though without any shew of reason, at least so far as I can see. For what is there on our part, or what do we perceive amongst all the ideas, sensations, notions, which are imprinted on our minds, either by sense or reflexion, from whence may be inferred the existence of an inert, thoughtless, unperceived occasion? and on the other hand, on the part of an *all-sufficient spirit*, what can there be that should make us believe, or even suspect, he is *directed* by an inert occasion to excite ideas in our minds?

75 It is a very extraordinary instance of the force of prejudice, and much to be lamented, that the mind of a man retains so great a fondness against all the evidence of reason, for a stupid thoughtless *somewhat*, by the interposition whereof it would, as it were, screen itself from the providence of God, and remove him farther off from the affairs of the world. But though we do the utmost we can, to secure the belief of *matter*, though when reason forsakes us, we endeavour to support our opinion on the bare possibility of the thing, and though we indulge ourselves in the full scope of an imagination not regulated by reason, to make out that poor *possibility*, yet the upshot of all is, that there are certain *unknown ideas* in the mind of God; for this, if anything, is all that I conceive to be meant by *occasion* with regard to God. And this, at the bottom, is no longer contending for the *thing*, but for the *name*.

76 Whether therefore there are such ideas in the mind of God, and whether they may be called by the name *matter*, I shall not dispute. But if you stick to the notion of an unthinking substance, or support of extension, motion, and other sensible qualities, then to me it is most evidently impossible there should be any such thing. Since it is a plain repugnancy, that those qualities should exist in or be supported by an unperceiving substance.

77 But say you, though it be granted that there is no thoughtless support of extension, and the other qualities or accidents which we perceive; yet there may, perhaps, be some inert unperceiving substance, or *substratum* of some other qualities, as incomprehensible to us as colours are to a man born blind, because we have not a sense adapted to them. But if we had a new sense, we should possibly no more doubt of their existence, than a blind man made to see does of the existence of light and colours. I answer, first, if what you mean by the word *matter* be only the unknown support of unknown qualities, it is no matter whether there is such a thing or no,

since it no way concerns us: and I do not see the advantage there is in disputing about we know not *what*, and we know not *why*.

78 But secondly, if we had a new sense, it could only furnish us with new ideas or sensations: and then we should have the same reason against their existing in an unperceiving substance, that has been already offered with relation to figure, motion, colour, and the like. Qualities, as hath been shewn, are nothing else but *sensations* or *ideas*, which exist only in a *mind* perceiving them; and this is true not only of the ideas we are acquainted with at present, but likewise of all possible ideas whatsoever.

79 But you will insist, what if I have no reason to believe the existence of matter, what if I cannot assign any use to it, or explain anything by it, or even conceive what is meant by that word? Yet still it is no contradiction to say that matter exists, and that this matter is *in general* a *substance*, or *occasion of ideas*; though, indeed, to go about to unfold the meaning, or adhere to any particular explication of those words, may be attended with great difficulties. I answer, when words are used without a meaning, you may put them together as you please, without danger of running into a contradiction. You may say, for example, that *twice two* is equal to *seven*, so long as you declare you do not take the words of that proposition in their usual acceptation, but for marks of you know not what. And by the same reason you may say, there is an inert thoughtless substance without accidents, which is the occasion of our ideas. And we shall understand just as much by one proposition, as the other.

80 In the last place, you will say, what if we give up the cause of material substance, and assert, that matter is an unknown *somewhat*, neither substance nor accident, spirit nor idea, inert, thoughtless, indivisible, immoveable, unextended, existing in no place? For, say you, whatever may be urged against *substance* or *occasion*, or any other positive or relative notion of matter, hath no place at all, so long as this *negative* definition of matter is adhered to. I answer, you may, if so it shall seem good, use the word *matter* in the same sense, that other men use *nothing*, and so make those terms convertible in your style. For after all, this is what appears to me to be the result of that definition, the parts whereof when I consider with attention, either collectively, or separate from each other, I do not find that there is any kind of effect or impression made on my mind, different from what is excited by the term *nothing*.

81 You will reply perhaps, that in the foresaid definition is included, what doth sufficiently distinguish it from nothing, the positive, abstract idea of *quiddity*, *entity*, or *existence*. I own indeed, that those who pretend to the faculty of framing abstract general ideas, do talk as if they had such an idea, which is, say they, the most abstract and general notion of all, that is to me the most incomprehensible of all others. That there are a great variety of spirits of different orders and capacities, whose faculties, both in number and extent, are far exceeding those the Author of my being has bestowed on me, I see no reason to deny. And for me to pretend to determine by my own few, stinted, narrow inlets of perception, what ideas the inexhaustible power of the Supreme Spirit may imprint upon them,

were certainly the utmost folly and presumption. Since there may be, for aught that I know, innumerable sorts of ideas or sensations, as different from one another, and from all that I have perceived, as colours are from sounds. But how ready soever I may be, to acknowledge the scantiness of my comprehension, with regard to the endless variety of spirits and ideas, that might possibly exist, yet for anyone to pretend to a notion of entity or existence, *abstracted* from *spirit* and *idea*, from perceiving and being perceived, is, I suspect, a downright repugnancy and trifling with words. It remains that we consider the objections, which may possibly be made on the part of religion.

82 Some there are who think, that though the arguments for the real existence of bodies, which are drawn from reason, be allowed not to amount to demonstration, yet the Holy Scriptures are so clear in the point, as will sufficiently convince every good Christian, that bodies do really exist, and are something more than mere ideas; there being in Holy Writ innumerable facts related, which evidently suppose the reality of timber, and stone, mountains, and rivers, and cities, and human bodies. To which I answer, that no sort of writings whatever, sacred or profane, which use those and the like words in the vulgar acceptation, or so as to have a meaning in them, are in danger of having their truth called in question by our doctrine. That all those things do really exist, that there are bodies, even corporeal substances, when taken in the vulgar sense, has been shown to be agreeable to our principles: and the difference betwixt *things* and *ideas*, *realities* and *chimeras*, has been distinctly explained.* And I do not think, that either what philosophers call *matter*, or the existence of objects without the mind, is anywhere mentioned in Scripture.

83 Again, whether there be, or be not external things, it is agreed on all hands, that the proper use of words, is the marking our conceptions, or things only as they are known and perceived by us; whence it plainly follows, that in the tenets we have laid down, there is nothing inconsistent with the right use and significancy of *language*, and that discourse of what kind soever, so far as it is intelligible, remains undisturbed. But all this seems so manifest, from what hath been set forth in the premises, that it is needless to insist any farther on it.

84 But it will be urged, that miracles do, at least, lose much of their stress and import by our principles. What must we think of Moses's rod, was it not *really* turned into a serpent, or was there only a change of *ideas* in the minds of the spectators? And can it be supposed, that our Saviour did no more at the marriage-feast in Cana, than impose on the sight, and smell, and taste of the guests, so as to create in them the appearance or idea only of wine? The same may be said of all other miracles: which, in consequence of the foregoing principles, must be looked upon only as so many cheats, or illusion of fancy. To this I reply, that the rod was changed into a real serpent, and the water into real wine. That this doth not, in the least, contradict what I have elsewhere said, will be evident from *Sect.* 34,

* Sect. 29, 30, 33, 36, &c.

and 35. But this business of *real* and *imaginary* hath been already so plainly and fully explained, and so often referred to, and the difficulties about it are so easily answered from what hath gone before, that it were an affront to the reader's understanding, to resume the explication of it in this place. I shall only observe, that if at table all who were present should see, and smell, and taste, and drink wine, and find the effects of it, with me there could be no doubt of its reality. So that, at bottom, the scruple concerning real miracles hath no place at all on ours, but only on the received principles, and consequently maketh rather *for*, than *against* what hath been said.

85 Having done with the objections, which I endeavoured to propose in the clearest light, and gave them all the force and weight I could, we proceed in the next place to take a view of our tenets in their consequences. Some of these appear at first sight, as that several difficult and obscure questions, on which abundance of speculation hath been thrown away, are entirely banished from philosophy. Whether corporeal substance can think? Whether matter be infinitely divisible? And how it operates on spirit? these and the like inquiries have given infinite amusement to philosophers in all ages. But depending on the existence of *matter*, they have no longer any place on our principles. Many other advantages there are, as well with regard to *religion* as the *sciences*, which it is easy for anyone to deduce from what hath been premised. But this will appear more plainly in the sequel.

86 From the principles we have laid down, it follows, human knowledge may naturally be reduced to two heads, that of *ideas*, and that of *spirits*. Of each of these I shall treat in order. And first as to ideas or unthinking things, our knowledge of these hath been very much obscured and confounded, and we have been led into very dangerous errors, by supposing a twofold existence of the objects of sense, the one *intelligible*, or in the mind, the other *real* and without the mind: whereby unthinking things are thought to have a natural subsistence of their own, distinct from being perceived by spirits. This which, if I mistake not, hath been shewn to be a most groundless and absurd notion, is the very root of *scepticism*; for so long as men thought that real things subsisted without the mind, and that their knowledge was only so far forth *real* as it was conformable to *real things*, it follows, they could not be certain that they had any real knowledge at all. For how can it be known, that the things which are perceived, are conformable to those which are not perceived, or exist without the mind?

87 Colour, figure, motion, extension and the like, considered only as so many *sensations* in the mind, are perfectly known, there being nothing in them which is not perceived. But if they are looked on as notes or images, referred to *things* or *archetypes* existing without the mind, then are we involved all in *scepticism*. We see only the appearances, and not the real qualities of things. What may be the extension, figure, or motion of any thing really and absolutely, or in itself, it is impossible for us to know, but only the proportion or the relation they bear to our senses. Things remaining the same, our ideas vary, and which of them, or even whether any of them at all represent the true quality really existing in the thing, it is out of our reach to determine. So that, for aught we know, all we see,

hear, and feel, may be only phantom and vain chimera, and not at all agree with the real things, existing in *rerum natura*. All this scepticism follows, from our supposing a difference between *things* and *ideas*, and that the former have a subsistence without the mind, or unperceived. It were easy to dilate on this subject, and shew how the arguments urged by *sceptics* in all ages, depend on the supposition of external objects.

88 So long as we attribute a real existence to unthinking things, distinct from their being perceived, it is not only impossible for us to know with evidence the nature of any real unthinking being, but even that it exists. Hence it is, that we see philosophers distrust their senses, and doubt of the existence of heaven and earth, of everything they see or feel, even of their own bodies. And after all their labour and struggle of thought, they are forced to own, we cannot attain to any self-evident or demonstrative knowledge of the existence of sensible things. But all this doubtfulness, which so bewilders and confounds the mind, and makes *philosophy* ridiculous in the eyes of the world, vanishes, if we annex a meaning to our words, and do not amuse ourselves with the terms *absolute, external, exist,* and such like, signifying we know not what. I can as well doubt of my own being, as of the being of those things which I actually perceive by sense: it being a manifest contradiction, that any sensible object should be immediately perceived by sight or touch, and at the same time have no existence in Nature, since the very existence of an unthinking being consists in *being perceived*.

89 Nothing seems of more importance, towards erecting a firm system of sound and real knowledge, which may be proof against the assaults of *scepticism*, than to lay the beginning in a distinct explication of what is meant by *thing, reality, existence*: for in vain shall we dispute concerning the real existence of things, or pretend to any knowledge thereof, so long as we have not fixed the meaning of those words. *Thing* or *being* is the most general name of all, it comprehends under it two kinds entirely distinct and heterogeneous, and which have nothing common but the name, to wit, *spirits* and *ideas*. The former are *active, indivisible substances*: the latter are *inert, fleeting, dependent beings,*[1] which subsist not by themselves, but are supported by, or exist in minds or spiritual substances. We comprehend our own existence by inward feeling or reflexion, and that of other spirits by reason. We may be said to have some knowledge or notion of our own minds, of spirits and active beings, whereof in a strict sense we have not ideas. In like manner we know and have a notion of relations between things or ideas, which relations are distinct from the ideas or things related, inasmuch as the latter may be perceived by us without our perceiving the former. To me it seems that ideas, spirits and relations are all in their respective kinds, the object of human knowledge and subject of discourse: and that the term *idea* would be improperly extended to signify everything we know or have any notion of.

---

[1] [First edition: indivisible, incorruptible substances: *the latter are* inert, fleeting perishable passions, *or* dependent beings.]

90 Ideas imprinted on the senses are real things, or do really exist; this we do not deny, but we deny they can subsist without the minds which perceive them, or that they are resemblances of any archetypes existing without the mind: since the very being of a sensation or idea consists in being perceived, and an idea can be like nothing but an idea. Again, the things perceived by sense may be termed *external*, with regard to their origin, in that they are not generated from within, by the mind itself, but imprinted by a spirit distinct from that which perceives them. Sensible objects may likewise be said to be without the mind, in another sense, namely when they exist in some other mind. Thus when I shut my eyes, the things I saw may still exist, but it must be in another mind.

91 It were a mistake to think, that what is here said derogates in the least from the reality of things. It is acknowledged on the received principles, that extension, motion, and in a word all sensible qualities, have need of a support, as not being able to subsist by themselves. But the objects perceived by sense, are allowed to be nothing but combinations of those qualities, and consequently cannot subsist by themselves. Thus far it is agreed on all hands. So that in denying the things perceived by sense, an existence independent of a substance, or support wherein they may exist, we detract nothing from the received opinion of their *reality*, and are guilty of no innovation in that respect. All the difference is, that according to us the unthinking beings perceived by sense, have no existence distinct from being perceived, and cannot therefore exist in any other substance, than those unextended, indivisible substances, or *spirits*, which act, and think, and perceive them: whereas philosophers vulgarly hold, that the sensible qualities exist in an inert, extended, unperceiving substance, which they call *matter*, to which they attribute a natural subsistence, exterior to all thinking beings, or distinct from being perceived by any mind whatsoever, even the eternal mind of the Creator, wherein they suppose only ideas of the corporeal substances created by him: if indeed they allow them to be at all created.

92 For as we have shewn the doctrine of matter or corporeal substance, to have been the main pillar and support of *scepticism*, so likewise upon the same foundation have been raised all the impious schemes of *atheism* and irreligion. Nay so great a difficulty hath it been thought, to conceive matter produced out of nothing, that the most celebrated among the ancient philosophers, even of these who maintained the being of a God, have thought matter to be uncreated and coeternal with him. How great a friend material substance hath been to *atheists* in all ages, were needless to relate. All their monstrous systems have so visible and necessary a dependence on it, that when this corner-stone is once removed, the whole fabric cannot choose but fall to the ground; insomuch that it is no longer worth while, to bestow a particular consideration on the absurdities of every wretched sect of *atheists*.

93 That impious and profane persons should readily fall in with those systems which favour their inclinations, by deriding immaterial substance, and supposing the soul to be divisible and subject to corruption as the

body; which exclude all freedom, intelligence, and design from the formation of things, and instead thereof make a self-existent, stupid, unthinking substance the root and origin of all beings. That they should hearken to those who deny a providence, or inspection of a superior mind over the affairs of the world, attributing the whole series of events either to blind chance or fatal necessity, arising from the impulse of one body on another. All this is very natural. And on the other hand, when men of better principles observe the enemies of religion lay so great a stress on *unthinking matter*, and all of them use so much industry and artifice to reduce everything to it; methinks they should rejoice to see them deprived of their grand support, and driven from that only fortress, without which your *Epicureans*, *Hobbists*, and the like, have not even the shadow of a pretence, but become the most cheap and easy triumph in the world.

94 The existence of matter, or bodies unperceived, has not only been the main support of *atheists* and *fatalists*, but on the same principle doth *idolatry* likewise in all its various forms depend. Did men but consider that the sun, moon, and stars, and every other object of the senses, are only so many sensations in their minds, which have no other existence but barely being perceived, doubtless they would never fall down, and worship their own *ideas*; but rather address their homage to that Eternal Invisible Mind which produces and sustains all things.

95 The same absurd principle, by mingling itself with the articles of our faith, hath occasioned no small difficulties to Christians. For example, about the *resurrection*, how many scruples and objections have been raised by Socinians and others? But do not the most plausible of them depend on the supposition, that a body is denominated the *same*, with regard not to the form or that which is perceived by sense, but the material substance which remains the same under several forms? Take away this *material substance*, about the identity whereof all the dispute is, and mean by *body* what every plain ordinary person means by that word, to wit, that which is immediately seen and felt, which is only a combination of sensible qualities, or ideas: and then their most unanswerable objections come to nothing.

96 Matter being once expelled out of Nature, drags with it so many sceptical and impious notions, such an incredible number of disputes and puzzling questions, which have been thorns in the sides of divines, as well as philosophers, and made so much fruitless work for mankind; that if the arguments we have produced against it, are not found equal to demonstration (as to me they evidently seem) yet I am sure all friends to knowledge, peace, and religion, have reason to wish they were.

97 Beside the external existence of the objects of perception, another great source of errors and difficulties, with regard to ideal knowledge, is the doctrine of *abstract ideas*, such as it hath been set forth in the Introduction. The plainest things in the world, those we are most intimately acquainted with, and perfectly know, when they are considered in an abstract way, appear strangely difficult and incomprehensible. Time, place, and motion, taken in particular or concrete, are what everybody knows; but having passed through the hands of a metaphysician, they become too

abstract and fine, to be apprehended by men of ordinary sense. Bid your servant meet you at such a *time*, in such a *place*, and he shall never stay to deliberate on the meaning of those words: in conceiving that particular time and place, or the motion by which he is to get thither, he finds not the least difficulty. But if *time* be taken, exclusive of all those particular actions and ideas that diversify the day, merely for the continuation of existence, or duration in abstract, then it will perhaps gravel even a philosopher to comprehend it.

98 Whenever I attempt to frame a simple idea of *time*, abstracted from the succession of ideas in my mind, which flows uniformly, and is participated by all beings, I am lost and embrangled in inextricable difficulties. I have no notion of it at all, only I hear others say, it is infinitely divisible, and speak of it in such a manner as leads me to entertain odd thoughts of my existence: since that doctrine lays one under an absolute necessity of thinking, either that he passes away innumerable ages without a thought, or else that he is annihilated every moment of his life: both which seem equally absurd. Time therefore being nothing, abstracted from the succession of ideas in our minds, it follows that the duration of any finite spirit must be estimated by the number of ideas or actions succeeding each other in that same spirit or mind. Hence it is a plain consequence that the soul always thinks: and in truth whoever shall go about to divide in his thoughts, or abstract the *existence* of a spirit from its *cogitation*, will, I believe, find it no easy task.

99 So likewise, when we attempt to abstract extension and motion from all other qualities, and consider them by themselves, we presently lose sight of them, and run into great extravagancies. All which depend on a two-fold abstraction: first, it is supposed that extension, for example, may be abstracted from all other sensible qualities; and secondly, that the entity of extension may be abstracted from its being perceived. But whoever shall reflect, and take care to understand what he says, will, if I mistake not, acknowledge that all sensible qualities are alike *sensations*, and alike *real*; that where the extension is, there is the colour too, to wit, in his mind, and that their archetypes can exist only in some other *mind*: and that the objects of sense are nothing but those sensations combined, blended, or (if one may so speak) concreted together: none of all which can be supposed to exist unperceived.

100 What it is for a man to be happy, or an object good, everyone may think he knows. But to frame an abstract idea of *happiness*, prescinded from all particular pleasure, or of *goodness*, from everything that is good, this is what few can pretend to. So likewise, a man may be just and virtuous, without having precise ideas of *justice* and *virtue*. The opinion that those and the like words stand for general notions abstracted from all particular persons and actions, seems to have rendered morality difficult, and the study thereof of less use to mankind. And in effect, the doctrine of *abstraction* has not a little contributed towards spoiling the most useful parts of knowledge.

101 The two great provinces of speculative science, conversant about

ideas received from sense and their relations, are *natural philosophy* and *mathematics*; with regard to each of these I shall make some observations. And first, I shall say somewhat of natural philosophy. On this subject it is, that the *sceptics* triumph: all that stock of arguments they produce to depreciate our faculties, and make mankind appear ignorant and low, are drawn principally from this head, to wit, that we are under an invincible blindness as to the *true* and *real* nature of things. This they exaggerate, and love to enlarge on. We are miserably bantered, say they, by our senses, and amused only with the outside and shew of things. The real essence, the internal qualities, and constitution of even the meanest object, is hid from our view; something there is in every drop of water, every grain of sand, which is beyond the power of human understanding to fathom or comprehend. But it is evident from what has been shewn, that all this complaint is groundless, and that we are influenced by false principles to that degree as to mistrust our senses, and think we know nothing of those things which we perfectly comprehend.

102 One great inducement to our pronouncing ourselves ignorant of the nature of things, is the current opinion that everything includes within itself the cause of its properties: or that there is in each object an inward essence, which is the source whence its discernible qualities flow, and whereon they depend. Some have pretended to account for appearances by occult qualities, but of late they are mostly resolved into mechanical causes, to wit, the figure, motion, weight, and such like qualities of insensible particles: whereas in truth, there is no other agent or efficient cause than *spirit*, it being evident that motion, as well as all other *ideas*, is perfectly inert. See *Sect.* 25. Hence, to endeavour to explain the production of colours or sounds, by figure, motion, magnitude and the like, must needs be labour in vain. And accordingly, we see the attempts of that kind are not at all satisfactory. Which may be said, in general, of those instances, wherein one idea or quality is assigned for the cause of another. I need not say, how many *hypotheses* and speculations are left out, and how much the study of Nature is abridged by this doctrine.

103 The great mechanical principle now in vogue is *attraction*. That a stone falls to the earth, or the sea swells towards the moon, may to some appear sufficiently explained thereby. But how are we enlightened by being told this is done by attraction? Is it that that word signifies the manner of the tendency, and that it is by the mutual drawing of bodies, instead of their being impelled or protruded towards each other? But nothing is determined of the manner or action, and it may as truly (for aught we know) be termed *impulse* or *protrusion* as *attraction*. Again, the parts of steel we see cohere firmly together, and this also is accounted for by attraction; but in this, as in the other instances, I do not perceive that anything is signified besides the effect itself; for as to the manner of the action whereby it is produced, or the cause which produces it, these are not so much as aimed at.

104 Indeed, if we take a view of the several *phenomena*, and compare them together, we may observe some likeness and conformity between them.

For example, in the falling of a stone to the ground, in the rising of the sea towards the moon, in cohesion and crystallization, there is something alike, namely an union or mutual approach of bodies. So that any one of these or the like *phenomena*, may not seem strange or surprising to a man who hath nicely observed and compared the effects of Nature. For that only is thought so which is uncommon, or a thing by itself, and out of the ordinary course of our observation. That bodies should tend towards the centre of the earth, is not thought strange, because it is what we perceive every moment of our lives. But that they should have a like gravitation towards the centre of the moon, may seem odd and unaccountable to most men, because it is discerned only in the tides. But a philosopher, whose thoughts take in a larger compass of Nature, having observed a certain similitude of appearances, as well in the heavens as the earth, that argue innumerable bodies to have a mutual tendency towards each other, which he denotes by the general name *attraction*, whatever can be reduced to that, he thinks justly accounted for. Thus he explains the tides by the attraction of the terraqueous globe towards the moon, which to him doth not appear odd or anomalous, but only a particular example of a general rule or law of Nature.

105 If therefore we consider the difference there is betwixt natural philosophers and other men, with regard to their knowledge of the *phenomena*, we shall find it consists, not in an exacter knowledge of the efficient cause that produces them, for that can be no other than the *will of a spirit*, but only in a greater largeness of comprehension, whereby analogies, harmonies, and agreements are discovered in the works of Nature, and the particular effects explained, that is, reduced to general rules, see *Sect*. 62, which rules grounded on the analogy, and uniformness observed in the production of natural effects, are most agreeable, and sought after by the mind; for that they extend our prospect beyond what is present, and near to us, and enable us to make very probable conjectures, touching things that may have happened at very great distances of time and place, as well as to predict things to come; which sort of endeavour towards omniscience, is much affected by the mind.

106 But we should proceed warily in such things: for we are apt to lay too great a stress on analogies, and to the prejudice of truth, humour that eagerness of the mind, whereby it is carried to extend its knowledge into general theorems. For example, gravitation, or mutual attraction, because it appears in many instances, some are straightway for pronouncing *universal*; and that to *attract, and be attracted by every other body, is an essential quality inherent in all bodies whatsoever*. Whereas it appears the fixed stars have no such tendency towards each other: and so far is that gravitation, from being *essential* to bodies, that, in some instances, a quite contrary principle seems to shew itself: as in the perpendicular growth of plants, and the elasticity of the air. There is nothing necessary or essential in the case, but it depends entirely on the will of the *governing spirit*, who causes certain bodies to cleave together, or tend towards each other, according to various laws, whilst he keeps others at a fixed distance; and

to some he gives a quite contrary tendency to fly asunder, just as he sees convenient.

107 After what has been premised, I think we may lay down the following conclusions. First, it is plain philosophers amuse themselves in vain, when they inquire for any natural efficient cause, distinct from a *mind* or *spirit*. Secondly, considering the whole creation is the workmanship of a *wise and good agent*, it should seem to become philosophers, to employ their thoughts (contrary to what some hold) about the final causes of things: and I must confess, I see no reason, why pointing out the various ends, to which natural things are adapted, and for which they were originally with unspeakable wisdom contrived, should not be thought one good way of accounting for them, and altogether worthy a philosopher. Thirdly, from what hath been premised no reason can be drawn, why the history of Nature should not still be studied, and observations and experiments made, which, that they are of use to mankind, and enable us to draw any general conclusions, is not the result of any immutable habitudes, or relations between things themselves, but only of God's goodness and kindness to men in the administration of the world. See *Sect.* 30 and 31. Fourthly, by a diligent observation of the *phenomena* within our view, we may discover the general laws of Nature, and from them deduce the other *phenomena*, I do not say *demonstrate*; for all deductions of that kind depend on a supposition that the Author of Nature always operates uniformly, and in a constant observance of those rules we take for principles: which we cannot evidently know.

108 Those men who frame general rules from the *phenomena*, and afterwards derive the *phenomena* from those rules, seem to consider signs rather than causes. A man may well understand natural signs without knowing their analogy, or being able to say by what rule a thing is so or so. And as it is very possible to write improperly, through too strict an observance of general grammar-rules: so in arguing from general rules of Nature, it is not impossible we may extend the analogy too far, and by that means run into mistakes.

109 As in reading other books, a wise man will choose to fix his thoughts on the sense and apply it to use, rather than lay them out in grammatical remarks on the language; so in perusing the volume of Nature, it seems beneath the dignity of the mind to affect an exactness in reducing each particular phenomenon to general rules, or shewing how it follows from them. We should propose to ourselves nobler views, such as to recreate and exalt the mind, with a prospect of the beauty, order, extent, and variety of natural things: hence, by proper inferences, to enlarge our notions of the grandeur, wisdom, and beneficence of the Creator: and lastly, to make the several parts of the Creation, so far as in us lies, subservient to the ends they were designed for, God's glory, and the sustentation and comfort of ourselves and fellow-creatures.

110 The best key for the aforesaid analogy, or natural science, will be easily acknowledged to be a certain celebrated treatise of *mechanics*: in the entrance of which justly admired treatise, time, space and motion,

are distinguished into *absolute* and *relative, true* and *apparent, mathematical* and *vulgar*: which distinction, as it is at large explained by the author, doth suppose those quantities to have an existence without the mind: and that they are ordinarily conceived with relation to sensible things, to which nevertheless in their own nature, they bear no relation at all.

111 As for *time*, as it is there taken in an absolute or abstracted sense, for the duration or perseverance of the existence of things, I have nothing more to add concerning it, after what hath been already said on that subject, *Sect.* 97 and 98. For the rest, this celebrated author holds there is an *absolute space*, which, being unperceivable to sense, remains in itself similar and immoveable: and relative space to be the measure thereof, which being moveable, and defined by its situation in respect of sensible bodies, is vulgarly taken for immoveable space. *Place* he defines to be that part of space which is occupied by any body. And according as the space is absolute or relative, so also is the place. *Absolute motion* is said to be the translation of a body from absolute place to absolute place, as relative motion is from one relative place to another. And because the parts of absolute space, do not fall under our senses, instead of them we are obliged to use their sensible measures: and so define both place and motion with respect to bodies, which we regard as immoveable. But it is said, in philosophical matters we must abstract from our senses, since it may be, that none of those bodies which seem to be quiescent, are truly so: and the same thing which is moved relatively, may be really at rest. As likewise one and the same body may be in relative rest and motion, or even moved with contrary relative motions at the same time, according as its place is variously defined. All which ambiguity is to be found in the apparent motions, but not at all in the true or absolute, which should therefore be alone regarded in philosophy. And the true, we are told, are distinguished from apparent or relative motions by the following properties. First, in true or absolute motion, all parts which preserve the same position with respect to the whole, partake of the motions of the whole. Secondly, the place being moved, that which is placed therein is also moved: so that a body moving in a place which is in motion, doth participate the motion of its place. Thirdly, true motion is never generated or changed, otherwise than by force impressed on the body itself. Fourthly, true motion is always changed by force impressed on the body moved. Fifthly, in circular motion barely relative, there is no centrifugal force, which nevertheless in that which is true or absolute, is proportional to the quantity of motion.

112 But notwithstanding what hath been said, it doth not appear to me, that there can be any motion other than *relative*: so that to conceive motion, there must be at least conceived two bodies, whereof the distance or position in regard to each other is varied. Hence if there was one only body in being, it could not possibly be moved. This seems evident, in that the idea I have of motion doth necessarily include relation.

113 But though in every motion it be necessary to conceive more bodies than one, yet it may be that one only is moved, namely that on which the

force causing the change of distance is impressed, or in other words, that to which the action is applied. For however some may define relative motion, so as to term that body *moved*, which changes its distance from some other body, whether the force or action causing that change were applied to it, or no: yet as relative motion is that which is perceived by sense, and regarded in the ordinary affairs of life, it should seem that every man of common sense knows what it is, as well as the best philosopher: now I ask anyone, whether in his sense of motion as he walks along the streets, the stones he passes over may be said to *move*, because they change distance with his feet? To me it seems, that though motion includes a relation of one thing to another, yet it is not necessary that each term of the relation be denominated from it. As a man may think of somewhat which doth not think, so a body may be moved to or from another body, which is not therefore itself in motion.

114 As the place happens to be variously defined, the motion which is related to it varies. A man in a ship may be said to be quiescent, with relation to the sides of the vessel, and yet move with relation to the land. Or he may move eastward in respect of the one, and westward in respect of the other. In the common affairs of life, men never go beyond the earth to define the place of any body: and what is quiescent in respect of that, is accounted *absolutely* to be so. But philosophers who have a greater extent of thought, and juster notions of the system of things, discover even the earth itself to be moved. In order therefore to fix their notions, they seem to conceive the corporeal world as finite, and the utmost unmoved walls or shell thereof to be the place, whereby they estimate true motions. If we sound our own conceptions, I believe we may find all the absolute motion we can frame an idea of, to be at bottom no other than relative motion thus defined. For as hath been already observed, absolute motion exclusive of all external relation is incomprehensible: and to this kind of relative motion, all the above-mentioned properties, causes, and effects ascribed to absolute motion, will, if I mistake not, be found to agree. As to what is said of the centrifugal force, that it doth not at all belong to circular relative motion: I do not see how this follows from the experiment which is brought to prove it. See *Philosophiæ Naturalis Principia Mathematica, in Schol. Def.* VIII. For the water in the vessel, at that time wherein it is said to have the greatest relative circular motion, hath, I think, no motion at all: as is plain from the foregoing section.

115 For to denominate a body *moved*, it is requisite, first, that it change its distance or situation with regard to some other body: and secondly, that the force or action occasioning that change be applied to it. If either of these be wanting, I do not think that agreeably to the sense of mankind, or the propriety of language, a body can be said to be in motion. I grant indeed, that it is possible for us to think a body, which we see change its distance from some other, to be moved, though it have no force applied to it (in which sense there may be apparent motion), but then it is, because the force causing the change of distance, is imagined by us to be applied or impressed on that body thought to move. Which indeed shews we

are capable of mistaking a thing to be in motion which is not, and that is all.[1]

116 From what hath been said, it follows that the philosophic consideration of motion doth not imply the being of an *absolute space*, distinct from that which is perceived by sense, and related to bodies: which that it cannot exist without the mind, is clear upon the same principles, that demonstrate the like of all other objects of sense. And perhaps, if we inquire narrowly, we shall find we cannot even frame an idea of *pure space*, exclusive of all body. This I must confess seems impossible, as being a most abstract idea. When I excite a motion in some part of my body, if it be free or without resistance, I say there is *space*: but if I find a resistance, then I say there is *body*: and in proportion as the resistance to motion is lesser or greater, I say the *space* is more or less *pure*. So that when I speak of pure or empty space, it is not to be supposed, that the word *space* stands for an idea distinct from, or conceivable without body and motion. Though indeed we are apt to think every noun substantive stands for a distinct idea, that may be separated from all others: which hath occasioned infinite mistakes. When therefore supposing all the world to be annihilated besides my own body, I say there still remains *pure space*: thereby nothing else is meant, but only that I conceive it possible, for the limbs of my body to be moved on all sides without the least resistance: but if that too were annihilated, then there could be no motion, and consequently no space. Some perhaps may think the sense of seeing doth furnish them with the idea of pure space; but it is plain from what we have elsewhere shewn, that the ideas of space and distance are not obtained by that sense. See the *Essay concerning Vision*.

117 What is here laid down, seems to put an end to all those disputes and difficulties, which have sprung up amongst the learned concerning the nature of *pure space*. But the chief advantage arising from it, is, that we are freed from that dangerous *dilemma*, to which several who have employed their thoughts on this subject, imagine themselves reduced, to wit, of thinking either that real space is God, or else that there is something beside God which is eternal, uncreated, infinite, indivisible, immutable. Both which may justly be thought pernicious and absurd notions. It is certain

---

[1] [First edition: . . . *but does not prove that, in the common acceptation of* motion, *a body is moved merely because it changes distance from another; since as soon as we are undeceived, and find that the moving force was not communicated to it, we no longer hold it to be moved. So on the other hand, when one only body (the parts whereof preserve a given position between themselves) is imagined to exist; some there are who think that it can be moved all manner of ways, tho' without any change of distance or situation to any other bodies; which we should not deny, if they meant only that it might have an impressed force, which, upon the bare creation of other bodies, would produce a motion of some certain quantity and determination. But that an actual motion (distinct from the impressed force, or power productive of change of place in case there were bodies present whereby to define it) can exist in such a single body, I must confess I am not able to comprehend.*]

that not a few divines, as well as philosophers of great note, have, from the difficulty they found in conceiving either limits or annihilation of space, concluded it must be *divine*. And some of late have set themselves particularly to shew, that the incommunicable attributes of God agree to it. Which doctrine, how unworthy soever it may seem of the Divine Nature, yet I do not see how we can get clear of it, so long as we adhere to the received opinions.

118 Hitherto of natural philosophy: we come now to make some inquiry concerning that other great branch of speculative knowledge, to wit, *mathematics*. These, how celebrated soever they may be, for their clearness and certainty of demonstration, which is hardly anywhere else to be found, cannot nevertheless be supposed altogether free from mistakes; if in their principles there lurks some secret error, which is common to the professors of those sciences with the rest of mankind. Mathematicians, though they deduce their theorems from a great height of evidence, yet their first principles are limited by the consideration of quantity: and they do not ascend into any inquiry concerning those transcendental maxims, which influence all the particular sciences, each part whereof, mathematics not excepted, doth consequently participate of the errors involved in them. That the principles laid down by mathematicians are true, and their way of deduction from those principles clear and incontestable, we do not deny. But we hold, there may be certain erroneous maxims of greater extent than the object of mathematics, and for that reason not expressly mentioned, though tacitly supposed throughout the whole progress of that science; and that the ill effects of those secret unexamined errors are diffused through all the branches thereof. To be plain, we suspect the mathematicians are, as well as other men, concerned in the errors arising from the doctrine of abstract general ideas, and the existence of objects without the mind.

119 *Arithmetic* hath been thought to have for its object abstract ideas of *number*. Of which to understand the properties and mutual habitudes is supposed no mean part of speculative knowledge. The opinion of the pure and intellectual nature of numbers in abstract, hath made them in esteem with those philosophers, who seem to have affected an uncommon fineness and elevation of thought. It hath set a price on the most trifling numerical speculations which in practice are of no use, but serve only for amusement: and hath therefore so far infected the minds of some, that they have dreamt of mighty *mysteries* involved in numbers, and attempted the explication of natural things by them. But if we inquire into our own thoughts, and consider what hath been premised, we may perhaps entertain a low opinion of those high flights and abstractions, and look on all inquiries about numbers, only as so many *difficiles nugæ*, so far as they are not subservient to practice, and promote the benefit of life.

120 Unity in abstract we have before considered in *Sect.* 13, from which and what hath been said in the Introduction, it plainly follows there is not any such idea. But number being defined a *collection of units*, we may conclude that, if there be no such thing as unity or unit in abstract, there are no ideas of number in abstract denoted by the numerical names and

figures. The theories therefore in arithmetic, if they are abstracted from the names and figures, as likewise from all use and practice, as well as from the particular things numbered, can be supposed to have nothing at all for their object. Hence we may see, how entirely the science of numbers is subordinate to practice, and how jejune and trifling it becomes, when considered as a matter of mere speculation.

121 However since there may be some, who, deluded by the specious shew of discovering abstracted verities, waste their time in arithmetical theorems and problems, which have not any use: it will not be amiss, if we more fully consider, and expose the vanity of that pretence; and this will plainly appear, by taking a view of arithmetic in its infancy, and observing what it was that originally put men on the study of that science, and to what scope they directed it. It is natural to think that at first, men, for ease of memory and help of computation, made use of counters, or in writing of single strokes, points or the like, each whereof was made to signify an unit, that is, some one thing of whatever kind they had occasion to reckon. Afterwards they found out the more compendious ways, of making one character stand in place of several strokes, or points. And lastly, the notation of the Arabians or Indians came into use, wherein by the repetition of a few characters or figures, and varying the signification of each figure according to the place it obtains, all numbers may be most aptly expressed: which seems to have been done in imitation of language, so that an exact analogy is observed betwixt the notation by figures and names, the nine simple figures answering the nine first numeral names and places in the former, corresponding to denominations in the latter. And agreeably to those conditions of the simple and local value of figures, were contrived methods of finding from the given figures or marks of the parts, what figures and how placed, are proper to denote the whole or *vice versa*. And having found the sought figures, the same rule or analogy being observed throughout, it is easy to read them into words; and so the number becomes perfectly known. For then the number of any particular things is said to be known, when we know the name or figures (with their due arrangement) that according to the standing analogy belong to them. For these signs being known, we can by the operations of arithmetic, know the signs of any part of the particular sums signified by them; and thus computing in signs (because of the connexion established betwixt them and the distinct multitudes of things, whereof one is taken for an unit), we may be able rightly to sum up, divide, and proportion the things themselves that we intend to number.

122 In *arithmetic* therefore we regard not the *things* but the *signs*, which nevertheless are not regarded for their own sake, but because they direct us how to act with relation to things, and dispose rightly of them. Now agreeably to what we have before observed, of words in general (*Sect. 19. Introd.*) it happens here likewise, that abstract ideas are thought to be signified by numeral names or characters, while they do not suggest ideas of particular things to our minds. I shall not at present enter into a more particular dissertation on this subject; but only observe that it is

evident from what hath been said, those things which pass for abstract truths and theorems concerning numbers, are, in reality, conversant about no object distinct from particular numerable things, except only names and characters; which originally came to be considered, on no other account but their being *signs*, or capable to represent aptly, whatever particular things men had need to compute. Whence it follows, that to study them for their own sake would be just as wise, and to as good purpose, as if a man, neglecting the true use or original intention and subserviency of language, should spend his time in impertinent criticisms upon words, or reasonings and controversies purely verbal.

123 From numbers we proceed to speak of *extension*, which considered as relative, is the object of geometry. The *infinite* divisibility of *finite* extension, though it is not expressly laid down, either as an axiom or theorem in the elements of that science, yet is throughout the same every-where supposed, and thought to have so inseparable and essential a connexion with the principles and demonstrations in geometry, that mathematicians never admit it into doubt, or make the least question of it. And as this notion is the source from whence do spring all those amusing geometrical paradoxes, which have such a direct repugnancy to the plain common sense of mankind, and are admitted with so much reluctance into a mind not yet debauched by learning: so is it the principal occasion of all that nice and extreme subtlety, which renders the study of *mathematics* so difficult and tedious. Hence if we can make it appear, that no finite extension contains innumerable parts, or is infinitely divisible, it follows that we shall at once clear the science of geometry from a great number of difficulties and contradictions, which have ever been esteemed a reproach to human reason, and withal make the attainment thereof a business of much less time and pains, than it hitherto hath been.

124 Every particular finite extension, which may possibly be the object of our thought, is an *idea* existing only in the mind, and consequently each part thereof must be perceived. If therefore I cannot perceive innumerable parts in any finite extension that I consider, it is certain they are not con-tained in it: but it is evident, that I cannot distinguish innumerable parts in any particular line, surface, or solid, which I either perceive by sense, or figure to myself in my mind: wherefore I conclude they are not contained in it. Nothing can be plainer to me, than that the extensions I have in view are no other than my own ideas, and it is no less plain, that I cannot resolve any one of my ideas into an infinite number of other ideas, that is, that they are not infinitely divisible. If by *finite extension* be meant something distinct from a finite idea, I declare I do not know what that is, and so cannot affirm or deny anything of it. But if the terms *extension*, *parts*, and the like, are taken in any sense conceivable, that is, for ideas; then to say a finite quantity or extension consists of parts infinite in num-ber, is so manifest a contradiction, that everyone at first sight acknowledged it to be so. And it is impossible it should ever gain the assent of any reasonable creature, who is not brought to it by gentle and slow degrees, as a converted Gentile to the belief of *transubstantiation*. Ancient and rooted

prejudices do often pass into principles: and those propositions which once obtain the force and credit of a *principle*, are not only themselves, but likewise whatever is deducible from them, thought privileged from all examination. And there is no absurdity so gross, which by this means the mind of man may not be prepared to swallow.

125 He whose understanding is prepossessed with the doctrine of abstract general ideas, may be persuaded, that (whatever be thought of the ideas of sense), extension in *abstract* is infinitely divisible. And one who thinks the objects of sense exist without the mind, will perhaps in virtue thereof be brought to admit, that a line but an inch long may contain innumerable parts really existing, though too small to be discerned. These errors are grafted as well in the minds of *geometricians*, as of other men, and have a like influence on their reasonings; and it were no difficult thing, to shew how the arguments from geometry made use of to support the infinite divisibility of extension, are bottomed on them. At present we shall only observe in general, whence it is that the mathematicians are all so fond and tenacious of this doctrine.

126 It hath been observed in another place, that the theorems and demonstrations in geometry are conversant about universal ideas. *Sect.* 15. *Introd.* Where it is explained in what sense this ought to be understood, to wit, that the particular lines and figures included in the diagram, are supposed to stand for innumerable others of different sizes: or in other words, the geometer considers them abstracting from their magnitude: which doth not imply that he forms an abstract idea, but only that he cares not what the particular magnitude is, whether great or small, but looks on that as a thing indifferent to the demonstration: hence it follows, that a line in the scheme, but an inch long, must be spoken of, as though it contained ten thousand parts, since it is regarded not in itself, but as it is universal; and it is universal only in its signification, whereby it represents innumerable lines greater than itself, in which may be distinguished ten thousand parts or more, though there may not be above an inch in it. After this manner the properties of the lines signified are (by a very usual figure) transferred to the sign, and thence through mistake thought to appertain to it considered in its own nature.

127 Because there is no number of parts so great, but it is possible there may be a line containing more, the inch-line is said to contain parts more than any assignable number; which is true, not of the inch taken absolutely, but only for the things signified by it. But men not retaining that distinction in their thoughts, slide into a belief that the small particular line described on paper contains in itself parts innumerable. There is no such thing as the ten-thousandth part of an *inch*; but there is of a *mile* or *diameter of the earth*, which may be signified by that inch. When therefore I delineate a triangle on paper, and take one side not above an inch, for example, in length to be the *radius*: this I consider as divided into ten thousand or an hundred thousand parts, or more. For though the ten-thousandth part of that line considered in itself, is nothing at all, and consequently may be neglected without any error or inconveniency; yet

these described lines being only marks standing for greater quantities, whereof it may be the ten-thousandth part is very considerable, it follows, that to prevent notable errors in practice, the *radius* must be taken of ten thousand parts, or more.

128 From what hath been said the reason is plain why, to the end any theorem may become universal in its use, it is necessary we speak of the lines described on paper, as though they contained parts which really they do not. In doing of which, if we examine the matter thoroughly, we shall perhaps discover that we cannot conceive an inch itself as consisting of, or being divisible into a thousand parts, but only some other line which is far greater than an inch, and represented by it. And that when we say a line is *infinitely divisible*, we must mean a line which is *infinitely great*. What we have here observed seems to be the chief cause, why to suppose the infinite divisibility of finite extension hath been thought necessary in geometry.

129 The several absurdities and contradictions which flowed from this false principle might, one would think, have been esteemed so many demonstrations against it. But by I know not what *logic*, it is held that proofs *a posteriori* are not to be admitted against propositions relating to infinity. As though it were not impossible even for an infinite mind to reconcile contradictions. Or as if anything absurd and repugnant could have a necessary connexion with truth, or flow from it. But whoever considers the weakness of this pretence, will think it was contrived on purpose to humour the laziness of the mind, which had rather acquiesce in an indolent scepticism, than be at the pains to go through with a severe examination of those principles it hath ever embraced for true.

130 Of late the speculations about infinites have run so high, and grown to such strange notions, as have occasioned no small scruples and disputes among the geometers of the present age. Some there are of great note, who not content with holding that finite lines may be divided into an infinite number of parts, do yet farther maintain, that each of those infinitesimals is itself subdivisible into an infinity of other parts, or infinitesimals of a second order, and so on *ad infinitum*. These, I say, assert there are infinitesimals of infinitesimals of infinitesimals, without ever coming to an end. So that according to them an inch doth not barely contain an infinite number of parts, but an infinity of an infinity of an infinity *ad infinitum* of parts. Others there be who hold all orders of infinitesimals below the first to be nothing at all, thinking it with good reason absurd, to imagine there is any positive quantity or part of extension, which though multiplied infinitely, can never equal the smallest given extension. And yet on the other hand it seems no less absurd, to think the square, cube, or other power of a positive real root, should itself be nothing at all; which they who hold infinitesimals of the first order, denying all of the subsequent orders, are obliged to maintain.

131 Have we not therefore reason to conclude, that they are *both* in the wrong, and that there is in effect no such thing as parts infinitely small, or an infinite number of parts contained in any finite quantity? But you will say, that if this doctrine obtains, it will follow the very foundations of

geometry are destroyed: and those great men who have raised that science to so astonishing an height, have been all the while building a castle in the air. To this it may be replied, that whatever is useful in geometry and promotes the benefit of human life, doth still remain firm and unshaken on our principles. That science considered as practical, will rather receive advantage than any prejudice from what hath been said. But to set this in a due light, may be the subject of a distinct inquiry. For the rest, though it should follow that some of the more intricate and subtle parts of *speculative mathematics* may be pared off without any prejudice to truth; yet I do not see what damage will be thence derived to mankind. On the contrary, it were highly to be wished, that men of great abilities and obstinate application would draw off their thoughts from those amusements, and employ them in the study of such things as lie nearer the concerns of life, or have a more direct influence on the manners.

132 If it be said that several theorems undoubtedly true, are discovered by methods in which infinitesimals are made use of, which could never have been, if their existence included a contradiction in it. I answer, that upon a thorough examination it will not be found, that in any instance it is necessary to make use of or conceive infinitesimal parts of finite lines, or even quantities less than the *minimum sensibile:* nay, it will be evident this is never done, it being impossible.

133 By what we have premised, it is plain that very numerous and important errors have taken their rise from those false principles, which were impugned in the foregoing parts of this treatise. And the opposites of those erroneous tenets at the same time appear to be most fruitful principles, from whence do flow innumerable consequences highly advantageous to true philosophy as well as to religion. Particularly, *matter* or *the absolute existence of corporeal objects*, hath been shewn to be that wherein the most avowed and pernicious enemies of all knowledge, whether human or divine, have ever placed their chief strength and confidence. And surely, if by distinguishing the real existence of unthinking things from their being perceived, and allowing them a subsistence of their own out of the minds of spirits, no one thing is explained in Nature; but on the contrary a great many inexplicable difficulties arise: if the supposition of matter is barely precarious, as not being grounded on so much as one single reason: if its consequences cannot endure the light of examination and free inquiry, but screen themselves under the dark and general pretence of *infinites being incomprehensible*: if withal the removal of this *matter* be not attended with the least evil consequence, if it be not even missed in the world, but everything as well, nay much easier conceived without it: if lastly, both *sceptics* and *atheists* are for ever silenced upon supposing only spirits and ideas, and this scheme of things is perfectly agreeable both to *reason* and *religion*: methinks we may expect it should be admitted and firmly embraced, though it were proposed only as an *hypothesis*, and the existence of matter had been allowed possible, which yet I think we have evidently demonstrated that it is not.

134 True it is, that in consequence of the foregoing principles, several

disputes and speculations, which are esteemed no mean parts of learning, are rejected as useless. But how great a prejudice soever against our notions, this may give to those who have already been deeply engaged, and made large advances in studies of that nature: yet by others, we hope it will not be thought any just ground of dislike to the principles and tenets herein laid down, that they abridge the labour of study, and make human sciences more clear, compendious, and attainable, than they were before.

135 Having dispatched what we intended to say concerning the knowledge of *ideas*, the method we proposed leads us, in the next place, to treat of *spirits*: with regard to which, perhaps human knowledge is not so deficient as is vulgarly imagined. The great reason that is assigned for our being thought ignorant of the nature of spirits, is, our not having an idea of it. But surely it ought not to be looked on as a defect in a human understanding, that it does not perceive the idea of *spirit*, if it is manifestly impossible there should be any such *idea*. And this, if I mistake not, has been demonstrated in *Sect*. 27: to which I shall here add that a spirit has been shown to be the only substance or support, wherein the unthinking beings or ideas can exist: but that this *substance* which supports or perceives ideas should itself be an *idea* or like an *idea*, is evidently absurd.

136 It will perhaps be said, that we want a sense (as some have imagined) proper to know substances withal, which if we had, we might know our own soul, as we do a triangle. To this I answer, that in case we had a new sense bestowed upon us, we could only receive thereby some new sensations of ideas of sense. But I believe nobody will say, that what he means by the terms *soul* and *substance*, is only some particular sort of idea or sensation. We may therefore infer, that all things duly considered, it is not more reasonable to think our faculties defective, in that they do not furnish us with an idea of spirit or active thinking substance, than it would be if we should blame them for not being able to comprehend a *round square*.

137 From the opinion that spirits are to be known after the manner of an idea or sensation, have risen many absurd and heterodox tenets, and much scepticism about the nature of the soul. It is even probable, that this opinion may have produced a doubt in some, whether they had any soul at all distinct from their body, since upon inquiry they could not find they had an idea of it. That an *idea* which is inactive, and the existence whereof consists in being perceived, should be the image or likeness of an agent subsisting by itself, seems to need no other refutation, than barely attending to what is meant by those words. But perhaps you will say, that though an *idea* cannot resemble a *spirit*, in its thinking, acting, or subsisting by itself, yet it may in some other respects: and it is not necessary that an idea or image be in all respects like the original.

138 I answer, if it does not in those mentioned, it is impossible it should represent it in any other thing. Do but leave out the power of willing, thinking, and perceiving ideas, and there remains nothing else wherein the idea can be like a spirit. For by the word *spirit* we mean only that which thinks, wills, and perceives; this, and this alone, constitutes the signification of that term. If therefore it is impossible that any degree of those powers

should be represented in an idea,[1] it is evident there can be no idea of a spirit.[2]

139 But it will be objected, that if there is no idea signified by the terms *soul, spirit,* and *substance,* they are wholly insignificant, or have no meaning in them. I answer, those words do mean or signify a real thing, which is neither an idea nor like an idea, but that which perceives ideas, and wills, and reasons about them. What I am myself, that which I denote by the term I, is the same with what is meant by *soul* or *spiritual substance.* If it be said[3] that this is only quarrelling at a word, and that since the immediate significations of other names are by common consent called *ideas,* no reason can be assigned, why that which is signified by the name *spirit* or *soul* may not partake in the same appellation. I answer, all the unthinking objects of the mind agree, in that they are entirely passive, and their existence consists only in being perceived: whereas a soul or spirit is an active being, whose existence consists not in being perceived, but in perceiving ideas and thinking. It is therefore necessary, in order to prevent equivocation and confounding natures perfectly disagreeing and unlike, that we distinguish between *spirit* and *idea.* See *Sect.* 27.

140 In a large sense indeed, we may be said to have an idea, or rather a notion[4] of *spirit,* that is, we understand the meaning of the word, otherwise we could not affirm or deny anything of it. Moreover, as we conceive the ideas that are in the minds of other spirits by means of our own, which we suppose to be resemblances of them: so we know other spirits by means of our own soul, which in that sense is the image or idea of them, it having a like respect to other spirits, that blueness or heat by me perceived hath to those ideas perceived by another.

141 It must not be supposed, that they who assert the natural immortality of the soul are of opinion, that it is absolutely incapable of annihilation even by the infinite power of the Creator who first gave it being: but only that it is not liable to be broken or dissolved by the ordinary Laws of Nature or motion. They indeed, who hold the soul of man to be only a thin vital flame, or system of animal spirits, make it perishing and cor-

---

[1] [First edition: *idea or notion.*]

[2] [*MS.: Again the soul is without composition of parts, one pure simple undivided being. Whatever distinction of faculties or parts we may conceive in it arises only from its various acts or operations about ideas. Hence it is repugnant that it should be known or represented in some parts and not in others, or that there should be an idea, which incompletely resembles it.*]

[3] [First edition: *But if I should say, that I was nothing, or that I was an idea or notion, nothing could be more evidently absurd than either of these propositions. You'll perhaps, insist, that this. . . .*]

[4] (*or rather a notion* not in first edition. *MS.* has *idea or notion* as in §§ 138 and 139, first edition. Evidently Berkeley originally thought of 'notion' as a synonym for 'idea', correspondingly ambiguous; but came to regard the former as more appropriate than the latter when, as in the case of thinking about spirits and their activity or essence, there can be no mind-dependent 'representative' resembling the object of thought. Cf. §§ 27 and 142, and DHP III *233.* The emendation is not to his doctrine, but to its expression.)

ruptible as the body, since there is nothing more easily dissipated than such a being, which it is naturally impossible should survive the ruin of the tabernacle, wherein it is enclosed. And this notion hath been greedily embraced and cherished by the worst part of mankind, as the most effectual antidote against all impressions of virtue and religion. But it hath been made evident, that bodies of what frame or texture soever, are barely passive ideas in the mind, which is more distant and heterogeneous from them, than light is from darkness. We have shewn that the soul is indivisible, incorporeal, unextended, and it is consequently incorruptible. Nothing can be plainer, than that the motions, changes, decays, and dissolutions which we hourly see befall natural bodies (and which is what we mean by the *course of Nature*) cannot possibly affect an active, simple, uncompounded substance: such a being therefore is indissoluble by the force of Nature, that is to say, *the soul of man is naturally immortal.*

142 After what hath been said, it is I suppose plain, that our souls are not to be known in the same manner as senseless inactive objects, or by way of *idea. Spirits* and *ideas* are things so wholly different, that when we say, *they exist, they are known*, or the like, these words must not be thought to signify anything common to both natures. There is nothing alike or common in them: and to expect that by any multiplication or enlargement of our faculties, we may be enabled to know a spirit as we do a triangle, seems as absurd as if we should hope to *see a sound.* This is inculcated because I imagine it may be of moment towards clearing several important questions, and preventing some very dangerous errors concerning the nature of the soul. We may not[1] I think strictly be said to have an idea of an active being, or of an action, although we may be said to have a notion of them. I have some knowledge or notion of my mind, and its acts about ideas, inasmuch as I know or understand what is meant by those words. What I know, that I have some notion of. I will not say, that the terms *idea* and *notion* may not be used convertibly, if the world will have it so. But yet it conduceth to clearness and propriety, that we distinguish things very different by different names. It is also to be remarked, that all relations including an act of the mind, we cannot so properly be said to have an idea, but rather a notion of the relations or habitudes between things. But if in the modern way the word *idea* is extended to spirits, and relations and acts; this is after all an affair of verbal concern.

143 It will not be amiss to add, that the doctrine of *abstract ideas* hath had no small share in rendering those sciences intricate and obscure, which are particularly conversant about spiritual things. Men have imagined they could frame abstract notions of the powers and acts of the mind, and consider them prescinded, as well from the mind or spirit itself, as from their respective objects and effects. Hence a great number of dark and ambiguous terms presumed to stand for abstract notions, have been introduced into metaphysics and morality, and from these have grown infinite distractions and disputes amongst the learned.

[1] [*We may not* . . . (to end of Section) not in first edition.]

144 But nothing seems more to have contributed towards engaging men in controversies and mistakes, with regard to the nature and operations of the mind, than the being used to speak of those things, in terms borrowed from sensible ideas. For example, the will is termed the *motion* of the soul: this infuses a belief, that the mind of man is as a ball in motion, impelled and determined by the objects of sense, as necessarily as that is by the stroke of a racket. Hence arise endless scruples and errors of dangerous consequence in morality. All which I doubt not may be cleared, and truth appear plain, uniform, and consistent, could but philosophers be prevailed on to retire into themselves, and attentively consider their own meaning.

145 From what hath been said, it is plain that we cannot know the existence of other spirits, otherwise than by their operations, or the ideas by them excited in us. I perceive several motions, changes, and combinations of ideas, that inform me there are certain particular agents like myself, which accompany them, and concur in their production. Hence the knowledge I have of other spirits is not immediate, as is the knowledge of my ideas; but depending on the intervention of ideas, by me referred to agents or spirits distinct from myself, as effects or concomitant signs.

146 But though there be some things which convince us, human agents are concerned in producing them; yet it is evident to everyone, that those things which are called the works of Nature, that is, the far greater part of the ideas or sensations perceived by us, are not produced by, or dependent on the wills of men. There is therefore some other spirit that causes them, since it is repugnant that they should subsist by themselves. See *Sect*. 29. But if we attentively consider the constant regularity, order, and concatenation of natural things, the surprising magnificence, beauty, and perfection of the larger, and the exquisite contrivance of the smaller parts of the creation, together with the exact harmony and correspondence of the whole, but above all, the never enough admired laws of pain and pleasure, and the instincts or natural inclinations, appetites, and passions of animals; I say if we consider all these things, and at the same time attend to the meaning and import of the attributes, one, eternal, infinitely wise, good, and perfect, we shall clearly perceive that they belong to the aforesaid spirit, *who works all in all*, and *by whom all things consist*.

147 Hence it is evident, that God is known as certainly and immediately as any other mind or spirit whatsoever, distinct from ourselves. We may even assert, that the existence of God is far more evidently perceived than the existence of men; because the effects of Nature are infinitely more numerous and considerable, than those ascribed to human agents. There is not any one mark that denotes a man, or effect produced by him, which doth not more strongly evince the being of that spirit who is the *Author of Nature*. For it is evident that in affecting other persons, the will of man hath no other object, than barely the motion of the limbs of his body; but that such a motion should be attended by, or excite any idea in the mind of another, depends wholly on the will of the Creator. He alone it is who *upholding all things by the Word of his Power*, maintains that intercourse

between spirits, whereby they are able to perceive the existence of each other. And yet this pure and clear light which enlightens everyone, is itself invisible.

148 It seems to be a general pretence of the unthinking herd, that they cannot see God. Could we but see him, say they, as we see a man, we should believe that he is, and believing obey his commands. But alas we need only open our eyes to see the sovereign Lord of all things with a more full and clear view, than we do any one of our fellow-creatures. Not that I imagine we see God (as some will have it) by a direct and immediate view, or see corporeal things, not by themselves, but by seeing that which represents them in the essence of God, which doctrine is I must confess to me incomprehensible.[1] But I shall explain my meaning. A human spirit or person is not perceived by sense, as not being an idea; when therefore we see the colour, size, figure, and motions of a man, we perceive only certain sensations or ideas excited in our own minds: and these being exhibited to our view in sundry distinct collections, serve to mark out unto us the existence of finite and created spirits like ourselves. Hence it is plain, we do not see a man, if by *man* is meant that which lives, moves, perceives, and thinks as we do: but only such a certain collection of ideas, as directs us to think there is a distinct principle of thought and motion like to ourselves, accompanying and represented by it. And after the same manner we see God; all the difference is, that whereas some one finite and narrow assemblage of ideas denotes a particular human mind, whithersoever we direct our view, we do at all times and in all places perceive manifest tokens of the divinity: everything we see, hear, feel, or any wise perceive by sense, being a sign or effect of the Power of God; as is our perception of those very motions, which are produced by men.

149 It is therefore plain, that nothing can be more evident to anyone that is capable of the least reflexion, than the existence of God, or a spirit who is intimately present to our minds, producing in them all that variety of ideas or sensations, which continually affect us, on whom we have an absolute and entire dependence, in short, *in whom we live, and move, and have our being.* That the discovery of this great truth which lies so near and obvious to the mind, should be attained to by the reason of so very few, is a sad instance of the stupidity and inattention of men, who, though they are surrounded with such clear manifestations of the Deity, are yet so little affected by them, that they seem as it were blinded with excess of light.

150 But you will say, hath Nature no share in the production of natural things, and must they be all ascribed to the immediate and sole operation of God? I answer, if by *Nature* is meant only the visible *series* of effects, or sensations imprinted on our minds according to certain fixed and general laws: then it is plain, that Nature taken in this sense cannot produce anything at all. But if by *Nature* is meant some being distinct from God, as well as from the Laws of Nature, and things perceived by sense, I must confess that word is to me an empty sound, without any intelligible

---

[1] [The reference is to Malebranche.]

meaning annexed to it. Nature in this acceptation is a vain *chimera* introduced by those heathens, who had not just notions of the omnipresence
and infinite perfection of God. But it is more unaccountable, that it should
be received among *Christians* professing belief in the Holy Scriptures,
which constantly ascribe those effects to the immediate hand of God,
that heathen philosophers are wont to impute to *Nature. The Lord, he
causeth the vapours to ascend; he maketh lightnings with rain; he bringeth
forth the wind out of his treasures,* Jerem. Chap. 10. ver. 13. *He turneth the
shadow of death into the morning, and maketh the day dark with night,*
Amos Chap. 5 ver. 8. *He visiteth the earth, and maketh it soft with showers:
he blesseth the springing thereof, and crowneth the year with his goodness;
so that the pastures are clothed with flocks, and the valleys are covered
over with corn.* See *Psalm* 65. But notwithstanding that this is the constant
language of Scripture; yet we have I know not what aversion from believing, that God concerns himself so nearly in our affairs. Fain would we
suppose him at a great distance off, and substitute some blind unthinking
deputy in his stead, though (if we may believe Saint Paul) *he be not far
from every one of us.*

151 It will I doubt not be objected, that the slow and gradual methods
observed in the production of natural things, do not seem to have for their
cause the immediate hand of an *almighty Agent.* Besides, monsters, un-
timely births, fruits blasted in the blossom, rains falling in desert places,
miseries incident to human life, are so many arguments that the whole frame
of Nature is not immediately actuated and superintended by a spirit of
infinite wisdom and goodness. But the answer to this objection is in a good
measure plain from *Sect.* 62, it being visible, that the aforesaid methods of
Nature are absolutely necessary, in order to working by the most simple
and general rules, and after a steady and consistent manner; which argues
both the *wisdom* and *goodness* of God. Such is the artificial contrivance of
this mighty machine of Nature, that whilst its motions and various phenomena strike on our senses, the hand which actuates the whole is itself
unperceivable to men of flesh and blood. *Verily* (saith the prophet) *thou
art a God that hidest thyself,* Isaiah Chap. 45. ver. 15. But though God
conceal himself from the eyes of the *sensual* and *lazy,* who will not be at
the least expense of thought; yet to an unbiassed and attentive mind,
nothing can be more plainly legible, than the intimate presence of an *all-
wise Spirit,* who fashions, regulates, and sustains the whole system of
beings. It is clear from what we have elsewhere observed, that the operating
according to general and stated laws, is so necessary for our guidance in the
affairs of life, and letting us into the secret of Nature, that without it, all
reach and compass of thought, all human sagacity and design could serve
to no manner of purpose: it were even impossible there should be any such
faculties or powers in the mind. See *Sect.* 31. Which one consideration
abundantly out-balances whatever particular inconveniences may thence
arise.

152 We should further consider, that the very blemishes and defects of
Nature are not without their use, in that they make an agreeable sort of

variety, and augment the beauty of the rest of the creation, as shades in a picture serve to set off the brighter and more enlightened parts. We would likewise do well to examine, whether our taxing the waste of seeds and embryos, and accidental destruction of plants and animals, before they come to full maturity, as an imprudence in the Author of Nature, be not the effect of prejudice contracted by our familiarity with impotent and saving mortals. In *man* indeed a thrifty management of those things, which he cannot procure without much pains and industry, may be esteemed *wisdom*. But we must not imagine, that the inexplicably fine machine of an animal or vegetable, costs the great Creator any more pains or trouble in its production than a pebble doth: nothing being more evident, than that an omnipotent spirit can indifferently produce every thing by a mere *fiat* or act of his will. Hence it is plain, that the splendid profusion of natural things should not be interpreted, weakness or prodigality in the agent who produces them, but rather be looked on as an argument of the riches of his power.

153 As for the mixture of pain or uneasiness which is in the world, pursuant to the general laws of Nature, and the actions of finite imperfect spirits: this, in the state we are in at present, is indispensably necessary to our well-being. But our prospects are too narrow: we take, for instance, the idea of some one particular pain into our thoughts, and account it *evil*; whereas if we enlarge our view, so as to comprehend the various ends, connexions, and dependencies of things, on what occasions and in what proportions we are affected with pain and pleasure, the nature of human freedom, and the design with which we are put into the world; we shall be forced to acknowledge that those particular things, which considered in themselves appear to be *evil*, have the nature of *good*, when considered as linked with the whole system of beings.

154 From what hath been said it will be manifest to any considering person, that it is merely for want of attention and comprehensiveness of mind, that there are any favourers of *atheism* or the *Manichean heresy* to be found. Little and unreflecting souls may indeed burlesque the works of Providence, the beauty and order whereof they have not capacity, or will not be at the pains to comprehend. But those who are masters of any justness and extent of thought, and are withal used to reflect, can never sufficiently admire the divine traces of wisdom and goodness that shine throughout the economy of Nature. But what truth is there which shineth so strongly on the mind, that by an aversion of thought, a wilful shutting of the eyes, we may not escape seeing it? Is it therefore to be wondered at, if the generality of men, who are ever intent on business or pleasure, and little used to fix or open the eye of their mind, should not have all that conviction and evidence of the being of God, which might be expected in reasonable creatures?

155 We should rather wonder, that men can be found so stupid as to neglect, than that neglecting they should be unconvinced of such an evident and momentous truth. And yet it is to be feared that too many of parts and leisure, who live in Christian countries, are merely through a supine and

dreadful negligence sunk into a sort of *atheism*. Since it is downright impossible, that a soul pierced and enlightened with a thorough sense of the omnipresence, holiness, and justice of that *Almighty Spirit*, should persist in a remorseless violation of his laws. We ought therefore earnestly to meditate and dwell on those important points; that so we may attain conviction without all scruple, *that the eyes of the Lord are in every place beholding the evil and the good; that he is with us and keepeth us in all places whither we go, and giveth us bread to eat, and raiment to put on;* that he is present and conscious to our innermost thoughts; and that we have a most absolute and immediate dependence on him. A clear view of which great truths cannot choose but fill our hearts with an awful circumspection and holy fear, which is the strongest incentive to *virtue*, and the best guard against *vice*.

156 For after all, what deserves the first place in our studies, is the consideration of *God*, and our *duty*; which to promote, as it was the main drift and design of my labours, so shall I esteem them altogether useless and ineffectual, if by what I have said I cannot inspire my readers with a pious sense of the presence of God: and having shewn the falseness or vanity of those barren speculations, which make the chief employment of learned men, the better dispose them to reverence and embrace the salutary truths of the Gospel, which to know and to practise is the highest perfection of human nature.

Three Dialogues Between Hylas and Philonous

The design of which is plainly to demonstrate the reality and perfection of human knowledge, the incorporeal nature of the soul, and the immediate providence of a Deity: in opposition to Sceptics and Atheists. Also to open a method for rendering the Sciences more easy, useful and compendious.[1]

Text based on the Third Edition of 1734
First printed in 1713

[1](Shortened in the third edition to *In opposition to Sceptics and Atheists*.)

To facilitate a standard method of reference the page numbers from the *Works* have been placed in the margins.

The Preface [1]

Though it seems the general opinion of the world, no less than the design of Nature and Providence, that the end of speculation be practice, or the improvement and regulation of our lives and actions; yet those, who are most addicted to speculative studies, seem as generally of another mind. And, indeed, if we consider the pains that have been taken, to perplex the plainest things, that distrust of the senses, those doubts and scruples, those abstractions and refinements that occur in the very entrance of the sciences; it will not seem strange, that men of leisure and curiosity should lay themselves out in fruitless disquisitions, without descending to the practical parts of life, or informing themselves in the more necessary and important parts of knowledge.

Upon the common principles of philosophers, we are not assured of the existence of things from their being perceived. And we are taught to distinguish their real nature from that which falls under our senses. Hence arise *scepticism* and *paradoxes*. It is not enough, that we see and feel, that we taste and smell a thing. Its true nature, its absolute external entity, is still concealed. For, though it be the fiction of our own brain, we have made it inaccessible to all our faculties. Sense is fallacious, reason defective. We spend our lives in doubting of those things which other men evidently know, and believing those things which they laugh at, and despise.

In order, therefore, to divert the busy mind of man from vain researches, it seemed necessary to inquire into the source of its perplexities; and, if possible, to lay down such principles, as, by an easy solution of them, together with their own native evidence, may, at once, recommend themselves for genuine to the mind, and rescue it from those endless pursuits it is engaged in. Which, with a plain demonstration of the immediate Providence of an all-seeing God, and the natural immortality of the soul, should seem the readiest preparation, as well as the strongest motive, to the study and practice of virtue.

This design I proposed, in the First Part of a Treatise concerning the *Principles of Human Knowledge*, published in the year 1710. But, before I proceed to publish the Second Part, I thought it requisite to treat more clearly and fully of certain principles laid down in the First, and to place them in a new light. Which is the business of the following *Dialogues*.

[1] [In editions of 1713 and 1725 only.]

In this treatise, which does not presuppose in the reader, any knowledge of what was contained in the former, it has been my aim to introduce the notions I advance, into the mind, in the most easy and familiar manner; especially, because they carry with them a great opposition to the prejudices of philosophers, which have so far prevailed against the common sense and natural notions of mankind.

If the principles, which I here endeavour to propagate, are admitted for true; the consequences which, I think, evidently flow from thence, are, that *atheism* and *scepticism* will be utterly destroyed, many intricate points made plain, great difficulties solved, several useless parts of science retrenched, speculation referred to practice, and men reduced from paradoxes to common sense.

And although it may, perhaps, seem an uneasy reflexion to some, that when they have taken a circuit through so many refined and unvulgar notions, they should at last come to think like other men: yet, methinks, this return to the simple dictates of nature, after having wandered through the wild mazes of philosophy, is not unpleasant. It is like coming home from a long voyage: a man reflects with pleasure on the many difficulties and perplexities he has passed through, sets his heart at ease, and enjoys himself with more satisfaction for the future.

As it was my intention to convince *sceptics* and *infidels* by reason, so it has been my endeavour strictly to observe the most rigid laws of reasoning. And, to an impartial reader, I hope, it will be manifest, that the sublime notion of a God, and the comfortable expectation of immortality, do naturally arise from a close and methodical application of thought: whatever may be the result of that loose, rambling way, not altogether improperly termed *free-thinking*, by certain libertines in thought, who can no more endure the restraints of *logic*, than those of *religion*, or *government*.

It will, perhaps, be objected to my design, that so far as it tends to ease the mind of difficult and useless inquiries, it can affect only a few speculative persons; but, if by their speculations rightly placed, the study of morality and the Law of Nature were brought more into fashion among men of parts and genius, the discouragements that draw to *scepticism* removed, the measures of right and wrong accurately defined, and the principles of natural religion reduced into regular systems, as artfully disposed and clearly connected as those of some other sciences: there are grounds to think, these effects would not only have a gradual influence in repairing the too much defaced sense of virtue in the world; but also, by shewing, that such parts of revelation, as lie within the reach of human inquiry, are most agreeable to right reason, would dispose all prudent, unprejudiced persons, to a modest and wary treatment of those sacred mysteries, which are above the comprehension of our faculties.

It remains, that I desire the reader to withold his censure of these Dialogues, till he has read them through. Otherwise, he may lay them aside in a mistake of their design, or on account of difficulties or objections which he would find answered in the sequel. A treatise of this nature would require to be once read over coherently, in order to comprehend its design, the proofs, solution of difficulties, and the connexion and disposition of its parts. If it be thought to deserve a second reading; this, I imagine, will make the entire scheme very plain: especially, if recourse be had to an Essay I wrote, some years since, upon *vision*, and the Treatise concerning the *Principles of Human Knowledge*. Wherein divers notions advanced in these *Dialogues*, are farther pursued, or placed in different lights, and other points handled, which naturally tend to confirm and illustrate them.

Three Dialogues Between Hylas and Philonous

THE FIRST DIALOGUE

PHILONOUS. Good morrow, Hylas: I did not expect to find you abroad *171* so early.

HYLAS. It is indeed something unusual; but my thoughts were so taken up with a subject I was discoursing of last night, that finding I could not sleep, I resolved to rise and take a turn in the garden.

PHILONOUS. It happened well, to let you see what innocent and agreeable pleasures you lose every morning. Can there be a pleasanter time of the day, or a more delightful season of the year? That purple sky, these wild but sweet notes of birds, the fragrant bloom upon the trees and flowers, the gentle influence of the rising sun, these and a thousand nameless beauties of nature inspire the soul with secret transports; its faculties too being at this time fresh and lively, are fit for those meditations, which the solitude of a garden and tranquillity of the morning naturally dispose us to. But I am afraid I interrupt your thoughts: for you seemed very intent on something.

HYLAS. It is true, I was, and shall be obliged to you if you will permit me to go on in the same vein; not that I would by any means deprive myself of your company, for my thoughts always flow more easily in conversation with a friend, than when I am alone: but my request is, that you would suffer me to impart my reflexions to you.

PHILONOUS. With all my heart, it is what I should have requested myself, if you had not prevented me.

HYLAS. I was considering the odd fate of those men who have in all ages, through an affectation of being distinguished from the vulgar, or some unaccountable turn of thought, pretended either to believe nothing at all, or to believe the most extravagant things in the world. This however might be borne, if their paradoxes and scepticism did not draw after them some consequences of general disadvantage to mankind. But the mischief lieth here; that when men of less leisure see them who are *172* supposed to have spent their whole time in the pursuits of knowledge, professing an entire ignorance of all things, or advancing such notions as are repugnant to plain and commonly received principles, they will be tempted to entertain suspicions concerning the most important truths, which they had hitherto held sacred and unquestionable.

PHILONOUS. I entirely agree with you, as to the ill tendency of the affected doubts of some philosophers, and fantastical conceits of others. I am

even so far gone of late in this way of thinking, that I have quitted
several of the sublime notions I had got in their schools for vulgar
opinions. And I give it you on my word, since this revolt from metaphysical notions to the plain dictates of nature and common sense,
I find my understanding strangely enlightened, so that I can now easily
comprehend a great many things which before were all mystery and
riddle.

HYLAS. I am glad to find there was nothing in the accounts I heard of you.

PHILONOUS. Pray, what were those?

HYLAS. You were represented in last night's conversation, as one who
maintained the most extravagant opinion that ever entered into the mind
of man, to wit, that there is no such thing as *material substance* in the
world.

PHILONOUS. That there is no such thing as what philosophers call *material
substance*, I am seriously persuaded: but if I were made to see anything
absurd or sceptical in this, I should then have the same reason to
renounce this, that I imagine I have now to reject the contrary opinion.

HYLAS. What! can anything be more fantastical, more repugnant to
common sense, or a more manifest piece of scepticism, than to believe
there is no such thing as *matter*?

PHILONOUS. Softly, good Hylas. What if it should prove, that you, who
hold there is, are by virtue of that opinion a greater *sceptic*, and maintain
more paradoxes and repugnancies to common sense, than I who believe
no such thing?

HYLAS. You may as soon persuade me, the part is greater than the whole,
as that, in order to avoid absurdity and scepticism, I should ever be
obliged to give up my opinion in this point.

PHILONOUS. Well then, are you content to admit that opinion for true,
which upon examination shall appear most agreeable to common sense,
and remote from scepticism?

HYLAS. With all my heart. Since you are for raising disputes about the
173   plainest things in Nature, I am content for once to hear what you have
to say.

PHILONOUS. Pray, Hylas, what do you mean by a *sceptic*?

HYLAS. I mean what all men mean, one that doubts of everything.

PHILONOUS. He then who entertains no doubt concerning some particular
point, with regard to that point cannot be thought a *sceptic*.

HYLAS. I agree with you.

PHILONOUS. Whether doth doubting consist in embracing the affirmative
or negative side of a question?

HYLAS. In neither; for whoever understands English, cannot but know
that *doubting* signifies a suspense between both.

PHILONOUS. He then that denieth any point, can no more be said to doubt
of it, than he who affirmeth it with the same degree of assurance.

HYLAS. True.

PHILONOUS. And consequently, for such his denial is no more to be
esteemed a *sceptic* than the other.

HYLAS. I acknowledge it.

PHILONOUS. How cometh it to pass then, Hylas, that you pronounce me a *sceptic*, because I deny what you affirm, to wit, the existence of matter? Since, for ought you can tell, I am as peremptory in my denial, as you in your affirmation.

HYLAS. Hold, Philonous, I have been a little out in my definition; but every false step a man makes in discourse is not to be insisted on. I said indeed, that a *sceptic* was one who doubted of everything; but I should have added, or who denies the reality and truth of things.

PHILONOUS. What things? Do you mean the principles and theorems of sciences? But these you know are universal intellectual notions, and consequently independent of matter; the denial therefore of this doth not imply the denying them.

HYLAS. I grant it. But are there no other things? What think you of distrusting the senses, of denying the real existence of sensible things, or pretending to know nothing of them. Is not this sufficient to denominate a man a *sceptic*?

PHILONOUS. Shall we therefore examine which of us it is that denies the reality of sensible things, or professes the greatest ignorance of them; since, if I take you rightly, he is to be esteemed the greatest *sceptic*?

HYLAS. That is what I desire.

174

PHILONOUS. What mean you by sensible things?

HYLAS. Those things which are perceived by the senses. Can you imagine that I mean anything else?

PHILONOUS. Pardon me, Hylas, if I am desirous clearly to apprehend your notions, since this may much shorten our inquiry. Suffer me then to ask you this farther question. Are those things only perceived by the senses which are perceived immediately? Or may those things properly be said to be *sensible*, which are perceived mediately, or not without the intervention of others?

HYLAS. I do not sufficiently understand you.

PHILONOUS. In reading a book, what I immediately perceive are the letters, but mediately, or by means of these, are suggested to my mind the notions of God, virtue, truth, &c. Now, that the letters are truly sensible things, or perceived by sense, there is no doubt: but I would know whether you take the things suggested by them to be so too.

HYLAS. No certainly, it were absurd to think *God* or *Virtue* sensible things, though they may be signified and suggested to the mind by sensible marks, with which they have an arbitrary connexion.

PHILONOUS. It seems then, that by *sensible things* you mean those only which can be perceived immediately by sense.

HYLAS. Right.

PHILONOUS. Doth it not follow from this, that though I see one part of the sky red, and another blue, and that my reason doth thence evidently conclude there must be some cause of that diversity of colours, yet that cause cannot be said to be a sensible thing, or perceived by the sense of seeing?

HYLAS. It doth.

PHILONOUS. In like manner, though I hear variety of sounds, yet I cannot be said to hear the causes of those sounds.

HYLAS. You cannot.

PHILONOUS. And when by my touch I perceive a thing to be hot and heavy, I cannot say with any truth or propriety, that I feel the cause of its heat or weight.

HYLAS. To prevent any more questions of this kind, I tell you once for all, that by *sensible things* I mean those only which are perceived by sense, and that in truth the senses perceive nothing which they do not perceive immediately: for they make ño inferences. The deducing *175* therefore of causes or occasions from effects and appearances, which alone are perceived by sense, entirely relates to reason.

PHILONOUS. This point then is agreed between us, that *sensible things are those only which are immediately perceived by sense.* You will farther inform me, whether we immediately perceive by sight any thing beside light, and colours, and figures: or by hearing, any thing but sounds: by the palate, any thing beside tastes: by the smell, beside odours: or by the touch, more than tangible qualities.

HYLAS. We do not.

PHILONOUS. It seems therefore, that if you take away all sensible qualities, there remains nothing sensible.

HYLAS. I grant it.

PHILONOUS. Sensible things therefore are nothing else but so many sensible qualities, or combinations of sensible qualities.

HYLAS. Nothing else.

PHILONOUS. Heat then is a sensible thing.

HYLAS. Certainly.

PHILONOUS. Doth the reality of sensible things consist in being perceived? or, is it something distinct from their being perceived, and that bears no relation to the mind?

HYLAS. To *exist* is one thing, and to be *perceived* is another.

PHILONOUS. I speak with regard to sensible things only: and of these I ask, whether by their real existence you mean a subsistence exterior to the mind, and distinct from their being perceived?

HYLAS. I mean a real absolute being, distinct from, and without any relation to their being perceived.

PHILONOUS. Heat therefore, if it be allowed a real being, must exist without the mind.

HYLAS. It must.

PHILONOUS. Tell me, Hylas, is this real existence equally compatible to all degrees of heat, which we perceive: or is there any reason why we should attribute it to some, and deny it others? And if there be, pray let me know that reason.

HYLAS. Whatever degree of heat we perceive by sense, we may be sure the same exists in the object that occasions it.

PHILONOUS. What, the greatest as well as the least?

HYLAS. I tell you, the reason is plainly the same in respect of both: they are both perceived by sense; nay, the greater degree of heat is more sensibly perceived; and consequently, if there is any difference, we are more certain of its real existence than we can be of the reality of a *176* lesser degree.

PHILONOUS. But is not the most vehement and intense degree of heat a very great pain?

HYLAS. No one can deny it.

PHILONOUS. And is any unperceiving thing capable of pain or pleasure?

HYLAS. No certainly.

PHILONOUS. Is your material substance a senseless being, or a being endowed with sense and perception?

HYLAS. It is senseless, without doubt.

PHILONOUS. It cannot therefore be the subject of pain.

HYLAS. By no means.

PHILONOUS. Nor consequently of the greatest heat perceived by sense, since you acknowledge this to be no small pain.

HYLAS. I grant it.

PHILONOUS. What shall we say then of your external object; is it a material substance, or no?

HYLAS. It is a material substance with the sensible qualities inhering in it.

PHILONOUS. How then can a great heat exist in it, since you own it cannot in a material substance? I desire you would clear this point.

HYLAS. Hold, Philonous, I fear I was was out in yielding intense heat to to be a pain. It should seem rather, that pain is something distinct from heat, and the consequence or effect of it.

PHILONOUS. Upon putting your hand near the fire, do you perceive one simple uniform sensation, or two distinct sensations?

HYLAS. But one simple sensation.

PHILONOUS. Is not the heat immediately perceived?

HYLAS. It is.

PHILONOUS. And the pain?

HYLAS. True.

PHILONOUS. Seeing therefore they are both immediately perceived at the same time, and the fire affects you only with one simple, or uncompounded idea, it follows that this same simple idea is both the intense heat immediately perceived, and the pain; and consequently, that the intense heat immediately perceived, is nothing distinct from a particular sort of pain.

HYLAS. It seems so.

PHILONOUS. Again, try in your thoughts, Hylas, if you can conceive a vehement sensation to be without pain, or pleasure.

HYLAS. I cannot.   *177*

PHILONOUS. Or can you frame to yourself an idea of sensible pain or pleasure in general, abstracted from every particular idea of heat, cold, tastes, smells? &c.

HYLAS. I do not find that I can.

PHILONOUS. Doth it not therefore follow, that sensible pain is nothing distinct from those sensations or ideas, in an intense degree?

HYLAS. It is undeniable; and to speak the truth, I begin to suspect a very great heat cannot exist but in a mind perceiving it.

PHILONOUS. What! are you then in that *sceptical* state of suspense, between affirming and denying?

HYLAS. I think I may be positive in the point. A very violent and painful heat cannot exist without the mind.

PHILONOUS. It hath not therefore, according to you, any real being.

HYLAS. I own it.

PHILONOUS. Is it therefore certain, that there is no body in nature really hot?

HYLAS. I have not denied there is any real heat in bodies. I only say, there is no such thing as an intense real heat.

PHILONOUS. But did you not say before, that all degrees of heat were equally real: or if there was any difference, that the greater were more undoubtedly real than the lesser?

HYLAS. True: but it was, because I did not then consider the ground there is for distinguishing between them, which I now plainly see. And it is this: because intense heat is nothing else but a particular kind of painful sensation; and pain cannot exist but in a perceiving being; it follows that no intense heat can really exist in an unperceiving corporeal substance. But this is no reason why we should deny heat in an inferior degree to exist in such a substance.

PHILONOUS. But how shall we be able to discern those degrees of heat which exist only in the mind, from those which exist without it?

HYLAS. That is no difficult matter. You know, the least pain cannot exist unperceived; whatever therefore degree of heat is a pain, exists only in the mind. But as for all other degrees of heat, nothing obliges us to think the same of them.

PHILONOUS. I think you granted before, that no unperceiving being was capable of pleasure, any more than of pain.

HYLAS. I did.

178 PHILONOUS. And is not warmth, or a more gentle degree of heat than what causes uneasiness, a pleasure?

HYLAS. What then?

PHILONOUS. Consequently it cannot exist without the mind in any unperceiving substance, or body.

HYLAS. So it seems.

PHILONOUS. Since therefore, as well those degrees of heat that are not painful, as those that are, can exist only in a thinking substance; may we not conclude that external bodies are absolutely incapable of any degree of heat whatsoever?

HYLAS. On second thoughts, I do not think it so evident that warmth is a pleasure, as that a great degree of heat is a pain.

PHILONOUS. I do not pretend that warmth is as great a pleasure as heat is a pain. But if you grant it to be even a small pleasure, it serves to make good my conclusion.

HYLAS. I could rather call it an *indolence*. It seems to be nothing more than a privation of both pain and pleasure. And that such a quality or state as this may agree to an unthinking substance, I hope you will not deny.

PHILONOUS. If you are resolved to maintain that warmth, or a gentle degree of heat, is no pleasure, I know not how to convince you otherwise, than by appealing to your own sense. But what think you of cold?

HYLAS. The same that I do of heat. An intense degree of cold is a pain; for to feel a very great cold, is to perceive a great uneasiness: it cannot therefore exist without the mind; but a lesser degree of cold may, as well as a lesser degree of heat.

PHILONOUS. Those bodies therefore, upon whose application to our own, we perceive a moderate degree of heat, must be concluded to have a moderate degree of heat or warmth in them: and those, upon whose application we feel a like degree of cold, must be thought to have cold in them.

HYLAS. They must.

PHILONOUS. Can any doctrine be true that necessarily leads a man into an absurdity?

HYLAS. Without doubt it cannot.

PHILONOUS. Is it not an absurdity to think that the same thing should be at the same time both cold and warm?

HYLAS. It is.

PHILONOUS. Suppose now one of your hands hot, and the other cold, and that they are both at once put into the same vessel of water, in an intermediate state; will not the water seem cold to one hand, and warm to *179* the other?

HYLAS. It will.

PHILONOUS. Ought we not therefore by your principles to conclude, it is really both cold and warm at the same time, that is, according to your own concession, to believe an absurdity.

HYLAS. I confess it seems so.

PHILONOUS. Consequently, the principles themselves are false, since you have granted that no true principle leads to an absurdity.

HYLAS. But after all, can anything be more absurd than to say, *there is no heat in the fire?*

PHILONOUS. To make the point still clearer; tell me, whether in two cases exactly alike, we ought not to make the same judgment?

HYLAS. We ought.

PHILONOUS. When a pin pricks your finger, doth it not rend and divide the fibres of your flesh?

HYLAS. It doth.

PHILONOUS. And when a coal burns your finger, doth it any more?

HYLAS. It doth not.

PHILONOUS. Since therefore you neither judge the sensation itself occasioned by the pin, nor any thing like it to be in the pin; you should not, conformably to what you have now granted, judge the sensation occasioned by the fire, or any thing like it, to be in the fire.

HYLAS. Well, since it must be so, I am content to yield this point, and acknowledge, that heat and cold are only sensations existing in our minds: but there still remain qualities enough to secure the reality of external things.

PHILONOUS. But what will you say, Hylas, if it shall appear that the case is the same with regard to all other sensible qualities, and that they can no more be supposed to exist without the mind, than heat and cold?

HYLAS. Then indeed you will have done something to the purpose; but that is what I despair of seeing proved.

PHILONOUS. Let us examine them in order. What think you of tastes, do they exist without the mind, or no?

HYLAS. Can any man in his senses doubt whether sugar is sweet, or wormwood bitter?

PHILONOUS. Inform me, Hylas. Is a sweet taste a particular kind of pleasure or pleasant sensation, or is it not?

180 HYLAS. It is.

PHILONOUS. And is not bitterness some kind of uneasiness or pain?

HYLAS. I grant it.

PHILONOUS. If therefore sugar and wormwood are unthinking corporeal substances existing without the mind, how can sweetness and bitterness, that is, pleasure and pain, agree to them?

HYLAS. Hold, Philonous, I now see what it was deluded me all this time. You asked whether heat and cold, sweetness and bitterness, were not particular sorts of pleasure and pain; to which I answered simply, that they were. Whereas I should have thus distinguished: those qualities, as perceived by us, are pleasures or pains, but not as existing in the external objects. We must not therefore conclude absolutely, that there is no heat in the fire, or sweetness in the sugar, but only that heat or sweetness, as perceived by us, are not in the fire or sugar. What say you to this?

PHILONOUS. I say it is nothing to the purpose. Our discourse proceeded altogether concerning sensible things, which you defined to be the things we *immediately perceive by our senses*. Whatever other qualities therefore you speak of, as distinct from these, I know nothing of them, neither do they at all belong to the point in dispute. You may indeed pretend to have discovered certain qualities which you do not perceive, and assert those insensible qualities exist in fire and sugar. But what use can be made of this to your present purpose, I am at a loss to conceive. Tell me then once more, do you acknowledge that heat and cold, sweetness and bitterness (meaning those qualities which are perceived by the senses) do not exist without the mind?

HYLAS. I see it is to no purpose to hold out, so I give up the cause as to those mentioned qualities. Though I profess it sounds oddly, to say that sugar is not sweet.

PHILONOUS. But for your farther satisfaction, take this along with you: that which at other times seems sweet, shall to a distempered palate appear bitter. And nothing can be plainer, than that divers persons perceive different tastes in the same food, since that which one man delights in, another abhors. And how could this be, if the taste was something really inherent in the food?

HYLAS. I acknowledge I know not how.

PHILONOUS. In the next place, odours are to be considered. And with regard to these, I would fain know, whether what hath been said of tastes doth not exactly agree to them? Are they not so many pleasing *181* or displeasing sensations?

HYLAS. They are.

PHILONOUS. Can you then conceive it possible that they should exist in an unperceiving thing?

HYLAS. I cannot.

PHILONOUS. Or can you imagine, that filth and ordure affect those brute animals that feed on them out of choice, with the same smells which we perceive in them?

HYLAS. By no means.

PHILONOUS. May we not therefore conclude of smells, as of the other forementioned qualities, that they cannot exist in any but a perceiving substance or mind?

HYLAS. I think so.

PHILONOUS. Then as to sounds, what must we think of them: are they accidents really inherent in external bodies, or not?

HYLAS. That they inhere not in the sonorous bodies, is plain from hence; because a bell struck in the exhausted receiver of an air-pump, sends forth no sound. The air therefore must be thought the subject of sound.

PHILONOUS. What reason is there for that, Hylas?

HYLAS. Because when any motion is raised in the air, we perceive a sound greater or lesser, in proportion to the air's motion; but without some motion in the air, we never hear any sound at all.

PHILONOUS. And granting that we never hear a sound but when some motion is produced in the air, yet I do not see how you can infer from thence, that the sound itself is in the air.

HYLAS. It is this very motion in the external air, that produces in the mind the sensation of *sound*. For, striking on the drum of the ear, it causeth a vibration, which by the auditory nerves being communicated to the brain, the soul is thereupon affected with the sensation called *sound*.

PHILONOUS. What! is sound then a sensation?

HYLAS. I tell you, as perceived by us, it is a particular sensation in the mind.

PHILONOUS. And can any sensation exist without the mind?

HYLAS. No certainly.

PHILONOUS. How then can sound, being a sensation exist in the air, if by the *air* you mean a senseless substance existing without the mind?

HYLAS. You must distinguish, Philonous, between sound as it is perceived
182 by us, and as it is in itself; or (which is the same thing) between the sound
we immediately perceive, and that which exists without us. The former
indeed is a particular kind of sensation, but the latter is merely a vibrative
or undulatory motion in the air.

PHILONOUS. I thought I had already obviated that distinction by the
answer I gave when you were applying it in a like case before. But to
say no more of that; are you sure then that sound is really nothing but
motion?

HYLAS. I am.

PHILONOUS. Whatever therefore agrees to real sound, may with truth be
attributed to motion.

HYLAS. It may.

PHILONOUS. It is then good sense to speak of *motion*, as of a thing that is
loud, sweet, acute, or *grave*.

HYLAS. I see you are resolved not to understand me. Is it not evident, those
accidents or modes belong only to sensible sound, or *sound* in the
common acceptation of the word, but not to *sound* in the real and
philosophic sense, which, as I just now told you, is nothing but a certain
motion of the air?

PHILONOUS. It seems then there are two sorts of sound, the one vulgar,
or that which is heard, the other philosophical and real.

HYLAS. Even so.

PHILONOUS. And the latter consists in motion.

HYLAS. I told you so before.

PHILONOUS. Tell me, Hylas, to which of the senses think you, the idea of
motion belongs: to the hearing?

HYLAS. No certainly, but to the sight and touch.

PHILONOUS. It should follow then, that according to you, real sounds
may possibly be *seen* or *felt*, but never *heard*.

HYLAS. Look you, Philonous, you may if you please make a jest of my
opinion, but that will not alter the truth of things. I own indeed, the
inferences you draw me into, sound something oddly; but common
language, you know, is framed by, and for the use of the vulgar: we
must not therefore wonder, if expressions adapted to exact philosophic
notions, seem uncouth and out of the way.

PHILONOUS. Is it come to that? I assure you, I imagine myself to have
gained no small point, since you make so light of departing from
common phrases and opinions; it being a main part of our inquiry, to
examine whose notions are widest of the common road, and most
183 repugnant to the general sense of the world. But can you think it no more
than a philosophical paradox, to say that *real sounds are never heard*,
and that the idea of them is obtained by some other sense. And is there
nothing in this contrary to nature and the truth of things?

HYLAS. To deal ingenuously, I do not like it. And after the concessions
already made, I had as well grant that sounds too have no real being
without the mind.

PHILONOUS. And I hope you will make no difficulty to acknowledge the same of colours.

HYLAS. Pardon me: the case of colours is very different. Can anything be plainer, than that we see them on the objects?

PHILONOUS. The objects you speak of are, I suppose, corporeal substances existing without the mind.

HYLAS. They are.

PHILONOUS. And have true and real colours inhering in them?

HYLAS. Each visible object hath that colour which we see in it.

PHILONOUS. How! Is there any thing visible but what we perceive by sight?

HYLAS. There is not.

PHILONOUS. And do we perceive any thing by sense, which we do not perceive immediately?

HYLAS. How often must I be obliged to repeat the same thing? I tell you, we do not.

PHILONOUS. Have patience, good Hylas; and tell me once more, whether there is any thing immediately perceived by the senses, except sensible qualities. I know you asserted there was not: but I would now be informed, whether you still persist in the same opinion.

HYLAS. I do.

PHILONOUS. Pray, is your corporeal substance either a sensible quality, or made up of sensible qualities?

HYLAS. What a question that is! who ever thought it was?

PHILONOUS. My reason for asking was, because in saying, *each visible object hath that colour which we see in it*, you make visible objects to be corporeal substances; which implies either that corporeal substances are sensible qualities, or else that there is something beside sensible qualities perceived by sight: but as this point was formerly agreed between us, and is still maintained by you, it is a clear consequence, that your corporeal substance is nothing distinct from sensible qualities.

HYLAS. You may draw as many absurd consequences as you please, and *184* endeavour to perplex the plainest things; but you shall never persuade me out of my senses. I clearly understand my own meaning.

PHILONOUS. I wish you would make me understand it too. But since you are unwilling to have your notion of corporeal substance examined, I shall urge that point no farther. Only be pleased to let me know, whether the same colours which we see, exist in external bodies, or some other.

HYLAS. The very same.

PHILONOUS. What! are then the beautiful red and purple we see on yonder clouds, really in them? Or do you imagine they have in themselves any other form, than that of a dark mist or vapour?

HYLAS. I must own, Philonous, those colours are not really in the clouds as they seem to be at this distance. They are only apparent colours.

PHILONOUS. *Apparent* call you them? how shall we distinguish these apparent colours from real?

HYLAS. Very easily. Those are to be thought apparent, which appearing only at a distance, vanish upon a nearer approach.

PHILONOUS. And those I suppose are to be thought real, which are discovered by the most near and exact survey.

HYLAS. Right.

PHILONOUS. Is the nearest and exactest survey made by the help of a microscope, or by the naked eye?

HYLAS. By a microscope, doubtless.

PHILONOUS. But a microscope often discovers colours in an object different from those perceived by the unassisted sight. And in case we had microscopes magnifying to any assigned degree; it is certain, that no object whatsoever viewed through them, would appear in the same colour which it exhibits to the naked eye.

HYLAS. And what will you conclude from all this? You cannot argue that there are really and naturally no colours on objects: because by artificial managements they may be altered, or made to vanish.

PHILONOUS. I think it may evidently be concluded from your own concessions, that all the colours we see with our naked eyes, are only apparent as those on the clouds, since they vanish upon a more close and accurate inspection, which is afforded us by a microscope. Then as to what you say by way of prevention: I ask you, whether the real
185   and natural state of an object is better discovered by a very sharp and piercing sight, or by one which is less sharp?

HYLAS. By the former without doubt.

PHILONOUS. Is it not plain from *dioptrics*, that microscopes make the sight more penetrating, and represent objects as they would appear to the eye, in case it were naturally endowed with a most exquisite sharpness?

HYLAS. It is.

PHILONOUS. Consequently the microscopical representation is to be thought that which best sets forth the real nature of the thing, or what it is in itself. The colours therefore by it perceived, are more genuine and real, than those perceived otherwise.

HYLAS. I confess there is something in what you say.

PHILONOUS. Besides, it is not only possible but manifest, that there actually are animals, whose eyes are by Nature framed to perceive those things, which by reason of their minuteness escape our sight. What think you of those inconceivably small animals perceived by glasses? Must we suppose they are all stark blind? Or, in case they see, can it be imagined their sight hath not the same use in preserving their bodies from injuries, which appears in that of all other animals? And if it hath, is it not evident, they must see particles less than their own bodies, which will present them with a far different view in each object, from that which strikes our senses? Even our own eyes do not always represent objects to us after the same manner. In the *jaundice*, everyone knows that all things seem yellow. Is it not therefore highly probable, those animals in whose eyes we discern a very different texture from that of ours, and whose bodies abound with different humours, do not see the same colours in every object that we do? From all which, should it not seem to follow, that all colours are equally apparent, and that none of those which we perceive are really inherent in any outward object?

HYLAS. It should.

PHILONOUS. The point will be past all doubt, if you consider, that in case colours were real properties or affections inherent in external bodies, they could admit of no alteration, without some change wrought in the very bodies themselves: but is it not evident from what hath been said, that upon the use of microscopes, upon a change happening in the humours of the eye, or a variation of distance, without any manner of real alteration in the thing itself, the colours of any object are either *186* changed, or totally disappear? Nay all other circumstances remaining the same, change but the situation of some objects, and they shall present different colours to the eye. The same thing happens upon viewing an object in various degrees of light. And what is more known, than that the same bodies appear differently coloured by candle-light, from what they do in the open day? Add to these the experiment of a prism, which separating the heterogeneous rays of light, alters the colour of any object; and will cause the whitest to appear of a deep blue or red to the naked eye. And now tell me, whether you are still of opinion, that every body hath its true real colour inhering in it; and if you think it hath, I would fain know farther from you, what certain distance and position of the object, what peculiar texture and formation of the eye, what degree or kind of light is necessary for ascertaining that true colour, and distinguishing it from apparent ones.

HYLAS. I own myself entirely satisfied, that they are all equally apparent; and that there is no such thing as colour really inhering in external bodies, but that it is altogether in the light. And what confirms me in this opinion is, that in proportion to the light, colours are still more or less vivid; and if there be no light, then are there no colours perceived. Besides, allowing there are colours on external objects, yet how is it possible for us to perceive them? For no external body affects the mind, unless it act first on our organs of sense. But the only action of bodies is motion; and motion cannot be communicated otherwise than by impulse. A distant object therefore cannot act on the eye, nor consequently make itself or its properties perceivable to the soul. Whence it plainly follows, that it is immediately some contiguous substance, which operating on the eye occasions a perception of colours: and such is light.

PHILONOUS. How! is light then a substance?

HYLAS. I tell you, Philonous, external light is nothing but a thin fluid substance, whose minute particles being agitated with a brisk motion, and in various manners reflected from the different surfaces of outward objects to the eyes, communicate different motions to the optic nerves; which being propagated to the brain, cause therein various impressions: and these are attended with the sensations of red, blue, yellow, &c.

PHILONOUS. It seems then, the light doth no more than shake the optic nerves.

HYLAS. Nothing else.

PHILONOUS. And consequent to each particular motion of the nerves the mind is affected with a sensation, which is some particular colour.

HYLAS. Right.

PHILONOUS. And these sensations have no existence without the mind.

HYLAS. They have not.

PHILONOUS. How then do you affirm that colours are in the light, since by *light* you understand a corporeal substance external to the mind?

HYLAS. Light and colours, as immediately perceived by us, I grant cannot exist without the mind. But in themselves they are only the motions and configurations of certain insensible particles of matter.

PHILONOUS. Colours then in the vulgar sense, or taken for the immediate objects of sight, cannot agree to any but a perceiving substance.

HYLAS. That is what I say.

PHILONOUS. Well then, since you give up the point as to those sensible qualities, which are alone thought colours by all mankind beside, you may hold what you please with regard to those invisible ones of the philosophers. It is not my business to dispute about them; only I would advise you to bethink yourself, whether considering the inquiry we are upon, it be prudent for you to affirm, *the red and blue which we see are not real colours, but certain unknown motions and figures which no man ever did or can see, are truly so.* Are not these shocking notions, and are not they subject to as many ridiculous inferences, as those you were obliged to renounce before in the case of sounds?

HYLAS. I frankly own, Philonous, that it is in vain to stand out any longer. Colours, sounds, tastes, in a word, all those termed *secondary qualities,* have certainly no existence without the mind. But by this acknowledgment I must not be supposed to derogate anything from the reality of matter or external objects, seeing it is no more than several philosophers maintain, who nevertheless are the farthest imaginable from denying matter. For the clearer understanding of this, you must know sensible qualities are by philosophers divided into *primary* and *secondary.* The former are extension, figure, solidity, gravity, motion, *188* and rest. And these they hold exist really in bodies. The latter are those above enumerated; or briefly, all sensible qualities beside the primary, which they assert are only so many sensations or ideas existing nowhere but in the mind. But all this, I doubt not, you are already apprised of. For my part, I have been a long time sensible there was such an opinion current among philosophers, but was never thoroughly convinced of its truth till now.

PHILONOUS. You are still then of opinion, that extension and figures are inherent in external unthinking substances.

HYLAS. I am.

PHILONOUS. But what if the same arguments which are brought against secondary qualities, will hold good against these also?

HYLAS. Why then I shall be obliged to think, they too exist only in the mind.

PHILONOUS. Is it your opinion, the very figure and extension which you perceive by sense, exist in the outward object or material substance?

HYLAS. It is.

PHILONOUS. Have all other animals as good grounds to think the same of the figure and extension which they see and feel?

HYLAS. Without doubt, if they have any thought at all.

PHILONOUS. Answer me, Hylas. Think you the senses were bestowed upon all animals for their preservation and well-being in life? or were they given to men alone for this end?

HYLAS. I make no question but they have the same use in all other animals.

PHILONOUS. If so, is it not necessary they should be enabled by them to perceive their own limbs, and those bodies which are capable of harming them?

HYLAS. Certainly.

PHILONOUS. A mite therefore must be supposed to see his own foot, and things equal or even less than it, as bodies of some considerable dimension; though at the same time they appear to you scarce discernible, or at best as so many visible points.

HYLAS. I cannot deny it.

PHILONOUS. And to creatures less than the mite they will seem yet larger.

HYLAS. They will.

PHILONOUS. Insomuch that what you can hardly discern, will to another extremely minute animal appear as some huge mountain.

HYLAS. All this I grant. 189

PHILONOUS. Can one and the same thing be at the same time in itself of different dimensions?

HYLAS. That were absurd to imagine.

PHILONOUS. But from what you have laid down it follows, that both the extension by you perceived, and that perceived by the mite itself, as likewise all those perceived by lesser animals, are each of them the true extension of the mite's foot, that is to say, by your own principles you are led into an absurdity.

HYLAS. There seems to be some difficulty in the point.

PHILONOUS. Again, have you not acknowledged that no real inherent property of any object can be changed, without some change in the thing itself?

HYLAS. I have.

PHILONOUS. But as we approach to or recede from an object, the visible extension varies, being at one distance ten or an hundred times greater than at another. Doth it not therefore follow from hence likewise, that it is not really inherent in the object?

HYLAS. I own I am at a loss what to think.

PHILONOUS. Your judgment will soon be determined, if you will venture to think as freely concerning this quality, as you have done concerning the rest. Was it not admitted as a good argument, that neither heat nor cold was in the water, because it seemed warm to one hand, and cold to the other?

HYLAS. It was.

PHILONOUS. Is it not the very same reasoning to conclude, there is no extension or figure in an object, because to one eye it shall seem little, smooth, and round, when at the same time it appears to the other, great, uneven, and angular?

HYLAS. The very same. But doth this latter fact ever happen?

PHILONOUS. You may at any time make the experiment, by looking with one eye bare, and with the other through a microscope.

HYLAS. I know not how to maintain it, and yet I am loth to give up *extension*, I see so many odd consequences following upon such a concession.

PHILONOUS. Odd, say you? After the concessions already made, I hope you will stick at nothing for its oddness. But on the other hand [1] should it not seem very odd, if the general reasoning which includes all other sensible qualities did not also include extension? If it be allowed that no idea nor any thing like an idea can exist in an unperceiving substance, then surely it follows, that no figure or mode of extension, which we can either perceive or imagine, or have any idea of, can be really inherent in matter; not to mention the peculiar difficulty there must be, in conceiving a material substance, prior to and distinct from extension, to be the *substratum* of extension. Be the sensible quality what it will, figure, or sound, or colour; it seems alike impossible it should subsist in that which doth not perceive it.

HYLAS. I give up the point for the present, reserving still a right to retract my opinion, in case I shall hereafter discover any false step in my progress to it.

PHILONOUS. That is a right you cannot be denied. Figures and extension being dispatched, we proceed next to *motion*. Can a real motion in any external body be at the same time both very swift and very slow?

HYLAS. It cannot.

PHILONOUS. Is not the motion of a body swift in a reciprocal proportion to the time it takes up in describing any given space? Thus a body that describes a mile in an hour, moves three times faster than it would in case it described only a mile in three hours.

HYLAS. I agree with you.

PHILONOUS. And is not time measured by the succession of ideas in our minds?

HYLAS. It is.

PHILONOUS. And is it not possible ideas should succeed one another twice as fast in your mind, as they do in mine, or in that of some spirit of another kind.

HYLAS. I own it.

PHILONOUS. Consequently the same body may to another seem to perform its motion over any space in half the time that it doth to you. And the same reasoning will hold as to any other proportion: that is to

---

[1] [*But on the other hand* . . . (to end of speech) added in 1734 edition.]

say, according to your principles (since the motions perceived are both really in the object) it is possible one and the same body shall be really moved the same way at once, both very swift and very slow. How is this consistent either with common sense, or with what you just now granted?

HYLAS. I have nothing to say to it.

PHILONOUS. Then as for *solidity*; either you do not mean any sensible *191* quality by that word, and so it is beside our inquiry: or if you do, it must be either hardness or resistance. But both the one and the other are plainly relative to our senses: it being evident, that what seems hard to one animal, may appear soft to another, who hath greater force and firmness of limbs. Nor is it less plain, that the resistance I feel is not in the body.

HYLAS. I own the very sensation of resistance, which is all you immediately perceive, is not in the *body*, but the cause of that sensation is.

PHILONOUS. But the causes of our sensations are not things immediately perceived, and therefore not sensible. This point I thought had been already determined.

HYLAS. I own it was; but you will pardon me if I seem a little embarrassed: I know not how to quit my old notions.

PHILONOUS. To help you out, do but consider, that if extension be once acknowledged to have no existence without the mind, the same must necessarily be granted of motion, solidity, and gravity, since they all evidently suppose extension. It is therefore superfluous to inquire particularly concerning each of them. In denying extension, you have denied them all to have any real existence.

HYLAS. I wonder, Philonous, if what you say be true, why those philosophers who deny the secondary qualities any real existence, should yet attribute it to the primary. If there is no difference between them, how can this be accounted for?

PHILONOUS. It is not my business to account for every opinion of the philosophers. But among other reasons which may be assigned for this, it seems probable, that pleasure and pain being rather annexed to the former than the latter, may be one. Heat and cold, tastes and smells, have something more vividly pleasing or disagreeable than the ideas of extension, figure, and motion, affect us with. And it being too visibly absurd to hold, that pain or pleasure can be in an unperceiving substance, men are more easily weaned from believing the external existence of the secondary, than the primary qualities. You will be satisfied there is something in this, if you recollect the difference you made between an intense and more moderate degree of heat, allowing the one a real existence, while you denied it to the other. But after all, there is no rational ground for that distinction; for surely an indifferent sensation is as truly *a sensation*, as one more pleasing or painful; and consequently *192* should not any more than they be supposed to exist in an unthinking subject.

HYLAS. It is just come into my head, Philonous, that I have somewhere heard of a distinction between absolute and sensible extension. Now though it be acknowledged that *great* and *small*, consisting merely in the relation which other extended beings have to the parts of our own bodies, do not really inhere in the substances themselves; yet nothing obliges us to hold the same with regard to *absolute extension*, which is something abstracted from *great* and *small*, from this or that particular magnitude or figure. So likewise as to motion, *swift* and *slow* are altogether relative to the succession of ideas in our own minds. But it doth not follow, because those modifications of motion exist not without the mind, that therefore absolute motion abstracted from them doth not.

PHILONOUS. Pray what is it that distinguishes one motion, or one part of extension from another? Is it not something sensible, as some degree of swiftness or slowness, some certain magnitude or figure peculiar to each?

HYLAS. I think so.

PHILONOUS. These qualities therefore stripped of all sensible properties, are without all specific and numerical differences, as the Schools call them.

HYLAS. They are.

PHILONOUS. That is to say, they are extension in general, and motion in general.

HYLAS. Let it be so.

PHILONOUS. But it is an universally received maxim, that *everything which exists, is particular*. How then can motion in general, or extension in general exist in any corporeal substance?

193 HYLAS. I will take time to solve your difficulty.

PHILONOUS. But I think the point may be speedily decided. Without doubt you can tell, whether you are able to frame this or that idea. Now I am content to put our dispute on this issue. If you can frame in your thoughts a distinct abstract idea of motion or extension, divested of all those sensible modes, as swift and slow, great and small, round and square, and the like, which are acknowledged to exist only in the mind, I will then yield the point you contend for. But if you cannot, it will be unreasonable on your side to insist any longer upon what you have no notion of.

HYLAS. To confess ingenuously, I cannot.

PHILONOUS. Can you even separate the ideas of extension and motion, from the ideas of all those qualities which they who make the distinction, term *secondary*?

HYLAS. What! is it not an easy matter, to consider extension and motion by themselves, abstracted from all other sensible qualities? Pray how do the mathematicians treat of them?

PHILONOUS. I acknowledge, Hylas, it is not difficult to form general propositions and reasonings about those qualities, without mentioning any other; and in this sense to consider or treat of them abstractedly. But how doth it follow that because I can pronounce the word *motion* by itself, I can form the idea of it in my mind exclusive of body? Or because theorems may be made of extension and figures, without any mention of *great* or *small*, or any other sensible mode or quality; that therefore it is possible such an abstract idea of extension, without any particular size or figure, or sensible quality, should be distinctly formed, and apprehended by the mind? Mathematicians treat of quantity, without regarding what other sensible qualities it is attended with, as being altogether indifferent to their demonstrations. But when laying aside the words, they contemplate the bare ideas, I believe you will find, they are not the pure abstracted ideas of extension.

HYLAS. But what say you to *pure intellect*? May not abstracted ideas be framed by that faculty?

PHILONOUS. Since I cannot frame abstract ideas at all, it is plain, I cannot frame them by the help of *pure intellect*, whatsoever faculty you understand by those words. Besides, not to inquire into the nature of pure *194* intellect and its spiritual objects, as *virtue, reason, God*, or the like; thus much seems manifest, that sensible things are only to be perceived by sense, or represented by the imagination. Figures therefore and extension being originally perceived by sense, do not belong to pure intellect. But for your farther satisfaction, try if you can frame the idea of any figure, abstracted from all particularities of size, or even from other sensible qualities.

HYLAS. Let me think a little—I do not find that I can.

PHILONOUS. And can you think it possible, that should really exist in Nature, which implies a repugnancy in its conception?

HYLAS. By no means.

PHILONOUS. Since therefore it is impossible even for the mind to disunite the ideas of extension and motion from all other sensible qualities, doth it not follow, that where the one exist, there necessarily the other exist likewise?

HYLAS. It should seem so.

PHILONOUS. Consequently the very same arguments which you admitted, as conclusive against the secondary qualities, are without any farther application of force against the primary too. Besides, if you will trust your senses, is it not plain all sensible qualities coexist, or to them, appear as being in the same place? Do they ever represent a motion, or figure, as being divested of all other visible and tangible qualities?

HYLAS. You need say no more on this head. I am free to own, if there be no secret error or oversight in our proceedings hitherto, that all sensible qualities are alike to be denied existence without the mind. But my fear is, that I have been too liberal in my former concessions, or overlooked some fallacy or other. In short, I did not take time to think.

PHILONOUS. For that matter, Hylas, you may take what time you please in reviewing the progress of our inquiry. You are at liberty to recover any slips you might have made, or offer whatever you have omitted, which makes for your first opinion.

HYLAS. One great oversight I take to be this: that I did not sufficiently distinguish the *object* from the *sensation*. Now though this latter may not exist without the mind, yet it will not thence follow that the former cannot.

PHILONOUS. What object do you mean? the object of the senses?

HYLAS. The same.

PHILONOUS. It is then immediately perceived.

195 HYLAS. Right.

PHILONOUS. Make me to understand the difference between what is immediately perceived, and a sensation.

HYLAS. The sensation I take to be an act of the mind perceiving; beside which, there is something perceived; and this I call the *object*. For example, there is red and yellow on that tulip. But then the act of perceiving those colours is in me only, and not in the tulip.

PHILONOUS. What tulip do you speak of? is it that which you see?

HYLAS. The same.

PHILONOUS. And what do you see beside colour, figure, and extension?

HYLAS. Nothing.

PHILONOUS. What you would say then is, that the red and yellow are coexistent with the extension; is it not?

HYLAS. That is not all; I would say, they have a real existence without the mind, in some unthinking substance.

PHILONOUS. That the colours are really in the tulip which I see, is manifest. Neither can it be denied, that this tulip may exist independent of your mind or mine; but that any immediate object of the senses, that is, any idea, or combination of ideas, should exist in an unthinking substance, or exterior to all minds, is in itself an evident contradiction. Nor can I imagine how this follows from what you said just now, to wit that the red and yellow were on the tulip *you saw*, since you do not pretend to *see* that unthinking substance.

HYLAS. You have an artful way, Philonous, of diverting our inquiry from the subject.

PHILONOUS. I see you have no mind to be pressed that way. To return then to your distinction between *sensation* and *object*; if I take you right, you distinguish in every perception two things, the one an action of the mind, the other not.

HYLAS. True.

PHILONOUS. And this action cannot exist in, or belong to any unthinking thing; but whatever beside is implied in a perception, may.

196 HYLAS. That is my meaning.

PHILONOUS. So that if there was a perception without any act of the mind, it were possible such a perception should exist in an unthinking substance.

HYLAS. I grant it. But it is impossible there should be such a perception.

PHILONOUS. When is the mind said to be active?

HYLAS. When it produces, puts an end to, or changes anything.

PHILONOUS. Can the mind produce, discontinue, or change anything but by an act of the will?

HYLAS. It cannot.

PHILONOUS. The mind therefore is to be accounted active in its perceptions, so far forth as volition is included in them.

HYLAS. It is.

PHILONOUS. In plucking this flower, I am active, because I do it by the motion of my hand, which was consequent upon my volition; so likewise in applying it to my nose. But is either of these smelling?

HYLAS. No.

PHILONOUS. I act too in drawing the air through my nose; because my breathing so rather than otherwise, is the effect of my volition. But neither can this be called *smelling*: for if it were, I should smell every time I breathed in that manner.

HYLAS. True.

PHILONOUS. Smelling then is somewhat consequent to all this.

HYLAS. It is.

PHILONOUS. But I do not find my will concerned any farther. Whatever more there is, as that I perceive such a particular smell or any smell at all, this is independent of my will, and therein I am altogether passive. Do you find it otherwise with you, Hylas?

HYLAS. No, the very same.

PHILONOUS. Then as to seeing, is it not in your power to open your eyes, or keep them shut; to turn them this or that way?

HYLAS. Without doubt.

PHILONOUS. But doth it in like manner depend on your will, that in looking on this flower, you perceive *white* rather than any other colour? Or directing your open eyes toward yonder part of the heaven, can you avoid seeing the sun? Or is light or darkness the effect of your volition?

HYLAS. No certainly.

PHILONOUS. You are then in these respects altogether passive.

HYLAS. I am.

197

PHILONOUS. Tell me now, whether *seeing* consists in perceiving light and colours, or in opening and turning the eyes?

HYLAS. Without doubt, in the former.

PHILONOUS. Since therefore you are in the very perception of light and colours altogether passive, what is become of that action you were speaking of, as an ingredient in every sensation? And doth it not follow from your own concessions, that the perception of light and colours, including no action in it, may exist in an unperceiving substance? And is not this a plain contradiction?

HYLAS. I know not what to think of it.

PHILONOUS. Besides, since you distinguish the *active* and *passive* in every perception, you must do it in that of pain. But how is it possible that pain, be it as little active as you please, should exist in an unperceiving substance? In short, do but consider the point, and then confess ingenuously, whether light and colours, tastes, sounds, &c. are not all equally passions or sensations in the soul. You may indeed call them *external objects,* and give them in words what subsistence you please.

But examine your own thoughts, and then tell me whether it be not as I say?

HYLAS. I acknowledge, Philonous, that upon a fair observation of what passes in my mind, I can discover nothing else, but that I am a thinking being, affected with variety of sensations; neither is it possible to conceive how a sensation should exist in an unperceiving substance. But then on the other hand, when I look on sensible things in a different view, considering them as so many modes and qualities, I find it necessary to suppose a material *substratum*, without which they cannot be conceived to exist.

PHILONOUS. *Material substratum* call you it? Pray, by which of your senses came you acquainted with that being?

HYLAS. It is not itself sensible; its modes and qualities only being perceived by the senses.

PHILONOUS. I presume then, it was by reflexion and reason you obtained the idea of it.

HYLAS. I do not pretend to any proper positive idea of it. However I conclude it exists, because qualities cannot be conceived to exist without a support.

PHILONOUS. It seems then you have only a relative notion of it, or that you conceive it not otherwise than by conceiving the relation it bears to sensible qualities.

198 HYLAS. Right.

PHILONOUS. Be pleased therefore to let me know wherein that relation consists.

HYLAS. Is it not sufficiently expressed in the term *substratum*, or *substance*?

PHILONOUS. If so, the word *substratum* should import, that it is spread under the sensible qualities or accidents.

HYLAS. True.

PHILONOUS. And consequently under extension.

HYLAS. I own it.

PHILONOUS. It is therefore somewhat in its own nature entirely distinct from extension.

HYLAS. I tell you, extension is only a mode, and matter is something that supports modes. And is it not evident the thing supported is different from the thing supporting?

PHILONOUS. So that something distinct from, and exclusive of extension, is supposed to be the *substratum* of extension.

HYLAS. Just so.

PHILONOUS. Answer me, Hylas. Can a thing be spread without extension? or is not the idea of extension necessarily included in *spreading*?

HYLAS. It is.

PHILONOUS. Whatsoever therefore you suppose spread under any thing, must have in itself an extension distinct from the extension of that thing under which it is spread.

HYLAS. It must.

PHILONOUS. Consequently every corporeal substance being the *substratum* of extension, must have in itself another extension by which it is qualified to be a *substratum*: and so on to infinity. And I ask whether this be not absurd in itself, and repugnant to what you granted just now, to wit, that the *substratum* was something distinct from, and exclusive of extension.

HYLAS. Ay but, Philonous, you take me wrong. I do not mean that matter is *spread* in a gross literal sense under extension. The word *substratum* is used only to express in general the same thing with *substance*.

PHILONOUS. Well then, let us examine the relation implied in the term *substance*. Is it not that it stands under accidents?

HYLAS. The very same.

PHILONOUS. But that one thing may stand under or support another, must it not be extended?

HYLAS. It must.

PHILONOUS. Is not therefore this supposition liable to the same absurdity *199* with the former?

HYLAS. You still take things in a strict literal sense: that is not fair, Philonous.

PHILONOUS. I am not for imposing any sense on your words: you are at liberty to explain them as you please. Only I beseech you, make me understand something by them. You tell me, matter supports or stands under accidents. How! is it as your legs support your body?

HYLAS. No; that is the literal sense.

PHILONOUS. Pray let me know any sense, literal or not literal, that you understand it in.—— How long must I wait for an answer, Hylas?

HYLAS. I declare I know not what to say. I once thought I understood well enough what was meant by matter's supporting accidents. But now the more I think on it, the less can I comprehend it; in short, I find that I know nothing of it.

PHILONOUS. It seems then you have no idea at all, neither relative nor positive of matter; you know neither what it is in itself, nor what relation it bears to accidents.

HYLAS. I acknowledge it.

PHILONOUS. And yet you asserted, that you could not conceive how qualities or accidents should really exist, without conceiving at the same time a material support of them.

HYLAS. I did.

PHILONOUS. That is to say, when you conceive the real existence of qualities, you do withal conceive something which you cannot conceive.

HYLAS. It was wrong I own. But still I fear there is some fallacy or other. Pray what think you of this? It is just come into my head, that the ground of all our mistakes lies in your treating of each quality by itself. Now, I grant that each quality cannot singly subsist without the mind. Colour cannot without extension, neither can figure without some other sensible quality. But as the several qualities united or blended together form entire sensible things, nothing hinders why such things may not be supposed to exist without the mind.

PHILONOUS. Either, Hylas, you are jesting, or have a very bad memory. Though indeed we went through all the qualities by name one after another; yet my arguments, or rather your concessions nowhere tended to prove, that the secondary qualities did not subsist each alone by itself; but that they were not *at all* without the mind. Indeed in treating of figure and motion, we concluded they could not exist without the mind, because it was impossible even in thought to separate them from all secondary qualities, so as to conceive them existing by themselves. But then this was not the only argument made use of upon that occasion. But (to pass by all that hath been hitherto said, and reckon it for nothing, if you will have it so) I am content to put the whole upon this issue. If you can conceive it possible for any mixture or combination of qualities, or any sensible object whatever, to exist without the mind, then I will grant it actually to be so.

HYLAS. If it comes to that, the point will soon be decided. What more easy than to conceive a tree or house existing by itself, independent of, and unperceived by any mind whatsoever? I do at this present time conceive them existing after that manner.

PHILONOUS. How say you, Hylas, can you see a thing which is at the same time unseen?

HYLAS. No, that were a contradiction.

PHILONOUS. Is it not as great a contradiction to talk of *conceiving* a thing which is *unconceived*?

HYLAS. It is.

PHILONOUS. The tree or house therefore which you think of, is conceived by you.

HYLAS. How should it be otherwise?

PHILONOUS. And what is conceived, is surely in the mind.

HYLAS. Without question, that which is conceived is in the mind.

PHILONOUS. How then came you to say, you conceived a house or tree existing independent and out of all minds, whatsoever?

HYLAS. That was I own an oversight; but stay, let me consider what led me into it.—It is a pleasant mistake enough. As I was thinking of a tree in a solitary place, where no one was present to see it, methought that was to conceive a tree as existing unperceived or unthought of, not considering that I myself conceived it all the while. But now I plainly see, that all I can do is to frame ideas in my own mind. I may indeed conceive in my own thoughts the idea of a tree, or a house, or a mountain, but this is all. And this is far from proving, that I can conceive them *existing out of the minds of all spirits*.

PHILONOUS. You acknowledge then that you cannot possibly conceive, how any one corporeal sensible thing should exist otherwise than in a mind.

HYLAS. I do.

PHILONOUS. And yet you will earnestly contend for the truth of that which you cannot so much as conceive.

HYLAS. I profess I know not what to think, but still there are some scruples remain with me. Is it not certain I see things at a distance? Do we not perceive the stars and moon, for example, to be a great way off? Is not this, I say, manifest to the senses?

PHILONOUS. Do you not in a dream too perceive those or the like objects?

HYLAS. I do.

PHILONOUS. And have they not then the same appearance of being distant?

HYLAS. They have.

PHILONOUS. But you do not thence conclude the apparitions in a dream to be without the mind?

HYLAS. By no means.

PHILONOUS. You ought not therefore to conclude that sensible objects are without the mind, from their appearance or manner wherein they are perceived.

HYLAS. I acknowledge it. But doth not my sense deceive me in those cases?

PHILONOUS. By no means. The idea or thing which you immediately perceive, neither sense nor reason inform you that it actually exists without the mind. By sense you only know that you are affected with such certain sensations of light and colours, &c. And these you will not say are without the mind.

HYLAS. True: but beside all that, do you not think the sight suggests something of *outness* or *distance*?

PHILONOUS. Upon approaching a distant object, do the visible size and figure change perpetually, or do they appear the same at all distances?

HYLAS. They are in a continual change.

PHILONOUS. Sight therefore doth not suggest or any way inform you, that the visible object you immediately perceive, exists at a distance,* or will be perceived when you advance farther onward, there being a continued series of visible objects succeeding each other, during the whole time of your approach.

HYLAS. It doth not; but still I know, upon seeing an object, what object I shall perceive after having passed over a certain distance: no matter whether it be exactly the same or no: there is still something of distance *202* suggested in the case.

PHILONOUS. Good Hylas, do but reflect a little on the point, and then tell me whether there be any more in it than this. From the ideas you actually perceive by sight, you have by experience learned to collect what other ideas you will (according to the standing order of Nature) be affected with, after such a certain succession of time and motion.

HYLAS. Upon the whole, I take it to be nothing else.

PHILONOUS. Now is it not plain, that if we suppose a man born blind was on a sudden made to see, he could at first have no experience of what may be suggested by sight.

HYLAS. It is.

* See the Essay towards a new Theory of Vision; and its Vindication.

PHILONOUS. He would not then according to you have any notion of distance annexed to the things he saw; but would take them for a new set of sensations existing only in his mind.

HYLAS. It is undeniable.

PHILONOUS. But to make it still more plain: is not *distance* a line turned endwise to the eye?

HYLAS. It is.

PHILONOUS. And can a line so situated be perceived by sight?

HYLAS. It cannot.

PHILONOUS. Doth it not therefore follow that distance is not properly and immediately perceived by sight?

HYLAS. It should seem so.

PHILONOUS. Again, is it your opinion that colours are at a distance?

HYLAS. It must be acknowledged, they are only in the mind.

PHILONOUS. But do not colours appear to the eye as coexisting in the same place with extension and figures?

HYLAS. They do.

PHILONOUS. How can you then conclude from sight, that figures exist without, when you acknowledge colours do not; the sensible appearance being the very same with regard to both?

HYLAS. I know not what to answer.

PHILONOUS. But allowing that distance was truly and immediately perceived by the mind, yet it would not thence follow it existed out of the mind. For whatever is immediately perceived is an idea: and can any *idea* exist out of the mind?

HYLAS. To suppose that, were absurd: but inform me, Philonous, can we perceive or know nothing beside our ideas?

PHILONOUS. As for the rational deducing of causes from effects, that is beside our inquiry. And by the senses you can best tell, whether you perceive any thing which is not immediately perceived. And I ask you, whether the things immediately perceived, are other than your own sensations or ideas? You have indeed more than once, in the course of this conversation, declared yourself on those points; but you seem by this last question to have departed from what you then thought.

HYLAS. To speak the truth, Philonous, I think there are two kinds of objects, the one perceived immediately, which are likewise called *ideas*; the other are real things or external objects perceived by the mediation of ideas, which are their images and representations. Now I own, ideas do not exist without the mind; but the latter sort of objects do. I am sorry I did not think of this distinction sooner; it would probably have cut short your discourse.

PHILONOUS. Are those external objects perceived by sense, or by some other faculty?

HYLAS. They are perceived by sense.

PHILONOUS. How! is there anything perceived by sense, which is not immediately perceived?

HYLAS. Yes, Philonous, in some sort there is. For example, when I look on a picture or statue of Julius Cæsar, I may be said after a manner to perceive him (though not immediately) by my senses.

PHILONOUS. It seems then, you will have our ideas, which alone are immediately perceived, to be pictures of external things: and that these also are perceived by sense, inasmuch as they have a conformity or resemblance to our ideas.

HYLAS. That is my meaning.

PHILONOUS. And in the same way that Julius Cæsar, in himself invisible, is nevertheless perceived by sight; real things in themselves imperceptible, are perceived by sense.

HYLAS. In the very same.

PHILONOUS. Tell me, Hylas, when you behold the picture of Julius Cæsar, do you see with your eyes any more than some colours and figures with a certain symmetry and composition of the whole?

HYLAS. Nothing else.

PHILONOUS. And would not a man, who had never known anything of Julius Cæsar, see as much?

HYLAS. He would.   204

PHILONOUS. Consequently he hath his sight, and the use of it, in as perfect a degree as you.

HYLAS. I agree with you.

PHILONOUS. Whence comes it then that your thoughts are directed to the Roman Emperor, and his are not? This cannot proceed from the sensations or ideas of sense by you then perceived; since you acknowledge you have no advantage over him in that respect. It should seem therefore to proceed from reason and memory: should it not?

HYLAS. It should.

PHILONOUS. Consequently it will not follow from that instance, that any thing is perceived by sense which is not immediately perceived. Though I grant we may in one acceptation be said to perceive sensible things mediately by sense: that is, when from a frequently perceived connexion, the immediate perception of ideas by one sense suggests to the mind others perhaps belonging to another sense, which are wont to be connected with them. For instance, when I hear a coach drive along the streets, immediately I perceive only the sound; but from the experience I have had that such a sound is connected with a coach, I am said to hear the coach. It is nevertheless evident, that in truth and strictness, nothing can be *heard* but *sound*: and the coach is not then properly perceived by sense, but suggested from experience. So likewise when we are said to see a red-hot bar of iron; the solidity and heat of the iron are not the objects of sight, but suggested to the imagination by the colour and figure, which are properly perceived by that sense. In short, those things alone are actually and strictly perceived by any sense, which would have been perceived, in case that same sense had then been first conferred on us. As for other things, it is plain they are only suggested to the mind by experience grounded on former perceptions. But to return to your comparison of Cæsar's picture, it is plain, if you keep to that, you must hold the real things or archetypes of our ideas are not perceived by sense, but by some internal faculty of the soul, as reason or memory. I would therefore fain know, what arguments you can draw from reason for the existence of what you call *real things* or *material objects*. Or whether you remember to have seen them formerly as they are in themselves? or if you have heard or read of anyone that did.

205 HYLAS. I see, Philonous, you are disposed to raillery; but that will never convince me.

PHILONOUS. My aim is only to learn from you, the way to come at the knowledge of *material beings*. Whatever we perceive, is perceived either immediately or mediately: by sense, or by reason and reflexion. But as you have excluded sense, pray shew me what reason you have to believe their existence; or what *medium* you can possibly make use of, to prove it either to mine or your own understanding.

HYLAS. To deal ingenuously, Philonous, now I consider the point, I do not find I can give you any good reason for it. But thus much seems pretty plain, that it is at least possible such things may really exist. And as long as there is no absurdity in supposing them, I am resolved to believe as I did, till you bring good reasons to the contrary.

PHILONOUS. What! is it come to this, that you only believe the existence of material objects, and that your belief is founded barely on the possi-bility of its being true? Then you will have me bring reasons against it: though another would think it reasonable, the proof should lie on him who holds the affirmative. And after all, this very point which you are now resolved to maintain without any reason, is in effect what you have more than once during this discourse seen good reason to give up. But to pass over all this; if I understand you rightly, you say our ideas do not exist without the mind; but that they are copies, images, or representations of certain originals that do.

HYLAS. You take me right.

PHILONOUS. They are then like external things.

HYLAS. They are.

PHILONOUS. Have those things a stable and permanent nature independent of our senses; or are they in a perpetual change, upon our producing any motions in our bodies, suspending, exerting, or altering our faculties or organs of sense?

HYLAS. Real things, it is plain, have a fixed and real nature, which remains the same, notwithstanding any change in our senses, or in the posture and motion of our bodies; which indeed may affect the ideas in our minds, but it were absurd to think they had the same effect on things existing without the mind.

PHILONOUS. How then is it possible, that things perpetually fleeting and variable as our ideas, should be copies or images of anything fixed and constant? Or in other words, since all sensible qualities, as

206 size, figure, colour, &c. that is, our ideas are continually changing upon every alteration in the distance, medium, or instruments of sensation;

how can any determinate material objects be properly represented or painted forth by several distinct things, each of which is so different from and unlike the rest? Or if you say it resembles some one only of our ideas, how shall we be able to distinguish the true copy from all the false ones?

HYLAS. I profess, Philonous, I am at a loss. I know not what to say to this.

PHILONOUS. But neither is this all. Which are material objects in themselves, perceptible or imperceptible?

HYLAS. Properly and immediately nothing can be perceived but ideas. All material things therefore are in themselves insensible, and to be perceived only by their ideas.

PHILONOUS. Ideas then are sensible, and their archetypes or originals insensible.

HYLAS. Right.

PHILONOUS. But how can that which is sensible be like that which is insensible? Can a real thing in itself *invisible* be like a *colour*; or a real thing which is not *audible*, be like a *sound*? In a word, can anything be like a sensation or idea, but another sensation or idea?

HYLAS. I must own, I think not.

PHILONOUS. Is it possible there should be any doubt in the point? Do you not perfectly know your own ideas?

HYLAS. I know them perfectly; since what I do not perceive or know, can be no part of my idea.

PHILONOUS. Consider therefore, and examine them, and then tell me if there be anything in them which can exist without the mind: or if you can conceive anything like them existing without the mind.

HYLAS. Upon inquiry, I find it is impossible for me to conceive or understand how anything but an idea can be like an idea. And it is most evident, that *no idea can exist without the mind*.

PHILONOUS. You are therefore by your principles forced to deny the reality of sensible things, since you made it to consist in an absolute existence exterior to the mind. That is to say, you are a downright *sceptic*. So I have gained my point, which was to shew your principles led to scepticism.

HYLAS. For the present I am, if not entirely convinced, at least silenced. 207

PHILONOUS. I would fain know what more you would require in order to a perfect conviction. Have you not had the liberty of explaining yourself all manner of ways? Were any little slips in discourse laid hold and insisted on? Or were you not allowed to retract or reinforce anything you had offered, as best served your purpose? Hath not everything you could say been heard and examined with all the fairness imaginable? In a word, have you not in every point been convinced out of your own mouth? And if you can at present discover any flaw in any of your former concessions, or think of any remaining subterfuge, any new distinction, colour, or comment whatsoever, why do you not produce it?

HYLAS. A little patience, Philonous. I am at present so amazed to see myself ensnared, and as it were imprisoned in the labyrinths you have drawn me into, that on the sudden it cannot be expected I should find my way out. You must give me time to look about me, and recollect myself.

PHILONOUS. Hark; is not this the college-bell?

HYLAS. It rings for prayers.

PHILONOUS. We will go in then if you please, and meet here again tomorrow morning. In the mean time you may employ your thoughts on this morning's discourse, and try if you can find any fallacy in it, or invent any new means to extricate yourself.

HYLAS. Agreed.

THE SECOND DIALOGUE

HYLAS. I beg your pardon, Philonous, for not meeting you sooner. All *208* this morning my head was so filled with our late conversation, that I had not leisure to think of the time of the day, or indeed of anything else.

PHILONOUS. I am glad you were so intent upon it, in hopes if there were any mistakes in your concessions, or fallacies in my reasonings from them, you will now discover them to me.

HYLAS. I assure you, I have done nothing ever since I saw you, but search after mistakes and fallacies, and with that view have minutely examined the whole series of yesterday's discourse: but all in vain, for the notions it led me into, upon review appear still more clear and evident; and the more I consider them, the more irresistibly do they force my assent.

PHILONOUS. And is not this, think you, a sign that they are genuine, that they proceed from Nature, and are conformable to right reason? Truth and beauty are in this alike, that the strictest survey sets them both off to advantage. While the false lustre of error and disguise cannot endure being reviewed, or too nearly inspected.

HYLAS. I own there is a great deal in what you say. Nor can anyone be more entirely satisfied of the truth of those odd consequences, so long as I have in view the reasonings that lead to them. But when these are out of my thoughts, there seems on the other hand something so satisfactory, so natural and intelligible in the modern way of explaining things, that I profess I know not how to reject it.

PHILONOUS. I know not what way you mean.

HYLAS. I mean the way of accounting for our sensations or ideas.

PHILONOUS. How is that?

HYLAS. It is supposed the soul makes her residence in some part of the brain, from which the nerves take their rise, and are thence extended to all parts of the body: and that outward objects by the different impressions they make on the organs of sense, communicate certain vibrative motions to the nerves; and these being filled with spirits, propagate them to the brain or seat of the soul, which according to the various impres- *209* sions or traces thereby made in the brain, is variously affected with ideas.

PHILONOUS. And call you this an explication of the manner whereby we are affected with ideas?

HYLAS. Why not, Philonous, have you anything to object against it?

PHILONOUS. I would first know whether I rightly understand your hypothesis. You make certain traces in the brain to be the causes or occasions of our ideas. Pray tell me, whether by the *brain* you mean any sensible thing?

HYLAS. What else think you I could mean?

PHILONOUS. Sensible things are all immediately perceivable; and those things which are immediately perceivable, are ideas; and these exist only in the mind. Thus much you have, if I mistake not, long since agreed to.

HYLAS. I do not deny it.

PHILONOUS. The brain therefore you speak of, being a sensible thing, exists only in the mind. Now, I would fain know whether you think it reasonable to suppose, that one idea or thing existing in the mind, occasions all other ideas. And if you think so, pray how do you account for the origin of that primary idea or brain itself?

HYLAS. I do not explain the origin of our ideas by that brain which is perceivable to sense, this being itself only a combination of sensible ideas, but by another which I imagine.

PHILONOUS. But are not things imagined as truly in the mind as things perceived?

HYLAS. I must confess they are.

PHILONOUS. It comes therefore to the same thing; and you have been all this while accounting for ideas, by certain motions or impressions in the brain, that is, by some alterations in an idea, whether sensible or imaginable it matters not.

HYLAS. I begin to suspect my hypothesis.

PHILONOUS. Beside spirits, all that we know or conceive are our own ideas. When therefore you say, all ideas are occasioned by impressions in the brain, do you conceive this brain or no? If you do, then you talk of ideas imprinted in an idea, causing that same idea, which is absurd. If you do not conceive it, you talk unintelligibly, instead of forming a reasonable hypothesis.

210 HYLAS. I now clearly see it was a mere dream. There is nothing in it.

PHILONOUS. You need not be much concerned at it: for after all, this way of explaining things, as you called it, could never have satisfied any reasonable man. What connexion is there between a motion in the nerves, and the sensations of sound or colour in the mind? or how is it possible these should be the effect of that?

HYLAS. But I could never think it had so little in it, as now it seems to have.

PHILONOUS. Well then, are you at length satisfied that no sensible things have a real existence; and that you are in truth an arrant *sceptic?*

HYLAS. It is too plain to be denied.

PHILONOUS. Look! are not the fields covered with a delightful verdure? Is there not something in the woods and groves, in the rivers and clear springs that soothes, that delights, that transports the soul? At the prospect of the wide and deep ocean, or some huge mountain whose top is lost in the clouds, or of an old gloomy forest, are not our minds filled with a pleasing horror? Even in rocks and deserts, is there not an agreeable wildness? How sincere a pleasure is it to behold the natural beauties of the earth! To preserve and renew our relish for them, is not the veil of night alternately drawn over her face, and doth she not change her dress with the seasons? How aptly are the elements disposed? What variety and use in the meanest productions of Nature? What delicacy, what beauty, what contrivance in animal and vegetable bodies? How exquisitely are all things suited, as well to their particular ends, as to constitute apposite parts of the whole! And while they mutually aid and support, do they not also set off and illustrate each other? Raise now your thoughts from this ball of earth, to all those glorious luminaries that adorn the high arch of heaven. The motion and situation of the planets, are they not admirable for use and order? Were those (miscalled *erratic*) globes ever known to stray, in their repeated journeys through the pathless void? Do they not measure areas round the sun ever proportioned to the times? So fixed, so immutable are the laws by which the unseen Author of Nature actuates the universe. How vivid and radiant is the lustre of the fixed stars! How magnificent and rich that negligent *211* profusion, with which they appear to be scattered throughout the whole azure vault! Yet if you take the telescope, it brings into your sight a new host of stars that escape the naked eye. Here they seem contiguous and minute, but to a nearer view immense orbs of light at various distances, far sunk in the abyss of space. Now you must call imagination to your aid. The feeble narrow sense cannot descry innumerable worlds revolving round the central fires; and in those worlds the energy of an all-perfect mind displayed in endless forms. But neither sense nor imagination are big enough to comprehend the boundless extent with all its glittering furniture. Though the labouring mind exert and strain each power to its utmost reach, there still stands out ungrasped a surplusage immeasurable. Yet all the vast bodies that compose this mighty frame, how distant and remote soever, are by some secret mechanism, some divine art and force linked in a mutual dependence and intercourse with each other, even with this earth, which was almost slipped from my thoughts, and lost in the crowd of worlds. Is not the whole system immense, beautiful, glorious beyond expression and beyond thought! What treatment then do those philosophers deserve, who would deprive these noble and delightful scenes of all reality? How should those principles be entertained, that lead us to think all the visible beauty of the creation a false imaginary glare? To be plain, can you expect this scepticism of yours will not be thought extravagantly absurd by all men of sense?

HYLAS. Other men may think as they please: but for your part you have nothing to reproach me with. My comfort is, you are as much a *sceptic* as I am.

PHILONOUS. There, Hylas, I must beg leave to differ from you.

HYLAS. What! have you all along agreed to the premises, and do you now deny the conclusion, and leave me to maintain those paradoxes by myself which you led me into? This surely is not fair.

PHILONOUS. I deny that I agreed with you in those notions that led to scepticism. You indeed said, the reality of sensible things consisted in an *absolute existence* out of the minds of spirits, or distinct from their being perceived. And pursuant to this notion of reality, you are obliged to

212 deny sensible things any real existence: that is, according to your own definition, you profess yourself a *sceptic*. But I neither said nor thought the reality of sensible things was to be defined after that manner. To me it is evident, for the reasons you allow of, that sensible things cannot exist otherwise than in a mind or spirit. Whence I conclude, not that they have no real existence, but that seeing they depend not on my thought, and have an existence distinct from being perceived by me, *there must be some other mind wherein they exist.* As sure therefore as the sensible world really exists, so sure is there an infinite omnipresent spirit who contains and supports it.

HYLAS. What! this is no more than I and all Christians hold; nay, and all others too who believe there is a God, and that he knows and comprehends all things.

PHILONOUS. Ay, but here lies the difference. Men commonly believe that all things are known or perceived by God, because they believe the being of a God, whereas I on the other side, immediately and necessarily conclude the being of a God, because all sensible things must be perceived by him.

HYLAS. But so long as we all believe the same thing, what matter is it how we come by that belief?

PHILONOUS. But neither do we agree in the same opinion. For philosophers, though they acknowledge all corporeal beings to be perceived by God, yet they attribute to them an absolute subsistence distinct from their being perceived by any mind whatever, which I do not. Besides, is there no difference between saying, *there is a God, therefore he perceives all things*: and saying, *sensible things do really exist: and if they really exist, they are necessarily perceived by an infinite mind: therefore there is an infinite mind, or God.* This furnishes you with a direct and immediate demonstration, from a most evident principle, of the *being of a God.* Divines and philosophers had proved beyond all controversy, from the beauty and usefulness of the several parts of the creation, that it was the workmanship of God. But that setting aside all help of astronomy and natural philosophy, all contemplation of the contrivance, order, and adjustment of things, an infinite mind should be necessarily inferred from the bare existence of the sensible world, is an advantage peculiar to them only who have made this easy reflexion: that the sensible world is that which we perceive by our several senses; and that nothing is perceived by the senses beside ideas; and that no idea or archetype of an

213 idea can exist otherwise than in a mind. You may now, without any laborious search into the sciences, without any subtlety of reason, or tedious length of discourse, oppose and baffle the most strenuous advo-

cate for atheism. Those miserable refuges, whether in an eternal succession of unthinking causes and effects, or in a fortuitous concourse of atoms; those wild imaginations of Vanini, Hobbes, and Spinoza; in a word the whole system of atheism, is it not entirely overthrown by this single reflexion on the repugnancy included in supposing the whole, or any part, even the most rude and shapeless of the visible world, to exist without a mind? Let any one of those abettors of impiety but look into his own thoughts, and there try if he can conceive how so much as a rock, a desert, a chaos, or confused jumble of atoms; how anything at all, either sensible or imaginable, can exist independent of a mind, and he need go no farther to be convinced of his folly. Can anything be fairer than to put a dispute on such an issue, and leave it to a man himself to see if he can conceive, even in thought, what he holds to be true in fact, and from a notional to allow it a real existence?

HYLAS. It cannot be denied, there is something highly serviceable to religion in what you advance. But do you not think it looks very like a notion entertained by some eminent moderns, of *seeing all things in God?*

PHILONOUS. I would gladly know that opinion; pray explain it to me.

HYLAS. They conceive that the soul being immaterial, is incapable of being united with material things, so as to perceive them in themselves, but that she perceives them by her union with the substance of God, which being spiritual is therefore purely intelligible, or capable of being the immediate object of a spirit's thought. Besides, the divine essence contains in it perfections correspondent to each created being; and which are for that reason proper to exhibit or represent them to the mind.

PHILONOUS. I do not understand how our ideas, which are things altogether passive and inert, can be the essence, or any part (or like any part) of the essence or substance of God, who is an impassive, in-
214   divisible, purely active being. Many more difficulties and objections there are, which occur at first view against this hypothesis; but I shall only add that it is liable to all the absurdities of the common hypotheses, in making a created world exist otherwise than in the mind of a spirit. Beside all which it hath this peculiar to itself; that it makes that material world serve to no purpose. And if it pass for a good argument against other hypotheses in the sciences, that they suppose Nature or the divine wisdom to make something in vain, or do that by tedious round-about methods, which might have been performed in a much more easy and compendious way, what shall we think of that hypothesis which supposes the whole world made in vain?

HYLAS. But what say you, are not you too of opinion that we see all things in God? If I mistake not, what you advance comes near it.

PHILONOUS. Few men think, yet all will have opinions. Hence men's opinions are superficial and confused. It is nothing strange that tenets, which in themselves are ever so different, should nevertheless be confounded with each other by those who do not consider them attentively. I shall not therefore be surprised, if some men imagine that I run into the enthusiasm of Malbranche, though in truth I am very remote from it. He builds on the most abstract general ideas, which I entirely disclaim. He asserts an absolute external world, which I deny. He maintains that we are deceived by our senses, and know not the real natures or the true forms and figures of extended beings; of all which I hold the direct contrary. So that upon the whole there are no principles more fundamentally opposite than his and mine.[1] It must be owned I entirely agree with what the holy Scripture saith, *that in God we live, and move, and have our being.* But that we see things in his essence after the manner above set forth, I am far from believing. Take here in brief my meaning.[2] It is evident that the things I perceive are my own ideas, and that no idea can exist unless it be in a mind. Nor is it less plain that these ideas or things by me perceived, either themselves or their archetypes, exist independently of my mind, since I know myself not to be their author, it being out of my power to determine at pleasure, what particular ideas I shall be affected with upon opening my eyes or ears. They must therefore exist in some other mind, whose will it is they should be exhibited to me. The things, I say, immediately perceived, are ideas or sensations, call them which you will. But how can any idea or sensation exist in, or be produced by, anything but a mind or spirit? This indeed is inconceivable; and to assert that which is inconceivable, is to talk nonsense: is it not?

HYLAS. Without doubt.

PHILONOUS. But on the other hand, it is very conceivable that they should exist in, and be produced by, a spirit; since this is no more than I daily experience in myself, inasmuch as I perceive numberless ideas; and

[1] [*Few men think ... than his and mine* added in 1734 edition.]
[2] [The difficult argument for God's existence here summarized occurs only in DHP. The thought is as follows: Since I am not the author of my ideas of sense, which are involuntary, they ('or their archetypes') must exist *quite* independently of my perceiving them (i.e., they would have existed, even if I had not perceived them.) Such ideas, *wholly* independent of me, must (since ideas are intrinsically dependent beings) exist in the mind of their author, upon whom they are *wholly* dependent. i.e. God now performs both functions of spiritual substance in relation to ideas of sense: whereas in PHK they are caused by God but 'exist in' or are 'supported by' their human perceiver (see editor's Introduction, p. xvi). Thus Berkeley has (1) adopted a conception of reality formally like the realist's, for whom physical objects are entirely independent of the perceiver, and (2) followed Locke *et al.* in taking the involuntariness of ideas of sense as evidence that there are such independent, real things (cf. Locke's *Essay* 4.11.5.). The phrase 'exhibited to me' suggests that these divine ideas are identical with the ideas that I perceive, but 'or their archetypes' (cf. DHP III *248* and *254*) seems designed to leave the question open. Both expressions suggest that God's ideas exist 'during the intervals between the times of my perceiving them', but Berkeley does not actually say so here. That must be because he took it as said, however, since later allusions back to the argument are explicit on the point: i.e. DHP III *230* and *236*. On peculiarities of God's ideas, see DHP III *241* and *254*.]

by an act of my Will can form a great variety of them, and raise them up in my imagination: though it must be confessed, these creatures of the fancy are not altogether so distinct, so strong, vivid, and permanent, as those perceived by my senses, which latter are called *real things*. From all which I conclude, *there is a mind which affects me every moment with all the sensible impressions I perceive*. And from the variety, order, and manner of these, I conclude the Author of them to be *wise, powerful, and good, beyond comprehension*. Mark it well; I do not say, I see things by perceiving that which represents them in the intelligible substance of God. This I do not understand; but I say, the things by me perceived are known by the understanding, and produced by the will, of an infinite spirit. And is not all this most plain and evident? Is there any more in it, than what a little observation of our own minds, and that which passes in them not only enableth us to conceive, but also obligeth us to acknowledge?

HYLAS. I think I understand you very clearly; and own the proof you give of a Deity seems no less evident, than it is surprising. But allowing that God is the Supreme and Universal Cause of all things, yet may not there be still a third nature besides spirits and ideas? May we not admit a subordinate and limited cause of our ideas? In a word, may there not for all that be *matter?*

PHILONOUS. How often must I inculcate the same thing? You allow the things immediately perceived by sense to exist nowhere without the mind: but there is nothing perceived by sense, which is not perceived immediately: therefore there is nothing sensible that exists without the mind. The matter therefore which you still insist on, is something intelligible, I suppose; something that may be discovered by reason, and not by sense.

HYLAS. You are in the right.

216 PHILONOUS. Pray let me know what reasoning your belief of matter is grounded on; and what this matter is in your present sense of it.

HYLAS. I find myself affected with various ideas, whereof I know I am not the cause; neither are they the cause of themselves, or of one another, or capable of subsisting by themselves, as being altogether inactive, fleeting, dependent beings. They have therefore some cause distinct from me and them: of which I pretend to know no more, than that it is *the cause of my ideas*. And this thing, whatever it be, I call matter.

PHILONOUS. Tell me, Hylas, hath everyone a liberty to change the current proper signification annexed to a common name in any language? For example, suppose a traveller should tell you, that in a certain country men might pass unhurt through the fire; and, upon explaining himself, you found he meant by the word *fire* that which others call *water*: or if he should assert there are trees which walk upon two legs, meaning men by the term *trees*. Would you think this reasonable?

HYLAS. No; I should think it very absurd. Common custom is the standard of propriety in language. And for any man to affect speaking improperly, is to pervert the use of speech, and can never serve to a better purpose, than to protract and multiply disputes where there is no difference in opinion.

PHILONOUS. And doth not *matter*, in the common current acceptation of the word, signify an extended, solid, moveable, unthinking, inactive substance?

HYLAS. It doth.

PHILONOUS. And hath it not been made evident, that no such substance can possibly exist? And though it should be allowed to exist, yet how can that which is *inactive* be a *cause*; or that which is *unthinking* be a *cause of thought*? You may indeed, if you please, annex to the word *matter* a contrary meaning to what is vulgarly received; and tell me you understand by it an unextended, thinking, active being, which is the cause of our ideas. But what else is this, than to play with words, and run into that very fault you just now condemned with so much reason? I do by no means find fault with your reasoning, in that you collect a cause from the *phenomena*: but I deny that the cause deducible by reason can properly be termed *matter*.

217 HYLAS. There is indeed something in what you say. But I am afraid you do not thoroughly comprehend my meaning. I would by no means be thought to deny that God or an Infinite Spirit is the supreme cause of all things. All I contend for, is, that subordinate to the supreme agent there is a cause of a limited and inferior nature, which concurs in the production of our ideas, not by any act of will or spiritual efficiency, but by that kind of action which belongs to matter, *viz. motion*.

PHILONOUS. I find, you are at every turn relapsing into your old exploded conceit, of a moveable and consequently an extended substance existing without the mind. What! Have you already forgot you were convinced, or are you willing I should repeat what has been said on that head? In truth this is not fair dealing in you, still to suppose the being of that which you have so often acknowledged to have no being. But not to insist farther on what has been so largely handled, I ask whether all your ideas are not perfectly passive and inert, including nothing of action in them?

HYLAS. They are.

PHILONOUS. And are sensible qualities anything else but ideas?

HYLAS. How often have I acknowledged that they are not?

PHILONOUS. But is not motion a sensible quality?

HYLAS. It is.

PHILONOUS. Consequently it is no action.

HYLAS. I agree with you. And indeed it is very plain, that when I stir my finger, it remains passive; but my will which produced the motion, is active.

PHILONOUS. Now I desire to know in the first place, whether motion being allowed to be no action, you can conceive any action besides volition: and in the second place, whether to say something and conceive nothing be not to talk nonsense: and lastly, whether having considered the premises, you do not perceive that to suppose any efficient or active cause of our ideas, other than *spirit*, is highly absurd and unreasonable?

HYLAS. I give up the point entirely. But though matter may not be a cause, yet what hinders its being an *instrument* subservient to the supreme agent in the production of our ideas?

PHILONOUS. An instrument, say you; pray what may be the figure, springs, wheels, and motions of that instrument?

HYLAS. Those I pretend to determine nothing of, both the substance and its qualities being entirely unknown to me.

PHILONOUS. What? You are then of opinion, it is made up of unknown parts, that it hath unknown motions, and an unknown shape.   *218*

HYLAS. I do not believe it hath any figure or motion at all, being already convinced, that no sensible qualities can exist in an unperceiving substance.

PHILONOUS. But what notion is it possible to frame of an instrument void of all sensible qualities, even extension itself?

HYLAS. I do not pretend to have any notion of it.

PHILONOUS. And what reason have you to think, this unknown, this inconceivable somewhat doth exist? Is it that you imagine God cannot act as well without it, or that you find by experience the use of some such thing, when you form ideas in your own mind?

HYLAS. You are always teasing me for reasons of my belief. Pray, what reasons have you not to believe it?

PHILONOUS. It is to me a sufficient reason not to believe the existence of anything, if I see no reason for believing it. But not to insist on reasons for believing, you will not so much as let me know what it is you would have me believe, since you say you have no manner of notion of it. After all, let me entreat you to consider whether it be like a philosopher, or even like a man of common sense, to pretend to believe you know not what, and you know not why.

HYLAS. Hold, Philonous. When I tell you matter is an *instrument*, I do not mean altogether nothing. It is true, I know not the particular kind of instrument; but however I have some notion of *instrument in general*, which I apply to it.

PHILONOUS. But what if it should prove that there is something, even in the most general notion of *instrument*, as taken in a distinct sense from *cause*, which makes the use of it inconsistent with the divine attributes?

HYLAS. Make that appear, and I shall give up the point.

PHILONOUS. What mean you by the general nature or notion of *instrument*?

HYLAS. That which is common to all particular instruments, composeth the general notion.

PHILONOUS. Is it not common to all instruments, that they are applied to the doing those things only, which cannot be performed by the mere act of our wills? Thus for instance, I never use an instrument to move my finger, because it is done by a volition. But I should use one, if I were to remove part of a rock, or tear up a tree by the roots. Are you of the same mind? Or can you shew any example where an instrument   *219* is made use of in producing an effect immediately depending on the will of the agent?

HYLAS. I own, I cannot.

PHILONOUS. How therefore can you suppose, that an all-perfect spirit, on whose will all things have an absolute and immediate dependence, should need an instrument in his operations, or not needing it make use of it? Thus it seems to me that you are obliged to own the use of a lifeless inactive instrument, to be incompatible with the infinite perfection of God; that is, by your own confession, to give up the point.

HYLAS. It doth not readily occur what I can answer you.

PHILONOUS. But methinks you should be ready to own the truth, when it hath been fairly proved to you. We indeed, who are beings of finite powers, are forced to make use of instruments. And the use of an instrument sheweth the agent to be limited by rules of another's prescription, and that he cannot obtain his end, but in such a way and by such conditions. Whence it seems a clear consequence, that the supreme unlimited agent useth no tool or instrument at all. The will of an omnipotent spirit is no sooner exerted than executed, without the application of means, which, if they are employed by inferior agents, it is not upon account of any real efficacy that is in them, or necessary aptitude to produce any effect, but merely in compliance with the laws of Nature, or those conditions prescribed to them by the first cause, who is himself above all limitation or prescription whatsoever.

HYLAS. I will no longer maintain that matter is an instrument. However, I would not be understood to give up its existence neither; since, notwithstanding what hath been said, it may still be an *occasion*.

PHILONOUS. How many shapes is your matter to take? Or how often must it be proved not to exist, before you are content to part with it? But to say no more of this (though by all the laws of disputation I may justly blame you for so frequently changing the signification of the principal term) I would fain know what you mean by affirming that matter is an occasion, having already denied it to be a cause. And when you have shewn in what sense you understand *occasion*, pray in the next place be pleased to shew me what reason induceth you to believe there is such an occasion of our ideas.

HYLAS. As to the first point: by *occasion* I mean an inactive unthinking being, at the presence whereof God excites ideas in our minds.

PHILONOUS. And what may be the nature of that inactive unthinking being?

HYLAS. I know nothing of its nature.

PHILONOUS. Proceed then to the second point, and assign some reason why we should allow an existence to this inactive, unthinking, unknown thing.

HYLAS. When we see ideas produced in our minds after an orderly and constant manner, it is natural to think they have some fixed and regular occasions, at the presence of which they are excited.

PHILONOUS. You acknowledge then God alone to be the cause of our ideas, and that he causes them at the presence of those occasions.

HYLAS. That is my opinion.

PHILONOUS. Those things which you say are present to God, without doubt He perceives.

HYLAS. Certainly; otherwise they could not be to Him an occasion of acting.

PHILONOUS. Not to insist now on your making sense of this hypothesis, or answering all the puzzling questions and difficulties it is liable to: I only ask whether the order and regularity observable in the series of our ideas, or the course of Nature, be not sufficiently accounted for by the wisdom and power of God; and whether it doth not derogate from those attributes, to suppose He is influenced, directed, or put in mind, when and what He is to act, by any unthinking substance. And lastly whether, in case I granted all you contend for, it would make anything to your purpose, it not being easy to conceive how the external or absolute existence of an unthinking substance, distinct from its being perceived, can be inferred from my allowing that there are certain things perceived by the mind of God, which are to Him the occasion of producing ideas in us.

HYLAS. I am perfectly at a loss what to think, this notion of *occasion* seeming now altogether as groundless as the rest.

PHILONOUS. Do you not at length perceive, that in all these different acceptations of *matter*, you have been only supposing you know not what, for no manner of reason, and to no kind of use?

HYLAS. I freely own myself less fond of my notions, since they have been so accurately examined. But still, methinks I have some confused perception that there is such a thing as *matter*.

PHILONOUS. Either you perceive the being of matter immediately, or *221* mediately. If immediately, pray inform me by which of the senses you perceive it. If mediately, let me know by what reasoning it is inferred from those things which you perceive immediately. So much for the perception. Then for the matter itself, I ask whether it is object, *substratum*, cause, instrument, or occasion? You have already pleaded for each of these, shifting your notions, and making matter to appear sometimes in one shape, then in another. And what you have offered hath been disapproved and rejected by yourself. If you have anything new to advance, I would gladly hear it.

HYLAS. I think I have already offered all I had to say on those heads. I am at a loss what more to urge.

PHILONOUS. And yet you are loth to part with your old prejudice. But to make you quit it more easily, I desire that, beside what has been hitherto suggested, you will farther consider whether, upon supposition that matter exists, you can possibly conceive how you should be affected by it? Or supposing it did not exist, whether it be not evident you might for all that be affected with the same ideas you now are, and consequently have the very same reasons to believe its existence that you now can have?

HYLAS. I acknowledge it is possible we might perceive all things just as we do now, though there was no matter in the world; neither can I conceive, if there be matter, how it should produce any idea in our minds. And I do farther grant, you have entirely satisfied me, that it is impossible there should be such a thing as matter in any of the foregoing acceptations. But still I cannot help supposing that there is *matter* in some sense or other. What that is I do not indeed pretend to determine.

PHILONOUS. I do not expect you should define exactly the nature of that unknown being. Only be pleased to tell me, whether it is a substance: and if so, whether you can suppose a substance without accidents; or in case you suppose it to have accidents or qualities, I desire you will let me know what those qualities are, at least what is meant by matter's supporting them.

HYLAS. We have already argued on those points. I have no more to say to them. But to prevent any farther questions, let me tell you, I at present understand by *matter* neither substance nor accident, thinking nor extended being, neither cause, instrument, nor occasion, but something entirely unknown, distinct from all these.

222 PHILONOUS. It seems then you include in your present notion of matter, nothing but the general abstract idea of *entity*.

HYLAS. Nothing else, save only that I super-add to this general idea the negation of all those particular things, qualities, or ideas that I perceive, imagine, or in any wise apprehend.

PHILONOUS. Pray where do you suppose this unknown matter to exist?

HYLAS. Oh Philonous! now you think you have entangled me; for if I say it exists in place, then you will infer that it exists in the mind, since it is agreed, that place or extension exists only in the mind: but I am not ashamed to own my ignorance. I know not where it exists; only I am sure it exists not in place. There is a negative answer for you: and you must expect no other to all the questions you put for the future about matter.

PHILONOUS. Since you will not tell me where it exists, be pleased to inform me after what manner you suppose it to exist, or what you mean by its *existence*.

HYLAS. It neither thinks nor acts, neither perceives, nor is perceived.

PHILONOUS. But what is there positive in your abstracted notion of its existence?

HYLAS. Upon a nice observation, I do not find I have any positive notion or meaning at all. I tell you again I am not ashamed to own my ignorance. I know not what is meant by its *existence*, or how it exists.

PHILONOUS. Continue, good Hylas, to act the same ingenuous part, and tell me sincerely whether you can frame a distinct idea of entity in general, prescinded from and exclusive of all thinking and corporeal beings, all particular things whatsoever.

HYLAS. Hold, let me think a little—I profess, Philonous, I do not find that I can. At first glance methought I had some dilute and airy notion of pure entity in abstract; but upon closer attention it hath quite vanished out of sight. The more I think on it, the more am I confirmed in my prudent resolution of giving none but negative answers, and not pretending to the least degree of any positive knowledge or conception of matter, its *where*, its *how*, its *entity*, or anything belonging to it.

PHILONOUS. When therefore you speak of the existence of matter, you have not any notion in your mind.

HYLAS. None at all.

PHILONOUS. Pray tell me if the case stands not thus: at first, from a belief of material substance you would have it that the immediate objects existed without the mind; then that their archetypes; then causes; next *223* instruments; then occasions: lastly, *something in general*, which being interpreted proves *nothing*. So matter comes to nothing. What think you, Hylas, is not this a fair summary of your whole proceeding?

HYLAS. Be that as it will, yet I still insist upon it, that our not being able to conceive a thing, is no argument against its existence.

PHILONOUS. That from a cause, effect, operation, sign, or other circumstance, there may reasonably be inferred the existence of a thing not immediately perceived, and that it were absurd for any man to argue against the existence of that thing, from his having no direct and positive notion of it, I freely own. But where there is nothing of all this; where neither reason nor revelation induce us to believe the existence of a thing; where we have not even a relative notion of it; where an abstraction is made from perceiving and being perceived, from spirit and idea: lastly, where there is not so much as the most inadequate or faint idea pretended to: I will not indeed thence conclude against the reality of any notion or existence of any thing: but my inference shall be, that you mean nothing at all: that you employ words to no manner of purpose, without any design or signification whatsoever. And I leave it to you to consider how mere jargon should be treated.

HYLAS. To deal frankly with you, Philonous, your arguments seem in themselves unanswerable, but they have not so great an effect on me as to produce that entire conviction, that hearty acquiescence which attends demonstration. I find myself still relapsing into an obscure surmise of I know not what, *matter*.

PHILONOUS. But are you not sensible, Hylas, that two things must concur to take away all scruple, and work a plenary assent in the mind? Let a visible object be set in never so clear a light, yet if there is any imperfection in the sight, or if the eye is not directed towards it, it will not be distinctly seen. And though a demonstration be never so well grounded and fairly proposed, yet if there is withal a stain of prejudice, or a wrong bias on the understanding, can it be expected on a sudden to perceive clearly and adhere firmly to the truth? No, there is need of time and pains: the attention must be awakened and detained by a frequent repetition of the same thing placed oft in the same, oft in different lights. I have said it already, and find I must still repeat and inculcate, that it is an unaccountable licence you take in pretending to maintain you *224* know not what, for you know not what reason, to you know not what purpose. Can this be paralleled in any art or science, any sect or profession of men? Or is there anything so barefacedly groundless and unreasonable to be met with even in the lowest of common conversation? But perhaps you will still say, matter may exist, though at the same time you neither know what is meant by *matter*, or by its *existence*. This indeed is surprising, and the more so because it is altogether voluntary, you not being led to it by any one reason; for I challenge you to shew me that thing in Nature which needs matter to explain or account for it.

HYLAS. The reality of things cannot be maintained without supposing the existence of matter. And is not this, think you, a good reason why I should be earnest in its defence?

PHILONOUS. The reality of things! What things, sensible or intelligible?

HYLAS. Sensible things.

PHILONOUS. My glove, for example?

HYLAS. That or any other thing perceived by the senses.

PHILONOUS. But to fix on some particular thing; is it not a sufficient evidence to me of the existence of this *glove*, that I see it, and feel it, and wear it? Or if this will not do, how is it possible I should be assured of the reality of this thing, which I actually see in this place, by supposing that some unknown thing which I never did or can see, exists after an unknown manner, in an unknown place, or in no place at all? How can the supposed reality of that which is intangible, be a proof that anything tangible really exists? or of that which is invisible, that any visible thing, or in general of any thing which is imperceptible, that a perceptible exists? Do but explain this, and I shall think nothing too hard for you.

HYLAS. Upon the whole, I am content to own the existence of matter is highly improbable; but the direct and absolute impossibility of it does not appear to me.

PHILONOUS. But granting matter to be possible, yet upon that account merely it can have no more claim to existence, than a golden mountain or a centaur.

HYLAS. I acknowledge it; but still you do not deny it is possible; and that which is possible, for aught you know, may actually exist.

PHILONOUS. I deny it to be possible; and have, if I mistake not, evidently
225 proved from your own concessions that it is not. In the common sense of the word *matter*, is there any more implied, than an extended, solid, figured, moveable substance existing without the mind? And have not you acknowledged over and over, that you have seen evident reason for denying the possibility of such a substance?

HYLAS. True, but that is only one sense of the term *matter*.

PHILONOUS. But is it not the only proper genuine received sense? And if matter in such a sense be proved impossible, may it not be thought with good grounds absolutely impossible? Else how could anything be proved impossible? Or indeed how could there be any proof at all one way or other, to a man who takes the liberty to unsettle and change the common signification of words?

HYLAS. I thought philosophers might be allowed to speak more accurately than the vulgar, and were not always confined to the common acceptation of a term.

PHILONOUS. But this now mentioned is the common received sense among philosophers themselves. But not to insist on that, have you not been allowed to take matter in what sense you pleased? And have you not used this privilege in the utmost extent, sometimes entirely changing, at others leaving out or putting into the definition of it whatever for the present best served your design, contrary to all the known rules of reason and logic? And hath not this shifting unfair method of yours spun out our dispute to an unnecessary length; matter having been particularly examined, and by your own confession refuted in each of those senses? And can any more be required to prove the absolute impossibility of a thing, than the proving it impossible in every particular sense, that either you or anyone else understands it in?

HYLAS. But I am not so thoroughly satisfied that you have proved the impossibility of matter in the last most obscure abstracted and indefinite sense.

PHILONOUS. When is a thing shewn to be impossible?

HYLAS. When a repugnancy is demonstrated between the ideas comprehended in its definition.

PHILONOUS. But where there are no ideas, there no repugnancy can be demonstrated between ideas.

HYLAS. I agree with you.

PHILONOUS. Now in that which you call the obscure indefinite sense of the word *matter*, it is plain, by your own confession, there was included no idea at all, no sense except an unknown sense, which is the same thing as none. You are not therefore to expect I should prove a repugnancy between ideas where there are no ideas; or the impossibility of matter taken in an *unknown* sense, that is no sense at all. My business was only to shew, you meant *nothing*; and this you were brought to own. So that in all your various senses, you have been shewed either to mean nothing at all, or if anything, an absurdity. And if this be not sufficient to prove the impossibility of a thing, I desire you will let me know what is.

HYLAS. I acknowledge you have proved that matter is impossible; nor do I see what more can be said in defence of it. But at the same time that I give up this, I suspect all my other notions. For surely none could be more seemingly evident than this once was: and yet it now seems as false and absurd as ever it did true before. But I think we have discussed the point sufficiently for the present. The remaining part of the day I would willingly spend, in running over in my thoughts the several heads of this morning's conversation, and to-morrow shall be glad to meet you here again about the same time.

PHILONOUS. I will not fail to attend you.

THE THIRD DIALOGUE

227 PHILONOUS. Tell me, Hylas, what are the fruits of yesterday's meditation? Hath it confirmed you in the same mind you were in at parting? or have you since seen cause to change your opinion?

HYLAS. Truly my opinion is, that all our opinions are alike vain and uncertain. What we approve to-day, we condemn to-morrow. We keep a stir about knowledge, and spend our lives in the pursuit of it, when, alas! we know nothing all the while: nor do I think it possible for us ever to know anything in this life. Our faculties are too narrow and too few. Nature certainly never intended us for speculation.

PHILONOUS. What! say you we can know nothing, Hylas?

HYLAS. There is not that single thing in the world, whereof we can know the real nature, or what it is in itself.

PHILONOUS. Will you tell me I do not really know what fire or water is?

HYLAS. You may indeed know that fire appears hot, and water fluid: but this is no more than knowing what sensations are produced in your own mind, upon the application of fire and water to your organs of sense. Their internal constitution, their true and real nature, you are utterly in the dark as to *that*.

PHILONOUS. Do I not know this to be a real stone that I stand on, and that which I see before my eyes to be a real tree?

HYLAS. *Know?* No, it is impossible you or any man alive should know it. All you know, is, that you have such a certain idea or appearance in your own mind. But what is this to the real tree or stone? I tell you, that colour, figure, and hardness, which you perceive, are not the real natures of those things, or in the least like them. The same may be said of all other real things or corporeal substances which compose the world. They have none of them anything in themselves, like those sensible qualities by us perceived. We should not therefore pretend to affirm or know anything of them as they are in their own nature.

PHILONOUS. But surely, Hylas, I can distinguish gold, for example, from
228 iron: and how could this be if I knew not what either truly was?

HYLAS. Believe me, Philonous, you can only distinguish between your own ideas. That yellowness, that weight, and other sensible qualities, think you they are really in the gold? They are only relative to the senses, and have no absolute existence in Nature. And in pretending to distinguish the species of real things, by the appearances in your mind, you may perhaps act as wisely as he that should conclude two men were of a different species, because their clothes were not of the same colour.

PHILONOUS. It seems then we are altogether put off with the appearances of things, and those false ones too. The very meat I eat, and the cloth I wear, have nothing in them like what I see and feel.

HYLAS. Even so.

PHILONOUS. But is it not strange the whole world should be thus imposed on, and so foolish as to believe their senses? And yet I know not how it is, but men eat, and drink, and sleep, and perform all the offices of life as comfortably and conveniently, as if they really knew the things they are conversant about.

HYLAS. They do so: but you know ordinary practice does not require a nicety of speculative knowledge. Hence the vulgar retain their mistakes, and for all that, make a shift to bustle through the affairs of life. But philosophers know better things.

PHILONOUS. You mean, they know that they *know nothing*.

HYLAS. That is the very top and perfection of human knowledge.

PHILONOUS. But are you all this while in earnest, Hylas; and are you seriously persuaded that you know nothing real in the world? Suppose you are going to write, would you not call for pen, ink, and paper, like another man; and do you not know what it is you call for?

HYLAS. How often must I tell you, that I know not the real nature of any one thing in the universe? I may indeed upon occasion make use of pen, ink, and paper. But what any one of them is in its own true nature, I declare positively I know not. And the same is true with regard to every other corporeal thing. And, what is more, we are not only ignorant of the true and real nature of things, but even of their existence. It cannot be denied that we perceive such certain appearances or ideas; but it cannot be concluded from thence that bodies really exist. Nay, now I think on it, I must agreeably to my former concessions farther 229 declare, that it is impossible any real corporeal thing should exist in Nature.

PHILONOUS. You amaze me. Was ever anything more wild and extravagant than the notions you now maintain: and is it not evident you are led into all these extravagancies by the belief of *material substance?* This makes you dream of those unknown natures in everything. It is this occasions your distinguishing between the reality and sensible appearances of things. It is to this you are indebted for being ignorant of what everybody else knows perfectly well. Nor is this all: you are not only ignorant of the true nature of everything, but you know not whether anything really exists, or whether there are any true natures at all; forasmuch as you attribute to your material beings an absolute or external existence, wherein you suppose their reality consists. And as you are forced in the end to acknowledge such an existence means either a direct repugnancy, or nothing at all, it follows that you are obliged to pull down your own hypothesis of material substance, and positively to deny the real existence of any part of the universe. And so you are plunged into the deepest and most deplorable *scepticism* that ever man was. Tell me, Hylas, is it not as I say?

HYLAS. I agree with you. *Material substance* was no more than an hypothesis, and a false and groundless one too. I will no longer spend my breath in defence of it. But whatever hypothesis you advance, or whatsoever scheme of things you introduce in its stead, I doubt not it will appear every whit as false: let me but be allowed to question you upon it. That is, suffer me to serve you in your own kind, and I warrant it shall conduct you through as many perplexities and contradictions, to the very same state of scepticism that I myself am in at present.

PHILONOUS. I assure you, Hylas, I do not pretend to frame any hypothesis at all. I am of a vulgar cast, simple enough to believe my senses, and leave things as I find them. To be plain, it is my opinion, that the real things are those very things I see and feel, and perceive by my senses. These I know, and finding they answer all the necessities and purposes of life, have no reason to be solicitous about any other unknown beings. A piece of sensible bread, for instance, would stay my stomach better than ten thousand times as much of that insensible, unintelligible, real bread you speak of. It is likewise my opinion, that colours and other
230 sensible qualities are on the objects. I cannot for my life help thinking that snow is white, and fire hot. You indeed, who by *snow* and *fire* mean certain external, unperceived, unperceiving substances, are in the right to deny whiteness or heat, to be affections inherent in them. But I, who understand by those words the things I see and feel, am obliged to think like other folks. And as I am no sceptic with regard to the nature of things, so neither am I as to their existence. That a thing should be really perceived by my senses, and at the same time not really exist, is to me a plain contradiction; since I cannot prescind or abstract, even in thought, the existence of a sensible thing from its being perceived. Wood, stones, fire, water, flesh, iron, and the like things, which I name and discourse of, are things that I know. And I should not have known them, but that I perceived them by my senses; and things perceived by the senses are immediately perceived; and things immediately perceived are ideas; and ideas cannot exist without the mind; their existence therefore consists in being perceived; when therefore they are actually perceived, there can be no doubt of their existence. Away then with all that scepticism, all those ridiculous philosophical doubts. What a jest is it for a philosopher to question the existence of sensible things, till he hath it proved to him from the veracity of God: or to pretend our knowledge in this point falls short of intuition or demonstration? I might as well doubt of my own being, as of the being of those things I actually see and feel.

HYLAS. Not so fast, Philonous: you say you cannot conceive how sensible things should exist without the mind. Do you not?

PHILONOUS. I do.

HYLAS. Supposing you were annihilated, cannot you conceive it possible, that things perceivable by sense may still exist?

PHILONOUS. I can; but then it must be in another mind. When I deny sensible things an existence out of the mind, I do not mean my mind in particular, but all minds. Now it is plain they have an existence exterior to my mind, since I find them by experience to be independent of it. There is therefore some other mind wherein they exist, during the intervals of my perceiving them: as likewise they did before *231* my birth, and would do after my supposed annihilation. And as the same is true, with regard to all other finite created spirits; it necessarily follows, there is an *omnipresent eternal Mind*, which knows and comprehends all things, and exhibits them to our view in such a manner, and according to such rules as he himself hath ordained, and are by us termed the *Laws of Nature*.

HYLAS. Answer me, Philonous. Are all our ideas perfectly inert beings? Or have they any agency included in them?

PHILONOUS. They are altogether passive and inert.

HYLAS. And is not God an agent, a being purely active?

PHILONOUS. I acknowledge it.

HYLAS. No idea therefore can be like unto, or represent the nature of God.

PHILONOUS. It cannot.

HYLAS. Since therefore you have no idea of the mind of God, how can you conceive it possible, that things should exist in his mind? Or, if you can conceive the mind of God without having an idea of it, why may not I be allowed to conceive the existence of matter, notwithstanding that I have no idea of it?

PHILONOUS. As to your first question; I own I have properly no idea, either of God or any other spirit; for these being active, cannot be represented by things perfectly inert, as our ideas are. I do nevertheless know, that I who am a spirit or thinking substance, exist as certainly, as I know my ideas exist. Farther, I know what I mean by the terms *I* and *myself*; and I know this immediately, or intuitively, though I do not perceive it as I perceive a triangle, a colour, or a sound. The mind, spirit or soul, is that indivisible unextended thing, which thinks, acts, and perceives. I say *indivisible*, because unextended; and *unextended*, because extended, figured, moveable things, are ideas; and that which perceives ideas, which thinks and wills, is plainly itself no idea, nor like an idea. Ideas are things inactive, and perceived: and spirits a sort of beings altogether different from them. I do not therefore say my soul is an idea, or like an idea. However, taking the word *idea* in a large sense, my soul may be said to furnish me with an idea, that is, an image, or likeness of God, though indeed extremely inadequate. For all the notion I have of God, is obtained by reflecting on my own soul heightening its powers, and removing its imperfections. I have therefore, though not an inactive *232* idea, yet in myself some sort of an active thinking image of the Deity. And though I perceive Him not by sense, yet I have a notion of Him, or know Him by reflexion and reasoning. My own mind and my own ideas I have an immediate knowledge of; and by the help of these, do mediately apprehend the possibility of the existence of other spirits and ideas. Farther, from my own being, and from the dependency I find in myself and my ideas, I do by an act of reason, necessarily infer the existence of a God, and of all created things in the mind of God. So much for your first question. For the second: I suppose by this time you can answer it yourself. For you neither perceive matter objectively, as you do an inactive being or idea, nor know it, as you do yourself by a reflex act: neither do you mediately apprehend it by similitude of the one or the other: nor yet collect it by reasoning from that which you know immediately. All which makes the case of *matter* widely different from that of the *Deity*.

HYLAS. You say your own soul[1] supplies you with some sort of an idea or image of God. But at the same time you acknowledge you have, properly speaking, no idea of your own soul. You even affirm that spirits are a sort of beings altogether different from ideas. Consequently that no idea can be like a spirit. We have therefore no idea of any spirit. You admit nevertheless that there is spiritual substance, although you have no idea of it; while you deny there can be such a thing as material substance, because you have no notion or idea of it. Is this fair dealing? To act consistently, you must either admit matter or reject spirit. What say you to this?

PHILONOUS. I say in the first place, that I do not deny the existence of material substance, merely because I have no notion of it, but because the notion of it is inconsistent, or in other words, because it is repugnant that there should be a notion of it. Many things, for ought I know, may exist, whereof neither I nor any other man hath or can have any idea or notion whatsoever. But then those things must be possible, that is, nothing inconsistent must be included in their definition. I say secondly, that although we believe things to exist which we do not perceive; yet we may not believe that any particular thing exists, without some reason for such belief; but I have no reason for believing the existence of matter. I have no immediate intuition thereof: neither can I mediately from my sensations, ideas, notions, actions or passions, infer an unthinking, unperceiving, inactive substance, either by probable deduction, or necessary consequence. Whereas the being of myself, that is, my own soul, mind or thinking principle, I evidently know by reflexion. You will forgive me if I repeat the same things in answer to the same objections. In the very notion or definition of material substance, there is included a manifest repugnance and inconsistency. But this cannot be said of the notion of spirit. That ideas should exist in what doth not perceive, or be produced by what doth not act, is repugnant. But it is no repugnancy to say, that a perceiving thing should be the subject of ideas, or an active thing the cause of them. It is granted we have neither an immediate evidence nor a demonstrative knowledge of the existence of other finite

233

---

[1] [*You say your own soul . . . between spirit and matter* (i.e., next four speeches) added in 1734 edition.]

spirits; but it will not thence follow that such spirits are on a foot with material substances: if to suppose the one be inconsistent, and it be not inconsistent to suppose the other; if the one can be inferred by no argument, and there is a probability for the other; if we see signs and effects indicating distinct finite agents like ourselves, and see no sign or symptom whatever that leads to a rational belief of matter. I say lastly, that I have a notion of spirit, though I have not, strictly speaking, an idea of it. I do not perceive it as an idea or by means of an idea, but know it by reflexion.

HYLAS. Notwithstanding all you have said, to me it seems, that according to your own way of thinking, and in consequence of your own principles, it should follow that you are only a system of floating ideas, without any substance to support them. Words are not to be used without a meaning. And as there is no more meaning in spiritual substance than in material substance, the one is to be exploded as well as the other.

PHILONOUS. How often must I repeat, that I know or am conscious of my own being; and that I myself am not my ideas, but somewhat else, a thinking active principle that perceives, knows, wills, and operates about ideas. I know that I, one and the same self, perceive both colours and *234* sounds: that a colour cannot perceive a sound, nor a sound a colour: that I am therefore one individual principle, distinct from colour and sound; and, for the same reason, from all other sensible things and inert ideas. But I am not in like manner conscious either of the existence or essence of matter. On the contrary, I know that nothing inconsistent can exist, and that the existence of matter implies an inconsistency. Farther, I know what I mean, when I affirm that there is a spiritual substance or support of ideas, that is, that a spirit knows and perceives ideas. But I do not know what is meant, when it is said, that an unperceiving substance hath inherent in it and supports either ideas or the archetypes of ideas. There is therefore upon the whole no parity of case between spirit and matter.

HYLAS. I own myself satisfied in this point. But do you in earnest think, the real existence of sensible things consists in their being actually perceived? If so; how comes it that all mankind distinguish between them? Ask the first man you meet, and he shall tell you, *to be perceived* is one thing, and *to exist* is another.

PHILONOUS. I am content, Hylas, to appeal to the common sense of the world for the truth of my notion. Ask the gardener, why he thinks yonder cherry-tree exists in the garden, and he shall tell you, because he sees and feels it; in a word, because he perceives it by his senses. Ask him, why he thinks an orange-tree not to be there, and he shall tell you, because he does not perceive it. What he perceives by sense, that he terms a real being, and saith it *is*, or *exists*; but that which is not perceivable, the same, he saith, hath no being.

HYLAS. Yes, Philonous, I grant the existence of a sensible thing consists in being perceivable, but not in being actually perceived.

PHILONOUS. And what is perceivable but an idea? And can an idea exist without being actually perceived? These are points long since agreed between us.

HYLAS. But be your opinion never so true, yet surely you will not deny it is shocking, and contrary to the common sense of men. Ask the fellow,
235 whether yonder tree hath an existence out of his mind: what answer think you he would make?

PHILONOUS. The same that I should myself, to wit, that it doth exist out of his mind. But then to a Christian it cannot surely be shocking to say, the real tree existing without his mind is truly known and comprehended by (that is, *exists in*) the infinite mind of God. Probably he may not at first glance be aware of the direct and immediate proof there is of this, inasmuch as the very being of a tree, or any other sensible thing, implies a mind wherein it is. But the point itself he cannot deny. The question between the materialists and me is not, whether things have a real existence out of the mind of this or that person, but whether they have an absolute existence, distinct from being perceived by God, and exterior to all minds. This indeed some heathens and philosophers have affirmed, but whoever entertains notions of the Diety suitable to the Holy Scriptures, will be of another opinion.

HYLAS. But according to your notions, what difference is there between real things, and chimeras formed by the imagination, or the visions of a dream, since they are all equally in the mind?

PHILONOUS. The ideas formed by the imagination are faint and indistinct; they have besides an entire dependence on the will. But the ideas perceived by sense, that is, real things, are more vivid and clear, and being imprinted on the mind by a spirit distinct from us, have not a like dependence on our will. There is therefore no danger of confounding these with the foregoing: and there is as little of confounding them with the visions of a dream, which are dim, irregular, and confused. And though they should happen to be never so lively and natural, yet by their not being connected, and of a piece with the preceding and subsequent transactions of our lives, they might easily be distinguished from realities. In short, by whatever method you distinguish *things* from *chimeras* on your own scheme, the same, it is evident, will hold also upon mine. For it must be, I presume, by some perceived difference, and I am not for depriving you of any one thing that you perceive.

HYLAS. But still, Philonous, you hold, there is nothing in the world but spirits and ideas. And this, you must needs acknowledge, sounds very oddly.

PHILONOUS. I own the word *idea*, not being commonly used for *thing*, sounds something out of the way. My reason for using it was, because a necessary relation to the mind is understood to be implied by that
236 term; and it is now commonly used by philosophers, to denote the immediate objects of the understanding. But however oddly the proposition may sound in words, yet it includes nothing so very strange or shocking in its sense, which in effect amounts to no more than this, to wit, that there are only things perceiving, and things perceived; or that

every unthinking being is necessarily, and from the very nature of its existence, perceived by some mind; if not by any finite created mind, yet certainly by the infinite mind of God, in whom *we live, and move, and have our being*. Is this as strange as to say, the sensible qualities are not on the objects: or, that we cannot be sure of the existence of things, or know anything of their real natures, though we both see and feel them, and perceive them by all our senses?

HYLAS. And in consequence of this, must we not think there are no such things as physical or corporeal causes; but that a spirit is the immediate cause of all the *phenomena* in Nature? Can there be anything more extravagant than this?

PHILONOUS. Yes, it is infinitely more extravagant to say, a thing which is inert, operates on the mind, and which is unperceiving, is the cause of our perceptions.[1] Besides, that which to you, I know not for what reason, seems so extravagant, is no more than the Holy Scriptures assert in a hundred places. In them God is represented as the sole and immediate Author of all those effects, which some heathens and philosophers are wont to ascribe to Nature, matter, fate, or the like unthinking principle. This is so much the constant language of Scripture, that it were needless to confirm it by citations.

HYLAS. You are not aware, Philonous, that in making God the immediate author of all the motions in Nature, you make him the author of murder, sacrilege, adultery, and the like heinous sins.

PHILONOUS. In answer to that, I observe first, that the imputation of guilt is the same, whether a person commits an action with or without an instrument. In case therefore you suppose God to act by the mediation of an instrument, or occasion, called *matter*, you as truly make Him the author of sin as I, who think Him the immediate agent in all those operations vulgarly ascribed to Nature. I farther observe, that sin or moral turpitude doth not consist in the outward physical action or *237* motion, but in the internal deviation of the will from the laws of reason and religion. This is plain, in that the killing an enemy in a battle, or putting a criminal legally to death, is not thought sinful, though the outward act be the very same with that in the case of murder. Since therefore sin doth not consist in the physical action, the making God an immediate cause of all such actions, is not making him the author of sin. Lastly, I have nowhere said that God is the only agent who produces all the motions in bodies. It is true, I have denied there are any other agents beside spirits: but this is very consistent with allowing to thinking rational beings, in the production of motions, the use of limited powers, ultimately indeed derived from God, but immediately under the direction of their own wills, which is sufficient to entitle them to all the guilt of their actions.

[1] [1713 and 1725 editions: *perceptions, without any regard either to consistency, or the old known axiom:* Nothing can give to another that which it hath not itself.]

HYLAS. But the denying matter, Philonous, or corporeal substance; there is the point. You can never persuade me that this is not repugnant to the universal sense of mankind. Were our dispute to be determined by most voices, I am confident you would give up the point, without gathering the votes.

PHILONOUS. I wish both our opinions were fairly stated and submitted to the judgment of men who had plain common sense, without the prejudices of a learned education. Let me be represented as one who trusts his senses, who thinks he knows the things he sees and feels, and entertains no doubts, of their existence; and you fairly set forth with all your doubts, your paradoxes, and your scepticism about you, and I shall willingly acquiesce in the determination of any indifferent person. That there is no substance wherein ideas can exist beside spirit, is to me evident. And that the objects immediately perceived are ideas, is on all hands agreed. And that sensible qualities are objects immediately perceived, no one can deny. It is therefore evident there can be no *substratum* of those qualities but spirit, in which they exist, not by way of mode or property, but as a thing perceived in that which perceives it. I deny therefore that there is any unthinking *substratum* of the objects of sense, and in that acceptation that there is any material substance. But if by *material substance* is meant only sensible body, that which is seen and felt (and the unphilosophical part of the world, I dare say, mean no more) then I am more certain of matter's existence than you, or any other philosopher, pretend to be. If there be anything which makes the generality of mankind averse from the notions I espouse, it is a misapprehension that I deny the reality of sensible things: but as it is you who are guilty of that and not I, it follows that in truth their aversion is against your notions, and not mine. I do therefore assert that I am as certain as of my own being, that there are bodies or corporeal substances (meaning the things I perceive by my senses), and that granting this, the bulk of mankind will take no thought about, nor think themselves at all concerned in the fate of those unknown natures, and philosophical quiddities, which some men are so fond of.

HYLAS. What say you to this? Since, according to you, men judge of the reality of things by their senses, how can a man be mistaken in thinking the moon a plain lucid surface, about a foot in diameter; or a square tower, seen at a distance, round; or an oar, with one end in the water, crooked?

PHILONOUS. He is not mistaken with regard to the ideas he actually perceives; but in the inferences he makes from his present perceptions. Thus in the case of the oar, what he immediately perceives by sight is certainly crooked; and so far he is in the right. But if he thence conclude, that upon taking the oar out of the water he shall perceive the same crookedness; or that it would affect his touch, as crooked things are wont to do: in that he is mistaken. In like manner, if he shall conclude from what he perceives in one station, that in case he advances toward the moon or tower, he should still be affected with the like ideas,

238

he is mistaken. But his mistake lies not in what he perceives immediately and at present (it being a manifest contradiction to suppose he should err in respect of that) but in the wrong judgment he makes concerning the ideas he apprehends to be connected with those immediately perceived: or concerning the ideas that, from what he perceives at present, he imagines would be perceived in other circumstances. The case is the same with regard to the Copernican system. We do not here perceive any motion of the earth: but it were erroneous thence to conclude, that in case we were placed at as great a distance from that, as we are now from the other planets, we should not then perceive its motion.

HYLAS. I understand you; and must needs own you say things plausible enough: but give me leave to put you in mind of one thing. Pray, Philonous, were you not formerly as positive that matter existed, as *239* you are now that it does not?

PHILONOUS. I was. But here lies the difference. Before, my positiveness was founded without examination, upon prejudice; but now, after inquiry, upon evidence.

HYLAS. After all, it seems our dispute is rather about words than things. We agree in the thing, but differ in the name. That we are affected with ideas from without is evident; and it is no less evident, that there must be (I will not say archetypes, but) powers without the mind, corresponding to those ideas. And as these powers cannot subsist by themselves, there is some subject of them necessarily to be admitted, which I call *matter*, and you call *spirit*. This is all the difference.

PHILONOUS. Pray, Hylas, is that powerful being, or subject of powers, extended?

HYLAS. It hath not extension; but it hath the power to raise in you the idea of extension.

PHILONOUS. It is therefore itself unextended.

HYLAS. I grant it.

PHILONOUS. Is it not also active ?

HYLAS. Without doubt: otherwise, how could we attribute powers to it?

PHILONOUS. Now let me ask you two questions: *first*, whether it be agreeable to the usage either of philosophers or others, to give the name *matter* to an unextended active being? And *secondly*, whether it be not ridiculously absurd to misapply names contrary to the common use of language?

HYLAS. Well then, let it not be called matter, since you will have it so, but some *third nature* distinct from matter and spirit. For, what reason is there why you should call it spirit? does not the notion of spirit imply, that it is thinking as well as active and unextended?

PHILONOUS. My reason is this: because I have a mind to have some notion or meaning in what I say; but I have no notion of any action distinct from volition, neither can I conceive volition to be anywhere but in a spirit: therefore when I speak of an active being, I am obliged to mean a spirit. Beside, what can be plainer than that a thing which hath no ideas

in itself, cannot impart them to me; and if it hath ideas, surely it must
be a spirit. To make you comprehend the point still more clearly if
240 it be possible: I assert as well as you, that since we are affected from
without, we must allow powers to be without in a being distinct from
ourselves. So far we are agreed. But then we differ as to the kind of this
powerful being. I will have it to be spirit, you matter, or I know not what
(I may add too, you know not what) third nature. Thus I prove it to be
spirit. From the effects I see produced, I conclude there are actions;
and because actions, volitions; and because there are volitions, there
must be a will. Again, the things I perceive must have an existence, they
or their archetypes, out of my mind: but being ideas, neither they
nor their archetypes can exist otherwise than in an understanding: there
is therefore an understanding. But will and understanding constitute in
the strictest sense a mind or spirit. The powerful cause therefore of my
ideas, is in strict propriety of speech a *spirit*.

HYLAS. And now I warrant you think you have made the point very clear,
little suspecting that what you advance leads directly to a contradiction.
Is it not an absurdity to imagine any imperfection in God?

PHILONOUS. Without doubt.

HYLAS. To suffer pain is an imperfection.

PHILONOUS. It is.

HYLAS. Are we not sometimes affected with pain and uneasiness by some
other being?

PHILONOUS. We are.

HYLAS. And have you not said that being is a spirit, and is not that spirit
God?

PHILONOUS. I grant it.

HYLAS. But you have asserted, that whatever ideas we perceive from
without, are in the mind which affects us. The ideas therefore of pain
and uneasiness are in God; or in other words, God suffers pain: that
is to say, there is an imperfection in the Divine Nature, which you
acknowledged was absurd. So you are caught in a plain contradiction.

PHILONOUS. That God knows or understands all things, and that He knows
among other things what pain is, even every sort of painful sensation,
and what it is for His creatures to suffer pain, I make no question. But
that God, though He knows and sometimes causes painful sensations
in us, can Himself suffer pain, I positively deny. We who are limited
and dependent spirits, are liable to impressions of sense, the effects of
241 an external agent, which being produced against our wills, are sometimes
painful and uneasy. But God, whom no external being can affect, who
perceives nothing by sense as we do, whose will is absolute and independent, causing all things, and liable to be thwarted or resisted by
nothing; it is evident, such a being as this can suffer nothing, nor be
affected with any painful sensation, or indeed any sensation at all. We
are chained to a body, that is to say, our perceptions are connected with
corporeal motions. By the Law of our Nature we are affected upon every
alteration in the nervous parts of our sensible body: which sensible

body rightly considered, is nothing but a complexion of such qualities or ideas, as have no existence distinct from being perceived by a mind: so that this connexion of sensations with corporeal motions, means no more than a correspondence in the order of Nature between two sets of ideas, or things immediately perceivable. But God is a pure spirit, disengaged from all such sympathy or natural ties. No corporeal motions are attended with the sensations of pain or pleasure in his mind. To know everything knowable is certainly a perfection; but to endure, or suffer, or feel anything by sense, is an imperfection. The former, I say, agrees to God, but not the latter. God knows or hath ideas; but His ideas are not convey'd to Him by sense, as ours are. Your not distinguishing where there is so manifest a difference, makes you fancy you see an absurdity where there is none.

HYLAS. But all this while you have not considered, that the quantity of matter hath been demonstrated to be proportional to the gravity of bodies. And what can withstand demonstration?

PHILONOUS. Let me see how you demonstrate that point.

HYLAS. I lay it down for a principle, that the moments or quantities of motion in bodies, are in a direct compounded reason of the velocities and quantities of matter contained in them. Hence, where the velocities are equal, it follows, the moments are directly as the quantity of matter in each. But it is found by experience, that all bodies (bating the small inequalities, arising from the resistance of the air) descend with an equal velocity; the motion therefore of descending bodies, and consequently their gravity, which is the cause or principle of that motion, is proportional to the quantity of matter: which was to be demonstrated.

PHILONOUS. You lay it down as a self-evident principle, that the quantity of motion in any body, is proportional to the velocity and *matter* taken together: and this is made use of to prove a proposition, from whence the 242 existence of *matter* is inferred. Pray is not this arguing in a circle?

HYLAS. In the premise I only mean, that the motion is proportional to the velocity, jointly with the extension and solidity.

PHILONOUS. But allowing this to be true, yet it will not thence follow, that gravity is proportional to *matter*, in your philosophic sense of the word; except you take it for granted, that unknown *substratum*, or whatever else you call it, is proportional to those sensible qualities; which to suppose, is plainly begging the question. That there is magnitude and solidity, or resistance, perceived by sense, I readily grant; as likewise that gravity may be proportional to those qualities, I will not dispute. But that either these qualities as perceived by us, or the powers producing them do exist in a *material substratum*; this is what I deny, and you indeed affirm, but notwithstanding your demonstration, have not yet proved.

HYLAS. I shall insist no longer on that point. Do you think however, you shall persuade me the natural philosophers have been dreaming all this while; pray what becomes of all their hypotheses and explications of the *phenomena*, which suppose the existence of matter?

PHILONOUS. What mean you, Hylas, by the *phenomena*?

HYLAS. I mean the appearances which I perceive by my senses.

PHILONOUS. And the appearances perceived by sense, are they not ideas?

HYLAS. I have told you so a hundred times.

PHILONOUS. Therefore, to explain the *phenomena*, is to shew how we come to be affected with ideas, in that manner and order wherein they are imprinted on our senses. Is it not?

HYLAS. It is.

PHILONOUS. Now if you can prove, that any philosopher hath explained the production of any one idea in our minds by the help of *matter*, I shall for ever acquiesce, and look on all that hath been said against it as nothing: but if you cannot, it is in vain to urge the explication of phenomena. That a being endowed with knowledge and will, should produce or exhibit ideas, is easily understood. But that a being which is utterly destitute of these faculties should be able to produce ideas, or in any sort to affect an intelligence, this I can never understand. This I say, though we had some positive conception of matter, though we knew its qualities, and could comprehend its existence, would yet be so far from explaining things, that it is itself the most inexplicable thing in the world. And yet for all this, it will not follow, that philosophers have been doing nothing; for by observing and reasoning upon the connexion of ideas, they discover the laws and methods of Nature, which is a part of knowledge both useful and entertaining.

HYLAS. After all, can it be supposed God would deceive all mankind? Do you imagine, he would have induced the whole world to believe the being of matter, if there was no such thing?

PHILONOUS. That every epidemical opinion arising from prejudice, or passion, or thoughtlessness, may be imputed to God, as the Author of it, I believe you will not affirm. Whatsoever opinion we father on him, it must be either because he has discovered it to us by supernatural revelation, or because it is so evident to our natural faculties, which were framed and given us by God, that it is impossible we should withhold our assent from it. But where is the revelation? or where is the evidence that extorts the belief of matter? Nay, how does it appear, that matter taken for something distinct from what we perceive by our senses, is thought to exist by all mankind, or indeed by any except a few philosophers, who do not know what they would be at? Your question supposes these points are clear; and when you have cleared them, I shall think myself obliged to give you another answer. In the mean time let it suffice that I tell you, I do not suppose God has deceived mankind at all.

HYLAS. But the novelty, Philonous, the novelty! There lies the danger. New notions should always be discountenanced; they unsettle men's minds, and nobody knows where they will end.

PHILONOUS. Why the rejecting a notion that hath no foundation either in sense or in reason, or in divine authority, should be thought to unsettle the belief of such opinions as are grounded on all or any of these,

I cannot imagine. That innovations in government and religion, are dangerous, and ought to be discountenanced, I freely own. But is there the like reason why they should be discouraged in philosophy? The making anything known which was unknown before, is an innovation in knowledge: and if all such innovations had been forbidden, men would have made a notable progress in the arts and sciences. But *244* it is none of my business to plead for novelties and paradoxes. That the qualities we perceive, are not on the objects: that we must not believe our senses: that we know nothing of the real nature of things, and can never be assured even of their existence: that real colours and sounds are nothing but certain unknown figures and motions: that motions are in themselves neither swift nor slow: that there are in bodies absolute extensions, without any particular magnitude or figure: that a thing stupid, thoughtless and inactive, operates on a spirit: that the least particle of a body, contains innumerable extended parts. These are the novelties, these are the strange notions which shock the genuine un- corrupted judgment of all mankind; and being once admitted, embarrass the mind with endless doubts and difficulties. And it is against these and the like innovations, I endeavour to vindicate common sense. It is true, in doing this, I may perhaps be obliged to use some *ambages*, and ways of speech not common. But if my notions are once thoroughly under- stood, that which is most singular in them, will in effect be found to amount to no more than this: that it is absolutely impossible, and a plain contradiction to suppose, any unthinking being should exist with- out being perceived by a mind. And if this notion be singular, it is a shame it should be so at this time of day, and in a Christian country.

HYLAS. As for the difficulties other opinions may be liable to, those are out of the question. It is your business to defend your own opinion. Can anything be plainer, than that you are for changing all things into ideas? You, I say, who are not ashamed to charge me with *scepticism*. This is so plain, there is no denying it.

PHILONOUS. You mistake me. I am not for changing things into ideas, but rather ideas into things; since those immediate objects of perception, which according to you, are only appearances of things, I take to be the real things themselves.

HYLAS. Things! you may pretend what you please; but it is certain, you leave us nothing but the empty forms of things, the outside only which strikes the senses.

PHILONOUS. What you call the empty forms and outside of things, seems to me the very things themselves. Nor are they empty or incomplete otherwise, than upon your supposition, that matter is an essential part of all corporeal things. We both therefore agree in this, that we perceive *245* only sensible forms: but herein we differ, you will have them to be empty appearances, I real beings. In short you do not trust your senses, I do.

HYLAS. You say you believe your senses; and seem to applaud yourself that in this you agree with the vulgar. According to you therefore, the true nature of a thing is discovered by the senses. If so, whence comes that disagreement? Why is not the same figure, and other sensible qualities, perceived all manner of ways? and why should we use a microscope, the better to discover the true nature of a body, if it were discoverable to the naked eye?

PHILONOUS. Strictly speaking, Hylas, we do not see the same object that we feel; neither is the same object perceived by the microscope, which was by the naked eye. But in case every variation was thought sufficient to constitute a new kind or individual, the endless number or confusion of names would render language impracticable. Therefore to avoid this as well as other inconveniencies which are obvious upon a little thought, men combine together several ideas, apprehended by divers senses, or by the same sense at different times, or in different circumstances, but observed however to have some connexion in Nature, either with respect to co-existence or succession; all which they refer to one name, and consider as one thing. Hence it follows that when I examine by my other senses a thing I have seen, it is not in order to understand better the same object which I had perceived by sight, the object of one sense not being perceived by the other senses. And when I look through a microscope, it is not that I may perceive more clearly what I perceived already with my bare eyes, the object perceived by the glass being quite different from the former. But in both cases my aim is only to know what ideas are connected together; and the more a man knows of the connexion of ideas, the more he is said to know of the nature of things. What therefore if our ideas are variable; what if our senses are not in all circumstances affected with the same appearances? It will not thence follow, they are not to be trusted, or that they are inconsistent either with themselves or anything else, except it be with your preconceived notion of (I know not what) one single, unchanged, unperceivable, real nature, marked by each name: which prejudice seems to have taken its rise from not rightly understanding the common language of men speaking of several distinct ideas, as united into one thing by the mind. And indeed there is cause to suspect several erroneous conceits of the philosophers are owing to the same original: while they began to build their schemes, not so much on notions as words, which were framed by the vulgar, merely for conveniency and dispatch in the common actions of life, without any regard to speculation.

HYLAS. Methinks I apprehend your meaning.

PHILONOUS. It is your opinion, the ideas we perceive by our senses are not real things, but images, or copies of them. Our knowledge therefore is no farther real, than as our ideas are the true representations of those originals. But as these supposed originals are in themselves unknown, it is impossible to know how far our ideas resemble them; or whether they resemble them at all. We cannot therefore be sure we have any real knowledge. Farther, as our ideas are perpetually varied, without any change in the supposed real things, it necessarily follows they cannot all be true copies of them: or if some are, and others are not, it is impossible to distinguish the former from the latter. And this plunges us yet deeper in uncertainty. Again, when we consider the point, we cannot conceive how any idea, or anything like an idea, should have an absolute existence out of a mind: nor consequently, according to you, how there should be any real thing in Nature. The result of all which is, that we are thrown into the most hopeless and abandoned *scepticism*. Now give me leave to ask you, *first*, whether your referring ideas to certain absolutely existing unperceived substances, as their originals, be not the source of all this *scepticism*? *Secondly*, whether you are informed, either by sense or reason, of the existence of those unknown originals? And in casee you are not, whether it be not absurd to suppose them? *Thirdly*, whether, upon inquiry, you find there is anything distinctly conceived or meant by the *absolute or external existence of unperceiving substances?* *Lastly*, whether the premises considered, it be not the wisest way to follow Nature, trust your senses, and laying aside all anxious thought about unknown natures or substances, admit with the vulgar those for real things, which are perceived by the senses?

HYLAS. For the present, I have no inclination to the answering part. I would much rather see how you can get over what follows. Pray are not the objects perceived by the senses of one, likewise perceivable to others present? If there were an hundred more here, they would all see *247* the garden, the trees, and flowers as I see them. But they are not in the same manner affected with the ideas I frame in my imagination. Does not this make a difference between the former sort of objects and the latter?

PHILONOUS. I grant it does. Nor have I ever denied a difference between the objects of sense and those of imagination. But what would you infer from thence? You cannot say that sensible objects exist unperceived, because they are perceived by many.

HYLAS. I own, I can make nothing of that objection: but it hath led me into another. Is it not your opinion that by our senses we perceive only the ideas existing in our minds?

PHILONOUS. It is.

HYLAS. But the same idea which is in my mind, cannot be in yours, or in any other mind. Doth it not therefore follow from your principles, that no two can see the same thing? And is not this highly absurd?

PHILONOUS. If the term *same* be taken in the vulgar acceptation, it is certain (and not at all repugnant to the principles I maintain) that different persons may perceive the same thing; or the same thing or idea exist in different minds. Words are of arbitrary imposition; and since men are used to apply the word *same* where no distinction or variety is perceived, and I do not pretend to alter their perceptions, it follows, that as men have said before, *several saw the same thing*, so they may upon like occasions still continue to use the same phrase, without any deviation either from propriety of language, or the truth of things. But if the terms *same* be used in the acceptation of philosophers, who pretend to an abstracted notion of identity, then, according to their sundry definitions of this notion (for it is not yet agreed wherein that philosophic identity consists), it may or may not be possible for divers persons to perceive the same thing. But whether philosophers shall think fit to call a thing the *same* or no, is, I conceive, of small importance. Let us suppose several men together, all endued with the same faculties, and consequently affected in like sort by their senses, and who had yet never known the use of language; they would without question agree in their perceptions. Though perhaps, when they came to the use of speech, some regarding the uniformness of what was perceived, might call it the *same* thing: others especially regarding the diversity of persons who perceived, might choose the denomination of different things. But who sees not that all the dispute is about a word? to wit, whether what is perceived by different persons, may yet have the term *same* applied to it? Or suppose a house, whose walls or outward shell remaining unaltered, the chambers are all pulled down, and new ones built in their place; and that you should call this the *same*, and I should say it was not the *same* house: would we not for all this perfectly agree in our thoughts of the house, considered in itself? and would not all the difference consist in a sound? If you should say, we differed in our notions; for that you superadded to your idea of the house the simple abstracted idea of identity, whereas I did not; I would tell you I know not what you mean by that *abstracted idea of identity*; and should desire you to look into your own thoughts, and be sure you understood yourself.— Why so silent, Hylas? Are you not yet satisfied, men may dispute about identity and diversity, without any real difference in their thoughts and opinions, abstracted from names? Take this farther reflexion with you: that whether matter be allowed to exist or no, the case is exactly the same as to the point in hand. For the materialists themselves acknowledge what we immediately perceive by our senses, to be our own ideas. Your difficulty therefore, that no two see the same thing, makes equally against the materialists and me.

HYLAS. But they suppose an external archetype, to which referring their several ideas, they may truly be said to perceive the same thing.

PHILONOUS. And (not to mention your having discarded those archetypes) so may you suppose an external archetype on my principles; *external*, I mean, to your own mind; though indeed it must be supposed to exist in that mind which comprehends all things; but then this serves all the ends of identity, as well as if it existed out of a mind. And I am sure you yourself will not say, it is less intelligible.

HYLAS. You have indeed clearly satisfied me, either that there is no difficulty at bottom in this point; or if there be, that it makes equally against both opinions.

PHILONOUS. But that which makes equally against two contradictory opinions, can be a proof against neither.

HYLAS. I acknowledge it. But after all, Philonous, when I consider the substance of what you advance against *scepticism*, it amounts to no more than this. We are sure that we really see, hear, feel; in a word, that we are affected with sensible impressions.

PHILONOUS. And how are we concerned any farther? I see this *cherry*, I feel it, I taste it: and I am sure *nothing* cannot be seen, or felt, or tasted: it is therefore *real*. Take away the sensations of softness, moisture, redness, tartness, and you take away the cherry. Since it is not a being distinct from sensations; a *cherry*, I say, is nothing but a congeries of sensible impressions, or ideas perceived by various senses: which ideas are united into one thing (or have one name given them) by the mind; because they are observed to attend each other. Thus when the palate is affected with such a particular taste, the sight is affected with a red colour, the touch with roundness, softness, &c. Hence, when I see, and feel, and taste, in sundry certain manners, I am sure the *cherry* exists, or is real; its reality being in my opinion nothing abstracted from those sensations. But if by the word *cherry* you mean an unknown nature distinct from all those sensible qualities, and by its existence something distinct from its being perceived; then indeed I own, neither you nor I, nor anyone else can be sure it exists.

HYLAS. But what would you say, Philonous, if I should bring the very same reasons against the existence of sensible things in a mind, which you have offered against their existing in a material *substratum*?

PHILONOUS. When I see your reasons, you shall hear what I have to say to them.

HYLAS. Is the mind extended or unextended?

PHILONOUS. Unextended, without doubt.

HYLAS. Do you say the things you perceive are in your mind?

PHILONOUS. They are.

HYLAS. Again, have I not heard you speak of sensible impressions?

PHILONOUS. I believe you may.

HYLAS. Explain to me now, O Philonous! how it is possible there should be room for all those trees and houses to exist in your mind. Can extended things be contained in that which is unextended? Or are we to imagine impressions made on a thing void of all solidity? You cannot say objects are in your mind, as books in your study: or that things are imprinted on it, as the figure of a seal upon wax. In what sense therefore are we to understand those expressions? Explain me this if you can: and I shall *250* then be able to answer all those queries you formerly put to me about my *substratum*.

PHILONOUS. Look you, Hylas, when I speak of objects as existing in the mind or imprinted on the senses; I would not be understood in the gross literal sense, as when bodies are said to exist in a place, or a seal to make an impression upon wax. My meaning is only that the mind comprehends or perceives them; and that it is affected from without, or by some being distinct from itself. This is my explication of your difficulty; and how it can serve to make your tenet of an unperceiving material *substratum* intelligible, I would fain know.

HYLAS. Nay, if that be all, I confess I do not see what use can be made of it. But are you not guilty of some abuse of language in this?

PHILONOUS. None at all: it is no more than common custom, which you know is the rule of language, hath authorized: nothing being more usual,

than for philosophers to speak of the immediate objects of the understanding as things existing in the mind. Nor is there anything in this,
but what is conformable to the general analogy of language; most
part of the mental operations being signified by words borrowed from
sensible things; as is plain in the terms *comprehend, reflect, discourse,
&c.* which being applied to the mind, must not be taken in their gross
original sense.

HYLAS. You have, I own, satisfied me in this point: but there still remains
one great difficulty, which I know not how you will get over, And indeed
it is of such importance, that if you could solve all others, without being
able to find a solution for this, you must never expect to make me a
proselyte to your principles.

PHILONOUS. Let me know this mighty difficulty.

HYLAS. The Scripture account of the Creation, is what appears to me
utterly irreconcileable with your notions. Moses tells us of a Creation:
a Creation of what? of ideas? No certainly, but of things, of real things,
solid corporeal substances. Bring your principles to agree with this, and
I shall perhaps agree with you.

PHILONOUS. Moses mentions the sun, moon, and stars, earth and sea,
plants and animals: that all these do really exist, and were in the
beginning created by God, I make no question. If by *ideas*, you mean
251   fictions and fancies of the mind, then these are no ideas. If by *ideas*, you
mean immediate objects of the understanding, or sensible things which
cannot exist unperceived, or out of a mind, then these things are ideas.
But whether you do, or do not call them *ideas*, it matters little. The
difference is only about a name. And whether that name be retained or
rejected, the sense, the truth and reality of things continues the same.
In common talk, the objects of our senses are not termed *ideas* but
things. Call them so still: provided you do not attribute to them any
absolute external existence, and I shall never quarrel with you for a
word. The Creation therefore I allow to have been a creation of things,
of *real* things. Neither is this in the least inconsistent with my principles,
as is evident from what I have now said; and would have been evident
to you without this, if you had not forgotten what had been so often
said before. But as for solid corporeal substances, I desire you to shew
where Moses makes any mention of them; and if they should be
mentioned by him, or any other inspired writer, it would still be in-
cumbent on you to shew those words were not taken in the vulgar
acceptation, for things falling under our senses, but in the philosophic acceptation, for matter, or an unknown quiddity, with an
absolute existence. When you have proved these points, then (and not
till then) may you bring the authority of Moses into our dispute.

HYLAS. It is in vain to dispute about a point so clear. I am content to
refer it to your own conscience. Are you not satisfied there is some
peculiar repugnancy between the Mosaic account of the Creation, and
your notions?

PHILONOUS. If all possible sense, which can be put on the first chapter of

Genesis, may be conceived as consistently with my principles as any other, then it has no peculiar repugnancy with them. But there is no sense you may not as well conceive, believing as I do. Since, beside spirits, all you conceive are ideas; and the existence of these I do not deny. Neither do you pretend they exist without the mind.

HYLAS. Pray let me see any sense you can understand it in.

PHILONOUS. Why, I imagine that if I had been present at the Creation, I should have seen things produced into being; that is, become perceptible, in the order described by the sacred historian. I ever before believed the Mosaic account of the Creation, and now find no alteration in my manner of believing it. When things are said to begin or end their existence, we do not mean this with regard to God, but his *252* creatures. All objects are eternally known by God, or which is the same thing, have an eternal existence in his mind: but when things before imperceptible to creatures, are by a decree of God, made perceptible to them; then are they said to begin a relative existence, with respect to created minds. Upon reading therefore the Mosaic account of the Creation, I understand that the several parts of the world became gradually perceivable to finite spirits, endowed with proper faculties; so that whoever such were present, they were in truth perceived by them. This is the literal obvious sense suggested to me, by the words of the Holy Scripture: in which is included no mention or no thought, either of *substratum,* instrument, occasion, or absolute existence. And upon inquiry, I doubt not, it will be found, that most plain honest men, who believe the Creation, never think of those things any more than I. What metaphysical sense you may understand it in, you only can tell.

HYLAS. But, Philonous, you do not seem to be aware, that you allow created things in the beginning, only a relative, and consequently hypothetical being: that is to say, upon supposition there were men to perceive them, without which they have no actuality of absolute existence, wherein Creation might terminate. Is it not therefore according to you plainly impossible, the Creation of any inanimate creatures should precede that of man? And is not this directly contrary to the Mosaic account?

PHILONOUS. In answer to that I say, *first,* created beings might begin to exist in the mind of other created intelligences, beside men. You will not therefore be able to prove any contradiction between Moses and my notions, unless you first shew, there was no other order of finite created spirits in being before man. I say farther, in case we conceive the Creation, as we should at this time a parcel of plants or vegetables of all sorts, produced by an invisible power, in a desert where nobody was present: that this way of explaining or conceiving it, is consistent with my principles, since they deprive you of nothing, either sensible or imaginable: that it exactly suits with the common, natural, undebauched notions of mankind: that it manifests the dependence of all things on God; and consequently hath all the good effect or influence, which it is possible that important article of our faith should have in

making men humble, thankful, and resigned to their Creator. I say
253   moreover, that in this naked conception of things, divested of words,
there will not be found any notion of what you call the *actuality of
absolute existence*. You may indeed raise a dust with those terms, and
so lengthen our dispute to no purpose. But I entreat you calmly to look
into your own thoughts, and then tell me if they are not an useless and
unintelligible jargon.

HYLAS. I own, I have no very clear notion annexed to them. But what say
you to this? Do you not make the existence of sensible things consist
in their being in a mind? And were not all things eternally in the mind of
God? Did they not therefore exist from all eternity, according to
you? And how could that which was eternal, be created in time? Can
anything be clearer or better connected than this?

PHILONOUS. And are not you too of opinion, that God knew all things
from eternity?

HYLAS. I am.

PHILONOUS. Consequently they always had a being in the Divine
Intellect.

HYLAS. This I acknowledge.

PHILONOUS. By your own confession therefore, nothing is new, or
begins to be, in respect of the mind of God. So we are agreed in that
point.

HYLAS. What shall we make then of the Creation?

PHILONOUS. May we not understand it to have been entirely in respect of
finite spirits; so that things, with regard to us, may properly be said to
begin their existence, or be created, when God decreed they should
become perceptible to intelligent creatures, in that order and manner
which he then established, and we now call the Laws of Nature? You
may call this a *relative*, or *hypothetical existence* if you please. But so
long as it supplies us with the most natural, obvious, and literal sense
of the Mosaic history of the Creation; so long as it answers all the
religious ends of that great article; in a word, so long as you can
assign no other sense or meaning in its stead; why should we reject this?
Is it to comply with a ridiculous sceptical humour of making everything
nonsense and unintelligible? I am sure you cannot say, it is for the glory
of God. For allowing it to be a thing possible and conceivable, that the
corporeal world should have an absolute subsistence extrinsical to the
mind of God, as well as to the minds of all created spirits: yet how
could this set forth either the immensity or omniscience of the Deity,
or the necessary and immediate dependence of all things on him? Nay,
254   would it not rather seem to derogate from those attributes?

HYLAS. Well, but as to this decree of God's, for making things perceptible:
what say you, Philonous, is it not plain, God did either execute that
decree from all eternity, or at some certain time began to will what he
had not actually willed before, but only designed to will. If the former,
then there could be no Creation or beginning of existence in finite things.
If the latter, then we must acknowledge something new to befall the

Deity; which implies a sort of change: and all change argues imperfection.

PHILONOUS. Pray consider what you are doing. Is it not evident, this objection concludes equally against a Creation in any sense; nay, against every other act of the Deity, discoverable by the light of Nature? None of which can we conceive, otherwise than as performed in time, and having a beginning. God is a being of transcendent and unlimited perfections: his nature therefore is incomprehensible to finite spirits. It is not therefore to be expected, that any man, whether *materialist* or *immaterialist*, should have exactly just notions of the Deity, his attributes, and ways of operation. If then you would infer anything against me, your difficulty must not be drawn from the inadequateness of our conceptions of the Divine Nature, which is unavoidable on any scheme; but from the denial of matter, of which there is not one word, directly or indirectly, in what you have now objected.

HYLAS. I must acknowledge, the difficulties you are concerned to clear, are such only as arise from the non-existence of matter, and are peculiar to that notion. So far you are in the right. But I cannot by any means bring myself to think there is no such peculiar repugnancy between the Creation and your opinion; though indeed where to fix it, I do not distinctly know.

PHILONOUS. What would you have! do I not acknowledge a twofold state of things, the one ectypal or natural, the other archetypal and eternal? The former was created in time; the latter existed from everlasting in the mind of God. Is not this agreeable to the common notions of divines? or is any more than this necessary in order to conceive the Creation? But you suspect some peculiar repugnancy, though you know not where it lies. To take away all possibility of scruple in the case, do but consider this one point. Either you are not able to conceive the Creation on any hypothesis whatsoever; and if so, there is no ground for dislike *255* or complaint against my particular opinion on that score: or you are able to conceive it; and if so, why not on my principles, since thereby nothing conceivable is taken away? You have all along been allowed the full scope of sense, imagination, and reason. Whatever therefore you could before apprehend, either immediately or mediately by your senses, or by ratiocination from your senses; whatever you could perceive, imagine or understand, remains still with you. If therefore the notion you have of the Creation by other principles be intelligible, you have it still upon mine; if it be not intelligible, I conceive it to be no notion at all; and so there is no loss of it. And indeed it seems to me very plain, that the supposition of matter, that is, a thing perfectly unknown and inconceivable, cannot serve to make us conceive anything. And I hope, it need not be proved to you, that if the existence of matter doth not make the Creation conceivable, the Creation's being without it inconceivable, can be no objection against its non-existence.

HYLAS. I confess, Philonous, you have almost satisfied me in this point of the Creation.

PHILONOUS. I would fain know why you are not quite satisfied. You tell me indeed of a repugnancy between the Mosaic history and immaterialism: but you know not where it lies. Is this reasonable, Hylas? Can you expect I should solve a difficulty without knowing what it is? But to pass by all that, would not a man think you were assured there is no repugnancy between the received notions of materialists and the inspired writings?

HYLAS. And so I am.

PHILONOUS. Ought the historical part of Scripture to be understood in a plain obvious sense, or in a sense which is metaphysical, and out of the way?

HYLAS. In the plain sense, doubtless.

PHILONOUS. When Moses speaks of herbs, earth, water, &c. as having been created by God; think you not the sensible things, commonly signified by those words, are suggested to every unphilosophical reader?

HYLAS. I cannot help thinking so.

PHILONOUS. And are not all ideas, or things perceived by sense, to be denied a real existence by the doctrine of the materialists?

HYLAS. This I have already acknowledged.

PHILONOUS. The Creation therefore, according to them, was not the
256   creation of things sensible, which have only a relative being, but of certain unknown natures, which have an absolute being, wherein Creation might terminate.

HYLAS. True.

PHILONOUS. Is it not therefore evident, the asserters of matter destroy the plain obvious sense of Moses, with which their notions are utterly inconsistent; and instead of it obtrude on us I know not what, something equally unintelligible to themselves and me?

HYLAS. I cannot contradict you.

PHILONOUS. Moses tells us of a Creation. A Creation of what? of unknown quiddities, of occasions, or *substratums*? No certainly; but of things obvious to the senses. You must first reconcile this with your notions, if you expect I should be reconciled to them.

HYLAS. I see you can assault me with my own weapons.

PHILONOUS. Then as to *absolute existence*; was there ever known a more jejune notion than that? Something it is, so abstracted and unintelligible, that you have frankly owned you could not conceive it, much less explain anything by it. But allowing matter to exist, and the notion of absolute existence to be as clear as light; yet was this ever known to make the Creation more credible? Nay hath it not furnished the *atheists* and *infidels* of all ages, with the most plausible argument against a Creation? That a corporeal substance, which hath an absolute existence without the minds of spirits, should be produced out of nothing by the mere will of a spirit, hath been looked upon as a thing so contrary to all reason, so impossible and absurd, that not only the most celebrated among the ancients, but even divers modern and Christian philosophers have thought matter coeternal with the Deity. Lay these things together, and then judge you whether materialism disposes men to believe the Creation of things.

HYLAS. I own, Philonous, I think it does not. This of the Creation is the last objection I can think of; and I must needs own it hath been sufficiently answered as well as the rest. Nothing now remains to be overcome, but a sort of unaccountable backwardness that I find in myself towards your notions.

PHILONOUS. When a man is swayed, he knows not why, to one side of a question; can this, think you, be anything else but the effect of prejudice, which never fails to attend old and rooted notions? And indeed in this respect I cannot deny the belief of matter to have very *257* much the advantage over the contrary opinion, with men of a learned education.

HYLAS. I confess it seems to be as you say.

PHILONOUS. As a balance therefore to this weight of prejudice, let us throw into the scale the great advantages that arise from the belief of immaterialism, both in regard to religion and human learning. The being of a God, and incorruptibility of the soul, those great articles of religion, are they not proved with the clearest and most immediate evidence? When I say the being of a *God*, I do not mean an obscure general cause of things, whereof we have no conception, but *God*, in the strict and proper sense of the word. A being whose spirituality, omnipresence, providence, omniscience, infinite power and goodness, are as conspicuous as the existence of sensible things, of which (notwithstanding the fallacious pretences and affected scruples of *sceptics*) there is no more reason to doubt, than of our own being. Then with relation to human sciences; in natural philosophy, what intricacies, what obscurities, what contradictions, hath the belief of matter led men into! To say nothing of the numberless disputes about its extent, continuity, homogeneity, gravity, divisibility, &c. do they not pretend to explain all things by bodies operating on bodies, according to the laws of motion? and yet, are they able to comprehend how any one body should move another? Nay, admitting there was no difficulty in reconciling the notion of an inert being with a cause; or in conceiving how an accident might pass from one body to another; yet by all their strained thoughts and extravagant suppositions, have they been able to reach the mechanical production of any one animal or vegetable body? Can they account by the laws of motion, for sounds, tastes, smells, or colours, or for the regular course of things? Have they accounted by physical principles for the aptitude and contrivance, even of the most inconsiderable parts of the universe? But laying aside matter and corporeal causes, and admitting only the efficiency of an all-perfect mind, are not all the effects of Nature easy and intelligible? If the *phenomena* are nothing else but *ideas*; God is a *spirit*, but matter an unintelligent, unperceiving being. If they demonstrate an unlimited power in their cause; God is active and omnipotent, but matter an inert mass. If the order,

258   regularity, and usefulness of them, can never be sufficiently admired; God is infinitely wise and provident, but matter destitute of all contrivance and design. These surely are great advantages in *physics*. Not to mention that the apprehension of a distant Deity, naturally disposes men to a negligence in their *moral* actions, which they would be more cautious of, in case they thought Him immediately present, and acting on their minds without the interposition of matter, or unthinking second causes. Then in *metaphysics*; what difficulties concerning entity in abstract, substantial forms, hylarchic principles, plastic natures, substance and accident, principle of individuation, possibility of matter's thinking, origin of ideas, the manner how two independent substances, so widely different as *spirit* and *matter*, should mutually operate on each other? What difficulties, I say, and endless disquisitions concerning these and innumerable other the like points, do we escape by supposing only spirits and ideas? Even the *mathematics* themselves, if we take away the absolute existence of extended things, become much more clear and easy; the most shocking paradoxes and intricate speculations in those sciences, depending on the infinite divisibility of finite extension, which depends on that supposition. But what need is there to insist on the particular sciences? Is not that opposition to all science whatsoever, that phrensy of the ancient and modern *sceptics*, built on the same foundation? Or can you produce so much as one argument against the reality of corporeal things, or in behalf of that avowed utter ignorance of their natures, which doth not suppose their reality to consist in an external absolute existence? Upon this supposition indeed, the objections from the change of colours in a pigeon's neck, or the appearances of a broken oar in the water, must be allowed to have weight. But those and the like objections vanish, if we do not maintain the being of absolute external originals, but place the reality of things in ideas, fleeting indeed, and changeable; however not changed at random, but according to the fixed order of Nature. For herein consists that constancy and truth of things, which secures all the concerns of life, and distinguishes that which is *real* from the irregular visions of the fancy.

259 HYLAS. I agree to all you have now said, and must own that nothing can incline me to embrace your opinion, more than the advantages I see it is attended with. I am by nature lazy; and this would be a mighty abridgement in knowledge. What doubts, what hypotheses, what labyrinths of amusement, what fields of disputation, what an ocean of false learning, may be avoided by that single notion of *immaterialism*?

PHILONOUS. After all, is there anything farther remaining to be done? You may remember you promised to embrace that opinion, which upon examination should appear most agreeable to common sense, and remote from *scepticism*. This by your own confession is that which denies matter, or the absolute existence of corporeal things. Nor is this all; the same notion has been proved several ways, viewed in different lights, pursued in its consequences, and all objections against it cleared.

Can there be a greater evidence of its truth? or is it possible it should have all the marks of a true opinion, and yet be false?

HYLAS. I own myself entirely satisfied for the present in all respects. But what security can I have that I shall still continue the same full assent to your opinion, and that no unthought-of objection or difficulty will occur hereafter?

PHILONOUS. Pray, Hylas, do you in other cases, when a point is once evidently proved, withhold your assent on account of objections or difficulties it may be liable to? Are the difficulties that attend the doctrine of incommensurable quantities, of the angle of contact, of the asymptotes to curves or the like, sufficient to make you hold out against mathematical demonstration? Or will you disbelieve the providence of God, because there may be some particular things which you know not how to reconcile with it? If there are difficulties attending immaterialism, there are at the same time direct and evident proofs for it. But for the existence of matter, there is not one proof, and far more numerous and insurmountable objections lie against it. But where are those mighty difficulties you insist on? Alas! you know not where or what they are; something which may possibly occur hereafter. If this be a sufficient pretence for withholding your full assent, you should never yield it to any proposition, how free soever from exceptions, how clearly and solidly soever demonstrated.

HYLAS. You have satisfied me, Philonous.

PHILONOUS. But to arm you against all future objections, do but consider, that which bears equally hard on two contradictory opinions, can be a proof against neither. Whenever therefore any difficulty occurs, try if *260* you can find a solution for it on the hypothesis of the *materialists*. Be not deceived by words; but sound your own thoughts. And in case you cannot conceive it easier by the help of *materialism*, it is plain it can be no objection against *immaterialism*. Had you proceeded all along by this rule, you would probably have spared yourself abundance of trouble in objecting; since of all your difficulties I challenge you to shew one that is explained by matter; nay, which is not more unintelligible with, than without that supposition, and consequently makes rather *against* than *for* it. You should consider in each particular, whether the difficulty arises from the *non-existence of matter*. If it doth not, you might as well argue from the infinite divisibility of extension against the divine prescience, as from such a difficulty against *immaterialism*. And yet upon recollection I believe you will find this to have been often, if not always the case. You should likewise take heed not to argue on a *petitio principii*. One is apt to say, the unknown substances ought to be esteemed real things, rather than the ideas in our minds: and who can tell but the unthinking external substance may concur as a cause or instrument in the production of our ideas? But is not this proceeding on a supposition that there are such external substances? And to suppose this, is it not begging the question? But above all things you should beware of imposing on yourself by that vulgar sophism, which is called *ignoratio*

elenchi. You talked often as if you thought I maintained the non-existence of sensible things: whereas in truth no one can be more thoroughly assured of their existence than I am: and it is you who doubt; I should have said, positively deny it. Every thing that is seen, felt, heard, or any way perceived by the senses, is on the principles I embrace, a real being, but not on yours. Remember, the matter you contend for is an unknown somewhat (if indeed it may be termed *somewhat*) which is quite stripped of all sensible qualities, and can neither be perceived by sense, nor apprehended by the mind. Remember, I say, that it is not any object which is hard or soft, hot or cold, blue or white, round or square, &c. For all these things I affirm do exist. Though indeed I deny they have an existence distinct from being perceived; or that they exist out of all minds whatsoever. Think on these points; let them be attentively considered and still kept in view. Otherwise you will not comprehend the state of the question; without which your objections will always be
261   wide of the mark, and instead of mine, may possibly be directed (as more than once they have been) against your own notions.

HYLAS. I must needs own, Philonous, nothing seems to have kept me from agreeing with you more than this same *mistaking the question.* In denying matter, at first glimpse I am tempted to imagine you deny the things we see and feel; but upon reflexion find there is no ground for it. What think you therefore of retaining the name *matter*, and applying it to sensible things? This may be done without any change in your sentiments: and believe me it would be a means of reconciling them to some persons, who may be more shocked at an innovation in words than in opinion.

PHILONOUS. With all my heart: retain the word *matter*, and apply it to the objects of sense, if you please, provided you do not attribute to them any subsistence distinct from their being perceived. I shall never quarrel with you for an expression. *Matter*, or *material substance*, are terms introduced by philosophers; and as used by them, imply a sort of independency, or a subsistence distinct from being perceived by a mind: but are never used by common people; or if ever, it is to signify the immediate objects of sense. One would think therefore, so long as the names of all particular things, with the terms *sensible, substance, body, stuff*, and the like, are retained, the word *matter* should be never missed in common talk. And in philosophical discourses it seems the best way to leave it quite out; since there is not perhaps any one thing that hath more favoured and strengthened the depraved bent of the mind toward *atheism*, than the use of that general confused term.

HYLAS. Well but, Philonous, since I am content to give up the notion of an unthinking substance exterior to the mind, I think you ought not to deny me the privilege of using the word *matter* as I please, and annexing it to a collection of sensible qualities subsisting only in the mind. I freely own there is no other substance in a strict sense, than *spirit*. But I have been so long accustomed to the term *matter*, that I know not how to part with it. To say, there is no *matter* in the world, is still shocking to me. Whereas to say, there is no *matter*, if by that term be meant an unthinking substance existing without the mind: but if by *matter* is meant some sensible thing, whose existence consists in being perceived, then there is *matter*: this distinction gives it quite another turn: and men will come into your notions with small difficulty, when they are proposed in that manner. For after all, the controversy about *matter* 262 in the strict acceptation of it, lies altogether between you and the philosophers; whose principles, I acknowledge, are not near so natural, or so agreeable to the common sense of mankind, and Holy Scripture, as yours. There is nothing we either desire or shun, but as it makes, or is apprehended to make some part of our happiness or misery. But what hath happiness or misery, joy or grief, pleasure or pain, to do with absolute existence, or with unknown entities, abstracted from all relation to us? It is evident, things regard us only as they are pleasing or displeasing: and they can please or displease, only so far forth as they are perceived. Farther therefore we are not concerned; and thus far you leave things as you found them. Yet still there is something new in this doctrine. It is plain, I do not now think with the philosophers, nor yet altogether with the vulgar. I would know how the case stands in that respect: precisely, what you have added to, or altered in my former notions.

PHILONOUS. I do not pretend to be a setter-up of *new notions*. My endeavours tend only to unite and place in a clearer light that truth, which was before shared between the vulgar and the philosophers: the former being of opinion, that *those things they immediately perceive are the real things*; and the latter, that *the things immediately perceived, are ideas which exist only in the mind*. Which two notions put together, do in effect constitute the substance of what I advance.

HYLAS. I have been a long time distrusting my senses; methought I saw things by a dim light, and through false glasses. Now the glasses are removed, and a new light breaks in upon my understanding. I am clearly convinced that I see things in their native forms; and am no longer in pain about their unknown natures or absolute existence. This is the state I find myself in at present: though indeed the course that brought me to it, I do not yet thoroughly comprehend. You set out upon the same principles that Academics, Cartesians, and the like sects, usually do; and for a long time it looked as if you were advancing their philosophical *scepticism*; but in the end your conclusions are directly opposite to theirs.

PHILONOUS. You see, Hylas, the water of yonder fountain, how it is forced upwards, in a round column, to a certain height; at which it breaks and falls back into the basin from whence it rose: its ascent as well as 263 descent, proceeding from the same uniform law or principle of *gravitation*. Just so, the same principles which at first view lead to *scepticism*, pursued to a certain point, bring men back to common sense.

De Motu

Sive de motus principio & natura et de causa
communicationis motuum

Translated by A. A. Luce
First printed in 1721

Of Motion

Or the principle and nature of motion and the cause of
the communication of motions

1 In the pursuit of truth we must beware of being misled by terms which
we do not rightly understand. That is the chief point. Almost all philosophers utter the caution; few observe it. Yet it is not so difficult to observe,
where sense, experience, and geometrical reasoning obtain, as is especially
the case in physics. Laying aside, then, as far as possible, all prejudice,
whether rooted in linguistic usage or in philosophical authority, let us
fix our gaze on the very nature of things. For no one's authority ought to
rank so high as to set a value on his words and terms unless they are found
to be based on clear and certain fact.

2 The consideration of motion greatly troubled the minds of the ancient
philosophers, giving rise to various exceedingly difficult opinions (not to
say absurd) which have almost entirely gone out of fashion, and not being
worth a detailed discussion need not delay us long. In works on motion
by the more recent and sober thinkers of our age, not a few terms of
somewhat abstract and obscure signification are used, such as *solicitation
of gravity*, *urge*, *dead forces*, etc., terms which darken writings in other
respects very learned, and beget opinions at variance with truth and the
common sense of men. These terms must be examined with great care, not
from a desire to prove other people wrong, but in the interest of truth.

3 *Solicitation* and *effort* or *conation* belong properly to animate beings
alone. When they are attributed to other things, they must be taken in a
metaphorical sense; but a philosopher should abstain from metaphor.
Besides, anyone who has seriously considered the matter will agree that
those terms have no clear and distinct meaning apart from all affection
of the mind and motion of the body.

4 While we support heavy bodies we feel in ourselves effort, fatigue, and
discomfort. We perceive also in heavy bodies falling an accelerated motion
towards the centre of the earth; and that is all the senses tell us. By reason,
however, we infer that there is some cause or principle of these phenomena,
and that is popularly called *gravity*. But since the cause of the fall of heavy
bodies is unseen and unknown, gravity in that usage cannot properly be
styled a sensible quality. It is, therefore, an occult quality. But what an
occult quality is, or how any quality can act or do anything, we can
scarcely conceive—indeed we cannot conceive. And so men would do better
to let the occult quality go, and attend only to the sensible effects. Abstract
terms (however useful they may be in argument) should be discarded in

meditation, and the mind should be fixed on the particular and the concrete, that is, on the things themselves.

5 *Force* likewise is attributed to bodies; and that word is used as if it meant a known quality, and one distinct from motion, figure, and every other sensible thing and also from every affection of the living thing. But examine the matter more carefully and you will agree that such force is nothing but an occult quality. Animal effort and corporeal motion are commonly regarded as symptoms and measures of this occult quality.

6 Obviously then it is idle to lay down gravity or force as the principle of motion; for how could that principle be known more clearly by being styled an occult quality? What is itself occult explains nothing. And I need not say that an unknown acting cause could be more correctly styled substance than quality. Again, *force, gravity*, and terms of that sort are more often used in the concrete (and rightly so) so as to connote the body in motion, the effort of resisting, *etc*. But when they are used by philosophers to signify certain natures carved out and abstracted from all these things, natures which are not objects of sense, nor can be grasped by any force of intellect, nor pictured by the imagination, then indeed they breed errors and confusion.

7 About general and abstract terms many men make mistakes; they see their value in argument, but they do not appreciate their purpose. In part the terms have been invented by common habit to abbreviate speech, and in part they have been thought out by philosophers for instructional purposes, not that they are adapted to the natures of things which are in fact singulars and concrete, but they come in useful for handing on received opinions by making the notions or at least the propositions universal.

8 We generally suppose that corporeal force is something easy to conceive. Those, however, who have studied the matter more carefully are of a different opinion, as appears from the strange obscurity of their language when they try to explain it. Torricelli says that force and impetus are abstract and subtle things and quintessences which are included in corporeal substance as in the magic vase of Circe.* Leibniz likewise in explaining the nature of force has this: 'Active primitive force which is ἐντελέχεια ἡ πρώτη corresponds to the soul or substantial form.' See *Acta Erudit. Lips.* Thus even the greatest men when they give way to abstractions are bound to pursue terms which have no certain significance and are mere shadows of scholastic things. Other passages in plenty from the writings of the younger men could be produced which give abundant proof that metaphysical abstractions have not in all quarters given place to mechanical science and experiment, but still make useless trouble for philosophers.

---

* Matter is nothing else than a magic vase of Circe, which serves as a receptacle of force and of the moments of the impetus. Force and the impetus are such subtle abstractions and such volatile quintessences that they cannot be shut up in any vessel except in the innermost substance of natural solids. See *Academic Lectures.*

9 From that source derive various absurdities, such as that dictum: 'The force of percussion, however small, is infinitely great'—which indeed supposes that gravity is a certain real quality different from all others, and that gravitation is, as it were, an act of this quality, really distinct from motion. But a very small percussion produces a greater effect than the greatest gravitation without motion. The former gives out some motion indeed, the latter none. Whence it follows that the force of percussion exceeds the force of gravitation by an infinite ratio, *i.e.* is infinitely great. See the experiments of Galileo, and the writings of Torricelli, Borelli, and others on the definite force of percussion.

10 We must, however, admit that no force is immediately felt by itself, nor known or measured otherwise than by its effect; but of a dead force or of simple gravitation in a body at rest, no change taking place, there is no effect; of percussion there is some effect. Since, then, forces are proportional to effects, we may conclude that there is no dead force, but we must not on that account infer that the force of percussion is infinite; for we cannot regard as infinite any positive quantity on the ground that it exceeds by an infinite ratio a zero-quantity or nothing.

11 The force of gravitation is not to be separated from momentum; but there is no momentum without velocity, since it is mass multiplied by velocity; again, velocity cannot be understood without motion, and the same holds therefore of the force of gravitation. Then no force makes itself known except through action, and through action it is measured; but we are not able to separate the action of a body from its motion; therefore as long as a heavy body changes the shape of a piece of lead put under it, or of a cord, so long is it moved; but when it is at rest, it does nothing, or (which is the same thing) it is prevented from acting. In brief, those terms *dead force* and *gravitation* by the aid of metaphysical abstraction are supposed to mean something different from moving, moved, motion, and rest, but, in point of fact, the supposed difference in meaning amounts to nothing at all.

12 If anyone were to say that a weight hung or placed on the cord acts on it, since it prevents it from restoring itself by elastic force, I reply that by parity of reasoning any lower body acts on the higher body which rests on it, since it prevents it from coming down. But for one body to prevent another from existing in that space which *it* occupies cannot be styled the action of that body.

13 We feel at times the pressure of a gravitating body. But that unpleasant sensation arises from the motion of the heavy body communicated to the fibres and nerves of our body and changing their situation, and therefore it ought to be referred to percussion. In these matters we are afflicted by a number of serious prejudices, which should be subdued, or rather entirely exorcised by keen and continued reflection.

14 In order to prove that any quantity is infinite, we have to show that some, finite, homogeneous part is contained in it an infinite number of times. But dead force is to the force of percussion, not as part to the whole, but as the point to the line, according to the very writers who maintain the

infinite force of percussion. Much might be added on this matter, but I am afraid of being prolix.

15 By the foregoing principles famous controversies which have greatly exercised the minds of learned men can be solved; for instance, that controversy about the proportion of forces. One side conceding that momenta, motions, and impetus, given the mass, are simply as the velocities, affirms that the forces are as the squares of the velocities. Everyone sees that this opinion supposes that the force of the body is distinguished from momentum, motion, and impetus, and without that supposition it collapses.

16 To make it still clearer that a certain strange confusion has been introduced into the theory of motion by metaphysical abstractions, let us watch the conflict of opinion about force and impetus among famous men. Leibniz confuses impetus with motion. According to Newton impetus is in fact the same as the force of inertia. Borelli asserts that impetus is only the degree of velocity. Some would make impetus and effort different, others identical. Most regard the motive force as proportional to the motion; but a few prefer to suppose some other force besides the motive, to be measured differently, for instance by the squares of the velocities into the masses. But it would be an endless task to follow out this line of thought.

17 *Force, gravity, attraction*, and terms of this sort are useful for reasonings and reckonings about motion and bodies in motion, but not for understanding the simple nature of motion itself or for indicating so many distinct qualities. As for attraction, it was certainly introduced by Newton, not as a true, physical quality, but only as a mathematical hypothesis. Indeed Leibniz when distinguishing elementary effort or solicitation from impetus, admits that those entities are not really found in nature, but have to be formed by abstraction.

18 A similar account must be given of the composition and resolution of any direct forces into any oblique ones by means of the diagonal and sides of the parallelogram. They serve the purpose of mechanical science and reckoning; but to be of service to reckoning and mathematical demonstrations is one thing, to set forth the nature of things is another.

19 Of the moderns many are of the opinion that motion is neither destroyed nor generated anew, but that the quantity of motion remains for ever constant. Aristotle indeed propounded that problem long ago—does motion come into being and pass away, or is it eternal? *Phys*. Bk. 8. That sensible motion perishes is clear to the senses, but apparently they will have it that the same impetus and effort remains, or the same sum of forces. Borelli affirms that force in percussion is not lessened, but expanded, that even contrary impetus are received and retained in the same body. Likewise Leibniz contends that effort exists everywhere and always in matter, and that it is understood by reason where it is not evident to the senses. But these points, we must admit, are too abstract and obscure, and of much the same sort as substantial forms and entelechies.

20 All those who, to explain the cause and origin of motion, make use of the hylarchic principle, or of a nature's want or appetite, or indeed of a natural instinct, are to be considered as having said something, rather than

thought it. And from these they* are not far removed who have supposed 'that the parts of the earth are self-moving, or even that spirits are implanted in them like a form' in order to assign the cause of the acceleration of heavy bodies falling. So too with him† who said 'that in the body besides solid extension, there must be something posited to serve as starting-point for the consideration of forces.' All these indeed either say nothing particular and determinate, or if there is anything in what they say, it will be as difficult to explain as that very thing it was brought forward to explain.

21 To throw light on nature it is idle to adduce things which are neither evident to the senses, nor intelligible to reason. Let us see then what sense and experience tell us, and reason that rests upon them. There are two supreme classes of things, body and soul. By the help of sense we know the extended thing, solid, mobile, figured, and endowed with other qualities which meet the senses, but the sentient, percipient, thinking thing we know by a certain internal consciousness. Further we see that those things are plainly different from one another, and quite heterogeneous. I speak of things known; for of the unknown it is profitless to speak.

22 All that which we know to which we have given the name *body* contains nothing in itself which could be the principle of motion or its efficient cause; for impenetrability, extension, and figure neither include nor connote any power of producing motion; nay, on the contrary, if we review singly those qualities of body, and whatever other qualities there may be, we shall see that they are all in fact passive and that there is nothing active in them which can in any way be understood as the source and principle of motion. As for gravity we have already shown above that by that term is meant nothing we know, nothing other than the sensible effect, the cause of which we seek. And indeed when we call a body heavy we understand nothing else except that it is borne downwards, and we are not thinking at all about the cause of this sensible effect.

23 And so about body we can boldly state as established fact that it is not the principle of motion. But if anyone maintains that the term *body* covers in its meaning occult quality, virtue, form, and essence, besides solid extension and its modes, we must just leave him to his useless disputation with no ideas behind it, and to his abuse of names which express nothing distinctly. But the sounder philosophical method, it would seem, abstains as far as possible from abstract and general notions (if *notions* is the right term for things which cannot be understood).

24 The contents of the idea of body we know; but what we know in body is agreed not to be the principle of motion. But those who as well maintain something unknown in body of which they have no idea and which they call the principle of motion, are in fact simply stating that the principle of motion is unknown, and one would be ashamed to linger long on subtleties of this sort.

25 Besides corporeal things there is the other class, *viz.* thinking things, and that there is in them the power of moving bodies we have learned by

---

* Borelli.   † Leibniz.

personal experience, since our mind at will can stir and stay the movements of our limbs, whatever be the ultimate explanation of the fact. This is certain that bodies are moved at the will of the mind, and accordingly the mind can be called, correctly enough, a principle of motion, a particular and subordinate principle indeed, and one which itself depends on the first and universal principle.

26 Heavy bodies are borne downwards, although they are not affected by any apparent impulse; but we must not think on that account that the principle of motion is contained in them. Aristotle gives this account of the matter, 'Heavy and light things are not moved by themselves; for that would be a characteristic of life, and they would be able to stop themselves.' All heavy things by one and the same certain and constant law seek the centre of the earth, and we do not observe in them a principle or any faculty of halting that motion, of diminishing it or increasing it except in fixed proportion, or finally of altering it in any way. They behave quite passively. Again, in strict and accurate speech, the same must be said of percussive bodies. Those bodies as long as they are being moved, as also in the very moment of percussion, behave passively, exactly as when they are at rest. Inert body so acts as body moved acts, if the truth be told. Newton recognizes that fact when he says that the force of inertia is the same as impetus. But body, inert and at rest, does nothing; therefore body moved does nothing.

27 Body in fact persists equally in either state, whether of motion or of rest. Its existence is not called its action; nor should its persistence be called its action. Persistence is only continuance in the same way of existing which cannot properly be called action. Resistance which we experience in stopping a body in motion we falsely imagine to be its action, deluded by empty appearance. For that resistance which we feel is in fact passion in ourselves, and does not prove that body acts, but that we are affected; it is quite certain that we should be affected in the same way, whether that body were to be moved by itself, or impelled by another principle.

28 Action and reaction are said to be in bodies, and that way of speaking suits the purposes of mechanical demonstrations; but we must not on that account suppose that there is some real virtue in them which is the cause or principle of motion. For those terms are to be understood in the same way as the term *attraction*; and just as attraction is only a mathematical hypothesis, and not a physical quality, the same must be understood also about action and reaction, and for the same reason. For in mechanical philosophy the truth and the use of theorems about the mutual attraction of bodies remain firm, as founded solely in the motion of bodies, whether that motion be supposed to be caused by the action of bodies mutually attracting each other, or by the action of some agent different from the bodies, impelling and controlling them. Similarly the traditional formulations of rules and laws of motions, along with the theorems thence deduced remain unshaken, provided that sensible effects and the reasonings grounded in them are granted, whether we suppose the action itself or the force that causes these effects to be in the body or in the incorporeal agent.

29 Take away from the idea of body extension, solidity, and figure, and nothing will remain. But those qualities are indifferent to motion, nor do they contain anything which could be called the principle of motion. This is clear from our very ideas. If therefore by the term *body* be meant that which we conceive, obviously the principle of motion cannot be sought therein, that is, no part or attribute thereof is the true, efficient cause of the production of motion. But to employ a term, and conceive nothing by it is quite unworthy of a philosopher.

30 A thinking, active thing is given which we experience as the principle of motion in ourselves. This we call *soul*, *mind*, and *spirit*. Extended thing also is given, inert, impenetrable, moveable, totally different from the former and constituting a new genus. Anaxagoras, wisest of men, was the first to grasp the great difference between thinking things and extended things, and he asserted that the mind has nothing in common with bodies, as is established from the first book of Aristotle's *De Anima*. Of the moderns Descartes has put the same point most forcibly. What was left clear by him others have rendered involved and difficult by their obscure terms.

31 From what has been said it is clear that those who affirm that active force, action, and the principle of motion are really in bodies are adopting an opinion not based on experience, are supporting it with obscure and general terms, and do not well understand their own meaning. On the contrary those who will have mind to be the principle of motion are advancing an opinion fortified by personal experience, and one approved by the suffrages of the most learned men in every age.

32 Anaxagoras was the first to introduce *nous* to impress motion on inert matter. Aristotle, too, approves that opinion and confirms it in many ways, openly stating that the first mover is immoveable, indivisible, and has no magnitude. And he rightly notes that to say that every mover must be moveable is the same as to say that every builder must be capable of being built. *Phys.* Bk. 8. Plato, moreover, in the Timaeus records that this corporeal machine, or visible world, is moved and animated by mind which eludes all sense. To-day indeed Cartesian philosophers recognize God as the principle of natural motions. And Newton everywhere frankly intimates that not only did motion originate from God, but that still the mundane system is moved by the same actus. This is agreeable to Holy Scripture; this is approved by the opinion of the Schoolmen; for though the Peripatetics tell us that nature is the principle of motion and rest, yet they interpret *natura naturans* to be God. They understand of course that all the bodies of this mundane system are moved by Almighty Mind according to certain and constant reason.

33 But those who attribute a vital principle to bodies are imagining an obscure notion and one ill suited to the facts. For what is meant by being endowed with the vital principle, except to live? And to live, what is it but to move oneself, to stop, and to change one's state? But the most learned philosophers of this age lay it down for an indubitable principle that every body persists in its own state, whether of rest or of uniform

movement in a straight line, except in so far as it is compelled from without to alter that state. The contrary is the case with mind; we feel it as a faculty of altering both our own state and that of other things, and that is properly called vital, and puts a wide distinction between soul and bodies.

34 Modern thinkers consider motion and rest in bodies as two states of existence in either of which every body, without pressure from external force, would naturally remain passive; whence one might gather that the cause of the existence of bodies is also the cause of their motion and rest. For no other cause of the successive existence of the body in different parts of space should be sought, it would seem, than that cause whence is derived the successive existence of the same body in different parts of time. But to treat of the good and great God, creator and preserver of all things, and to show how all things depend on supreme and true being, although it is the most excellent part of human knowledge, is, however, rather the province of first philosophy or metaphysics and theology than of natural philosophy which to-day is almost entirely confined to experiments and mechanics. And so natural philosophy either presupposes the knowledge of God or borrows it from some superior science. Although it is most true that the investigation of nature everywhere supplies the higher sciences with notable arguments to illustrate and prove the wisdom, the goodness, and the power of God.

35 The imperfect understanding of this situation has caused some to make the mistake of rejecting the mathematical principles of physics on the ground that they do not assign the efficient causes of things. It is not, however, in fact the business of physics or mechanics to establish efficient causes, but only the rules of impulsions or attractions, and, in a word, the laws of motions, and from the established laws to assign the solution, not the efficient cause, of particular phenomena.

36 It will be of great importance to consider what properly a principle is, and how that term is to be understood by philosophers. The true, efficient and conserving cause of all things by supreme right is called their fount and principle. Yet it is proper to describe as the 'principles' of experimental philosophy the foundations upon which it rests, the springs from which flows, not the existence, but our knowledge of corporeal things: I mean, the senses and experience. Similarly in mechanical philosophy those are to be called principles, in which the whole discipline is grounded and contained, those primary laws of motions which have been proved by experiments, elaborated by reason and rendered universal. These laws of motion are conveniently called principles, since from them are derived both general mechanical theorems and particular explanations of the phenomena.

37 A thing can be said to be explained mechanically then indeed when it is reduced to those most simple and universal principles, and shown by accurate reasoning to be in agreement and connection with them. For once the laws of nature have been found out, then it is the philosopher's task to show that each phenomenon is in constant conformity with those laws, that is, necessarily follows from those principles. In that consist the explanation

and solution of phenomena and the assigning their cause, *i.e.* the reason why they take place.

38 The human mind delights in extending and expanding its knowledge; and for this purpose general notions and propositions have to be formed in which particular propositions and cognitions are in some way comprised, which then, and not till then, are believed to be understood. Geometers know this well. In mechanics also notions are premised, *i.e.* definitions and first and general statements about motion from which afterwards by mathematical method conclusions more remote and less general are deduced. And just as by the application of geometrical theorems, the sizes of particular bodies are measured, so also by the application of the universal theorems of mechanics, the movements of any parts of the mundane system, and the phenomena thereon depending, become known and are determined. And that is the sole mark at which the physicist must aim.

39 And just as geometers for the sake of their art make use of many devices which they themselves cannot describe nor find in the nature of things, even so the mechanician makes use of certain abstract and general terms, imagining in bodies force, action, attraction, solicitation, *etc.* which are of first utility for theories and formulations, as also for computations about motion, even if in the truth of things, and in bodies actually existing, they would be looked for in vain, just like the geometers' fictions made by mathematical abstraction.

40 We actually perceive by the aid of the senses nothing except the effects or sensible qualities and corporeal things entirely passive, whether in motion or at rest; and reason and experience advise us that there is nothing active except mind or soul. Whatever else is imagined must be considered to be of a kind with other hypotheses and mathematical abstractions. This ought to be laid to heart; otherwise we are in danger of sliding back into the obscure subtlety of the Schoolmen, which for so many ages like some dread plague, has corrupted philosophy.

41 Mechanical principles and universal laws of motions or of nature, happy discoveries of the last century, treated and applied by aid of geometry, have thrown a remarkable light upon philosophy. But metaphysical principles and real efficient causes of the motion and existence of bodies or of corporeal attributes in no way belong to mechanics or experiment, nor throw light on them, except in so far as by being known beforehand they may serve to define the limits of physics, and in that way to remove imported difficulties and problems.

42 Those who derive the principle of motion from spirits mean by *spirit* either a corporeal thing or an incorporeal; if a corporeal thing, however tenuous, yet the difficulty recurs; if an incorporeal thing, however true it may be, yet it does not properly belong to physics. But if anyone were to extend natural philosophy beyond the limits of experiments and mechanics, so as to cover a knowledge of incorporeal and inextended things, that broader interpretation of the term permits a discussion of soul, mind, or vital principle. But it will be more convenient to follow the usage which is fairly well accepted, and so to distinguish between the

sciences as to confine each to its own bounds; thus the natural philosopher should concern himself entirely with experiments, laws of motions, mechanical principles, and reasonings thence deduced; but if he shall advance views on other matters, let him refer them for acceptance to some superior science. For from the known laws of nature very elegant theories and mechanical devices of practical utility follow; but from the knowledge of the Author of nature Himself by far the most excellent considerations arise, but they are metaphysical, theological, and moral.

43 So far about principles; now we must speak of the nature of motion. Motion though it is clearly perceived by the senses has been rendered obscure rather by the learned comments of philosophers than by its own nature. Motion never meets our senses apart from corporeal mass, space, and time. There are indeed those who desire to contemplate motion as a certain simple and abstract idea, and separated from all other things. But that very fine-drawn and subtle idea eludes the keen edge of intellect, as anyone can find for himself by meditation. Hence arise great difficulties about the nature of motion, and definitions far more obscure than the thing they are meant to illustrate. Such are those definitions of Aristotle and the Schoolmen, who say that motion is the act 'of the moveable in so far as it is moveable, or the act of a being in potentiality in so far as it is in potentiality.' Such is the saying of a famous man of modern times, who asserts that 'there is nothing real in motion except that momentary thing which must be constituted when a force is striving towards a change.' Again, it is agreed that the authors of these and similar definitions had it in mind to explain the abstract nature of motion, apart from every consideration of time and space; but how that abstract quintessence, so to speak, of motion, can be understood I do not see.

44 Not content with this they go further and divide and separate from one another the parts of motion itself, of which parts they try to make distinct ideas, as if of entities in fact distinct. For there are those who distinguish movement from motion, looking on the movement as an instantaneous element in the motion. Moreover, they would have velocity, conation, force, and impetus to be so many things differing in essence, each of which is presented to the intellect through its own abstract idea separated from all the rest. But we need not spend any more time on these discussions if the principles laid down above hold good.

45 Many also define motion by *passage*, forgetting indeed that passage itself cannot be understood without motion, and through motion ought to be defined. So very true is it that definitions throw light on some things, and darkness again on others. And certainly hardly anyone could by defining them make clearer or better known the things we perceive by sense. Enticed by the vain hope of doing so, philosophers have rendered easy things very difficult, and have ensnared their own minds in difficulties which for the most part they themselves produced. From this desire of defining and abstracting many very subtle questions both about motion and other things take their rise. Those useless questions have tortured the minds of men to no purpose; so that Aristotle often actually confesses that

motion is 'a certain act difficult to know,' and some of the ancients became such past-masters in trifling as to deny the existence of motion altogether.

46 But one is ashamed to linger on minutiæ of this sort; let it suffice to have indicated the sources of the solutions; but this, too, I must add. The traditional mathematical doctrines of the infinite division of time and space have, from the very nature of the case, introduced paradoxes and thorny theories (as are all those that involve the infinite) into speculations about motion. All such difficulties motion shares with space and time, or rather has taken them over from that source.

47 Too much abstraction, on the one hand, or the division of things truly inseparable, and on the other hand composition or rather confusion of very different things have perplexed the nature of motion. For it has become usual to confuse motion with the efficient cause of motion. Whence it comes about that motion appears, as it were, in two forms, presenting one aspect to the senses, and keeping the other aspect covered in dark night. Thence obscurity, confusion, and various paradoxes of motion take their rise, while what belongs in truth to the cause alone is falsely attributed to the effect.

48 This is the source of the opinion that the same quantity of motion is always conserved; anyone will easily satisfy himself of its falsity unless it be understood of the force and power of the cause, whether that cause be called nature or *nous*, or whatever be the ultimate agent. Aristotle indeed (*Phys.* Bk. 8) when he asks whether motion be generated and destroyed, or is truly present in all things from eternity like life immortal, seems to have understood the vital principle rather than the external effect or change of place.

49 Hence it is that many suspect that motion is not mere passivity in bodies. But if we understand by it that which in the movement of a body is an object to the senses, no one can doubt that it is entirely passive. For what is there in the successive existence of body in different places which could relate to action, or be other than bare, lifeless effect?

50 The Peripatetics who say that motion is the one act of both the mover and the moved do not sufficiently divide cause from effect. Similarly those who imagine effort or conation in motion, or think that the same body at the same time is borne in opposite directions, seem to be the sport of the same confusion of ideas, and the same ambiguity of terms.

51 Diligent attention in grasping the concepts of others and in formulating one's own is of great service in the science of motion as in all other things; and unless there had been a failing in this respect I do not think that matter for dispute could have come from the query, Whether a body is indifferent to motion and to rest, or not. For since experience shows that it is a primary law of nature that a body persists exactly in 'a state of motion and rest as long as nothing happens from elsewhere to change that state,' and on that account it is inferred that the force of inertia is under different aspects either resistance or impetus, in this sense assuredly a body can be called indifferent in its own nature to motion or rest. Of course it is as difficult to induce rest in a moving body as motion in a resting body;

but since the body conserves equally either state, why should it not be said to be indifferent to both?

52 The Peripatetics used to distinguish various kinds of motion corresponding to the variety of changes which a thing could undergo. To-day those who discuss motion understand by the term only local motion. But local motion cannot be understood without understanding the meaning of *locus*. Now *locus* is defined by moderns as 'the part of space which a body occupies,' whence it is divided into relative and absolute corresponding to space. For they distinguish between absolute or true space and relative or apparent space. That is they postulate space on all sides measureless, immoveable, insensible, permeating and containing all bodies, which they call absolute space. But space comprehended or defined by bodies, and therefore an object of sense, is called relative, apparent, vulgar space.

53 And so let us suppose that all bodies were destroyed and brought to nothing. What is left they call absolute space, all relation arising from the situation and distances of bodies being removed together with the bodies. Again, that space is infinite, immoveable, indivisible, insensible, without relation and without distinction. That is, all its attributes are privative or negative. It seems therefore to be mere nothing. The only slight difficulty arising is that it is extended, and extension is a positive quality. But what sort of extension, I ask, is that which cannot be divided nor measured, no part of which can be perceived by sense or pictured by the imagination? For nothing enters the imagination which from the nature of the thing cannot be perceived by sense, since indeed the imagination is nothing else than the faculty which represents sensible things either actually existing or at least possible. Pure intellect, too, knows nothing of absolute space. That faculty is concerned only with spiritual and inextended things, such as our minds, their states, passions, virtues, and such like. From absolute space then let us take away now the words of the name, and nothing will remain in sense, imagination, or intellect. Nothing else then is denoted by those words than pure privation or negation, *i.e.* mere nothing.

54 It must be admitted that in this matter we are in the grip of serious prejudices, and to win free we must exert the whole force of our minds. For many, so far from regarding absolute space as nothing, regard it as the only thing (God excepted) which cannot be annihilated; and they lay down that it necessarily exists of its own nature, that it is eternal and uncreate, and is actually a participant in the divine attributes. But in very truth since it is most certain that all things which we designate by names are known by qualities or relations, at least in part (for it would be stupid, to use words to which nothing known, no notion, idea or concept, were attached), let us diligently inquire whether it is possible to form any idea of that pure, real, and absolute space continuing to exist after the annihilation of all bodies. Such an idea, moreover, when I watch it somewhat more intently, I find to be the purest idea of nothing, if indeed it can be called an idea. This I myself have found on giving the matter my closest attention; this, I think, others will find on doing likewise.

55 We are sometimes deceived by the fact that when we imagine the

removal of all other bodies, yet we suppose our own body to remain. On this supposition we imagine the movement of our limbs fully free on every side; but motion without space cannot be conceived. None the less if we consider the matter again we shall find, 1st, relative space conceived defined by the parts of our body; 2nd, a fully free power of moving our limbs obstructed by no obstacle; and besides these two things nothing. It is false to believe that some third thing really exists, *viz.* immense space which confers on us the free power of moving our body; for this purpose the absence of other bodies is sufficient. And we must admit that this absence or privation of bodies is nothing positive.*

56 But unless a man has examined these points with a free and keen mind, words and terms avail little. To one who meditates, however, and reflects, it will be manifest, I think, that predications about pure and absolute space can all be predicated about nothing. By this argument the human mind is easily freed from great difficulties, and at the same time from the absurdity of attributing necessary existence to any being except to the good and great God alone.

57 It would be easy to confirm our opinion by arguments drawn, as they say *a posteriori*, by proposing questions about absolute space, *e.g.* Is it substance or accidents? Is it created or uncreated? and showing the absurdities which follow from either answer. But I must be brief. I must not omit, however, to state that Democritus of old supported this opinion with his vote. Aristotle is our authority for the statement, *Phys.* Bk. 1, where he has these words, 'Democritus lays down as principles the solid and the void, of which the one, he says, is as what is, the other as what is not.' That the distinction between absolute and relative space has been used by philosophers of great name, and that on it as on a foundation many fine theorems have been built, may make us scruple to accept the argument, but those are empty scruples as will appear from what follows.

58 From the foregoing it is clear that we ought not to define the true place of the body as the part of absolute space which the body occupies, and true or absolute motion as the change of true or absolute place; for all place is relative just as all motion is relative. But to make this appear more clearly we must point out that no motion can be understood without some determination or direction, which in turn cannot be understood unless besides the body in motion our own body also, or some other body, be understood to exist at the same time. For *up*, *down*, *left*, and *right* and all places and regions are founded in some relation, and necessarily connote and suppose a body different from the body moved. So that if we suppose the other bodies were annihilated and, for example, a globe were to exist alone, no motion could be conceived in it; so necessary is it that another body should be given by whose situation the motion should be understood to be determined. The truth of this opinion will be very clearly seen if we

* See the arguments against absolute space in my book on *The Principles of Human Knowledge* in the English tongue published ten years ago.

shall have carried out thoroughly the supposed annihilation of all bodies, our own and that of others, except that solitary globe.

59 Then let two globes be conceived to exist and nothing corporeal besides them. Let forces then be conceived to be applied in some way; whatever we may understand by the application of forces, a circular motion of the two globes round a common centre cannot be conceived by the imagination. Then let us suppose that the sky of the fixed stars is created; suddenly from the conception of the approach of the globes to different parts of that sky the motion will be conceived. That is to say that since motion is relative in its own nature, it could not be conceived before the correlated bodies were given. Similarly no other relation can be conceived without correlates.

60 As regards circular motion many think that, as motion truly circular increases, the body necessarily tends ever more and more away from its axis. This belief arises from the fact that circular motion can be seen taking its origin, as it were, at every moment from two directions, one along the radius and the other along the tangent, and if in this latter direction only the impetus be increased, then the body in motion will retire from the centre, and its orbit will cease to be circular. But if the forces be increased equally in both directions the motion will remain circular though accelerated—which will not argue an increase in the forces of retirement from the axis, any more than in the forces of approach to it. Therefore we must say that the water forced round in the bucket rises to the sides of the vessel, because when new forces are applied in the direction of the tangent to any particle of water, in the same instant new equal centripetal forces are not applied. From which experiment it in no way follows that absolute circular motion is necessarily recognized by the forces of retirement from the axis of motion. Again, how those terms *corporeal forces* and *conation* are to be understood is more than sufficiently shown in the foregoing discussion.

61 A curve can be considered as consisting of an infinite number of straight lines, though in fact it does not consist of them. That hypothesis is useful in geometry; and just so circular motion can be regarded as arising from an infinite number of rectilinear directions—which supposition is useful in mechanics. Not, however, on that account must it be affirmed that it is impossible that the centre of gravity of each body should exist successively in single points of the circular periphery, no account being taken of any rectilineal direction in the tangent or the radius.

62 We must not omit to point out that the motion of a stone in a sling or of water in a whirled bucket cannot be called truly circular motion as that term is conceived by those who define the true places of bodies by the parts of absolute space, since it is strangely compounded of the motions, not alone of bucket or sling, but also of the daily motion of the earth round her own axis, of her monthly motion round the common centre of gravity of earth and moon, and of her annual motion round the sun. And on that account each particle of the stone or the water describes a line far removed from circular. Nor in fact does that supposed axifugal conation exist,

since it is not concerned with some one axis in relation to absolute space, supposing that such a space exists; accordingly I do not see how that can be called a single conation to which a truly circular motion corresponds as to its proper and adequate effect.

63 No motion can be recognized or measured, unless through sensible things. Since then absolute space in no way affects the senses, it must necessarily be quite useless for the distinguishing of motions. Besides, determination or direction is essential to motion; but that consists in relation. Therefore it is impossible that absolute motion should be conceived.

64 Further, since the motion of the same body may vary with the diversity of relative place, nay actually since a thing can be said in one respect to be in motion and in another respect to be at rest, to determine true motion and true rest, for the removal of ambiguity and for the furtherance of the mechanics of these philosophers who take the wider view of the system of things, it would be enough to bring in, instead of absolute space, relative space as confined to the heavens of the fixed stars, considered as at rest. But motion and rest marked out by such relative space can conveniently be substituted in place of the absolutes, which cannot be distinguished from them by any mark. For however forces may be impressed, whatever conations there are, let us grant that motion is distinguished by actions exerted on bodies; never, however, will it follow that that space, absolute place, exists, and that change in it is true place.

65 The laws of motions and the effects, and theorems containing the proportions and calculations of the same for the different configurations of the paths, likewise for accelerations and different directions, and for mediums resisting in greater or less degree, all these hold without bringing absolute motion into account. As is plain from this that since according to the principles of those who introduce absolute motion, we cannot know by any indication whether the whole frame of things is at rest, or is moved uniformly in a direction, clearly we cannot know the absolute motion of any body.

66 From the foregoing it is clear that the following rules will be of great service in determining the true nature of motion: (1) to distinguish mathematical hypotheses from the natures of things; (2) to beware of abstractions; (3) to consider motion as something sensible, or at least imaginable; and to be content with relative measures. If we do so, all the famous theorems of the mechanical philosophy by which the secrets of nature are unlocked, and by which the system of the world is reduced to human calculation, will remain untouched; and the study of motion will be freed from a thousand minutiæ, subtleties, and abstract ideas. And let these words suffice about the nature of motion.

67 It remains to discuss the cause of the communication of motions. Most people think that the force impressed on the moveable body is the cause of motion in it. However that they do not assign a known cause of motion, and one distinct from the body and the motion is clear from the preceding argument. It is clear, moreover, that force is not a thing certain

and determinate, from the fact that great men advance very different opinions, even contrary opinions, about it, and yet in their results attain the truth. For Newton says that impressed force consists in action alone, and is the action exerted on the body to change its state, and does not remain after the action. Torricelli contends that a certain heap or aggregate of forces impressed by percussion is received into the mobile body, and there remains and constitutes impetus. Borelli and others say much the same. But although Newton and Torricelli seem to be disagreeing with one another, they each advance consistent views, and the thing is sufficiently well explained by both. For all forces attributed to bodies are mathematical hypotheses just as are attractive forces in planets and sun. But mathematical entities have no stable essence in the nature of things; and they depend on the notion of the definer. Whence the same thing can be explained in different ways.

68 Let us lay down that the new motion in the body struck is conserved either by the natural force by reason of which any body persists in its own uniform state of motion or of rest, or by the impressed force, received (while the percussion lasts) into the body struck, and there remaining; it will be the same in fact, the difference existing only in name. Similarly when the striking moveable body loses motion, and the struck body acquires it, it is not worth disputing whether the acquired motion is numerically the same as the motion lost; the discussion would lead into metaphysical and even verbal minutiæ about identity. And so it comes to the same thing, whether we say that motion passes from the striker to the struck, or that motion is generated *de novo* in the struck, and is destroyed in the striker. In either case it is understood that one body loses motion, the other acquires it, and besides that, nothing.

69 That the Mind which moves and contains this universal, bodily mass, and is the true efficient cause of motion, is the same cause, properly and strictly speaking, of the communication thereof I would not deny. In physical philosophy, however, we must seek the causes and solutions of phenomena among mechanical principles. Physically, therefore, a thing is explained not by assigning its truly active and incorporeal cause, but by showing its connection with mechanical principles, such as *action and reaction are always opposite and equal*. From such laws as from the source and primary principle, those rules for the communication of motions are drawn, which by the moderns for the great good of the sciences have been already found and demonstrated.

70 I, for my part, will content myself with hinting that that principle could have been set forth in another way. For if the true nature of things, rather than abstract mathematics, be regarded, it will seem more correct to say that in attraction or percussion, the passion of bodies, rather than their action, is equal on both sides. For example, the stone tied by a rope to a horse is dragged towards the horse just as much as the horse towards the stone; for the body in motion impinging on a quiescent body suffers the same change as the quiescent body. And as regards real effect, the striker is just as the struck, and the struck as the striker. And that change

on both sides, both in the body of the horse and in the stone, both in the moved and in the resting, is mere passivity. It is not established that there is force, virtue, or bodily action truly and properly causing such effects. The body in motion impinges on the quiescent body; we speak, however, in terms of action and say that that impels this; and it is correct to do so in mechanics where mathematical ideas, rather than the true natures of things, are regarded.

71 In physics sense and experience which reach only to apparent effects hold sway; in mechanics the abstract notions of mathematicians are admitted. In first philosophy or metaphysics we are concerned with incorporeal things, with causes, truth, and the existence of things. The physicist studies the series or successions of sensible things, noting by what laws they are connected, and in what order, what precedes as cause, and what follows as effect. And on this method we say that the body in motion is the cause of motion in the other, and impresses motion on it, draws it also or impels it. In this sense second corporeal causes ought to be understood, no account being taken of the actual seat of the forces or of the active powers or of the real cause in which they are. Further, besides body, figure, and motion, even the primary axioms of mechanical science can be called causes or mechanical principles, being regarded as the causes of the consequences.

72 Only by meditation and reasoning can truly active causes be rescued from the surrounding darkness and be to some extent known. To deal with them is the business of first philosophy or metaphysics. Allot to each science its own province; assign its bounds; accurately distinguish the principles and objects belonging to each. Thus it will be possible to treat them with greater ease and clarity.

The Theory of Vision

or Visual Language shewing the immediate Presence and
Providence of a Deity

Vindicated and Explained

First printed in 1733

The Theory of Vision
Vindicated and Explained

IN ANSWER TO AN ANONYMOUS WRITER

1 An ill state of health, which permits me to apply myself but seldom and by short intervals to any kind of studies, must be my apology, Sir, for not answering your Letter* sooner. This would have altogether excused me from a controversy upon points either personal or purely speculative, or from entering the lists with declaimers, whom I leave to the triumph of their own passions. And indeed to one of this character, who contradicts himself and misrepresents me, what answer can be made more than to desire his readers not to take his word for what I say, but to use their own eyes, read, examine, and judge for themselves? And to their common sense I appeal. For such a writer, such an answer may suffice. But argument, I allow, hath a right to be considered, and, where it doth not convince, to be opposed with reason. And being persuaded that the *Theory of Vision*, annexed to the *Minute Philosopher*, affords to thinking men a new and unanswerable proof of the existence and immediate operation of God, and the constant condescending care of his providence, I think myself concerned, as well as I am able, to defend and explain it, at a time wherein atheism hath made a greater progress than some are willing to own, or others to believe.

2 He who considers that the present avowed enemies of Christianity begun their attacks against it under the specious pretext of defending the Christian Church and its rights, when he observes the same men pleading for natural religion, will be tempted to suspect their views, and judge of their sincerity in one case from what they have shewed in the other. Certainly the notion of a watchful, active, intelligent, free Spirit, with whom we have to do, and in whom we live and move and have our being, is not the most prevailing in the books and conversation even of those who are called deists. Besides, as their schemes take effect, we may plainly perceive moral virtue and the religion of nature to decay, and see, both from reason and experience, that the destroying revealed religion must end in atheism or idolatry. It must be owned, many minute philosophers would not like at present to be accounted atheists. But how many, twenty years ago, would have been affronted to be thought infidels, who would now be much more affronted to be thought Christians! As it would be unjust to charge those with atheism who are not really tainted with it; so it will be allowed very uncharitable and imprudent to overlook it in those who are,

* Published in the *Daily Post-boy* of September the ninth, 1732.

and suffer such men under specious pretexts to spread their principles, and in the event to play the same game with natural religion that they have done with revealed.

3 It must, without question, shock some innocent admirers of a certain plausible pretender to deism and natural religion, if a man should say, there are strong signatures of atheism and irreligion in every sense, natural as well as revealed, to be found even in that admired writer:[1] and yet, to introduce taste instead of duty, to make man a necessary agent, to deride a future judgment, seem to all intents and purposes atheistical, or subversive of all religion whatsoever. And these every attentive reader may plainly discover to be his principles; although it be not always easy to fix a determinate sense on such a loose and incoherent writer. There seems to be a certain way of writing, whether good or bad, tinsel or sterling, sense or nonsense, which, being suited to that size of understanding that qualifies its owners for the minute philosophy, doth marvellously strike and dazzle those ingenious men, who are by this means conducted they know not how, and they know not whither. Doubtless that atheist who gilds and insinuates, and, even while he insinuates, disclaims his principles, is the likeliest to spread them. What availeth it in the cause of virtue and natural religion, to acknowledge the strongest traces of wisdom and power throughout the structure of the universe, if this wisdom is not employed to observe, nor this power to recompense our actions, if we neither believe ourselves accountable, nor God our judge?

4 All that is said of a vital principle of order, harmony, and proportion; all that is said of the natural decorum and fitness of things; all that is said of taste and enthusiasm, may well consist and be supposed, without a grain even of natural religion, without any notion of law or duty, any belief of a lord or judge, or any religious sense of a God; the contemplation of the mind upon the ideas of beauty, and virtue, and order, and fitness, being one thing, and a sense of religion another. So long as we admit no principle of good actions but natural affection, no reward but natural consequences; so long as we apprehend no judgment, harbour no fears, and cherish no hopes of a future state, but laugh at all these things, with the author of the *Characteristics*, and those whom he esteems the liberal and polished part of mankind,* how can we be said to be religious in any sense? Or what is here that an atheist may not find his account in as well as a theist? To what moral purpose might not fate or nature serve as well as a Deity, on such a scheme? And is not this, at bottom, the amount of all those fair pretences?

5 Certainly that atheistical men, who hold no principles of any religion, natural or revealed, are an increasing number, and this too among people of no despicable rank, hath long since been expressly acknowledged† by one who will be allowed a proper judge, even this same plausible pretender

---

* *Characteristics*, vol. 3. Miscel. 3. ch. 2.
† *Moralists*, Part II. Sect. III.
[1] [The Earl of Shaftesbury (1671–1713).]

himself to deism and enthusiasm. But if any well-meaning persons, deluded by artful writers in the minute philosophy, or wanting the opportunity of an unreserved conversation with some ingenious men of that sect, should think that *Lysicles*[1] hath overshot the mark, and misrepresented their principles: to be satisfied of the contrary, they need only cast an eye on the *Philosophical Dissertation upon Death*,[2] lately published by a minute philosopher. Perhaps some man of leisure may think it worth while to trace the progress and unfolding of their principles, down from the writer in defence of the *Rights of the Christian Church*,[3] to this plain-dealer, the admirable author upon *Death*. During which period of time, I think one may observe a laid design gradually to undermine the belief of the divine attributes and natural religion; which scheme runs parallel with their gradual, covert, insincere proceedings, in respect of the Gospel.

6 That atheistical principles have taken deeper root, and are farther spread than most people are apt to imagine, will be plain to whoever considers that pantheism, materialism, fatalism are nothing but atheism a little disguised; that the notions of *Hobbes*, *Spinoza*, *Leibnitz*, and *Bayle* are relished and applauded; that as they who deny the freedom and immortality of the soul in effect deny its being, even so they do, as to all moral effects and natural religion, deny the being of God, who deny Him to be an observer, judge, and rewarder of human actions; that the course of arguing pursued by infidels leads to atheism as well as infidelity.

[An instance of this may be seen in the proceeding of the author of a book entitled, *A Discourse of Free-thinking occasioned by the Rise and Growth of a Sect called Free-thinkers*,[4] who, having insinuated his infidelity from men's various pretences and opinions concerning revealed religion, in like manner appears to insinuate his atheism from the differing notions of men concerning the nature and attributes of God, particularly from the opinion of our knowing God by analogy,* as it hath been misunderstood and misinterpreted by some of late years. Such is the ill effect of unto-ward defences and explanations of our faith; and such advantage do incautious friends give its enemies. If there be any modern well-meaning writer, who (perhaps from not having considered the fifth book of *Euclid*) writes much of analogy without understanding it, and thereby hath slipped his foot into this snare, I wish him to slip it back again, and, instead of causing scandal to good men and triumph to atheists, discreetly explain away his first sense; and return to speak of God and his attributes in the style of other Christians, allowing that knowledge and wisdom do, in the proper sense of the words, belong to God, and that we have some notion, though infinitely inadequate, of those divine attributes, yet still more than a man blind from his birth can have of light and colours.]

* See page 42 of the mentioned book.
[1] [A 'free-thinker' in Berkeley's *Alciphron*.]
[2] [1732. Attributed to A. Radicati.]
[3] [1706. By M. Tindal.]
[4] [1713. By Anthony Collins.]

But to return, if I see it in their writings, if they own it in their conversation, if their ideas imply it, if their ends are not answered but by
supposing it, if their leading author hath pretended to demonstrate
atheism, but thought fit to conceal his demonstration from the public;
if this was known in their clubs, and yet that author was nevertheless
followed, and represented to the world as a believer of natural religion;
if these things are so (and I know them to be so), surely what the favourers
of their schemes would palliate, it is the duty of others to display and refute.

7 And although the characters of divinity are large and legible throughout the whole creation to men of plain sense and common understanding,
yet it must be considered that we have other adversaries to oppose, other
proselytes to make, men prejudiced to false systems and proof against
vulgar arguments, who must be dealt with on a different foot. Conceited,
metaphysical, disputing men must be paid in another coin; we must shew
that truth and reason in all shapes are equally against them, except we
resolve to give them up, what they are very fond of being thought to
engross, all pretensions to philosophy, science, and speculation.

8 Meanwhile thus much is evident: those good men who shall not
care to employ their thoughts on this *Theory of Vision* have no reason
to find fault. They are just where they were, being left in full possession
of all other arguments for a God, none of which are weakened by this.
And as for those who shall be at the pains to examine and consider this
subject, it is hoped they may be pleased to find, in an age wherein so many
schemes of atheism are restored or invented, a new argument of a singular
nature in proof of the immediate care and providence of a God, present to
our minds, and directing our actions. As these considerations convince
me that I cannot employ myself more usefully than in contributing to
awaken and possess men with a thorough sense of the Deity inspecting,
concurring, and interesting itself in human actions and affairs: so, I hope
it will not be disagreeable to you that, in order to this, I make my appeal
to reason, from your remarks upon what I have wrote concerning vision;
since men who differ in the means may yet agree in the end, and in the same
candour and love of truth.

9 By a sensible object I understand that which is properly perceived by
sense. Things properly perceived by sense are immediately perceived.
Beside things properly and immediately perceived by any sense, there may
be also other things suggested to the mind by means of those proper and
immediate objects. Which things so suggested are not objects of that sense,
being in truth only objects of the imagination, and originally belonging to
some other sense or faculty. Thus, sounds are the proper object of hearing,
being properly and immediately perceived by that, and by no other sense.
But, by the mediation of sounds or words all other things may be suggested
to the mind, and yet things so suggested are not thought the object of
hearing.

10 The peculiar objects of each sense, although they are truly or strictly
perceived by that sense alone, may yet be suggested to the imagination
by some other sense. The objects therefore of all the senses may become

objects of imagination, which faculty represents all sensible things. A colour, therefore, which is truly perceived by sight alone, may, nevertheless, upon hearing the words *blue* or *red*, be apprehended by the imagination. It is in a primary and peculiar manner the object of sight: in a secondary manner it is the object of imagination: but cannot properly be supposed the object of hearing.

11 The objects of sense, being things immediately perceived, are otherwise called ideas. The cause of these ideas, or the power producing them, is not the object of sense, not being itself perceived, but only inferred by reason from its effects, to wit, those objects or ideas which are perceived by sense. From our ideas of sense the inference of reason is good to a Power, Cause, Agent. But we may not therefore infer that our ideas are like unto this Power, Cause, or active Being. On the contrary, it seems evident that an idea can be only like another idea, and that in our ideas or immediate objects of sense, there is nothing of power, causality, or agency included.

12 Hence it follows that the Power or Cause of ideas is not an object of sense, but of reason. Our knowledge of the cause is measured by the effect, of the power by our idea. To the absolute nature, therefore, of outward causes or powers, we have nothing to say: they are no objects of our sense or perception. Whenever, therefore, the appellation of sensible *object* is used in a determined intelligible sense, it is not applied to signify the absolutely existing outward cause or power, but the ideas themselves produced thereby.

13 Ideas which are observed to be connected together are vulgarly considered under the relation of cause and effect, whereas, in strict and philosophic truth, they are only related as the sign to the thing signified. For we know our ideas; and therefore know that one idea cannot be the cause of another. We know that our ideas of sense are not the cause of themselves. We know also that we do not cause them. Hence we know they must have some other efficient cause distinct from them and us.

14 In treating of vision, it was my purpose to consider the effects and appearances, the objects perceived by my senses, the ideas of sight as connected with those of touch; to inquire how one idea comes to suggest another belonging to a different sense, how things visible suggest things tangible, how present things suggest things remote and future, whether by likeness, by necessary connexion, by geometrical inference, or by arbitrary institution.

15 It hath indeed been a prevailing opinion and undoubted principle among mathematicians and philosophers that there were certain ideas common to both senses: whence arose the distinction of primary and secondary qualities. But I think it hath been demonstrated that there is no such thing as a common object, as an idea, or kind of idea perceived both by sight and touch.

16 In order to treat with due exactness on the nature of vision, it is necessary in the first place accurately to consider our own ideas: to distinguish where there is a difference: to call things by their right names:

to define terms, and not confound ourselves and others by their ambiguous use: the want or neglect whereof hath so often produced mistakes. Hence it is that men talk as if one idea was the efficient cause of another: hence they mistake inferences of reason for perceptions of sense: hence they confound the power residing in somewhat external with the proper object of sense, which is in truth no more than our own idea.

17 When we have well understood and considered the nature of vision, we may, by reasoning from thence, be better able to collect some knowledge of the external, unseen cause of our ideas, whether it be one or many, intelligent or unintelligent, active or inert, body or spirit. But, in order to understand and comprehend this theory, and discover the true principles thereof, we should consider the likeliest way is not to attend to unknown substances, external causes, agents, or powers, nor to reason or infer anything about or from things obscure, unperceived, and altogether unknown.

18 As in this inquiry we are concerned with what objects we perceive, or our own ideas, so, upon them our reasonings must proceed. To treat of things utterly unknown as if we knew them, and so lay our beginning in obscurity, would not surely seem the properest means for the discovering of truth. Hence it follows that it would be wrong if one about to treat of the nature of vision, should, instead of attending to visible ideas, define the object of sight to be that obscure cause, that invisible power or agent, which produced visible ideas in our minds. Certainly such cause or power doth not seem to be the object either of the sense or the science of vision, inasmuch as what we know thereby we know only of the effects. Having premised thus much, I now proceed to consider the principles laid down in your letter, which I shall take in order as they lie.

19 In your first paragraph or section, you say that 'whatever it is without which is the cause of any idea within, you call the object of sense.' And you tell us soon after this,* 'that we cannot possibly have an idea of any object without.' Hence it follows that by an object of sense you mean something that we can have no manner of idea of. This making the objects of sense to be things utterly insensible or unperceivable seems to me contrary to common sense and the use of language. That there is nothing in the reason of things to justify such a definition is, I think, plain from what hath been premised:† and that it is contrary to received custom and opinion, I appeal to the experience of the first man you meet, who I suppose will tell you that by an object of sense he means that which is perceived by sense, and not a thing utterly unperceivable and unknown. The beings, substances, powers which exist without may indeed concern a treatise on some other science, and may there become a proper subject of inquiry. But, why they should be considered as objects of the visive faculty, in a treatise of optics, I do not comprehend.

20 The real objects of sight we see, and what we see we know. And these true objects of sense and knowledge, to wit, our own ideas, are to be considered, compared, distinguished, in order to understand the true theory

---

* Sect. 4.   † *Supra*, sect. 9, 11, 12.

of vision. As to the outward cause of these ideas, whether it be one and the same, or various and manifold, whether it be thinking or unthinking, spirit or body, or whatever else we conceive or determine about it, the visible appearances do not alter their nature, our ideas are still the same. Though I may have an erroneous notion of the cause, or though I may be utterly ignorant of its nature; yet this doth not hinder my making true and certain judgments about my ideas: my knowing which are the same, and which different: wherein they agree, and wherein they disagree: which are connected together, and wherein this connexion consists: whether it be founded in a likeness of nature, in a geometrical necessity, or merely in experience and custom.

21 In your second section, you say 'that if we had but one sense, we might be apt to conclude there were no objects at all without us: but that, since the same object is the cause of ideas by different senses, thence we infer its existence.' Now, in the first place, I observe, that I am at a loss concerning the point which is here assumed, and would fain be informed how we come to know that the same object causeth ideas by different senses. In the next place, I must observe that, if I had only one sense, I should nevertheless infer and conclude there was some cause without me (which you, it seems, define to be an object), producing the sensations or ideas perceived by that sense. For, if I am conscious that I do not cause them, and know that they are not the cause of themselves, both which points seem very clear, it plainly follows that there must be some other third cause distinct from me and them.

22 In your third section, you acknowledge with me 'that the connexion between ideas of different senses ariseth only from experience.' Herein we are agreed. In your fourth section you say 'that a word denoting an external object, is the representative of no manner of idea: neither can we possibly have an idea of what is solely without us.' What is here said of an external unknown object hath been already considered.*

23 In the following section of your Letter, you declare 'that our ideas have only an arbitrary connexion with outward objects: that they are nothing like the outward objects: and that a variation in our ideas doth not imply or infer a change in the objects, which may still remain the same.' Now, to say nothing about the confused use of the word object, which hath been more than once already observed, I shall only remark that the points asserted in this section do not seem to consist with some others that follow.

24 For in the sixth section you say 'that in the present situation of things, there is an infallible certain connexion between the idea and the object.' But how can we perceive this connexion, since according to you† we never perceive such object, nor can have any idea of it? Or, not perceiving it, how can we know this connexion to be infallibly certain?

25 In the seventh section it is said 'that we may, from our infallible experience, argue from our idea of one sense to that of another.' But, I

---

* Supra, sect. 19.   † *Letter*, sect. 4.

think it is plain that our experience of the connexion between ideas of sight and touch is not infallible: since, if it were, there could be no *deceptio visus*, neither in painting, perspective, dioptrics, nor any other wise.

26 In the last section you affirm 'that experience plainly teaches us that a just proportion is observed in the alteration of the ideas of each sense, from the alteration of the object.' Now, I cannot possibly reconcile this section with the fifth, or comprehend how experience should shew us that the alteration of the object produceth a proportionable alteration in the ideas of different senses; or how indeed it should shew us anything at all either from or about the alteration of an object utterly unknown, of which we neither have nor can have any manner of idea. What I do not perceive or know, how can I perceive or know to be altered? And, knowing nothing of its alterations, how can I compute anything by them, deduce anything from them, or be said to have any experience about them?

27 From the observations you have premised, rightly understood and considered, you say it follows 'that my *New Theory of Vision* must in a great measure fall to the ground; and the laws of optics will be found to stand upon the old unshaken bottom.' But, though I have considered and endeavoured to understand your remarks, yet I do not in the least comprehend how this conclusion can be inferred from them. The reason you assign for such inference is, 'because, though our ideas in one sense are entirely different from our ideas in another; yet we may justly argue from one to the other, as they have one common cause without; of which, you say, we cannot possibly have even the faintest idea.' Now, my theory nowhere supposeth that we may not justly argue from the ideas of one sense to those of another, by analogy and by experience: on the contrary, this very point is affirmed, proved, or supposed throughout.*

28 Indeed I do not see how the inferences which we make from visible to tangible ideas include any consideration of one common unknown external cause, or depend thereon, but only on mere custom or habit. The experience which I have had that certain ideas of one sense are attended or connected with certain ideas of a different sense is, I think, a sufficient reason why the one may suggest the other.

29 In the next place you affirm 'that something without, which is the cause of all the variety of ideas within in one sense, is the cause also of the variety in another: and as they have a necessary connexion with it, we very justly demonstrate from our ideas of feeling, of the same object, what will be our ideas of seeing.' As to which, give me leave to remark that to inquire whether that unknown something be the same in both cases, or different, is a point foreign to optics; inasmuch as our perceptions by the visive faculty will be the very same, however we determine that point. Perhaps I think that the same Being which causeth our ideas of sight doth cause not only our ideas of touch likewise, but also all our ideas of all the other senses, with all the varieties thereof. But this, I say, is foreign to the purpose.

* *Theory of Vision*, sect. 38 and 78, &c.

30 As to what you advance, that our ideas have a *necessary* connexion with such cause, it seems to me *gratis dictum*: no reason is produced for this assertion; and I cannot assent to it without a reason. The ideas or effects I grant are evidently perceived: but the cause, you say, is utterly unknown.* How, therefore, can you tell whether such unknown cause acts arbitrarily or necessarily? I see the effects or appearances: and I know that effects must have a cause: but I neither see nor know that their connexion with that cause is necessary. Whatever there may be, I am sure I see no such necessary connexion, nor, consequently, can demonstrate by means thereof from ideas of one sense to those of another.

31 You add that although to talk of seeing by tangible angles and lines be direct nonsense, yet, to demonstrate from angles and lines in feeling to the ideas in seeing that arise from the same common object is very good sense. If by this no more is meant than that men might argue and compute geometrically by lines and angles in optics, it is so far from carrying in it any opposition to my theory that I have expressly declared the same thing.† This doctrine, as admitted by me, is indeed subject to certain limitations, there being divers cases wherein the writers of optics thought we judged by lines and angles, or by a sort of natural geometry; with regard to which I think they were mistaken, and I have given my reasons for it. And those reasons, as they are untouched in your letter, retain their force with me.

32 I have now gone through your reflexions, which the conclusion intimates to have been written in haste, and, having considered them with all the attention I am master of, must now leave it to the thinking reader to judge whether they contain anything that should oblige me to depart from what I have advanced in my *Theory of Vision*. For my own part, if I were ever so willing, it is not on this occasion in my power to indulge myself in the honest satisfaction it would be frankly to give up a known error, a thing so much more right and reputable to renounce than to defend. On the contrary, it should seem that the theory will stand secure: since you agree with me that men do not see by lines and angles: since I, on the other hand, agree with you that we may nevertheless compute in optics by lines and angles, as I have expressly shewed: since all that is said in your letter about the object, the same object, the alteration of the object, is quite foreign to the theory, which considereth our ideas as the object of sense, and hath nothing to do with that unknown, unperceived, unintelligible thing which you signify by the word object.‡ Certainly the laws of optics will not stand on the old, unshaken bottom, if it be allowed that we do not see by geometry:§ if it be evident that explications of phenomena given by the received theories in optics are insufficient and faulty: if other principles are found necessary for explaining the nature of vision: if there be no idea, nor kind of idea, common to both senses,¶ contrary to the old received universal supposition of optic writers.

33 We not only impose on others but often on ourselves, by the unsteady

* *Letter*, sect. 1 and 4. † *Theory of Vision*, sect. 78.
‡ *Supra*, sect. 14. § *Letter*, sect. 8.
¶ *Theory of Vision*, sect. 127.

or ambiguous use of terms. One would imagine that an object should be perceived. I must own, when that word is employed in a different sense, that I am at a loss for its meaning, and consequently cannot comprehend any arguments or conclusions about it: and I am not sure that, on my own part, some inaccuracy of expression, as well as the peculiar nature of the subject, not always easy either to explain or to conceive, may not have rendered my treatise concerning vision difficult to a cursory reader. But, to one of due attention, and who makes my words an occasion of his own thinking, I conceive the whole to be very intelligible. And, when it is rightly understood, I scarce doubt but it will be assented to. One thing at least I can affirm, that, if I am mistaken, I can plead neither haste nor inattention, having taken true pains and much thought about it.

34 And had you, Sir, thought it worth while to have dwelt more particularly on the subject, to have pointed out distinct passages in my treatise, to have answered any of my objections to the received notions, refuted any of my arguments in behalf of mine, or made a particular application of your own; I might without doubt have profited by your reflexions. But it seems to me we have been considering, either different things, or else the same things in such different views as the one can cast no light on the other. I shall, nevertheless, take this opportunity to make a review of my theory, in order to render it more easy and clear; and the rather because, as I had applied myself betimes to this subject, it became familiar: and in treating of things familiar to ourselves, we are too apt to think them so to others.

35 It seemed proper, if not unavoidable, to begin in the accustomed style of optic writers, admitting divers things as true, which in a rigorous sense are not such, but only received by the vulgar and admitted for such. There hath been a long and close connexion in our minds between the ideas of sight and touch. Hence they are considered as one thing: which prejudice suiteth well enough with the purposes of life; and language is suited to this prejudice. The work of science and speculation is to unravel our prejudices and mistakes, untwisting the closest connexions, distinguishing things that are different, instead of confused and perplexed, giving us distinct views, gradually correcting our judgment, and reducing it to a philosophical exactness. And, as this work is the work of time, and done by degrees, it is extremely difficult, if at all possible, to escape the snares of popular language, and the being betrayed thereby to say things strictly speaking neither true nor consistent. This makes thought and candour more especially necessary in the reader. For, language being accommodated to the prænotions of men and use of life, it is difficult to express therein the precise truth of things, which is so distant from their use, and so contrary to our prænotions.

36 In the contrivance of vision, as in that of other things, the wisdom of Providence seemeth to have consulted the operation, rather than the theory, of man; to the former things are admirably fitted, but, by that very means, the latter is often perplexed. For, as useful as these immediate suggestions and constant connexions are to direct our actions; so is our distinguishing between things confounded, and our separating things

connected, and as it were blended together, no less necessary to the speculation and knowledge of truth.

37 The knowledge of these connexions, relations, and differences of things visible and tangible, their nature, force, and significancy hath not been duly considered by former writers in optics, and seems to have been the great *desideratum* in that science, which for want thereof was confused and imperfect. A treatise, therefore, of this philosophical kind, for the understanding of vision, is at least as necessary as the physical consideration of the eye, nerve, coats, humours, refractions, bodily nature and motion of light, or the geometrical application of lines and angles for *praxis* or theory, in dioptric glasses and mirrors, or computing and reducing to some rule and measure our judgments, so far as they are proportional to the objects of geometry. In these three lights vision should be considered, in order to a complete theory of optics.

38 It is to be noted that, in considering the theory of vision, I observed a certain known method, wherein, from false and popular suppositions, men do often arrive at truth. Whereas in the synthetical method of delivering science or truth already found, we proceed in an inverted order, the conclusions in the analysis being assumed as principles in the synthesis. I shall therefore now begin with that conclusion, that *vision is the language of the Author of Nature*, from thence deducing theorems and solutions of phenomena, and explaining the nature of visible things and the visive faculty.

39 Ideas which are observed to be connected with other ideas come to be considered as signs, by means whereof things not actually perceived by sense are signified or suggested to the imagination, whose objects they are, and which alone perceives them. And as sounds suggest other things, so characters suggest those sounds; and, in general, all signs suggest the things signified, there being no idea which may not offer to the mind another idea which hath been frequently joined with it. In certain cases a sign may suggest its correlate as an image, in others as an effect, in others as a cause. But where there is no such relation of similitude or causality, nor any necessary connexion whatsoever, two things, by their mere coexistence, or two ideas, merely by being perceived together, may suggest or signify one the other, their connexion being all the while arbitrary; for it is the connexion only, as such, that causeth this effect.

40 A great number of arbitrary signs, various and apposite, do constitute a language. If such arbitrary connexion be instituted by men, it is an artificial language; if by the Author of Nature, it is a natural language. Infinitely various are the modifications of light and sound, whence they are each capable of supplying an endless variety of signs, and, accordingly, have been each employed to form languages; the one by the arbitrary appointment of mankind, the other by that of God Himself.* A connexion established by the Author of Nature, in the ordinary course of things, may surely be called natural; as that made by men will be named artificial.

---

* *Minute Philosopher*, Dial. IV. sect. 7, 11.

And yet this doth not hinder but the one may be as arbitrary as the other. And, in fact, there is no more likeness to exhibit, or necessity to infer, things tangible from the modifications of light, than there is in language to collect the meaning from the sound.* But, such as the connexion is of the various tones and articulations of voice with their several meanings, the same is in between the various modes of light and their respective correlates; or, in other words, between the ideas of sight and touch.

41 As to light, and its several modes or colours, all thinking men are agreed that they are ideas peculiar only to sight; neither common to the touch, nor of the same kind with any that are perceived by that sense. But herein lies the mistake, that, beside these, there are supposed other ideas common to both senses, being equally perceived by sight and touch, such as extension, size, figure, and motion. But that there are in reality no such common ideas, and that the objects of sight, marked by those words, are entirely different and heterogeneous from whatever is the object of feeling, marked by the same names, hath been proved in the *Theory*,† and seems by you admitted. Though I cannot conceive how you should in reason admit this, and at the same time contend for the received theories, which are as much ruined as mine is established by this main part and pillar thereof.

42 To perceive is one thing; to judge is another. So likewise, to be suggested is one thing, and to be inferred another. Things are suggested and perceived by sense. We make judgments and inferences by the understanding. What we immediately and properly perceive by sight is its primary object, light and colours. What is suggested or perceived by mediation therefore, are tangible ideas which may be considered as secondary and improper objects of sight. We infer causes from effects, effects from causes, and properties one from another, where the connection is necessary. But, how comes it to pass that we apprehend by the ideas of sight certain other ideas, which neither resemble them, nor cause them, nor are caused by them, nor have any necessary connexion with them? The solution of this problem, in its full extent, doth comprehend the whole theory of vision. Thus stating of the matter placeth it on a new foot, and in a different light from all preceding theories.

43 To explain how the mind or soul of man simply sees is one thing, and belongs to philosophy. To consider particles as moving in certain lines, rays of light as refracted or reflected, or crossing, or including angles, is quite another thing, and appertaineth to geometry. To account for the sense of vision by the mechanism of the eye is a third thing, which appertaineth to anatomy and experiments. These two latter speculations are of use in practice, to assist the defects and remedy the distempers of sight, agreeably to the natural laws obtaining in this mundane system. But the former theory is that which makes us understand the true nature of vision, considered as a faculty of the soul. Which theory, as I have already ob-

* *Theory of Vision*, sect. 144 and 147.
† *Theory of Vision*, sect. 127.

served, may be reduced to this simple question, to wit—how comes it to pass that a set of ideas, altogether different from tangible ideas, should nevertheless suggest them to us, there being no necessary connexion between them? To which the proper answer is, that this is done in virtue of an arbitrary connexion, instituted by the Author of Nature.

44 The proper, immediate object of vision is light, in all its modes and variations, various colours in kind, in degree, in quantity; some lively, others faint; more of some and less of others; various in their bounds or limits; various in their order and situation. A blind man, when first made to see, might perceive these objects, in which there is an endless variety; but he would neither perceive nor imagine any resemblance or connexion between these visible objects and those perceived by feeling.* Lights, shades, and colours would suggest nothing to him about bodies, hard or soft, rough or smooth: nor would their quantities, limits, or order suggest to him geometrical figures, or extension, or situation, which they must do upon the received supposition, that these objects are common to sight and touch.

45 All the various sorts, combinations, quantities, degrees, and dispositions of light and colours, would, upon the first perception thereof, be considered in themselves only as a new set of sensations or ideas. As they are wholly new and unknown, a man born blind would not, at first sight, give them the names of things formerly known and perceived by his touch. But, after some experience, he would perceive their connexion with tangible things, and would, therefore, consider them as signs, and give them (as is usual in other cases) the same names with the things signified.

46 More and less, greater and smaller, extent, proportion, interval are all found in time as in space; but it will not therefore follow that these are homogeneous quantities. No more will it follow, from the attribution of common names, that visible ideas are homogeneous with those of feeling. It is true that terms denoting tangible extension, figure, location, motion, and the like, are also applied to denote the quantity, relation, and order of the proper visible objects or ideas of sight. But this proceeds only from experience and analogy. There is a *higher* and *lower* in the notes of music. Men speak in a high or a low key. And this, it is plain, is no more than metaphor or analogy. So likewise, to express the order of visible ideas, the words *situation, high* and *low, up* and *down*, are made use of, and their sense, when so applied, is analogical.

47 But, in the case of vision we do not rest in a supposed analogy between different and heterogeneous natures. We suppose an identity of nature, or one and the same object common to both senses. And this mistake we are led into; forasmuch as the various motions of the head, upward and downward, to the right and to the left, being attended with a diversity in the visible ideas, it cometh to pass that those motions and situations of the head, which in truth are tangible, do confer their own

* *Theory of Vision,* sect. 41 and 106.

attributes and appellations on visible ideas wherewith they are connected, and which by that means come to be termed high and low, right and left, and to be marked by other names betokening the modes of position;* which, antecedently to such experienced connexion, would not have been attributed to them, at least not in the primary and literal sense.

48 From hence we may see how the mind is enabled to discern by sight the situation of distant objects. Those immediate objects whose mutual respect and order come to be expressed by terms relative to tangible place, being connected with the real objects of touch, what we say and judge of the one, we say and judge of the other, transferring our thought or apprehension from the signs to the things signified: as it is usual, in hearing or reading a discourse, to overlook the sounds or letters, and instantly pass on to the meaning.†

49 But there is a great difficulty relating to the situation of objects, as perceived by sight. For, since the pencils of rays issuing from any luminous object do, after their passage through the pupil, and their refraction by the crystalline, delineate inverted pictures in the retina, which pictures are supposed the immediate proper objects of sight, how comes it to pass that the objects whereof the pictures are thus inverted do yet seem erect and in their natural situation? For the objects not being perceived otherwise than by their pictures, it should follow that, as these are inverted, those should seem so too. But this difficulty, which is inexplicable on all the received principles and theories, admits of a most natural solution, if it be considered that the retina, crystalline, pupil, rays crossing refracted and reunited in distinct images correspondent and similar to the outward objects, are things altogether of a tangible nature.

50 The pictures, so called, being formed by the radious pencils, after their above-mentioned crossing and refraction, are not so truly pictures as images, or figures, or projections, tangible figures projected by tangible rays on a tangible retina, which are so far from being the proper objects of sight that they are not at all perceived thereby, being by nature altogether of the tangible kind, and apprehended by the imagination alone, when we suppose them actually taken in by the eye. These tangible images on the retina have some resemblance unto the tangible objects from which the rays go forth; and in respect of those objects I grant they are inverted. But then I deny that they are, or can be, the proper immediate objects of sight. This, indeed, is vulgarly supposed by the writers of optics: but it is a vulgar error: which being removed, the forementioned difficulty is removed with it, and admits a just and full solution, being shewn to arise from a mistake.

51 Pictures, therefore, may be understood in a twofold sense, or as two kinds quite dissimilar and heterogeneous, the one consisting of light, shade, and colours; the other not properly pictures, but images projected on the retina. Accordingly, for distinction, I shall call those *pictures*, and these *images*. The former are visible, and the peculiar objects of sight. The latter are so far otherwise, that a man blind from his birth may perfectly

* *Theory of Vision*, sect. 99.   † *Min. Phil.*, Dial IV. sect. 12.

imagine, understand, and comprehend them. And here it may not be amiss to observe that figures and motions which cannot be actually felt by us, but only imagined, may nevertheless be esteemed tangible ideas, forasmuch as they are of the same kind with the objects of touch, and as the imagination drew them from that sense.

52 Throughout this whole affair the mind is wonderfully apt to be deluded by the sudden suggestions of fancy, which it confounds with the perceptions of sense, and is prone to mistake a close and habitual connexion between the most distinct and different things for an identity of nature.* The solution of this knot about inverted images seems the principal point in the whole optic theory, the most difficult perhaps to comprehend, but the most deserving of our attention, and, when rightly understood, the surest way to lead the mind into a thorough knowledge of the true nature of vision.

53 It is to be noted of those inverted images on the retina that, although they are in kind altogether different from the proper objects of sight or pictures, they may nevertheless be proportional to them; as indeed the most different and heterogeneous things in nature may, for all that, have analogy, and be proportional each to other. And although those images, when the distance is given, should be simply as the radiating surfaces; and although it be consequently allowed that the pictures are in that case proportional to those radiating surfaces, or the tangible real magnitude of things; yet it will not thence follow that in common sight we perceive or judge of those tangible real magnitudes simply by the visible magnitudes of the pictures; for therein the distance is not given, tangible objects being placed at various distances: and the diameters of the images, to which images the pictures are proportional, are inversely as those distances, which distances are not immediately perceived by sight.† And admitting they were, it is nevertheless certain that the mind, in apprehending the magnitudes of tangible objects by sight, doth not compute them by means of the inverse proportion of the distances, and the direct proportion of the pictures. That no such inference or reasoning attends the common act of seeing, everyone's experience may inform him.

54 To know how we perceive or apprehend by sight the real magnitude of tangible objects, we must consider the immediate visible objects, and their properties or accidents. These immediate objects are the pictures. These pictures are some more lively, others more faint. Some are higher, others are lower in their own order or peculiar location, which, though in truth quite distinct, and altogether different from that of tangible objects, hath nevertheless a relation and connexion with it, and thence comes to be signified by the same terms, *high*, *low*, and so forth. Now by the greatness of the pictures, their faintness and their situation, we perceive the magnitude of tangible objects, the greater, the fainter, and the upper pictures suggesting the greater tangible magnitude.

55 For the better explication of this point, we may suppose a dia-

---

* *Theory of Vision*, sect. 144.   † *Theory of Vision*, sect. 2.

phanous plane erected near the eye, perpendicular to the horizon, and divided into small equal squares. A straight line from the eye to the utmost limit of the horizon, passing through this diaphanous plane, will mark a certain point or height to which the horizontal plane, as projected or represented in the perpendicular plane, would rise. The eye sees all the parts and objects in the horizontal plane, through certain corresponding squares of the perpendicular diaphanous plane. Those that occupy most squares have a greater visible extension, which is proportional to the squares. But the tangible magnitudes of objects are not judged proportional thereto. For those which are seen through the upper squares shall appear vastly bigger than those seen through the lower squares, though occupying the same, or a much greater number of those equal squares in the diaphanous plane.

56 Rays issuing from every point of each part or object in the horizontal plane, through the diaphanous plane to the eye, do to the imagination exhibit an image of the horizontal plane and all its parts, delineated in the diaphanous plane, and occupying the squares thereof to a certain height marked out by a right line reaching from the eye to the farthest limit of the horizon. A line drawn through the forementioned height or mark, upon the diaphanous plane, and parallel to the horizon, I call the horizontal line. Every square contains an image of some corresponding part of the horizontal plane. And this entire image we may call the horizontal image, and the picture answering to it the horizontal picture. In which representation, the upper images suggest much greater magnitudes than the lower. And these images suggesting the greater magnitudes are also fainter as well as upper. Whence it follows that faintness and situation concur with visible magnitude to suggest tangible magnitude. For the truth of all which I appeal to the experience and attention of the reader who shall add his own reflexion to what I have written.

57 It is true this diaphanous plane, and the images supposed to be projected thereon, are altogether of a tangible nature:* but then there are pictures relative to those images: and those pictures have an order among themselves, answering to the situation of the images, in respect of which order they are said to be higher and lower.† These pictures also are more or less faint, they, and not the images, being in truth the visible objects. Therefore, what hath been said of the images must in strictness be understood of the corresponding pictures, whose faintness, situation, and magnitude, being immediately perceived by sight, do all three concur in suggesting the magnitude of tangible objects, and this only by an experienced connexion.

58 The magnitude of the picture will perhaps be thought by some to have a necessary connexion with that of the tangible object, or (if not confounded with it) to be at least the sole means of suggesting it. But so far is this from being true, that of two visible pictures, equally large, the one, being fainter and upper, shall suggest an hundred times greater tangible

* *Theory of Vision*, sect. 158.   † *Supra*, sect. 46.

magnitude than the other:* which is an evident proof that we do not judge of the tangible magnitude merely by the visible: but that our judgment or apprehension is to be rated rather by other things, which yet, not being conceived to have so much resemblance with tangible magnitude, may therefore be overlooked.

59 It is farther to be observed that, beside this magnitude, situation, and faintness of the pictures, our prænotions concerning the kind, size, shape, and nature of things do concur in suggesting to us their tangible magnitudes. Thus, for instance, a picture equally great, equally faint, and in the very same situation, shall in the shape of a man suggest a lesser tangible magnitude than it would in the shape of a tower.

60 Where the kind, faintness, and situation of the horizontal pictures† are given, the suggested tangible magnitude will be as the visible. The distances and magnitudes that we have been accustomed to measure by experience of touch, lying in the horizontal plane, it thence comes to pass that situations of the horizontal pictures suggest the tangible magnitudes, which are not in like manner suggested by vertical pictures. And it is to be noted that, as an object gradually ascends from the horizon towards the zenith, our judgment concerning its tangible magnitude comes by degrees to depend more entirely on its visible magnitude. For the faintness is lessened as the quantity of intercepted air and vapours is diminished: and as the object riseth, the eye of the spectator is also raised above the horizon: so that the two concurring circumstances, of faintness and horizontal situation, ceasing to influence the suggestion of tangible magnitude, this same suggestion or judgment doth, in proportion thereto, become the sole effect of the visible magnitude and the prænotions. But it is evident that if several things (for instance, the faintness, situation, and visible magnitude) concur to enlarge an idea, upon the gradual omission of some of those things, the idea will be gradually lessened. This is the case of the moon,‡ when she ascends above the horizon, and gradually diminisheth her apparent dimension, as her altitude increaseth.

61 It is natural for mathematicians to regard the visual angle and the apparent magnitude as the sole or principal means of our apprehending the tangible magnitude of objects. But it is plain from what hath been premised, that our apprehension is much more influenced by other things,§ which have no similitude or necessary connexion therewith.

62 And these same means, which suggest the magnitude of tangible things, do also suggest their distance,¶ and in the same manner, that is to say, by experience alone, and not by any necessary connexion or geometrical inference. The faintness, therefore, and vividness, the upper and lower situation, together with the visible size of the pictures, and our prænotions concerning the shape and kind of tangible objects, are the true medium by which we apprehend the various degrees of tangible distance.

---

* *Theory of Vision*, sect. 78.   † *Supra*, sect. 56.
‡ *Theory of Vision*, sect. 73.   § *Supra*, sect. 58.
¶ *Theory of Vision*, sect. 77.

Which follows from what hath been premised, and will indeed be evident to whoever considers that those visual angles, with their arches or subtenses, are neither perceived by sight, nor by experience of any other sense. Whereas it is certain that the pictures, with their magnitudes, situations, and degrees of faintness, are alone the proper objects of sight. So that whatever is perceived by sight must be perceived by means thereof. To which perception the prænotions also, gained by experience of touch, or of sight and touch conjunctly, do contribute.

63 And indeed we need only reflect on what we see, to be assured that the less the pictures are, the fainter they are, and the higher (provided still they are beneath the horizontal* line or its picture), by so much the greater will the distance seem to be. And this upper situation of the picture is in strictness what must be understood when, after a popular manner of speech, the eye is said to perceive fields, lakes, and the like, interjacent† between it and the distant object, the pictures corresponding to them being only perceived to be lower than that of the object.‡ Now it is evident that none of these things have in their own nature any necessary connexion with the various degrees of distance. It will also appear, upon a little reflexion, that sundry circumstances of shape, colour, and kind, do influence our judgments or apprehensions of distance: all which follows from our prænotions, which are merely the effect of experience.

64 As is it natural for mathematicians to reduce things to the rule and measure of geometry, they are prone to suppose that the apparent magnitude hath a greater share than we really find, in forming our judgment concerning the distance of things from the eye. And, no doubt, it would be an easy and ready rule to determine the apparent place of an object, if we could say that its distance was inversely as the diameter of its apparent magnitude, and so judge by this alone, exclusive of every other circumstance. But that this would be no true rule is evident, there being certain cases in vision, by refracted or reflected light, wherein the diminution of the apparent magnitude is attended with an apparent diminution of distance.

65 But further to satisfy us that our judgments or apprehensions, either of the greatness or distance of an object, do not depend absolutely on the apparent magnitude, we need only ask the first painter we meet, who, considering nature rather than geometry, well knows that several other circumstances contribute thereto: and since art can only deceive us as it imitates nature, we need but observe pieces of perspective and landscapes to be able to judge of this point.

66 When the object is so near that the interval between the pupils beareth some sensible proportion to it, the sensation which attends the turn or straining of the eyes, in order to unite the two optic axes therein, is to be considered as one means of our perceiving distance.§ It must be owned, this sensation belongeth properly to the sense of feeling; but as it waits upon and hath a constant regular connexion with distinct vision of

---

* *Supra*, sect. 56.   † *Theory of Vision*, sect. 3.
‡ *Supra*, sect. 55.   § *Theory of Vision*, sect. 16, 17.

near distance (the nearer this, the greater that), so it is natural that it should become a sign thereof, and suggest it to the mind.* And that it is so in fact follows from that known experiment of hanging up a ring edge-wise to the eye, and then endeavouring, with one eye shut, by a lateral motion, to insert into it the end of a stick; which is found more difficult to perform than with both eyes open, from the want of this means of judging by the sensation attending the nearer meeting or crossing of the two optic axes.

67 True it is that the mind of man is pleased to observe in nature rules or methods, simple, uniform, general, and reducible to mathematics, as a means of rendering its knowledge at once easy and extensive. But we must not, for the sake of uniformities or analogies, depart from truth and fact, nor imagine that in all cases the apparent place or distance of an object must be suggested by the same means. And, indeed, it answers the ends of vision to suppose that the mind should have certain additional means or helps, for judging more accurately of the distance of those objects which are the nearest, and consequently most concern us.

68 It is also to be observed that when the distance is so small that the breadth of the pupil bears a considerable proportion to it, the object appears confused. And this confusion being constantly observed in poring on such near objects, and increasing as the distance lessens, becomes thereby a means of suggesting the place of an object.† For one idea is qualified to suggest another, merely by being often perceived with it. And if the one increaseth either directly or inversely as the other, various degrees of the former will suggest various degrees of the latter, by virtue of such habitual connexion, and proportional increase or diminution. And thus the gradual changing confusedness of an object may concur to form our apprehension of near distance, when we look only with one eye. And this alone may explain Dr. Barrow's difficulty, the case as proposed by him regarding only one visible point.‡ And when several points are considered, or the image supposed an extended surface, its increasing confusedness will, in that case, concur with the increasing magnitude to diminish its distance, which will be inversely as both.

69 Our experience in vision is got by the naked eye. We apprehend or judge from this same experience, when we look through glasses. We may not, nevertheless, in all cases, conclude from the one to the other, because that certain circumstances, either excluded or added, by the help of glasses, may sometimes alter our judgments, particularly as they depend upon prænotions.

70 What I have here written may serve as a commentary on my *Essay towards a New Theory of Vision*; and, I believe, will make it plain to thinking men. In an age wherein we hear so much of thinking and reasoning, it may seem needless to observe, how useful and necessary it is to think, in order to obtain just and accurate notions, to distinguish things that are different, to speak consistently, to know even our own meaning. And yet

* *Supra*, sect. 39. † *Theory of Vision*, sect. 21.
‡ *Theory of Vision*, sect. 29.

for want of this, we may see many, even in these days, run into perpetual blunders and paralogisms. No friend, therefore, to truth and knowledge would lay any restraint or discouragement on thinking. There are, it must be owned, certain general maxims, the result of ages, and the collected sense of thinking persons, which serve instead of thinking, for a guide or rule to the multitude, who, not caring to think for themselves, it is fit they should be conducted by the thought of others. But those who set up for themselves, those who depart from the public rule, or those who would reduce them to it, if they do not think, what will men think of them? As I pretend not to make any discoveries which another might not as well have made, who should have thought it worth his pains: so I must needs say that without pains and thought no man will ever understand the true nature of vision, or comprehend what I have wrote concerning it.

71 Before I conclude, it may not be amiss to add the following extract from the *Philosophical Transactions*, relating to a person blind from his infancy, and long after made to see: 'When he first saw, he was so far from making any judgment about distances that he thought all objects whatever touched his eyes (as he expressed it) as what he felt did his skin; and thought no objects so agreeable as those which were smooth and regular, though he could form no judgment of their shape, or guess what it was in any object that was pleasing to him. He knew not the shape of anything, nor any one thing from another, however different in shape or magnitude: but upon being told what things were, whose form he before knew from feeling, he would carefully observe that he might know them again: but having too many objects to learn at once, he forgot many of them: and (as he said) at first he learned to know, and again forgot, a thousand things in a day. Several weeks after he was couched, being deceived by pictures, he asked which was the lying sense, feeling or seeing? He was never able to imagine any lines beyond the bounds he saw. The room he was in, he said, he knew to be but part of the house, yet he could not conceive that the whole house could look bigger. He said every new object was a new delight, and the pleasure was so great that he wanted ways to express it.'* Thus, by fact and experiment, those points of the theory which seem the most remote from common apprehension were not a little confirmed, many years after I had been led into the discovery of them by reasoning.

* *Phil. Transact*, Num. 402.

Philosophical Commentaries

Berkeley's Notebooks of 1707–8
First printed in 1871

I	Introduction
M	Matter
P	Primary and Secondary Qualities
E	Existence
T	Time

S	Soul—Spirit
G	God
Mo	Moral Philosophy
N	Natural Philosophy

EDITOR'S NOTE

In order to avoid imposing a polished form on Berkeley's thoughts, the text has been left unmodernized and unaltered except in the case of a few obvious slips of the pen.

Notebook B precedes A because they were first printed and named, as they had been bound, in the wrong order.

Berkeley's key to the marginal signs, reproduced above, was placed by him at the beginning of Notebook A, before entry 400. For further information see editor's Introduction, section 6.

Entries are numbered as in the *Works*. The affix 'a' indicates a verso entry, i.e. a later comment on the original entry. The editorial mark †indicates doubt about the reading of the preceding word or expression.

Notebook B

M   ffall of Adam, rise of Idolatry, rise of Epicurism &   17
       Hobbism dispute about divisibility of matter &c expounded
       by material substances

       Extension a sensation, therefore not without the mind.   18

       In ye immaterial hypothesis the wall is white, fire hot etc   19

       Primary ideas prov'd not to exist in matter, after the same   20
       manner y^t secondary ones are prov^d not to exist therein.

×   Demonstrations of the infinite divisibility of extension   21
       suppose length without breadth ∧ wch is absurd.

       or invisible length   21a

^{1}M   World wthout thought is nec quid nec quantum nec   22
       quale etc

M   'tis wondrous to contemplate ye world empty'd of intelli-   23
       gences.

+   Nothing properly but persons i.e. conscious things do exist,   24
       all other things are not so much existences as manners of
       ye existence of persons.

+   Qu: about the Soul or rather person whether it be not   25
       compleatly known.

×   Infinite divisibility of extension does suppose ye external   26
       existence of extension but the later is false, ergo ye former
       also.

^{13}×   Qu: Blind man made to see would he know motion at   27
       1st sight.

^{13}×   Motion, figure & extension perceivable by sight are   28
       different from those ideas perceived by touch wch goe by
       the same name.

+   Diagonal incommensurable wth y^e side Quaere how this   29
       can be in my doctrine?

N   Qu: how to reconcile Newtons 2 sorts of motion wth my   30
       doctrine.

×   Terminations of surfaces and lines not imaginable per se.   31

$^{13}\times$ Molyneux's Blind man would not know   32
         the sphere or cube to be bodies or extended at first sight.

$+$ Extension so far from being incompatible wth y^t 'tis   33
         impossible it should exist without thought.

M.S.   Extension it self or any thing extended cannot think these   34
         being meer ideas or sensations whose essence we
         thoroughly know

$^{13}\times$ No extension but surface perceivable by sight.   35

ob:M   W^n we imagine 2 bowls v.g. moving in vacuo, 'tis onely   36
         conceiving a person affected wth those sensations.

^{1}M.   Extension to exist in a thoughtless thing Λ is a contra-   37
         diction.

M^1 or rather in a thing void of perception. Thought seeming   37a
         to imply action.

$+$ Qu: if visible motion be proportional to tangible motion.   38

T   In some dreams succession of ideas swifter than at other   39
         times.

^{1}M   If a piece of matter have extension y^t must be determin'd   40
         to a particular bigness & figure, but etc.

$+$ Nothing corresponds to our primary ideas wthout but   41
         powers, hence a direct & brief demonstration of an active
         powerfull being distinct from us on whom we depend. etc.

$+$ The name of colours actually given to tangible qualitys   42
         by the relation of y^e story of y^e German Count.

$^{13}\times$ Qu: how came visible & tangible qualitys by the same   43
         name in all languages?

$+$ Qu: whether being might not be the substance of y^e soul.   44
         or (otherwise thus) whether being added to y^e faculties
         compleat the real essence and adequate definition of the
         soul?

N   Qu: whether on the supposition of external Bodies it be   45
         possible for us to know that any Body is absolutely at rest,
         since that supposing ideas much slower than at present
         bodies now apparently moving would then be apparently
         at rest.

M   Qu: w^t can be like a sensation but a sensation?   46

      Qu: Did ever any man see any other things besides his   47
      own ideas, that he should compare them to these & make
      these like unto them?

T   The age of a fly for ought that we know may be as long   48
      as y^t of a man.

³¹×   Visible distance heterogeneous from tangible distance   49
      demonstrated 3 several ways.

³¹×   1st if a tangible inch be equal or in any other reason to a
      visible inch, thence it will follow y^t unequals are equals
      wch is absurd. for at w^t distance would the visible inch be
      placed to make it equal to the tangible inch?

³¹×   2^d One made to see y^t had not yet seen his own limbs or
      anything he touch'd, upon sight of a foot length would
      know it to be a foot length if tangible foot & visible foot
      were the same idea, sed falsum id ergo & hoc.

³¹×· 3dly from Molyneux's problem wch otherwise is falsely
      solv^d by Locke & him.

¹M   Nothing but ideas perceivable.   50

      A man cannot compare 2 things together without per-   51
      ceiving them each, ergo he cannot say any thing wch is
      not an idea is like or unlike an idea.

+   Bodies etc do exist even w^n not perceiv'd they being   52
      powers in the active Being.

+   Succession a simple idea ∧ Locke cap. 7.   53

      Succession is an abstract *i.e.* an unconceivable idea.   53a

³¹×   Visible extension [is proportional to tangible extension,   54
      also] is encreas'd & diminish'd by parts, hence taken for
      the same.

×   If extension be without the mind in bodies qu: whether   55
      tangible or visible or abstractible or both.

¹×   Mathematical propositions about extension & motion   56
      true in a double sense.

      Extension thought peculiarly inert because not accom-   57
      pany'd wth pleasure & pain; hence thought to exist in
      matter as also for y^t it was conceiv'd common to 2 senses.

as also the constant perception of 'em   57a

$^{11}\times$. Blind at 1st sight could not tell how near w^t he saw was   58
to him, nor even whether it be w^{th}out him or in his eye.
Qu: would he not think y^t later.

$^8\times^1$ Blind at 1st sight could not know y^t w^t he saw was   59
extended, untill he had seen & touch'd some one self same
thing. Not knowing how minimum tangibile would look.

M.   Mem: y^t Homogeneous particles be brought in to answer   60
the objection of Gods creating sun, plants etc before
animals.

$\times$ In every Bodie 2 infinite series of extension the one of   61
tangible the other of visible.

$+$ All things to a Blind at 1st seen in a point.   62

$+$ Ignorance of Glasses made men think extension to be in   63
bodies.

M   Homogeneous portions of matter usefull to contemplate   64
them.

$+$ Extension if in matter changes its relation wth minimum   65
visibile wch seems to be fixt.

$+$ Qu: whether m.v. be fix'd.   66

^{1}M.   Each particle of matter if extended must be infinitely   67
extended. or have an infinite series of extension.

^{1}M   If the world be granted to consist of matter tis the mind   68
gives it beauty & proportion.

$^3\times^1$ W^t I have said onely proves there is no proportion at all   69
times & in all men between a visible & tangible inch v.g.

$^8\times^1$ Tangible & visible extension heterogeneous because they   70
have no common measure: also because their simplest,
constituent parts or elements are specifically distinct viz.
punctum visibile & tangibile. N.B. The former seems to
be no good reason.

M : N. By immateriality is solv'd the cohesion of bodies, or rather   71
the dispute ceases.

×   Our idea we call extension neither way capable of   72
       infinity. i.e. neither infinitely small or great.

+   Greatest possible extension seen under an angle wch must   73
       be less than 180 degrees; the legs of wch angle proceed
       from the ends of the extension.

M   Allowing there be extended solid etc substances without   74
       the mind tis impossible the mind should know or perceive
       them. the mind even according to ye materialists perceiving
       onely the impressions made upon its brain or rather
       the ideas attending those impressions.

×   Unite in abstracto not at all divisible it being as it were   75
       a point or wth Barrow nothing at all in concreto not
       divisible ad infinitum there being no one idea diminishable
       ad infinitum.

M   Any subject can have of each sort of primary qualities but   76
1   one particular at once. Locke b.4. c 3.S.15.

+   Qu: whether we have clear ideas of large numbers them-   77
       selves, or onely of their relations.

^{1}M Of solidity see L.b 2.c.4S.1.S.5 S.6. If any one ask w^t 78
       solidity is let him put a flint between his hands & he will
       know. Extension of Body is continuity of solid etc,
       extension of space is continuity of unsolid etc.

^{3}×^{1} Why may not I say visible extension is a continuity of   78a
       visible points tangible extension is a Continuity of tangible
       points.

M   Mem. that I take notice that I do not fall in wth Sceptics 79
       Fardella etc, in y^t I make bodies to exist certainly, w^{ch}
       they doubt of.

M   I am more certain of ye existence & reality of Bodies than   80
       Mr Locke since he pretends onely to w^t he calls sensitive
       knowledge, whereas I think I have demonstrative know-
       ledge of their Existence, by them meaning combinations
       of powers in an unknown substratum.

^{1}M Our ideas we call figure & extension not images of the   81
       figure & extension of matter, these (if such there be) being
       infinitely divisible, those not so.

+   Tis impossible a Material cube should exist, because the   82
edges of a Cube will appear broad to an acute sense.

+   Men die or are in state of annihilation oft in a day.   83

S   Powers Quaere whether more or one onely?   84

+   Lengths abstract from breadths are the work of the mind,   85
such do intersect in a point at all angles, after the same
way colour is abstract from extension. every position
alters the line

×   Quaere, whether ideas of extension are made up of other   86
ideas v.g. idea of a foot made up of severall ideas of an
inch etc?

+   The idea of an inch length not one determin'd idea Hence   87
enquire the reason why we are out in judging of extension
by the sight, for wch purpose 'tis meet also to consider the
frequent & sudden changes of extension, by position.

$^{2}\times^{1}$ No stated ideas of length without a minimum   88

M   Material substance banter'd by Locke b.2 c.13 S.19   89

M   In my doctrine all absurditys from infinite space etc cease.   90

$^{12}\times^{1}$ Qu: whether if (speaking grosly) the things we see were all   91
of them at all times too small to be felt we should have
confounded tangible & visible extension & figure?

T   Qu: whether if succession of ideas in the Eternal mind,   92
a day does not seem to God a 1000 years rather than a
1000 years a day?

+   But one only Colour & it's degrees.   93

+   Enquiry about a grand mistake in writers of Dioptricks in   94
assigning the cause of Microscopes magnifying objects.

+   Qu: whether a blind made to see would at 1st give the   95
×   name of distance to any idea intromitted by sight since he
would take distance y^{t} he had perceiv'd by touch to be
something existing without his mind, but he would certainly think that no thing seen was without his mind.

S   Space wthout any bodies being in rerum natura, would not   96
+   be extended as not having parts in that parts are assigned
to it wth respect to body from whence also the notion of
distance is taken, now without either parts or distance or
mind how can there be space or anything beside one
uniform no thing?

+   Two demonstrations that blind made to see would not   97
×   take all things he saw to be without his mind or not in a
point, ye one from microscopic eyes, the other from not
perceiving distance i.e. radius of the visual sphere.

M   The Trees are in the Park, that is, whether I will or no   98
whether I imagine any thing about them or no, let me but
go thither & open my Eyes by day & I shall not avoid
seeing them.

+   Tho swiftness or slowness of motion depends on our ideas   99
it does not therefore follow, that the same force can impell
**a body over a greater or less space in proportion to
slowness or swiftness of our ideas.**

³×¹   By extension blind would mean either the perception   100
caused in his touch by something he calls extended, or
else the power of raising that perception, wch power is
without in the thing term'd extended. Now he could
not know either of these to be in things visible till he had
try'd.

×   **Geometry seems to have for its object tangible extension,**   101
figures & motion & not visible.

a   The reason explain'd why we see things erect their images   102
³×¹ being inverted in the eye.

³²×¹   A man will say a body will seem as big as before, tho the   103
visible idea it yields be less than w^t it was, therefore the
bigness or tangible extension of the body is different from
the visible extension.

×   Number not without the mind in any thing, because tis the   104
mind by considering things as one that makes complex
ideas of 'em, tis the mind combines into one, wch by
otherwise considering its ideas might make a score of w^t
was but one just now.

×   Extension or space no simple idea, length, breadth &   105
solidity being three severall ideas.

³×¹   Depth or solidity nor perceiv'd by sight.   106

+   Strange impotence of men. Man without God.   107
       Wretcheder than a stone or tree, he having onely the
       power to be miserable by his unperformed wills, these
       having no power at all.

       Length, perceivable by hearing, length & breadth by   108
       sight, Length breadth & depth by touch.

G   W^t affects us must be a thinking thing for w^t thinks not   109
       cannot subsist.

+   Number not in bodies it being the creature of the mind   110
       depending entirely on it's consideration & being more or
       less as the mind pleases.

+¹   Mem: Quaere whether extension be equally a sensation   111
       with colour?

×   The Mob use not the word Extension. tis an abstract term   111a
       of the Schools.

P   Round figure a perception or sensation in the mind but   112
       in the body is a power L.b. 2 c.8 S.8.

       Mem: mark well the later part of the last cited Section.   113

³×¹   Solids or any other tangible things are no otherwise seen   114
       than colours felt by the German Count

M   Of & thing causes of mistake   115

³×¹   The visible point of he who has microscopical eyes will   116
       not be greater or less than mine.

×   Qu: whether the propositions & even axioms of Geometry   117
       do not divers of them suppose the existence of lines etc
       without the mind.

T   Whether motion be the measure of Duration See Locke.   118
       b.2 c.14 S.19

×   Lines & points conceiv'd as terminations different ideas   119
       from those conceiv'd absolutely.

×   Every position alters a line.   120

× Blind at 1st would not take colours to be without his mind,   121
S   but colours would seem to be in the same place with the
    colour'd extension, therefore extension would not seem to
    be without the mind.

²×¹ All visible concentric circles whereof the eye is the center   122
     are absolutely equall.

+   Infinite number why absurd. not rightly solv'd by Locke.   123

³×¹ Qu: how tis possible we should see flats or right lines.   124

²×¹ Qu: why the Moon appears greatest in the Horizon?   125

a
³×¹ Qu: why we see things erect when painted inverted   126

T   Question put by Mr Deering touching the thief & paradise.   127

M¹   Matter tho' allow'd to exist may be no greater than a   128
     pin's head.

+   Motion is proportionable to space describ'd in given time.   129

+   Velocity not proportionable to Space describ'd in given   130
     time.

M¹   No active power but the will, therefore matter if it exists   131
     affects us not.

+   Magnitude when barely taken for the ratio partium extra   132
     partes or rather for coexistence & succession without con-
     sidering the parts coexisting & succeeding, is infinitely or
     rather indefinitely or not at all perhaps divisible because it
     is it self infinite or indefinite, but definite, determin'd
     magnitudes i.e. lines or surfaces consisting of points,
     whereby (together wᵗʰ distance & position) they are deter-
     min'd, are resoluble into those points.

+   Again, magnitude taken for coexistence and succession is   133
     not at all divisible but is one simple idea.

+   Simple ideas include no parts nor relations, hardly   134
     separated & considered in themselves, not yet rightly
     singl'd by any Authour. instance in power, red, extension
     etc

M Space not imaginable by any idea receiv'd from sight, not 135
imaginable, without body moving not even then necessarily
existing (I speak of infinite Space) for w^t the body has past
may be conceiv'd annihilated.

^{1}M Qu: w^t we see beside colours, w^t can 136
we feel beside, hard, soft cold warm pleasure pain

$^3\times^1$ Qu: why not taste & smell extension? 137

$^3\times^1$ Qu: why not tangible & visible extensions thought 138
heterogeneous extensions, so well as gustable & olfactible
perceptions thought heterogeneous perceptions. or at least
why not as heterogeneous as blue & red?

+ Preliminary discourse about singling & abstracting simple 139
ideas.

$^2\times^1$ Moon w^n Horizontal does not appear bigger as to visible 140
extension than at other times, hence difficulties & disputes
about things seen under equal Angles etc cease.

+ All Potentiae alike indifferent. 141

+ A.B. w^t does he mean by his potentia, is it the will, desire, 142
person or all or neither, or sometimes one sometimes
t'other.

+ No agent can be conceiv'd indifferent as to pain or 143
pleasure,

+ We do not properly speaking in a strict philosophical 144
sense make objects more or less pleasant, but the laws of
Nature do that.

Mo.S A finite intelligence might have foreseen 4 thousand years 145
agoe the place & circumstances, even the most minute &
trivial of my present existence.

S.Mo. This true on supposition that uneasiness determines the 145a
Will.

S.Mo. Doctrines of liberty, prescience etc explain'd by Billiard 146
balls.

+ W^t should we think of an object plac'd as in the 147
difficulty if we saw it clearly?

a   W^t judgement would he make of uppermost & lowermost   148
$^3\times^1$ who had always seen thro' an inverting glass.

S.Mo.   According to Locke we have not liberty as to vertue &   149
           vice, the Liberty he allows consisting in an Indifferency of
           the operative Faculties, wch is consecutive to the will, but
           virtue & vice consist in the will ergo etc.

$^2\times^1$ All lines subtending the same optic angle congruunt (as   150
           is evident by an easy experiment) therefore they are equal.

+   We have not pure, simple ideas of blue, red or any   151
           other colour (except perhaps black) because all bodies
           reflect heterogeneal light.

+   Qu: whether this be true as to sounds (& other sensations) 152
           there being, perhaps, Rays of air wch will onely exhibit
           one particular sound, as rays of light one particular colour.

+   Colours not definable, not because they are pure, unmixt   153
           thoughts, but because we cannot easily distinguish &
           separate the thoughts they include, or because we want
           names for their component ideas.

+   By Soul is meant onely a Complex idea made up of   154
           existence, willing & perception in a large sense. therefore
           its is known & it may be defin'd

S   We cannot possibly conceive any active power but the Will. 155

+   In moral matters Men think (tis true) that they are free, 156
           but this freedom is only the freedom of doing as they
           please, wch freedom is consecutive to the Will, respecting
           onely the operative faculties.

+   Men impute their actions to themselves because they will'd 157
           them & that not out of ignorance but whereas they knew
           the consequences, of them whether good or bad.

+   This does not prove men to be indifferent in respect of   158
           desiring.

+   If any thing is meant by the potentia of A.B. it must be   159
           desire. but I appeal to any man if his desire be indifferent,
           or (to speak more to the purpose) whether he himself be
           indifferent in respect of w^t he desires, till after he has
           desir'd it. for as for desire it self or the faculty of desiring
           that is indifferent as all other faculties are.

+   Actions leading to heaven are in my power if I will them,   160
therefore I will will them.

+   Qu: concerning the progression of wills in infinitum.   161

+   Herein Mathematiques have the advantage over Meta-   162
physiques & Morality. Their Definitions being of words
not yet known to ye Learner are not Disputed, but words
in Metaphisiques & Morality being mostly known to all
the definitions of them may chance to be controverted.

M   The short jejune way in Mathematiques will not do in   163
Metaphysiques & Ethiques, for y^t about Mathematical
propositions men have no prejudices, no anticipated
opinions to be encounter'd, they not having yet thought
on such matters. tis not so in the other 2 mention'd
sciences, a man must not onely demonstrate the truth, he
must also vindicate it against scruples & establish'd
opinions wch contradict it. In short the dry strigose rigid
way will not suffice. he must be more ample & copious,
else his demonstration tho never so exact will not go down
wth most.

+   Extension seems to consist in variety of homogeneal   164
thoughts coexisting without mixture.

+   or rather visible extension seems to be the coexistence of   165
colours in ye mind.

S.Mo.   Enquiring & judging are actions wch depend on the   166
operative faculties wch depend on ye will wch is determin'd
by some uneasiness ergo etc. Suppose an agent which is
finite perfectly indifferent, & as to desiring not determin'd
by any prospect or consideration of good I say, this Agent
cannot do an action morally Good. Hence 'tis evident
the suppositions of A:B: are insignificant.

×   Extension, motion, time Number no simple ideas, but   167
include succession in them wch seems to be a simple idea.

×   Mem: to enquire into the angle of Contact. & into   168
fluxions etc.

^{2}×^{1} The sphere of vision is equal whether I look onely in my   169
hand, or on the open firmament. for 1st in both cases the
Retina is full. 2d. the Radius's of both spheres are equall
or rather nothing at all to ye sight 3dly equall number of
points in one & t'other.

¹×¹   In the Barrovian Case purblind would judge aright   170

+×¹   Why the Horizontal Moon greater?   171

+×¹   Why objects seen erect?   172

 N   To w^t purpose certain figure & texture connected w^th   173
      other perceptions?

²×¹   Men estimate magnitudes, both by angles & distance.   174
      Blind at 1st could not know distance, or by pure sight
      abstracting from experience of connexion of sight & tangible
      ideas we can't perceive distance. therefore by pure sight we
      cannot perceive or judge of extension:

²×¹   Qu: whether it be possible to enlarge our sight or make   175
      us see at once more or more points than we do by
      diminishing the punctum visibile below 30″?

I.S. Speech metaphorical more than we imagine insensible   176
      things & their modes circumstances &c being exprest for
      ye most part by words borrow'd from things sensible. the
      reason's plain. Hence Manyfold Mistakes.

 S   The grand Mistake is that we think we have Ideas of the   176a
      Operations of our Minds. certainly this Metaphorical dress
      is an argument we have not.

 G   Qu: How can our idea of God be complex or com-   177
      pounded, w^n his essence is simple & uncompounded v.
      Locke b.2.S 35

 G   omnes reales rerum proprietates continentur in Deo w^t   177a
      means Le Clerc &c by this?

 +   The impossibility of defining or discoursing clearly of   178
      most things proceeds from the fault & scantiness of language,
      as much, perhaps, as from obscurity & confusion of
      Thought. Hence I may clearly & fully understand
      my own Soul extension, etc & not be able to define them.

 M   The substance wood a collection of simple ideas see Locke 179
      B.2 C.26. S.1.

 +   Mem: concerning strait lines seen to look at them thro' an 180
      orbicular Lattice.

²×¹   Qu: whether possible that those visible ideas wᶜʰ are now   181
        connected with greater extensions could have been con-
        nected with lesser extensions. there seeming to be no
        necessary connexion between those thoughts.

+×   Speculums seem to diminish or enlarge objects not by   182
        altering the optique angle but by altering the Apparent
        distance.

+   Hence Qu: if blind would think things diminish'd by   183
        convexes, or enlarged by concaves?

P.N.   Motion not one idea, it cannot be perceiv'd at once.   184

M.P.   Mem: to allow existence to colours in the dark, persons   185
        not thinking &c but not an absolute actual existence. 'Tis
        prudent to correct mens mistakes without altering their
        language. This makes truth glide into their souls
        insensibly.

M.P.   Colours in yᵉ dark do exist really *i.e.* were there light or as   185a
        soon as light comes we shall see them provided we open
        our eyes. & that whether we will or no.

+   How the Retina is fill'd by a Looking glass?   186

+   Convex speculums have the same effect wᵗʰ concave glasses.   187

+   Qu: whether concave speculums have the same effect wᵗʰ   188
        Convex glasses?

²×¹   The reason why convex speculums diminish & concave   189
        magnify not yet fully assign'd by any writer I know.

+   Qu: why not objects seen confus'd when yᵗ they seem   190
        inverted thro a convex lens?

+   Qu: how to make a glass or speculum which shall   191
        magnify or diminish by altering the distance without
        altering the angle?

+   No identity other than perfect likeness in any individuals   192
        besides persons.

N.   As well make tastes, smells, fear, shame, wit, vertue, vice   193
        & all thoughts move wᵗʰ Local motion as immaterial spirit.

+   On account of my doctrine the identity of finite substances   194
       must consist in some thing else than continued existence,
       or relation to determin'd time and place of beginning to
       exist. the existence of our thoughts (wch being combin'd
       make all substances) being frequently interrupted, & they
       having divers beginnings, & endings.

S   Qu: Whether Identity of Person consists not in the Will   194a

$^2\times^1$ No necessary connexion between great or little optique   195
       angles & great or little extension.

$^2\times^1$ Distance is not perceiv'd, optique angles are not perceiv'd.   196
       how then is extension perceiv'd by sight?

$^2\times^1$ Apparent magnitude of a line is not simply as the Optique   197
       angle, but directly as the Optique angle, & reciprocally as
       the confusion etc (i.e. the other sensations or want of sensa-
       tion that attend near vision) hence great mistakes in assign-
       ing the magnifying power of glasses. vid: Moly: p. 182.

$^2\times^1$ Glasses or speculums may perhaps magnify or lessen   198
       without altering the Optique angle but to no purpose.

$^2\times^1$ Qu: whether Purblind would think objects so much   199
       diminish'd by a convex speculum as another?

+   Qu: wherein consists identity of Person? not in actual   200
       consciousness, for then I'm not the same person I was this
       day twelvemonth, but while I think of w^t I then did.
       Not in potential for then all persons may be the same for
       ought we know.

+   Mem: story of Mr Deering's Aunt.   201

+   two sorts of Potential consciousnesses Natural &   202
       praeternatural in the last § but one I mean the latter.

$^2\times^1$ If by magnitude be meant the proportion any thing bears   203
       to a determin'd tangible extension as inch, foot etc this 'tis
       plain cannot be properly & per se perceiv'd by sight. & as
       for determin'd visible inches, feet etc there can be no such
       thing obtain'd by the meer act of seeing abstracted from
       experience etc.

$^2\times^1$ The greatness per se perceivable of the sight, is onely the   204
       proportion any visible appearance bears to the others seen

at the same time; or (wch is the same thing) the proportion of any particular part of the visual orb to the whole.
but mark that we perceive not it is an orb, any more than
a plain but by reasoning. This is all the greatness the
pictures have per se.

²×¹   Hereby meerly man cannot at all judge of the extension   205
of any object, it not availing to know the object makes such
a part of a sphaerical surface except we also know the
greatness of the sphaerical surface. for a point may subtend
the same angle wth a mile & so create as great an image in
the Retina, i.e. take up as much of the Orb.

²×¹   Men judge of magnitude by faintness & vigorousness, by   206
distinctness & confusion, wth some other circumstances by
great & little angles. Hence 'tis plain the ideas of sight
wch are now connected with greatness, might have been
connected wth smalness & vice versâ. there being no
necessary reason why great angle faintness & distinctness
without straining sould stand for great extension, any
more than than a great angle, vigorousness & confusion.

+   My end is not to deliver Metaphysiques altogether in a   207
General Scholastique way but in some measure to accom-
modate them to the Sciences, & shew how they may be
usefull in Optiques, Geometry &c.

²×¹   Qu: whether per se proportion of visible magnitudes be   208
perceivable by sight. this is put on account of distinctness
& confusedness the act of perception seeming to be as great
in viewing any point of the visual orb distinctly as in viewing the whole confusedly.

+   Mem: to correct my Language & make it as Philosophi-   209
cally nice as possible to avoid giving handle.

²×¹   If men could without straining alter the convexity of their   210
Crystallines they might magnify or diminish the apparent
diameters of objects the same optic angle remaining.

²×¹   The bigness in one sense of the pictures in the fund is not   211
determin'd, for the nearer a man views them, the images
of them (as well as other objects) will take up the greater
room in the fund of his eye.

+   Mem: Introduction to contain the design of the whole the   212
nature & manner of demonstrating &c.

²×¹ Two sorts of bigness accurately to be distinguish'd they   213
being perfectly & Toto Coelo different. the one the proportion that any one appearance has to the sum of appearances perceiv'd at the same time wᵗʰ it, wᶜʰ is proportional
to angles or if a surface to segments of sphaerical surfaces,
the other is tangible bigness.

²×¹ Qu: wᵗ would happen if the sphaerae of the Retina were   214
enlarg'd or diminish'd?

×+   We think by the meer act of vision we perceive distance   215
from us, yet we do not. also that we perceive solids yet we
do not, also the inequality of things seen under the same
angle, yet we do not. Why may I not add? we think we
see extension by meer vision, yet we do not.

×+   Extension seems to be perceiv'd by the eye as thoughts by   216
the ear.

×   We seem to have clear & distinct ideas of large numbers   217
v.g. 1000 no otherwise than by considering 'em as form'd
by the multiplying of small numbers.

²×¹ As long as the same angle determines the minimum visible   218
to two persons, no different conformation of the Eye can
make a different appearance of magnitude in the same
thing. But it being possible to try the Angle, we may
certainly know whether the same thing appears differently
big to 2 persons on account of their Eyes.

²×¹ If a man could see ″ objects would appear larger to him   219
than to another: hence there is another sort of purely
visible magnitude beside the proportion any appearance
bears to the Visual sphere, viz. its proportion to the m.v.

¹×³ Were there but one & the same Language in the World,   220
& did children speak it naturally as soon as born, & were
it not in the Power of men to conceal their thoughts or
deceive others but that there were an inseparable connexion between words and thoughts, so yᵗ posito uno
ponitur alterum by the Laws of Nature. Qu: would not
men think they heard thoughts as much as that they see
[extension] Distance

+   All our ideas are adequate, our knowledge of the Laws of   221
nature is not perfect & adequate.

M.P.   Men are in the right in judging their simple ideas to be   222
in the things themselves, certainly Heat & colour is as
much without the mind as figure, motion, time etc

We know many things wch we want words to express.   223
Great things discoverable upon this Principle, for want of
considering wch divers men have run into sundry mistakes
endeavouring to set forth their knowledge by sounds, w^{ch}
foundering them they thought the defect was in their
knowledge w^n in truth it was in their Language.

a
$^3 \times^1$ Query whether the sensations of sight arising from a man's   224
head be liker the sensation of touch proceeding from
thence or from his legs?

a
$^3 \times^1$ Or is it onely the constant & long association of ideas   225
entirely different that makes me judge them the same?

a
$^1 \times^3$ W^t I see is onely variety of colours & light. w^t I feel is   226
hard or soft, hot or cold, rough or smooth &c. w^t resem-
blance have these thoughts with those?

a
$^{13} \times$ A picture painted wth great variety of colours affects the   227
touch in one uniform manner. I cannot therefore con-
clude that because I see 2 I shall feel 2, because I see
angles or inequalitys I shall feel angles or inequalitys.
How therefore can I before experience teaches me know
that the visible leggs are (because 2) connected wth the
tangible ones, or the visible head (because one) connected
wth the tangible head?

^{1}M   All things by us conceivable are 1st thoughts 2dly powers   228
to receive thoughts, 3dly powers to cause thoughts neither
of all wch can possibly exist in an inert, senseless thing.

$^1 \times^2$ An object wthout a glass may be seen under as great an   229
angle as wth a glass. a glass therefore does not magnify the
appearance by the angle.

S   Absurd that men should know the soul by idea ideas being   230
inert, thoughtless, Hence Malbranch confuted.

$^1 \times^1$
^{23} I saw gladness in his looks, I saw shame in his face so I   231
see figure or Distance

$^1 \times^2$ Qu: why things seen confusedly thro a convex glass are   232
not magnify'd?

[1]×[2]   Tho we should judge the Horizontal Moon to be more   233
distant, why should we therefore judge her to be greater
what Connexion betwixt, the same Angle, farther distant
& greaterness?

N   My Doctrine affects the Essences of the Corpuscularians.   234

×   Perfect Circles &c exist not without (for none can so exist   235
whether perfect or no) but in the mind

×   Lines thought Divisible ad infinitum because they are   236
suppos'd to exist without. Also because they are thought
the same when view'd by the naked eye & w^n view'd thro
magnifying glasses.

×   They who knew not Glasses had not so fair a pretence for   237
the Divisibility ad infinitum.

×   No idea of Circle etc in abstract.   238

+   Metaphisiques as capable of Certainty as Ethiques but not   239
so capable to be demonstrated in a Geometrical way
because men see clearer & have not so many prejudices in
Ethiques.

[3]×[1] Visible ideas come into the mind very distinct, so do   240
tangible ideas, Hence Extension seen & felt. sounds tastes
etc are more blended.

[3]×[1] Qu: why not extension intromitted by the taste in   241
conjunction wth the smell seeing tastes & smells are very
distinct ideas.

×   Blew & yellow particles mixt while they exhibit an   242
uniform green, their extension is not perceiv'd, but as soon
as they exhibit distinct sensations of Blew & yellow then
their Extension is perceiv'd.

[3]×[1] Distinct perception of visible ideas not so perfect as of   243
tangible, tangible ideas being many at once equally vivid.
Hence heterogeneous Extension.

[2]×[1] Object: why a mist encreases not the Apparent magnitude   244
of an object in proportion to the faintness?

+   Mem: to Enquire touching the squaring of the Circle etc.   245

a   That wch seems smooth & round to the touch may to sight   246
ᵇ×¹   seem quite otherwise. Hence no necessary connexion
      betwixt visible ideas & tangible ones.

×   In Geometry it is not prov'd that an inch is divisible ad   247
     infinitum.

×   Geometry not conversant about our compleat determin'd   248
     ideas of figures, for these are not divisible ad infinitum.

×   Particular Circles may be squar'd, for the circumference   249
     being given a Diameter may be found betwixt w^{ch} & y^e
     true there is not any perceivable difference. therefore there
     is no difference. Extension being a perception & a
     perception not perceiv'd is contradiction, nonsense, nothing.
     In vain to alledge the difference may be seen by
     Magnifying Glasses. for in y^t case there is ('tis true) a
     difference perceiv'd but not between the same ideas but
     others much greater entirely different therefrom.

×   Any visible circle possibly perceivable of any man may be   250
     squar'd, by the Common way most accurately, or even
     perceivable by any other being see he never so acute i.e.
     never so small an arch of a Circle this being w^t makes the
     distinction between acute & dull sight & not ye m:v: as
     men are, perhaps apt to think.

×   The same is True of any Tangible Circle, therefore farther   251
     Enquiry of Accuracy in squaring or other curves is
     perfectly needless & time thrown away.

×   Mem: to press w^t last precedes more homely & to think   252
     on't again.

×   A meer line or distance is not made up of points, does   253
     not exist, cannot be imagin'd or have an idea fram'd
     thereof no more than meer colour without extension.

×   Mem: a great difference between considering length   254
     wthout breadth, and having an idea of or imagining length
     without breadth.

+   Malbranch out touching the Xtallines diminishing. l.1.c.6.   255

¹×²   Tis possible (& perhaps not very improbable that it is   256
     sometimes so) we may have the greatest pictures from the
     least objects. therefore no necessary connexion betwixt
     visible & tangible ideas. these ideas viz. great relation to

the Sphaera Visualis or to the M : V : (wch is all that I
would have meant by our having a greater picture) and
faintness, might possibly have stood for or signify'd small
tangible extensions. Certainly the greater relation to
S.V: & M:V. does frequently in y^t men view little objects
near the Eye.

¹²× Malbranch out in asserting we cannot possibly know   257
whether there are 2 men in the world that see a thing of
the same bigness. v.L.ɪ c.6

× Diagonal of particular square commensurable wth its side   258
they both containing a certain number of M: V:

× I do not think that surfaces consist of lines *i.e* meer   259
distances. Hence perhaps may be solv'd that sophism w^{ch}
would prove the oblique line equal to the perpendicular
between 2 parallels.

× Suppose an inch represent a mile. $\frac{1}{1000}$ of an inch is   260
nothing, but $\frac{1}{1000}$ of y^e mile represented is something
therefore $\frac{1}{1000}$ of an inch tho' nothing is not to be neglected,
because it represents something *i.e.* $\frac{1}{1000}$ of a mile.

× Particular Determin'd lines are not divisible ad infinitum,   261
but lines as us'd by Geometers are so they not being
determin'd to any particular finite number of points. Yet
a Geometer (He knows not why) will very readily say he
can demonstrable an inch line is divisible ad infinitum.

¹×³ A Body moving in the Optique axis not perceiv'd to move   262
by sight meerly & w^{th}out experience. there is (tis true) a
successive change of ideas it seems less & less, but besides
this there is no visible change of place.

× Mem: To Enquire most diligently Concerning the   263
Incommensurability of Diagonal & side. whether it Does
not go on the supposition of unit being divisible ad
infinitum, i.e. of the extended thing spoken of being
divisible ad infinitum (unit being nothing also V. Barrow
Lect. Geom:). & so the infinite indivisibility deduc'd
therefrom is a petitio principii.

× The Diagonal is commensurable with the Side.   264

M ffrom Malbranch, Locke & my first arguings it cant be   265
P prov'd that extension is not in matter ffrom Lockes
arguings it can't be prov'd that Colours are not in Bodies.

       Mem: that I was distrustful at 8 years old and Conse-   266
quently by nature disposed for these new Doctrines.

×   Qu: How can a line consisting of an unequal number of   267
points be divisible [ad infinitum] in two equals

[1]×   Mem: To discuss copiously how & why we do not see the   268
[2]   Pictures.

M.   Allowing extensions to exist in matter, we cannot know   269
P.   even their proportions Contrary to Malbranch.

[1]M I wonder how men cannot see a truth so obvious, as that   270
extension cannot exist without a thinking substance.

M   Species of all sensible things made by the mind, This   271
prov^d either by turning Men's Eyes into magnifyers or
diminishers.

[2]   Y^r M.V. is suppose less than mine. Let a 3d person have   272
[1]× perfect ideas of both our M:V:s. His idea of my M.V.
contains his idea of y^{rs} & somewhat more, therefore tis
made up of parts, therefore his Idea of my v.m. is not
perfect or just wch everts the Hypothesis.

[2]×[1] Qu: whether a m.v. or T be extended?   273

[1]×[2] Mem. The strange errours men run into about the   274
pictures.

×   We think them small, because should a man be suppos'd   275
[1] [2] to see them their Pictures would take up but little room in
the fund of his Eye.

×   It seems all lines can't be bisected in 2 equall parts, Mem: 276
to examine how the Geometers prove the contrary.

[1] [2] Tis impossible there should be a M.V. less than mine. if   277
×   there be mine may become equal to it (because they are
homogeneous) by detraction of some part or parts, but it
consists not of parts Ergo. &c

a   Suppose inverting perspectives bound to ye eyes of a child,   278
[1] [3] & continu'd to the years of Manhood, When he looks up
×   or turns up his head he shall behold w^t we call under.
Qu: w^t would he think of up & down?

M   I wonder not at my sagacity in discovering the obvious tho'   279
      amazing truth, I rather wonder at my stupid inadvertency
      in not finding it out before. 'tis no witchcraft to see†

¹M   Our simple ideas are so many simple thoughts or percep-   280
      tions, & that a perception cannot exist without a thing to
      perceive it or any longer than it is perceiv'd, that a thought
      cannot be in an unthinking thing, that one uniform simple
      thought can be like to nothing but another uniform simple
      thought. Complex thoughts or ideas are onely an
      assemblage of simple ideas and can be the image of
      nothing or like unto nothing but another assemblage of
      simple ideas. &c

M   The Cartesian opinion of light & Colours etc is orthodox   281
      enough even in their eyes who think the Scripture expres-
      sion may favour the common opinion. why may not mine
      also? But there is nothing in Scripture that can possibly
      be wrested to make against me, but, perhaps, many things
      for me.

+   Bodies etc do exist whether we think of 'em or no, they   282
      being taken in a twofold sense. Collections of thoughts &
      collections of powers to cause those thoughts. these later
      exist, tho perhaps a parte rei it may be one simple
      perfect power.

¹¹ × ² Qu. whether the extension of a plain look'd at straight &   283
      slantingly, survey'd minutely & distinctly or in the Bulk
      and confusedly at once, be the same. N.B. the plain is
      suppos'd to keep the same distance.

¹¹ × ² the ideas we have by a successive, curious, inspection of   284
      yᵉ minute parts of a plain do not seem to make up the
      extension of that plain view'd & consider'd all together.

+   Ignorance in some sort requisite in yᵉ Person that should   285
      Discover the Principle.

+   Thoughts do most properly signify or are mostly taken for   286
      the interior operations of the mind, wherein the mind is
      active, those yᵗ obey not the acts of Volition, & in wᶜʰ the
      mind is passive are more properly call'd sensations or per-
      ceptions, But yᵗ is all a case.

×   Extension being the Collection or distinct coexistence of   287
      Minimums i.e. of perceptions intromitted by sight or touch,
      it cannot be conceiv'd without a perceiving substance.

P Malbranch does not prove that the figures & extensions 288
exist not w[n] they are not perceiv'd. Consequently he does
not prove nor can it be prov'd on his principles, that y[e]
sorts are the work of the mind & onely in the mind.

M.P.[1] The great argument to prove that Extension cannot be in 288a
an unthinking substance is that it cannot be conceiv'd
distinct from or without all tangible or visible quality

M[1] Tho matter be extended wth an indefinite Extension, yet 289
the mind makes the sorts, they were not before the mind
perceiving them. & even now they are not without the
mind. Houses trees, &c tho' indefinitely extended matter
do exist. are not without the mind.

M The great danger of making extension exist without the 290
mind. in y[t] if it does it must be acknowledg'd infinite
immutable eternal etc. w[ch] will be to make either God
extended (w[ch] I think dangerous) or an eternal, immutable,
infinite, increate being beside God.

M[1] The Principle easily prov'd by plenty of arguments ad 291
absurdum.

I× finiteness of our mind no excuse for the Geometers. 292

+ The twofold signification of Bodies viz. combinations of 293
thoughts & combinations of powers to raise thoughts.
These, I say, in conjunction wth homogeneous particles,
may solve much better the objections from the Creation.
than y[e] supposition that matter does exist upon w[ch]
supposition, I think, they cannot be solv[d].

+ Bodies taken for Powers do exist w[n] not perceiv'd but this 293a
existence is not actual. w[n] I say a power exists no more is
meant than that if in y[e] light I open my eyes & look that
way I shall see it i.e y[e] body &c.

+ Quer: whether Blind before sight may not have an idea of 294
light & colours & visible extension. After the same manner
as we perceive them wth Eyes shut or in y[e] dark. not
imagining but seeing after a sort.

×[19] Visible extension cannot be conceiv'd added to tangible 295
extension. visible & tangible points can't make one sum.
therefore these extensions are heterogeneous.

¹×¹ A Probable method propos'd whereby one may judge   296
whether in near vision there is a greater distance between
the Xtalline & fund than usual. or whether yᵉ Xtalline be
onely render'd more convex if the former, then the V.S
is enlargᵈ & yᵉ m.v. corresponds to less than 30″ or
wᵗever it us'd to correspond to.

¹²× little extension, by distinction made great   296a

¹×³ Stated measures, inches, feet etc are tangible not visible   297
extension.

M Locke, More, Raphson etc seem to make God extended.   298
'tis nevertheless of great use to religion to take extension
out of our idea of God & put a power in its place. it
seems dangerous to suppose extension wᶜʰ is manifestly
inert in God.

M But say you the thought or perception I call extension   299
is not itself in an unthinking thing or matter But it is
like something wᶜʰ is in matter. Well, says I, do you
apprehend & conceive wᵗ you say extension is like unto
or do you not. If the later, how know you they are alike,
how can you compare any things besides yʳ own ideas.
if the former it must be an idea i.e perception thought,
or sensation wᶜʰ to be in an unperceiving thing is a
Contradiction.

I. I abstain from all flourish & pomp of words & figures   300
using a great plainness & simplicity of stile having oft
found it difficult to understand those that use the Lofty
& Platonic or Subtil & Scholastique strain.

M¹ Whatsoever has any of our ideas in it must perceive, it   301
being that very having, that passive reception of ideas that
denominates the mind perceiving. that being the very
essence of perception, or that wherein perception consists.

¹×² The faintness wᶜʰ alters the Appearance of the Horizontal   302
Moon, rather proceeds from the quantity or Grossness of
the intermediate Atmosphere, than from any change of
Distance wᶜʰ is perhaps not considerable enough to be a
total Cause but may be a partial cause of the Phaeno-
menon. N.B. the Visual angle is less in the Horizon.

¹
¹× We judge of the distance of bodies as by other things so   302a
also by the situation of their pictures in the eye. (wᶜʰ

is the same thing) according as they appear higher or
lower those wch seem higher are farther of etc

¹²×   Qu: why we see objects greater in y^e dusk whether this   303
       can be solv'd by any but my principles.

M   The Reverse of y^e Principle introduc'd Scepticism.   304

M   N.B. On my Principles there is a reality, there are things,   305
       there is a rerum Natura.

×   Mem. The surds, Doubling the Cube &c   306

×^a_13 We think that if just made to see we shou'd Judge of the   307
       Distance & Magnitude of things as we do now. but this
       is false. So also w^t we think so positively of the situation
       of objects.

×   Hayes' Keil's etc method of proving the infinitesimals   308
       of y^e 3d order absurd, & perfectly contradictious.

×   Angles of Contact, & vr̄ly all angles comprehended by a   309
       right line & a curve, cannot be measur'd, the arches
       intercepted not being similar.

+   The danger of Expounding the H: Trinity by extension.   310

M.P.¹ Qu: why should the magnitude seen at a near distance   311
       be deem'd the true one rather than that seen at a farther
       distance? Why should the Sun be thought many 1000
       miles rather than one foot in diameter: both being equally
       apparent diameters? Certainly Men judg'd of the Sun
       not in himself but wth relation to themselves.

M   4 Principles whereby to answer objections viz—   312
         1. Bodies do really exist tho not perceiv'd by us.
         2. There is a law or course of Nature.
         3. Language & knowledge are all about ideas, words
            stand for nothing else.
         4. Nothing can be a proof against one side of a con-
            tradiction that bears equally hard upon the other.

×   What shall I say? dare I pronounce the admir'd $\alpha\kappa\rho\iota\beta\epsilon\iota\alpha$ 313
       Mathematica, that Darling of the Age a trifle?

×   Most certainly no finite Extension divisible ad Infinitum.   314

×   Mem: Difficulties about Concentric Circles.   315

N.   Mem. to Examine & accurately discuss the scholium of   316
     the 8th Definition of Mr Newton's Principia.

×   Ridiculous in the Mathematicians to despise sense.   317

+   Qu. is it not impossible there should be General ideas?   318
     All ideas come from without, they are all particular.
     The mind, tis true, can consider one thing wthout another,
     but then consider'd asunder they make not 2 ideas. both
     together can make but one as for instance Colour & Visible
     extension.

×   The end of a Mathematical line is nothing. Locke's   319
     argument that the end of his pen is black or white
     concludes nothing here.

×   Mem: take care how you pretend to define extension,   320
     for fear of the Geometers.

×   Qu: why difficult to imagine a minimum. Ans. because   321
     we are not us'd to take notice of 'em singly, they not
     being able singly to pleasure or hurt us thereby to deserve
     our regard.

×   Mem. to prove against Keil y^t the infinite divisibility of   322
     matter makes the half have an equal number of equal
     parts with the whole.

×   Mem. to examine how far the not comprehending infinity   323
     may be admitted as a plea.

×   Qu. why may not the Mathematicians reject all the exten-   324
     sions below the M. as well as the d d s etc wch are allow'd
     to be somthing & consequently may be magnify'd by
     glasses into inches, feet etc as well as the quantitys next
     below the m?

+   Bigg, little & number are the works of the mind. How   325
     therefore can ye extension you suppose in matter be big
     or little how can it consist of any number of points?

P   Mem: strictly to remark L.b. 2 c.8 S.8   326

+   Schoolmen compar'd with the Mathematicians   327

×   Extension is blended wth tangible or visible ideas, & by   328
     the mind praescinded therefrom.

×   Mathematiques made easy the Scale does almost all.   329
the Scale can tell us the subtangent in yᵉ Parabola is 2ble
the abscisse.

×   Wᵗ need of the Utmost accuracy wⁿ the Mathematicians   330
own in rerum natura they cannot find any thing corresponding wᵗʰ their nice ideas.

×   Newton in sad plight about his Cave intellexeris   331
finitas.

×   One should indeavour to find a progression by trying wᵗʰ   332
the Scale.

×   Newton's fluxions needless. any thing below a M. might   333
serve for Leibnitz's Differential Calculus.

×   How can they hang together so well since there are in   334
them (I mean the mathematiques) so many Contra-
dictoriae argutiae v. Barrow Lect:

×   A man may read a book of Conics with ease knowing   335
how to try if they are right. he may take 'em on the
credit of the Authour.

×   Where's the need of certainty in such trifles? the thing   336
that makes it so much esteem'd in them is that we are
thought not capable of getting it elsewhere. But we may
in Ethiques & Metaphysiques.

×   The not Leading men into mistakes no argument for the   337
truth of the infinitesimals. they being nothings may,
perhaps, do neither good nor harm. except wⁿ they are
taken for som thing: & then the contradiction begets a
Contradiction.

× $a + 500$ nothings $= a + 50$ nothings an innocent silly   338
truth

M   My Doctrine excellently corresponds wᵗʰ the Creation I   339
suppose no matter, no stars, sun &c to have existed before.

×   It seems all Circles are not similar figures there not being   340
the same proportion betwixt all circumferences & their
diameters.

×.   When a small line upon Paper represents a mile the   341
Mathematicians do not calculate the $\frac{1}{10000}$ of the Paper

line they Calculate the $\frac{1}{10000}$ of the mile 'tis to this they
have regard, tis of this they think if they think or have
any idea at all. the inch perhaps might represent to their
imaginations the mile but y^e $\frac{1}{10000}$ of the inch can not be
made to represent anything it not being imaginable.

×   But the $\frac{1}{10000}$ of a mile being somwhat they think the   341a
$\frac{1}{10000}$ of the inch is somwhat, w^n they think of y^t they
imagine they think on this.

×   3 faults occur in the arguments of the Mathematicians,   342
for divisibility ad infinitum. 1. they suppose extension
to exist without the mind or not perceiv'd. 2. they
suppose that we have an idea of length without breadth.
* or that length without breadth does exist. 3. that unite is
is divisible ad infinitum.

× *   or rather that invisible length does exist.   342a

×   To suppose a M.S. divisible is to say there are   343
distinguishable ideas where there are no distinguishable
ideas.

×   The M.S. is not near so inconceivable as this Signum   344
in magnitudine individuum.

×   Mem: To examine the Math: about their point w^t it is   345
something or nothing, & how it differs from the M.S.

×   All might be demonstrated by a new method of   346
indivisibles, easier perhaps & juster than that of Cavalle-
rius.

M.P.[1]   Unperceivable perception a contradiction.   347

G.   Proprietates reales rerum omnium in Deo tam corporum   348
quam spirituum continentur. Clerici Log: cap. 8m.

+   Let my adversaries answer any one of mine I'll yield—   349
If I don't answer every one of theirs I'll yield.

+   The Loss of the excuse may hurt Transubstantiation,   350
but not the Trinity

By ye excuse is meant the finiteness of our mind making   350a
it possible for contradictions to appear true to us.

×   We need not strain our Imaginations to conceive such   351
little things. Bigger may do as well for infinitesimals since
the integer must be an infinite.

×   Evident y^t wch has an infinite number of parts must be   352
infinite.

×   Qu: whether extension be resoluble into points it does   353
not consist of.

×   Axiom. No reasoning about things whereof we have no   354
idea. Therefore no reasoning about Infinitesimals.

×   nor can it be objected that we reason about Numbers wch 354a
are only words & not ideas, for these Infinitesimals are
words of no use if not suppos'd to stand for Ideas.

×   Much less infinitesimals of infinitesimals &c.   355

+   Axiom. No word to be used without an idea.   356

S   If uneasiness be necessary to set the will at work. Qu: 357
How shall we will in Heaven.

+   Malbranche's & Bayle's arguments do not seem to prove   358
against Space, but onely Bodies.

M.P.[1]   Our Eyes & Senses inform us not of the existence of   359
Matter or ideas existing without the mind. They
are not to be Blam'd for the mistake.

×   I defy any man to assign a Right line equal to a Para-   360
boloeid, but that w^n lookt at thro a Microscope they may
appear unequall.

M   Newton's Harangue amounts to no more than that   361
gravity is proportional to gravity.

×   One can't imagine an extended thing without color. v.   362
Barrow L.G.

M   Qu: whether I had not better allow Colours to exist   362a
P   without the Mind taking the Mind for the Active thing
wch I call I, my self. Y^t seems to be distinct from y^e
Understanding.

P   Men allow colours, sounds &c not to exist without the   363
mind tho they had no Demonstration they do not. Why
may they not allow my Principle with a Demonstration.

P.   The taking extension to be distinct from all other tangible   363a
      & visible qualities & to make an idea by it self. has made
      Men take it to be without the Mind.

×   Keils filling the world with a mite this follows from the   364
M   Divisibility of extension ad infinitum.

+   Extension or length without breadth seems to be nothing   365
      save the number of points that lie betwixt any 2 points.
      it seems to consist in meer proportion meer reference of
      the mind.

×   Extension without breadth i.e. invisible, intangible length   365a
      is not conceivable tis a mistake we are led into by the
      Doctrine of Abstraction.

+   To what purpose is it to Determine the Focus's of Glasses   366
×   Geometrically.

M   Innumerable vessels if Matter v. Cheyne   367

+   I'll not admire the Mathematicians. tis w^t any one of   368
      common sense might attain to by repeated acts. I know
      it by experience, I am but one of common sense, and I etc

+   By thing I either mean Ideas or that wch has ideas.   369

+   Nullum Praeclarum ingenium unquam fuit Magnus   370
      Mathematicus. Scaliger.

+   A Great Genius cannot stoop to such trifles & minute-   371
      nesses as they consider.

+   I see no wit in any of them but Newton, The rest are   372
      meer triflers, meer Nihilarians.

×   The folly of the Mathematicians in not judging of   373
      sensations by their senses. Reason was given us for nobler
      uses.

×   Sir Isaac owns his book could have been demonstrated   374
      on the supposition of indivisibles.

+   Mathematicians have some of them good parts, the more   375
      is the pity. Had they not been Mathematicians they had
      been good for nothing. they were such fools they knew not
      how to employ their parts.

+ The Mathematicians could not so much as tell wherein 376
× truth & certainty consisted till Locke told 'em. I see the
  best of them talk of light & colours as if wthout the mind.

M.[1] An idea cannot exist unperceiv'd   377

+1 All significant words stand for Ideas 378
 2 All knowlege about our ideas
+3 All ideas come from without or from within.
 4 If from without it must be by the senses & they are
  call'd sensations.
+5 If from within they are the operations of the mind &
  are called thoughts.
 6 No sensation can be in a senseless thing.
 7 No thought can be in a thoughtless thing.
+8 All our ideas are either sensations or thoughts, by 3.4.5.
 9 None of our ideas can be in a thing wch is both thoughtless & senseless. 6.7.8.
10 the bare passive reception or having of ideas is call'd
  perception

11 Whatever has in it an idea, tho it be never so passive,
  tho it exert no manner of act about it, yet it must
  perceive. 10
12 all ideas either are simple ideas, or made up of simple
  ideas.
+13 that thing wch is like unto another thing must agree
  wth it in one or more simple ideas.
14 whatever is like a simple idea must either be another
+ simple idea of the same sort or contain a simple idea of
  the same sort. 13.
15 nothing like an idea can be in an unperceiving thing.
  11. 14.

     another demonstration of the same thing
16 Two things cannot be said to be alike or unlike till
  they have been compar'd
17 Comparing is the viewing two ideas together, & marking
  w^t they agree in & w^t they disagree in.
18 The mind can compare nothing but its' own ideas. 17.
19 Nothing like an idea can be in an ūperceiving
  thing. 11. 16. 18.

These arguments must be proposed shorter & more 378a
separate in the Treatise.

N.B. Other arguments innumerable both a priori & a 379

posteriori drawn from all the sciences, from the clearest plainest most obvious truths whereby to Demonstrate the Principle i.e. that neither our Ideas nor any thing like our ideas can possibly be in an unperceiving thing.

N.B.   Not one argument, of any kind w^tsoever, certain   380
or probable, a priori or a posteriori from any art or
science, from either sense or reason against it.

×   Mathematicians have no right idea of angles. hence   381
angles of Contact wrongly apply'd to prove extension
divisible ad infinitum.

×   We have got the Algebra of pure intelligences   382

×   We can prove Newton's propositions * more accurately   383
more easily & upon truer principles than himself.

*   to the utmost accuracy wanting nothing of perfection.   383a
×   their solution of Problems themselves must own to fall
infinitely short of perfection

×   Barrow owns the Downfall of Geometry. However I'll   384
Endeavour to Rescue it. so far as it is usefull or real or
imaginable or intelligible, but for the nothings I'll leave
them to their admirers.

×   I'll teach any one the whole course of Mathematiques in   385
$\frac{1}{100}$ prt the time that another will.

×   Much Banter got from the prefaces of the Mathe-   386
maticians.

+   Innumerable vessels if Matter v. Cheyne.   387

P.   Newton says colour is in the subtil matter. hence Mal-   388
branch proves nothing or is mistaken in asserting there
is onely figure & motion therein.

×   The Billys use a finite visible line for an$\frac{1}{m}$ 389

T   Marsilius ficinus his appearing the moment he died solv'd   390
by my idea of time.

M   The Philosophers lose their Matter, The Mathematicians   391
loose their insensible sensations, the Profane their
extended Deity Pray w^t do the Rest of Mankind lose, as

for bodies &c we have them still. N.B. the future
Philosoph: & Mathem: get vastly by yᵉ bargain.

P   There are men who say there are insensible extensions,   392
there are others who say the Wall is not white, the fire is
not hot &c We Irish men cannot attain to these truths.

×   The Mathematicians think there are insensible lines, about   393
these they harangue, these cut in a point, at all angles
these are divisible ad infinitum. We Irish men can conceive no such lines.

×   The Mathematicians talk of wᵗ they call a point, this   394
they say is not altogether nothing nor is it downright
somthing, now we Irish men are apt to think something
& nothing are next neighbours.

×   I can square the circle, &c they cannot, wᶜʰ goes on the   395
best principles

+   Engagements to P. on account of yᵉ treatise that grew   396
up under his Eye, on account also of his approving my
harangue. Glorious for P. to be the Protectour of usefull
tho newly discover'd Truths.

+   How could I venture thoughts into the world, before I   397
knew they would be of use to the world? and how could
I know that till I had try'd how they suited other men's
ideas.

+   I Publish not this so much for anything else as to know   398
whether other men have the same Ideas as we Irishmen.
this is my end and not to be inform'd as to my own
Particular.

+   The Materialists & Nihilarians need not be of a party.   399

Notebook A

¹×³ Qu: if there be not two kinds of visible extension. one   400
perceiv'd by a confus'd view, the other by a distinct
successive direction of the optique axis to each point.

I No general Ideas, the contrary a cause of mistake or con-   401
fusion in Mathematiques etc. this to be intimated in yᵉ
Introduction.

+ The Principle may be apply'd to the difficulties of   402
Conservation cooperation etc.

N Trifling for the Philosophers to enquire the cause of   403
Magnetical attractions etc, They onely search after
coexisting ideas.

M.P. Quaecunque in Scriptura militant adversus Copernicum,   404
militant pro me.

M.P. All things in the Scripture wᶜʰ side with the Vulgar   405
against the Learned side with me also. I side in all
things with the Mob.

I know there is a mighty sect of Men will oppose me.   406
but yet I may expect to be supported by those whose
minds are not so far overgrown wᵗʰ madness, these are
far the greatest part of Mankind. Especially Moralists,
Divines, Politicians, in a word all but Mathematicians
& Natural Philosophers (I mean only the Hypothetical
Gentlemen). Experimental Philosophers have nothing
whereat to be offended in me.

+ Newton begs his Principle, † I Demonstrate mine.   407

M.E. I must be very particular in explaining wᵗ is meant by   408
things existing in Houses, chambers, fields, caves etc wⁿ
not perceiv'd as well as wⁿ perceiv'd. & shew how the

Vulgar notion agrees with mine when we narrowly inspect into the meaning & definition of the word Existence wch is no simple idea distinct from perceiving & being perceiv'd.

+ The Schoolmen have noble subjects but handle them ill. 409
The Mathematicians have trifling subjects but reason admirably about them. certainly their Method & arguing are excellent.

+ God knows how far our knowledge of Intellectual beings 410
may be enlarg'd from the Principle.

M. The Reverse of the Principle I take to have been the 411
chief source of all that scepticism & folly all those contradictions & inextricable puzling absurdities, that have in all ages been a reproach to Human Reason. as well as of that Idolatry whether of Images or of Gold etc that blinds the Greatest part of the World. as well as of that shamefull immorality that turns us into Beasts.

E היה vixit & fuit. 412

+E ουσια the name for substance used by Aristotle the 413
fathers etc.

× If at the same time we shall make the Mathematiques 414
much more easie & much more accurate, w^t can be objected to us?

× We need not force our Imagination to conceive such very 415
small lines for infinitesimals. they may every whit as well be imagin'd big as little since that the integer must be infinite.

× Evident that wch has an ifinite number of parts must be 416
infinite.

× We cannot imagine a line or space infinitely great 417
therefore absurd to talk or make propositions about it.

× We cannot imagine a line, space etc quovis dato majus. 418
Since y^t what we imagine must be datum aliquod. & a thing can't be greater than it self.

× If you call infinite that wch is greater than any assignable 419
by another, then I say in that sence there may be an infinite square, sphere or any other figure wch is absurd.

×   Qu. if extension be resoluble into points it does not consist of.   420

×   No reasoning about things whereof we have no ideas therefore no Reasoning about Infinitesimals.   421

+   No word to be used without an idea.   422

S   If uneasiness be necessary to set the will at work. Qu: How shall we will in Heaven.   423

+   Bayle's Malbranch's etc arguments do not seem to prove against space, but onely against Bodies.   424

M P   I agree in Nothing wth the Cartesians as to ye existence of Bodies & qualities   424a

+   Aristotle as good a Man as Euclid but He was allow'd to have been mistaken.   425

×   Lines not proper for Demonstration   426

M   We see the Horse it self, the Church it self it being an Idea & nothing more   427

M   The Horse it self the Church it self is an Idea i:e object immediate object of thought.   427a

×   Instead of injuring our Doctrine much Benefits Geometry.   428

E   Existere is percipi or percipere $\wedge$. the horse is in the stable, the Books are in the study as before.   429

         $\wedge$ or velle i:e. agere   429a

N   In Physiques I have a vast view of things soluble hereby but have not Leisure.   430

N   Hyps & such like unaccountable things confirm my Doctrine.   431

×   Angle not well Defin'd see Pardie's Geometry by Harris etc: this one ground of Trifling   432

+   One idea not the cause of another, one power not the cause of another. The cause of all natural things is onely God. Hence trifling to enquire after second Causes. This Doctrine gives a most suitable idea of the Divinity.   433

N   Absurd to study Astronomy & other the like Doctrines   434
as speculative sciences.

N   The absurd account of Memory by the Brain etc makes   435
for me.

+   How was light created before man? even so were Bodies   436
created before man.

E¹   Impossible any thing Besides that wch thinks & is thought   437
on should exist.

       Making thought to be active   437a

×   That wch is visible cannot be made up of invisible things.   438

×   M.S. is that wherein there are not contain'd distinguish-   439
able sensible parts. now how can that wch hath not
sensible parts be divided into sensible parts? if you say
it may be divided into insensible parts. I say these
are nothings.

×   Extension abstract from sensible qualities is no sensation,   440
I grant, but then there is no such idea as any one may
try. there is onely a Considering the number of points
without the sort of them, & this makes more for me.
since it must be in a Considering thing.

¹×¹²   Mem: before I have shewn the Distinction between   441
visible & tangible extension I must not mention them as
distinct, I must not mention M.T. & M.V. but in general
M.S. etc.

×   this belongs to Geometry   441a

¹×³   Qu: whether a M.V. be of any colour? a M.T. of any   442
tangible quality?

¹×³   If visible extension be the object of Geometry 'tis that   443
which is survey'd by the optique axis.

P   I may say the pain is in my finger etc according to my   444
Doctrine.

×   Mem: nicely to discuss w^t is meant when we say a line   445
consists of a certain number of inches or points etc A
Circle of a certain number of square inches, points etc.

Certainly we may think of a Circle, or have it's idea in
our mind without thinking of points or square inches etc.
whence it should seem the idea of a Circle is not made
up of the ideas of points square inches etc.

×   Qu: is any more than this meant by the foregoing Expres-   446
      sions viz. that squares or points may be perceived in or
      made out of a Circle etc. or that squares points etc are
      actually in it i.e. are perceivable in it.

×+   A line in abstract or distance is the number of points   447
      between two points. There is also distance between a
      Slave & an Emperour, between a Peasant & Philosopher,
      between a drachm & a pound, a farthing & a Crown etc
      in all wch distance signifies the number of intermediate
      ideas.

×   Halley's Doctrine about the Proportion between   448
      Infinitely great quantities vanishes. When men speak
      of Infinite quantities, either they mean finite quantities
*   or else talk of [that whereof they have] no idea. both
      wch are absurd.

*   that need not have been blotted out, 'tis good sense if we   448a
      do but determine w^t we mean by thing and Idea.

×   If the Disputations of the Schoolemen are blam'd for   449
      intricacy triflingness & confusion, yet it must be acknow-
      leg'd that in the main they treated of great & important
      subjects. If we admire the Method & acuteness of the
      Math: the length, the subtilty, the exactness of their
      Demonstrations, we must nevertheless be forced to grant
      that they are for the most part about trifling subjects &
      perhaps nothing at all.

+   Motion on 2^d thoughts seems to be a simple idea   450

P^1   Motion distinct from ye thing moved is not Conceivable.   450a

N   Mem: to take notice of Newton for Defining it also of   451
      Locke's wisdom in leaving it undefin'd.

+   ut ordo partium Temporis est immutabilis, sic etiam ordo   452
      partium Spatii. Moveantur hae de locis suis et move-
      buntur, (ut ita dicam) de seipsis. Truly Number is im-
      moveable that we will allow with Newton.

P   Ask a Cartesian whether he is wont to imagine his   453
globules without colour, pellucidness is a colour. The
colour of ordinary light of the Sun is white. Newton in
the right in assigning colours to the rays of light.

$^{1}\times^{1}$ A man born Blind would not imagine Space as we do.   454
we give it always some dilute or duskish
or dark colour. in short we imagine it as visible or
intromitted by the Eye wch he would not do.

N   Proinde vim inferunt sacris literis qui voces hasce   455
(v. tempus, spatium, motus) de quantitatibus mensuratis
ibi interpretantur. Newton p. 10.

N   I differ from Newton in that I think the recession ab axe   456
motus is not the effect or index or measure of motion,
but of the vis impressa. it sheweth not w^{t} is truly
moved but w^{t} has the force impress'd on it. or rather
that wch hath an impressed force.

$\times$ D & P are not proportional in all Circles. dd is to $\frac{1}{4}$dp   457
as d to $\frac{p}{4}$ but d & $\frac{p}{4}$ are not in the same proportion in
all Circles. Hence 'tis nonsense to seek the terms of one
general proportion whereby to rectify all peripheries or of
another whereby to square all Circles.

$\times$ N.B. if the Circle be squar'd Arithmetically, 'tis squar'd   458
Geometrically. Arithmetic or numbers being nothing but
lines & proportions of lines when apply'd to Geometry.

$\times+$ Mem. to remark Cheyne & his Doctrine of infinites   459

$\times$ Extension, motion, Time do each of them include the   460
idea of succession. & so far forth they seem to be of
Mathematical Consideration. Number consisting in
succession & distinct perception wch also consists in
succession for things at once perceiv'd are jumbled &
mixt together in the mind. Time and motion cannot be
conceiv'd without succession, & extension qua Mathemat:
cannot be conceiv'd but as consisting of parts wch may be
distinctly & successively perceiv'd. Extension perceiv'd
at once & in confuso does not belong to Math.

$+$ The simple idea call'd Power seems obscure or rather   461
none at all. but onely the relation 'twixt cause & Effect.
W^{n} I ask whether A can move B. if A be an intelligent

thing. I mean no more than whether the volition of A
that B move be attended with the motion of B, if A be
senseless whether the impulse of A against B be
follow'd by yᵉ motion of B.

×   Barrows arguing against indivisibles, lect. 1. p. 16 is a   462
petitio principii, for the Demonstration of Archimedes
supposeth the circumference to consist of more than 24
points. moreover it may perhaps be necessary to suppose
the divisibility ad infinitum, in order to Demonstrate that
the radius is equal to the side of the Hexagon.

×   Shew me an argument against indivisibles that does   463
not go on some false supposition.

×   A great number of insensibles. or thus. two invisibles   464
say you put together become visible therefore that m.v.
contains or is made up of Invisibles. I answer. the m.v.
does not comprise, is not compos'd of Invisibles. all the
matter amounts to this viz. whereof I had no idea a while
agoe I have an idea now. It remains for you to prove
that I came by the present idea because there were 2
invisibles added together. I say the invisibles are nothings,
cannot exist, include a contradiction.

+   I am young, I am an upstart, I am a pretender, I am   465
vain, very well. I shall Endeavour patiently to bear up
under the most lessening, vilifying appellations the pride
& rage of man can devise. But one thing, I know, I am
not guilty of. I do not pin my faith on the sleeve of any
great man. I act not out of prejudice & prepossession.
I do not adhere to any opinion because it is an old one,
a receiv'd one, a fashionable one, or one that I have
spent much time in the study and cultivation of.

×   Sense rather than Reason & demonstration ought to be   466
employ'd about lines & figures, these being things sensible,
for as for those you call insensible we have prov'd them
to be nonsense, nothing.

I   If in some things I differ from a Philosopher I profess   467
to admire, 'tis for that very thing on account whereof I
admire him namely the love of truth. this etc

I   wherever my Reader finds me talk very positively I   468
desire he'd not take it ill. I see no reason why certainty
should be confin'd to the Mathematicians

×   I say there are no incommensurables, no surds, I say the   469
side of any square may be assign'd in numbers. Say you
assign unto me the side of the square 10. I ask w^t 10,
10 feet, inches etc or 10 points. if the later; I deny there
is any such square, tis impossible 10 points should compose
a square. if the former, resolve y^r 10 square inches, feet
etc into points & the number of points must necessarily be
a square number whose side is easily assignable.

×   A mean proportional cannot be found betwixt any two   470
given lines. it can onely be found betwixt those the
numbers of whose points multiply'd together produce a
square number. thus betwixt a line of 2 inches & a line
of 5 inches, a mean geometrical cannot be found except
the number of points contain'd in 2 inches multiply'd by
ye number of points contain'd in 5 inches make a square
number.

×   If the wit & industry of the Nihilarians were employ'd   471
about the usefull & practical Mathematiques, w^t advantage
had it brought to Mankind?

M.E   You ask me whether the books are in the study now w^n 472
no one is there to see them. I answer yes. you ask
me are we not in the wrong for imagining things to exist
w^n they are not actually perceiv'd by the senses. I
answer no. the existence of our ideas consists in being
perceiv'd, imagin'd thought on whenever they are
imagin'd or thought on they do exist. Whenever they are
mention'd or discours'd of they are imagin'd & thought
on therefore you can at no time ask me whether they
exist or no, but by reason of y^t very question they must
necessarily exist.

E   But say you then a Chimaera does exist. I answer it   473
doth in one sense. i.e. it is imagin'd. but it must be well
noted that existence is vulgarly restrain'd to actuall perception. & that I use the word Existence in a larger sense
than ordinary.

+   N.B. according to my Doctrine all things are entia   474
rationis i.e. solum habent esse in Intellectu.

E   according to my Doctrine all are not entia rationis the   474a
distinction between ens rationis & ens reale is kept up by it
as well as any other Doctrine.

×   You ask me whether there can be an infinite Idea? I   475
answer in one sense there may. thus the visual sphere
tho ever so small is infinite. i.e. has no end. But if by
infinite you mean extension consisting of innumerable
points. then I ask y^r pardon. points tho never so many
may be number'd the multitude of points or feet, inches
etc hinders not their numberableness in the least.* Many
or most are numerable as well as few or least. also if
by infinite idea. you mean an idea too great to be comprehended or perceiv'd all at once. you must excuse me.
I think such an infinite is no less than a contradiction.

*   i.e. hinders not their being nameable.   475a

M ¹   The sillyness of the Currant Doctrine makes much for me.   476
they commonly suppose a material world, figures,
motions, bulks of various sizes etc according to their
own confession to no purpose, all our sensations may be
& sometimes actually are without them. nor can men so
much as conceive it possible they should concur in any
wise to the production of them.

M ¹   Ask a man I mean a Cartesian why he supposes this vast   477
structure, this compages of Bodies. he shall be at a stand,
he'll not have One word to say. wch sufficiently shews the
folly of the hypothesis:

M   or rather why he supposes all ye Matter, for bodies &   477a
their qualitys I do allow to exist independently of Our
mind.

S   Qu: how is the soul distinguish'd from it's ideas?   478
certainly if there were no sensible ideas there could be no
soul, no perception, remembrance, love, fear etc. no
faculty could be exerted.

S   The soul is the will properly speaking & as it is distinct   478a
from Ideas.

S   The grand, puzling question whether I sleep or wake?   479
easily solv'd.

×   Qu: whether minima or near minima may not be   480
compar'd by their sooner & later evanescency as well as
by more or less points. So that one sensible may be
greater than another tho it exceeds it not by one point.

×   Circles on several radius's are not similar figures they   481
having neither all nor any an infinite number of sides.
Hence in Vain to enquire after 2 terms of one & ye same
proportion that should constantly express the reason of
the d to the p in all Circles.

×   Mem: to remark Wallis's harangue that the aforesaid   482
Proportion can neither be express'd by rational numbers
nor surds.

×   We can no more have an idea of length without breadth   483
or visibility than of a General figure.

     One idea may be like another idea tho' they Contain no   484
common simple idea. thus the simple idea red is in some
+   sense like the simple idea blue. tis liker it than sweet or
shrill. But then those ideas wch are so said to be alike
agree both in their connexion with another simple idea
viz. extension & in their being receiv'd by one & ye same
sense. But after all nothing can be like an idea but an
idea.

     This I do not altogether approve of   484a

+   No sharing betwixt God & Nature or second Causes in   485
my Doctrine.

M   Materialists must allow the Earth to be actually mov'd   486
by the Attractive power of every stone that falls from
the air. with many other the like absurditys.

×   Enquire concerning the Pendulum Clock etc. whether   487
those inventions of Huygens etc may be attained to by
my Doctrine.

+   The *" " & " "' & " " "* etc of time are to be cast away &   488
neglected as so many noughts or nothings.

+   Mem. to make experiments concerning Minimums & their   489
colours. whether they have any or no. & whether they can
be of that green wch seems to be compounded of yellow &
blue.

S   Qu: whether it were not better not to call the operations   490
of the mind ideas, confining this term to things sensible?

E   Mem: Diligently to set forth how that many of the   491
Ancient philosophers run into so great absurditys as even

to deny the existence of motion and those other things
they perceiv'd actually by their senses. this sprung from
their not knowing w^t existence was and wherein it consisted this the source of all their Folly, 'tis on the Discovering of the nature & meaning & import of Existence
that I chiefly insist. This puts a wide difference betwixt
the Sceptics & me. This I think wholly new. I am
sure 'tis new to me

×   We have learn'd from Mr. Locke. that there may be   492
     and that there are several glib, coherent, methodical
     Discourses wch nevertheless amount to just nothing. this
     by him intimated with relation to the Scholemen. We
     may apply it to the Mathematicians.

+   Power no simple Idea. it means nothing but the Relation   493
     between Cause & Effect.

+   Qu: How can all words be said to stand for ideas? The   494
     word Blue stands for a Colour without any extension or
     abstract from extension. But we have not an idea of
     Colour without extension. we cannot imagine Colour
     without extension.

+   Locke seems wrongly to assign a Double use of words one   495
     for communicating & the other for recording our thoughts.
     Tis absurd to use words for the recording our thoughts to
     our selves: or in our private meditations.

+   No one abstract simple idea like another two simple   496
     ideas may be connected with one & the same 3d simple
     idea, or be intromitted by one & the same sense. But
     consider'd in themselves they can have nothing common
     & consequently no likeness.

+   Qu: How can there be any abstract ideas of Colours?   497
     it seems not so easily as of tastes or sounds. But then all
     abstract ideas whatsoever are particular. I can by no
     means conceive a general idea. 'Tis one thing to abstract
     one idea from another of a different kind. & another
     thing to abstract an idea from all particulars of the same
     kind.

N   Mem. much to Recommend & approve of Experimental   498
     Philosophy.

S   What means Cause as distinguish'd from Occasion?   499
     nothing but a Being wch wills w^n the Effect follows the

volition. Those things that happen from without we are
not the Cause of therefore there is some other Cause of
them i.e. there is a being that wills these perceptions in us.

S   it should be said nothing but a Will, a being wch wills   499a
     being unintelligible.

×   One square cannot be double of another. Hence the   500
     Pythagoric Theorem is false.

$^1×^1$ Some writers of Catoptrics absurd enough to place the   501
     apparent place of y^e objects in the Barrovian Case behind
     the eye.

+   Blew & yellow chequers still diminishing terminate in   502
     green. This may help to prove the composition of green.

+   There is in green 2 foundations of 2 relations of likeness   503
     to blew & yellow. therefore Green is compounded.

+   A mixt cause will produce a mixt Effect therefore   504
     Colours are all compounded that we see.

+   Mem: to Consider Newton's two sorts of Green.   505

+   N.B. my Abstract & general Doctrines ought not to be   506
     condemn'd by the Royall Society Tis w^t Their Meeting
     did ultimately intend. v. Sprat's History S.R.

I   Mem. to Premise a Definition of Idea.   507

Mo.   The 2 great Principles of Morality. the Being of a God   508
     & the Freedom of Man: these to be handled in the
     beginning of the Second Book.

×   Subvertitur Geometria ut non practica sed Speculativa.   509

×   Archimedes's proposition about squaring the Circle has   510
     nothing to do with circumferences containing less than
     96 points. & if the circumference contain 96 points it
     may be apply'd but nothing will follow against indivisibles.
     v. Barrow.

×   Those Curve lines that you can Rectify Geometrically.   511
     Compare them with their equal right lines & by a
     Microscope you shall discern an inequality. Hence my
     squaring of the Circle as good & exact as the best.

M   Qu: whether the substance of Body or any thing else,   512
be any more than the Collection of Ideas included in that
thing. Thus the substance of any particular Body is
extension solidity figure. & of General Body no idea.

I   Mem: most carefully to inculcate & set forth how that   513
the Endeavouring to Express abstract philosophic Thoughts
by words unavoidably runs a man into Difficulties. This
to be done in the Introduction.

×   Mem: to Endeavour most accurately to understand w^t is   514
meant by this axiom: Quae sibi mutuo congruunt
aequalia sunt.

×   Qu: w^t the Geometers mean by equality of lines &   515
whether according to their definition of equality a curve
line can possibly be equal to a right line.

×   If wth me you call those lines equal wch contain an equal   516
number of points. then there will be no difficulty. that
curve is equal to a right line wch contains as [many]†
points as the right.one doth.

M   I take not away substances. I ought not to be accus'd of   517
discarding Substance out of the reasonable World. I
onely reject the Philosophic sense (wch in effect is no sense)
of the word substance. Ask a man non tainted with
their jargon w^t he means by corporeal substance, or the
substance of Body, He shall answer Bulk, Solidity & such
like sensible qualitys. These I retain. the Philosophic nec
quid nec quantum nec quale whereof I have no idea I
discard. if a man may be said to discard that wch never
had any being was never so much as imagin'd or
conceiv'd.

M   N.B. I am more for reality than any other Philosophers,   517a
they make a thousand doubts & know not certainly but
we may be deceiv'd. I assert the direct Contrary.

M   In short be not angry you lose nothing. whether real or   518
chimerical w^{t}ever you can in any wise conceive or
imagine be it ever so wild so extravagant & absurd much
good may it do you. you may enjoy it for me. I'll not
deprive you of it.

×   A line in the sense of Mathematicians is not meer distance.   519
this evident in that there are curve lines.

×   Curves perfectly incomprehensible inexplicable, absurd   520
except we allow points.

I   If men look for a thing where it's not to be found. be they   521
never so sagacious it is lost labour. if a simple clumsey
man know where the Game lies. He tho afoot † shall
catch it sooner than the most fleet & dexterous that seek
it elsewhere. Men choose to hunt for truth & knowledge
any where rather than in their own Understanding where
'tis to be found.

¹M   All knowlege onely about ideas. V. Locke B.4 c.1.   522

S   It seems improper & liable to difficulties to make the   523
Word Person stand for an Idea, or to make our selves
Ideas or thinking things ideas.

I   General Ideas Cause of much Trifling & Mistake.   524

×   Mathematicians seem not to speak clearly & coherently   525
of Equality. They no where define w^t they mean by that
word when apply'd to Lines.

+   Locke says the modes of simple Ideas besides extension &   526
numbers are counted by degrees. I deny there are any
modes or degrees of simple Ideas. W^t He terms such are
complex Ideas as I have prov'd in Green.

×   W^t do the Mathematicians mean by Considering Curves   527
as Polygons? either they are Polygons or they are not.
if they are why do they give them the Name of Curves?
why do not they constantly call them Polygons & treat
them as such. If they are not polygons I think it absurd
to use polygons in their stead. w^t is this but to pervert
language to adapt an idea to a name that belongs not to it
but to a different idea?

×   The Mathematicians should look to their axiom Quae   528
congruunt sunt aequalia. I know not what they mean
by bidding me put one Triangle on another. the under
Triangle is no Triangle, nothing at all, it not being
perceiv'd. I ask must sight be judge of this Congruentia
or not. if it must then all Lines seen under the same Angle
are equal wch they will not acknowlege. Must the
Touch be Judge? But we cannot touch or feel Lines &
Surfaces, such as Triangles etc according to the Mathematicians themselves. Much less can we feel a line or
Triangle that's cover'd by another Line or Triangle.

×   Do you mean by saying one triangle is equall to another   529
     that they both take up equal spaces. But then the
     Question recurs w^t mean you by equal spaces, if you
     mean spatia congruentia answer the above difficulties.

×   I can mean (for my part) nothing else by equal Triangles   530
     than Triangles containing equal numbers of Points.

×   I can mean nothing by equal lines but lines wch tis   530a
     indifferent whether of them I take, lines in wch I observe
     by my senses no difference, & wch therefore have
     the same Name.

×   Must the Imagination be Judge in the aforemention'd   531
     Case. but then Imagination cannot go beyond the
     Touch & Sight. Say you Pure Intellect must be Judge. I
     reply that Lines & Triangles are not operations of the
     Mind.

     If I speak positively & with the air of a Mathematician   532
     in things of which I am certain. tis to avoid Disputes to
     make Men careful to think before they censure. To
     Discuss my Arguments before they go to refute them. I
     would by no means injure truth & Certainty by an
     affected modesty & submission to Better Judgements.
     W^t I lay before you are undoubted Theorems not
     plausible conjectures of my own nor learn'd opinions of
     other men. I pretend not to prove them by figures,
     analogy or Authority. Let them stand or fall by their
     own Evidence.

N   When you speak of the Corpuscularian Essences of Bodys   533
     mem: to reflect on sect: 11 & 12 b.4.c.3. Locke. Motion
     supposes not solidity a meer Colour'd Extension may give
     us the Idea of motion.

P   Any subject can have of each sort of primary Qualities   534
     but one particular at once. Lib. 4.c. 3 S 15 Locke.

M   Well say you according to this new Doctrine all is but   535
     meer Idea, there is nothing wch is not an ens rationis. I
     answer things are as real & exist in rerum natura as much
     as ever. the distinction betwixt entia Realia & entia
     rationis may be made as properly now as ever. Do but
     think before you speak. Endeavour rightly to compre-
     hend my meaning & you'll agree with me in this.

N   ffruitless the Distinction twixt real & nominal Essences.   536

We are not acquainted with the meaning of our words, 537
Real, Extension, Existence, power, matter, Lines, Infinite,
point, & many more are frequently in our mouths when
little clear & determin'd answers them in our Understandings. This must be well inculcated.

M   Vain is the Distinction twixt Intellectual & Material 538
World V. Locke Lib. 4.c.3. S 27 where he says that is far
more beautifull than this.

S.Mo. ffoolish in Men to despise the senses, if it were not for 539
them yᵉ mind could have no knowlege no thought at all.
All . . . .† of Introversion, meditation, contemplation &
spiritual acts as if these could be exerted before we had
ideas from without by the senses are manifestly absurd.
This may be of great use in that it makes the Happyness
of the Life to come more conceivable & agreeable to our
present nature. The Schoolemen & Refiners in
Philosophy Gave the Greatest part of Mankind no more
tempting Idea of Heaven or the Joys of the Blest.

×   The Vast, Widespread, Universal Cause of our Mistakes. 540
Is that we do not consider our own notions, I mean
consider them in them selves, fix, settle & determine
them. We regarding them with relation to each other
only. In short we are much out in studying the relations of
things before we study them absolutely & in themselves.
Thus we study to find out the Relations of figures to one
another, the Relations also of Number. without Endeavouring rightly to understand the Nature of Extension
& Number in themselves This we think is of no concern
of no difficulty but if I mistake not tis of the last
Importance.

Mo   I allow not of the Distinction there is made twix't Profit 541
& Pleasure.

Mo   I'd never blame a Man for acting upon Interest. he's 542
a fool that acts on any other Principle. the not considering these things has been of ill consequence in
Morality.

+   My positive Assertions are no less modest than those that 543
are introduc'd wᵗʰ it seems to me, I suppose etc since I
declare once for all, that all I write or think is entirely
about things as they appear to me. It concerns no man
else any farther than his thoughts agree with mine. This
in the Preface.

I   Two things are apt to confound men in their Reasonings   544
one with another. 1st. words signifying the operations
of the mind are taken from sensible Ideas. 2dly. words as
Used by the Vulgar are taken in some Latitude, their
signification is confused. Hence if a man use y^m in a
determin'd settled signification he is at a hazard either
of not being understood or of speaking improperly. All
this remedyed by studying the Understanding.

×   Unite no simple Idea. I have no Idea meerly answering   545
the word one. all Number consists in Relations.

+   Entia realia & Entia rationis a foolish distinction of the   546
Schoolemen.

       Words there not so foolish neither   546a

M.P.   We have an intuitive Knowlege of the Existence of   547
other things besides our selves & even praecedaneous to the
Knowlege of our own Existence. in that we must have
Ideas or else we cannot think.

S   We move our Legs our selves. 'tis we that will their   548
movement. Herein I differ from Malbranch.

Mo×   Mem: nicely to discuss Lib.4.c.4. Locke.   549

       it is of ye Reality of Knowledge   549a

M   Mem: again & again to mention & illustrate the Doctrine   550
of the Reality of Things Rerum Natura etc.

M   W^t I say is Demonstration, perfect Demonstration.   551
Whenever men have fix'd & determin'd Ideas annex'd
to their words they can hardly be mistaken. Stick but
to my Definition of Likeness & tis a Demonstration y^t
Colours are not simple Ideas. All Reds being like etc.
So also in other things. This to be heartily insisted on.

E   The abstract Idea of Being or Existence is never thought   552
of by the Vulgar. they never use those words standing for
abstract Ideas.

M   I must not say the words thing, substance etc have been   553
the Cause of mistakes. But the not reflecting on their
meaning. I will be still for retaining the words. I only
desire that men would think before they speak & settle
the meaning of their words.

Mo   I approve not of that which Locke says viz truth consists   554
×   in the joyning & separating of signs.

I   Locke cannot explain general Truth or Knowlege without   555
     treating of words & propositions. This makes for me
     against general Ideas — v. Locke Lib.4:ch:6.

I   Men have been very industrious in travelling forward   556
     they have gone a great way. But few or none have gone
     backward beyond the Principles. On that side there lys
     much terra incognita to be travel'd over & discover'd by
     me. A vast field for invention:

×   Twelve inches not the same Idea with a foot. Because a   557
     Man may perfectly conceive a foot who never thought of
     an inch.

×   A foot is equal to or the same with twelve inches in this   558
     respect viz. they contain both the same number of points.

+   [Forasmuch as] to be used.   559

     Mem: to mention somewhat wch may Encourage the   560
     study of Politiques & testify of me y^t I am well dispos'd
     toward them.

I   If men did not use words for Ideas they would never have   561
     thought of abstract ideas. certainly genera & species are
     not abstract general ideas. These include a contradiction
     in their nature v. Locke Lib.4 S.9.c.7.

     A various or mixt cause must necessarily produce a various   562
     or mixt effect. This demonstrable from the Definition of a
     Cause. wch way of Demonstrating must be frequently made
     use of in my Treatise & to that end Definitions often
     praemis'd. Hence 'tis evident that according to Newton's
     Doctrines Colours can not be simple ideas.

M   I am the farthest from Scepticism of any. man. I know   563
     with an intuitive knowledge the existence of other things
     as well as my own Soul. this is w^t Locke nor scarce any
     other Thinking Philosopher will pretend to.

I   Doctrine of Abstraction of very evil consequence in all   564
     the Sciences. Mem: Bacon's remark. Entirely owing to
     Language.

+   Locke greatly out in reckoning the recording our Ideas   565
     by words amongst the uses & not the abuses of Language.

I   Of great use & yᵉ last Importance to Contemplate a man   566
     put into the world alone wᵗʰ admirable abilitys. & see
     how after long experience he would know wᵗʰout words.
     Such a one would never think of Genera & Species or
     abstract general Ideas.

I   Wonderful in Locke that he could wⁿ advanc'd in years   567
     see at all thro a mist yᵗ had been so long a gathering &
     was consequently thick. This more to be admir'd than
     yᵗ he didn't see farther.

+   Identity of Ideas may be taken in a Double sense either as   568
     including or excluding Identity or Circumstances. such as
     time, place etc. .

Mo   I am glad the People I converse with are not all richer,   569
     wiser etc than I. This is agreeable to Reason, is no sin.
     Tis certain that if the Happyness of my Acquaintance
     encreases & mine not proportionably, mine much decrease.
     The not understanding this & the Doctrine about relative
     Good discuss'd with French, Madden etc to be noted as
     2 Causes of mistake in Judging of moral Matters.

+   Mem: to observe (wⁿ you talk of the Division of Ideas   570
     into simple & complex) that there may be another cause
     of the Undefinableness of certain Ideas besides that which
     Locke gives viz. the want of Names.

M   Mem: To begin the 1st Book not with mention of   571
     Sensation & Reflection but instead of those to use
     perception or thought in general.

S   I Defy any man to Imagine or conceive perception   572
     without an Idea or an Idea without perception

E   Locke's very supposition that matter & motion should   573
     exist before thought is absurd, includes a manifest
     Contradiction.

×   Locke's harangue about coherent, methodical Discourses   574
     amounting to nothing, apply'd to the Mathematicians.

×   They talk of determining all the points of a Curve by an   575
     Aequation wᵗ mean they by this. wᵗ would they signify by
     the word points. Do they stick to the Definition of Euclid.

S   We think we know not the Soul because we have no   576
imaginable or sensible Idea annex'd to that sound. This
the Effect of prejudice.

S   Certainly we do not know it. this will be plain if we   576a
examine w^t we mean by the word knowlege. Neither
doth this argue any defect in our knowlege no more than
our not knowing a contradiction

+   The very existence of Ideas constitutes the soul.   577

S   Consciousness, perception, existence of Ideas seem to be   578
all one.

+   Consult, ransack y^r Understanding w^t find you there   579
besides several perceptions or thoughts. W^t mean you
by the word mind you must mean something that you
perceive or y^t you do not perceive. a thing not perceived
is a contradiction. to mean (also) a thing you do not perceive
is a contradiction. We are in all this matter strangely
abused by words.

+   Mind is a congeries of Perceptions. Take away Per-   580
ceptions & you take away the Mind put the Perceptions
& you put the mind.

+   Say you the Mind is not the Perceptions. but that thing   581
wch perceives. I answer you are abus'd by the words that
& thing these are vague empty words wthout a meaning.

S   The having Ideas is not the same thing with Perception.   582
a Man may have Ideas when he only Imagines. But
then this Imagination presupposeth Perception.

M.   That wch extreamly strengthens us in prejudice is y^t we   583
think we see an empty space. wch I shall Demonstrate to
be false in the 3d Book.

There may be Demonstrations used even in Divinity. I   584
mean in reveal'd Theology, as contradistinguish'd from
natural. for tho the Principles may be founded in Faith
yet this hinders not but that legitimate Demonstrations
might be built thereon. Provided still that we define the
words we use & never go beyond our Ideas. Hence
'twere no very hard matter for those who hold Episcopacy
or Monarchy to be establish'd jure Divino. to demonstrate
their Doctrines if they are true. But to pretend to demon-

strate or reason any thing about the Trinity is absurd here
an implicit Faith becomes us.

S   Qu: if there be any real Difference betwixt certain Ideas   585
of Reflexion & others of Sensation. e.g. 'twixt perception
& white, black, sweet etc. wherein I pray you does the
perception of white differ from white. Mea . . . . †

I shall Demonstrate all my Doctrines. the Nature of   586
Demonstration to be set forth & insisted on in the Introduction. In that I must needs differ from Locke forasmuch as he makes all Demonstration to be about abstract
Ideas wch I say we have not nor can have.

S   The Understanding seemeth not to differ from its per-   587
ceptions or Ideas. Qu: w^t must one think of the Will &
passions.

E   A good Proof that Existence is nothing without or distinct   588
from Perception may be Drawn from Considering a Man
put into the World without company.

E   There was a smell i.e. there was a smell perceiv'd. Thus   589
we see that common speech confirms my Doctrine

T   No broken Intervals of Death or Annihilation. Those   590
Intervals are nothing. Each Person's time being measured
to him by his own Ideas.

I   We are frequently puzzl'd & at a loss in obtaining clear &   591
determin'd meanings of words commonly in use. & that
because we imagine words stand for general Ideas which
are altogether inconceivable.

I   A stone is a stone. this a nonsensical Proposition. & such   592
as the Solitary Man would never think on. nor do I
believe he would ever think on this viz. The whole is
equal to it's Parts. etc.

E   Let it not be said that I take away Existence. I onely   593
declare the meaning of the Word so far as I can comprehend it.

I   If you take away abstraction, how do men differ from   594
Beasts. I answer by shape. By Language rather by
Degrees of more & less.

+   W^t means Locke by inferences in words, consequences   595
          of Words as somthing different from consequences of
          Ideas. I conceive no such thing.

I   N.B. Much Complaint about the Imperfection of   596
          Language.

M   But perhaps some man may say an inert thoughtless   597
          substance may exist tho' not extended, moved etc. but wth
          other properties whereof we have no Idea. But even
          this I shall demonstrate to be Impossible w^n I come
          to treat more particularly of Existence.

+   Will not rightly distinguish'd from Desire by Locke. it   598
          seeming to superadd nothing to the Idea of an Action
          but the Uneasiness for it's absence or non Existence.

S   Mem: to enquire diligently into that strange Mistery viz.   599
          How it is that I can cast about, think of this or that Man,
          place, action w^n nothing appears to Introduce them into
          my thoughts. w^n they have no perceivable connexion wth
          the Ideas suggested by my senses at the present.

I   Tis not to be imagin'd w^t a marvellous emptiness &   600
          scarcity of Ideas that man shall descry who will lay aside
          all use of Words in his Meditations.

M   Incongruous in Locke to fancy we want a sense proper to   601
          see substances withal.

I   Locke owns that Abstract Ideas were made in order to   602
          naming.

[1] × M   The common Errour of the Opticians, that we judge of   603
          Distance by Angles strengthens' men in their prejudice that
          they see things without and distant from their mind.

E   I am persuaded would Men but examine w^t they mean by   604
          the Word Existence they wou'd agree with me.

×   c.20 S.8 B.4 of Locke makes for me against the Mathe-   605
          maticians.

M   The supposition that things are distinct from Ideas takes   606
          away all real Truth, & consequently brings in a Universal
          Scepticism, since all our knowlege & contemplation is
          confin'd barely to our own Ideas.

I   Qu: whether the Solitary Man would not find it necessary 607
to make use of words to record his Ideas if not in memory
or meditation yet, at least, in writing without which he
could scarce retain his Knowlege.

+   We read in History there was a time when fears & jea- 608
lousies, Privileges of Parliament, Malignant Party & such
like expressions of too unlimited & doubtfull a meaning
were words of much sway. Also the Words Church, Whig,
Tory etc. contribute very much to faction & Dispute.

S   The Distinguishing betwixt an Idea and perception of the 609
Idea has been one great cause of Imagining material
substances.

S   That God & Blessed Spirits have Will is a manifest 610
Argument against Lockes proofs that the will cannot be
conceiv'd put into action without a Previous Uneasiness.

S   The act of the Will or volition is not uneasiness for that 611
uneasiness may be without volition.

S   It is not so very evident that an Idea or at least Un- 611a
easiness may be without all Volition or act.

S   Volition is distinct from the object or Idea for the same 612
reason.

S   Also from uneasiness & Idea together. 613

    the Understanding not distinct from particular percep- 614
tions or Ideas.

*   The Understanding taken for a faculty is not really distinct 614a
from ye Will.

*   The Will not distinct from Particular volitions. 615

    This alter'd hereafter 615a

S   To ask whether a man can will either side is an absurd 616
question. for the word can presupposes volition.

N   Anima Mundi. Substantial fforms, Omniscient radical 617
Heat. Plastic vertue. Hylarchic principle. All these
vanish.

M   Newton proves that gravity is proportional to gravity.   618
         I think that's all.

+   Qu: whether it be the vis inertiae that makes it difficult   619
         to move a stone or the vis attractrix or both or neither.

         Mem: to express the Doctrines as fully & copiously &   620
         clearly as may be. also to be full and particular in
         answering objections.

S   To say yᵉ Will is a power. Volition is an act. This is   621
         idem per idem.

+   Wᵗ makes men despise extension motion etc & separate   622
         them from the essence of the soul is that they imagine
         them to be distinct from thought & to exist in unthinking
         substance.

+   An extended may have passive modes of thinking, not   623
         active

+   There might be Idea, there might be uneasiness. there   624
         might be the greatest uneasiness. wᵗʰout any volition.
         therefore the

M.+ Matter once allow'd. I defy any man to prove that God   625
         is not matter.

S   Man is free. There is no difficulty in this proposition   626
         if we but settle the signification of the word free, if we had
         an Idea annext to the word free & would but contemplate
         that Idea.

S   We are imposed on by the words, will, determine, agent,   627
         free, can etc.

S   Uneasiness precedes not every Volition. This evident   628
         by experience.

S   Trace an Infant in the Womb. mark the train & Succes-   629
         sion of its Ideas. observe how volition comes into the
         Mind. This may perhaps acquaint you with its nature.

S   Complacency seems rather to determine or precede or   630
         coincide wᵗʰ & constitute the Essence of volition than
         uneasiness.

S   You tell me according to my Doctrine a Man is not free.   631
     I answer. tell me w^t you mean by the word free & I
     shall resolve you.

N   Qu: w^t do men mean when they talk of one Body's   632
     touching another. I say you never saw one Body touch.
     or (rather) I say I never saw one Body that I could say
     touch'd this or that other. for that if my optiques were
     improv'd I should see intervalls & other bodies betwixt
     those wch now seem to touch.

×   Mem: upon all occasions to use the Utmost Modesty. to   633
     Confute the Mathematicians wth the utmost civility &
     respect. not to stile them Nihilarians etc:

     N.B. to rein in y^r Satyrical nature.   634

S   Tis folly to define volition an act of the mind ordering.   635
     for neither act nor ordering can them selves be
     understood without Volition.

     Blame me not if I use my words sometimes in some   636
     latitude. 'tis w^t cannot be helpt. Tis the fault of Language
     that you cannot always apprehend the clear & determinate
     meaning of my words.

+   Say you there must be a thinking substance. Somthing   637
     unknown wch perceives & supports & ties together the
     Ideas. Say I, make it appear there is any need of it &
     you shall have it for me. I care not to take away any
     thing I can see the least reason to think should exist.

+   I affirm 'tis manifestly absurd. no excuse in ye world can   638
     be given why a man should use a word without an idea.
     Certainly we shall find that w^tever word we make use
     of in matter of pure reasoning has or ought to have a
     compleat Idea annext to it. i.e.: it's meaning or the sense
     we take it in must be compleatly known.

+   Tis demonstrable a Man can never be brought to Imagine   639
     any thing should exist whereof he has no Idea. Whoever
     says he does, banters himself with Words.

G   We Imagine a great difference & distance in respect of   640
     Knowlege, power &c betwixt a Man & a Worm. the like
     distance betwixt Man & God may be Imagin'd. or
     Infinitely greater.

G   We find in our own minds a great Number of different   641
Ideas. We may Imagine in God a Greater Number. i.e.
that Our's in Number or the Number of ours is inconsiderable in respect thereof. The Words difference &
number old & known we apply to that wch is unknown.
but I am embrangled in words. tis scarce possible it should
be otherwise.

        the chief thing I do or pretend to do is onely to remove   642
the mist or veil of Words. This has occasion'd Ignorance
& confusion. This has ruin'd the Scholemen & Mathematicians, Lawyers & Divines.

S   The grand Cause of perplexity & darkness in treating of   643
the Will, is that we Imagine it to be an object of thought
(to speak wth the vulgar), we think we may perceive,
contemplate & view it like any of our Ideas whereas in
truth 'tis no idea. Nor is there any Idea of it. tis toto
coelo different from the Understanding i.e. from all our
Ideas. If you say the will or rather a Volition is something I answer there is an Homonymy in the word thing
w^n apply'd to Ideas & volitions & understanding & will.
all ideas are passive, volitions active.

S   Thing & Idea are much w^t words of the same extent &   644
meaning. why therefore do I not use the word thing?
Answ: because thing is of greater latitude than Idea.
Thing comprehends also volitions or actions. now these
are no ideas.

S   There can be perception w^{th}out volition. Qu: whether   645
there can be volition without perception.

E   Existence not conceivable without perception or volition   646
not distinguish'd therefrom.

T   N.B. severall distinct Ideas can be perceiv'd by Sight &   647
Touch at once. not so by the other senses. 'Tis this
diversity of sensations in other senses chiefly but sometimes in touch & sight (as also diversity of volitions
whereof there cannot be more than one at once, or rather
it seems there cannot for of that I doubt) gives us the Idea
of Time. or is Time it self.

×   W^t would the Solitary Man think of number?   648

S   There are innate Ideas i.e. Ideas created with us.   649

S Locke seems to be mistaken w^n he says thought is not 650
   essential to the mind.

S Certainly the mind always & constantly thinks & we 651
   know this too In Sleep & trances the mind exists not
   there is no time no succession of Ideas.

S To say the mind exists' without thinking is a Contradic- 652
   tion, nonsense, nothing.

S Folly to enquire w^t determines the Will. Uneasiness etc 653
   are Ideas, therefore unactive, therefore can do nothing
   therefore cannot determine the Will.

S Again. w^t mean you by determine? 654

N.T. for want of rightly Understanding, time, motion, existence 655
   etc Men are forc'd into such absurd contradictions as this
   v.g. light moves 16 diameters of Earth in a second of Time.

S Twas the opinion that Ideas could exist unperceiv'd or 656
   before perception that made Men think perception was
   somewhat different from the Idea perceiv'd, y^t it was an
   Idea of Reflexion whereas the thing perceiv'd was an idea
   of Sensation. I say twas this made 'em think the understanding took it in receiv'd it from without wch could
   never be did not they think it existed without.

S To ask have we an idea of ye Will or volition is nonsense. 657
   an idea can resemble nothing but an idea.

M properly speaking Idea is the picture of the Imagination's 657a
   making this is ye likeness of & refer'd to the real Idea or
   (if you will) thing.

S If you ask w^t thing it is that wills. I answer if you mean 658
   Idea by the Word thing or any thing like any Idea, then
   I say tis no thing at all that wills'. This how extravagant soever it may seem yet is a certain truth. we are
   cheated by these general terms, thing, is etc.

S+ Again if by is you mean is perceived or dos' perceive. I 659
   say nothing wch is perceived or does perceive Wills.

S The referring Ideas to things wch are not Ideas, the using 660
   the Term, Idea of, is one great cause of mistake, as in
   other matters so also in this.

S   Some words there are wch do not stand for Ideas v.g.   661
    particles Will etc

S   particles stand for volitions & their concomitant Ideas   661a

+   There seem to be but two Colours wch are simple Ideas.   662
    viz. those exhibited by the most & least refrangible Rays.
    being the Intermediate ones may be formed by com-
    position.

S   I have no Idea of a Volition or act of the mind neither has   663
    any other Intelligence for that were a contradiction.

+   N.B. Simple Ideas viz. Colours are not devoid of all sort   664
    of Composition. tho it must be granted they are not made
    up of distinguishable Ideas. yet there is another sort of
    composition. Men are wont to call those things com-
    pounded in which we do not actually discover the
    component ingredients. Bodies are said to be com-
    pounded of Chymical Principles wch nevertheless come
    not into view till after the dissolution of the Bodies. &
    wch were not could not be discerned in the Bodies whilst
    remaining entire.

S   If by Idea you mean object of the Understanding. Then   665
    certainly the Will is no Idea, or we have no idea annext
    to the word Will.

I   All our knowlege is about particular ideas according to   666
    Locke. All our sensations are particular Ideas as is
    evident. w^t use then do we make of general Ideas, since
    we neither know, nor perceive them.

S   Tis allow'd that Particles stand not for Ideas & yet they   667
    are not said to be empty useless sounds. The truth on't
    is they stand for the operations of the mind i.e. volitions.

Mo. Locke says all our knowledge is about Particulars. if so,   668
    pray w^t is the following ratiocination but a jumble of
    words Omnis Homo est animal, omne animal vivit, ergo
    omnis Homo vivit. it amounts (if you annex particular
    Ideas to the Words animal & vivit) to no more than this.
    Omnis Homo est Homo, omnis Homo est Homo, ergo
    omnis Homo est Homo. A mere Sport & trifling with
    sounds.

Mo   We have no Ideas of vertues & vices, no Ideas of Moral   669
      Actions wherefore it may be Question'd whether we are
      capable of arriving at Demonstration about them, the
      morality consisting in the Volition chiefly.

E   Strange it is that Men should be at a loss to find their Idea   670
      of Existence since that (if such there be distinct from Per-
      ception) it is brought into the mind by all the Ways of
      Sensation & Reflection; methinks it should be most
      familiar to us & we best Acquainted with it.

E   This I am sure I have no such idea of Existence or annext   671
      to the Word Existence. & if others have that's nothing to
      me. they can Never make me sensible of it, simple Ideas
      being uncommunicable by Language.

S   Say you the unknown substratum of Volitions & Ideas,   672
      is somthing whereof I have no Idea. I ask is there any
      other Being wch has or can have an Idea of it. if there be
      then it must be it self an Idea wch you will think absurd.

S   There is somewhat active in most perceptions i.e. such as   672a
      ensue upon our Volitions, such as we can prevent & stop
      v.g. I turn my eyes towards the Sun I open them all this
      is active.

S   Things are two-fold active or inactive, The Existence of   673
      Active things is to act, of inactive to be perceiv'd.

S.E. Distinct from or without perception there is no volition;   674
      therefore neither is their existence without perception.

G   God May comprehend all Ideas even the Ideas wch are   675
      painfull & unpleasant without being in any degree pained
      thereby. Thus we our selves can imagine the pain of a
      burn etc without any misery or uneasiness at all.

N Mo.× Truth. three sorts thereof Natural, Mathematical & Moral.   676

Mo   Agreement of relation onely where Numbers do obtain. of   677
×   Coexistence in nature, of signification or Including or
      thinking by Including in Morality.

I   Gyant who shakes the Mountain that's on him must be   678
      acknowleg'd. I   or rather Thus. I am no more to be
      reckon'd stronger than Locke than a pigmy should be
      reckon'd stronger than a Gyant because he could throw

of the Molehill wch lay upon him, & the Gyant could onely shake or shove the Mountain that oppressed him This in the Preface.

I	Promise to extend our knowlege & clear it of those shamefull Contradictions wch Embarrass it. Something like this to begin the Introduction in a modest way.	679

I Whoever shall pretend to censure any part—I desire He   680
would read out the Whole, else he may perhaps not
understand me.   in the Preface or Introd:

S Doctrine of Identity best explain'd by Taking the Will for   681
Volitions, the Understanding for Ideas. The difficulty of
Consciousness of w^t are never acted etc solv'd hereby.

I I must acknowlege my self beholding to the Philosophers   682
have gone before me. They have given good rules tho
perhaps they do not always observe them. Similitude of
Adventurers who tho they them selves attained not the
desir'd Port, they by their wrecks have made known the
Rocks & sands, whereby the Passage of aftercomers is
made more secure & easy. Pref: or Introd:

Mo The opinion that men had Ideas of Moral actions has   683
render'd the Demonstrating Ethiques very difficult to them.

S An Idea being it self unactive cannot be the resemblance   684
or image of an Active thing.

I Excuse to be made in the Introduction for the using the   685
Word Idea viz. because it has obtain'd. But a Caution
must be added.

Scripture & possibility are the onely proofs with Mal-   686
branch add to these w^t he calls a great propension to
think so. this perhaps may be question'd. perhaps men
if they think before they speak will not be found so
thoroughly perswaded of the Existence of Matter.

M On second thoughts I am, on t'other extream I am   686a
certain of that wch Malbranch seems to doubt of. viz the
existence of Bodies.

I. & c. Mem: to bring the killing blow at the last v.g. in the   687
matter of Abstraction to bring Lockes general triangle at
the last.

I   They give good rules tho perhaps they themselves do not   688
        always observe them. they speak much of clear & distinct
        Ideas. tho at the same they talk of General, abstract ideas
        etc I'll instance in Lockes opinion of abstraction he
        being as clear a writer as I have met with. Such was the
        Candour of this great Man that I perswade my Self were
        he alive. he would not be offended that I differ from him
        seeing that even in so doing. I follow his advice viz. to
        use my own Judgement, see with my own eyes & not
        with anothers. Introd:

S   The word thing as comprising or standing for Idea &   689
        volition usefull. as standing for Idea and Archetype with-
        out the Mind Mischievous & useless.

Mo   To demonstrate Morality it seems one need only make a   690
        Dictionary of Words & see which included which. at least.
        This is the greatest part & bulk of the Work.

IMo.   Lockes instances of Demonstration in Morality are   691
        according to his own Rule trifling Propositions.

P.S.   Qu: How comes it that some Ideas are confessedly allow'd   692
        by all to be onely in the mind, & others as generally taken
        to be without the mind. if according to you All are equally
        only in the mind. Ans. because that in proportion to the
        Pleasure & pain Ideas are attended with desire aversion
        & other actions wch include volition now volition is by all
        grant'd to be in Spirit.

I   If Men would lay aside words in thinking 'tis impossible   693
        they should ever mistake save only in Matters of Fact. I
        mean it seems impossible they should Be positive & secure
        that any thing was true wch in truth is not so. certainly I
        cannot err in matter of simple perception. so far as we
        can in reasoning go without the help of signs there we
        have certain knowlege. indeed in long deductions made
        by signs there may be slips of Memory.

MO.   From my Doctrine there follows a cure for Pride. we are   694
        only to be praised for those things wch are our own, or of
        our own Doing, Natural Abilitys are not consequences
        of Our Volitions.

M   Mem: candidly to take Notice that Locke holds some   695
        dangerous opinions. such as the Infinity & eternity of
        space. The Possibility of Matter's Thinking.

I   Once more I desire my Reader may be upon his guard   696
against the Fallacy of Words, Let him beware that I do
not impose on him by plausible empty talk that common
dangerous way of cheating men into absurditys. Let him
not regard my Words any otherwise than as occasions of
bringing into his mind determin'd significations so far as
they fail of this they are Gibberish, Jargon & deserve not
the name of Language. I desire & warn him not to
expect to find truth in my Book or any where but in his
own Mind. w^{t}ever I see my self tis impossible I can paint
it out in words.

Mo.   N.B. To Consider well w^t is meant by that wch Locke   697
saith Concerning Algebra that it supplys intermediate
Ideas. Also to think of a Method affording the same
use in Morals etc that this doth in Mathematiques.

Mo   Homo is not proved to be Vivens by means of any inter-   698
×   mediate Idea. I dont fully agree wth Locke in w^t he says
concerning Sagacity in finding out Intermediate Ideas in
Matter capable of Demonstration & the use thereof; as
if that were the onely Means of Improving & enlarging
Demonstrative Knowlege.

S   There is a difference betwixt Power & Volition. There   699
may be volition without Power. But there can be no
Power without Volition. Power implyeth volition & at the
same time a Connotation of the Effect's following the
Volition.

M.S.   We have assuredly an Idea of substance. twas absurd of   700
Locke to think we had a name without a Meaning. this
might prove Acceptable to the Stillingfleetians.

M.S.   The substance of Body we know, the substance of Spirit   701
we do not know it not being knowable. it being purus
actus.

I   Words have ruin'd & over run all the Sciences, Law   702
Physique Chymistry, Astrology. etc

I   Abstract Ideas only to be had amongst the Learned. The   703
Vulgar never think they have any such, nor truly do they
find any want of them. Genera & Species & abstract
Ideas are terms unknown to them.

S   Locke's out. The case is different. we can have an Idea   704
of Body without motion, but not of Soul without Thought.

Mo.   God Ought to be worship'd. This Easily demonstrated   705
      when once we ascertain the signification of the word God,
      worship, ought.

S   No Perception according to Locke is active. Therefore   706
      no perception (i.e. no Idea) can be the image of or like
      unto that wch is altogether active & not at all passive
      i.e. the Will.

S   I can will the calling to mind somthing that is past, tho 707
      at the same time that wch I call to mind was not in my
      thoughts before that Volition of mine, & consequently I
      could have had no uneasiness for the want of it.

S   The will & the Understanding may very well   708
      be thought two distinct beings.

S   Sed quia voluntas raro agit nisi ducente desiderio. v.   709
      Locke's Epistles p. 479 ad Limburgum.

¹×³   You cannot say the M.T. is like or one with the M.V.   710
      because they be both Minima, just perceiv'd & next door
      to nothing. You may as well say the M.T. is the same
      with or like unto a sound so small that it is scarce per-
      ceiv'd.

+   Extension seems to be a Mode of some tangible or   711
      sensible quality according as it is seen or felt.

S   The Spirit the Active thing that wch is Soul & God   712
      is the Will alone The Ideas are effects impotent things.

S   The Concrete of the Will & understanding I must call   713
      Mind not person, lest offence be given, there being but one
      volition acknowleged to be God. Mem: Carefully to
      omit Defining of Person, or making much mention of it.

S   You ask do these volitions make one Will. w^t you ask is   714
      meerly about a Word. Unite being no more.

      N.B. To use utmost Caution not to give the least Handle   715
      of offence to the Church or Church-men.

I   Even to speak somwhat favourably of the Schoolmen &   716
      shew that they who blame them for Jargon are not free
      from it themselves. Introd:

Introd Locke's great oversight seems to be that he did not 717
Begin wth his Third Book at least that he had not some
thought of it at first. Certainly the 2 1st books don't
agree wth w^t he says in ye 3d.

M If Matter is once allow'd to exist Clippings of beards & 718
parings of nails may Think for ought that Locke can tell
Tho he seems positive of the Contrary.

Since I say men cannot mistake in short reasoning about 719
things demonstrable if they lay aside words. it will be
expected This treatise will Contain nothing but w^t is
certain & evident Demonstration. & in truth I Hope you
will find nothing in it but w^t is such. certainly I take it
all for such. Introd:

I When I say I will reject all Propositions wherein I know 720
not fully & adequately & clearly so far as knowable the
Thing meant thereby This is not to be extended to propositions in the Scripture. I speak of Matters of Reason
& Philosophy not Revelation, In this I think an Humble
Implicit faith becomes us just (where we cannot comprehend & Understand the proposition) such as a popish
peasant gives to propositions he hears at Mass in Latin.
This proud men may call blind, popish, implicit, irrational.
for my part I think it more irrational to pretend to dispute
at cavil & ridicule holy mysteries i.e. propositions about
things out of our reach that are altogether above our
knowlege out of our reach. w^n I shall come to plenary
knowlege of the meaning of any Text then I shall yield an
explicit belief. Introd.

Complexation of Ideas twofold. y^s refers to colours being 721
complex Ideas.

× Cōsidering length without breadth is considering any 722
length be the Breadth w^t it will.

M I may say earth, plants etc were created before Man 723
there being other intelligences to perceive them before
Man was created.

M There is a Philosopher who says we can get an idea of 724
substance by no way of Sensation or Reflection. & seems
to imagine that we want a sense proper for it. Truly if
we had a new sense it could only give us a new Idea.
now I suppose he will not say substance according to him

is an Idea. for my part I own I have no Idea can
stand for substance in his or yᵉ Schoolmen's sense of
that word. But take it in the common vulgar sense &
then we see & feel substance.

E   N.B. That not common usage but the Schools coined   725
       the Word Existence supposed to stand for an abstract
       general Idea.

¹×   Writers of Optics mistaken in their principles both in   726
       judging of Magnitudes & distances.

I   Tis evident yᵗ wⁿ the Solitary man should be taught to   727
       speak the words would give him no other new Ideas (save
       only the sounds) beside wᵗ he had before. If he had not
       could not have an abstract Idea before, he cannot have it
       after he is taught to speak.

I   & complex Ideas wᶜʰ tho' unknown before may be signi-   727a
       fy'd by Language.

Mo   Homo est Homo etc comes at last to Petrus est Petrus etc   728
       Now if these identical Propositions are sought after in the
       Mind they will not be found. there are no identical mental
       Propositions tis all about sounds & terms.

Mo   Hence we see the Doctrine of Certainty by Ideas & prov-   729
       ing by intermediate Ideas comes to Nothing.

MO   We may have certainty & knowlege without Ideas Λ.   730

Mo   Λ i.e without other Ideas than the Words & their standing   730a
       for one idea i.e. their being to be used indifferently.

*   It seems to me that we have no certainty about Ideas.   731
Mo   but onely about words. tis improper to say I am certain
       I see, I feel etc. there are no Mental propositions form'd
       answering to these Words & in simple perception tis
       allowed by all there is no affirmation or negation &
       consequently no certainty.

*   this seems wrong certainty real certainty is of sensible Ideas   731a
       pro hic & nunc. I may be certain without affirmation
       or negation.

Mo   The reason why we can demonstrate so well about signs   732
×   is that they are perfectly arbitrary & in our power, made
       at pleasure.

Mo   The Obscure ambiguous term Relation wch is said to be   733
×   the largest field of Knowlege confounds us, deceives us.

Mo   Let any Man shew me a Demonstration not verbal that   734
×   does not depend either on some false principle or at best
×   on some principle of Nature which is ye effect of God's
will and we know not how soon it may be changed.

I   Qu: w^t becomes of the aeternae veritates? Ans^r they   735
vanish.

I   But say you I find it very difficult to look beneath the   736
words & uncover my Ideas. Say I use will make it easy.
In the sequel of My Book the Cause of this difficulty shall
be more clearly made out.

I   To view the deformity of Errour we need onely undress it.   737

E   Cogito ergo sum, Tautology, no mental Proposition.   738
answering thereto.

N   Knowlege or certainty or perception of agreement of   739
Mo   Ideas as to Identity & diversity & real existence Vanisheth
×   of relation becometh meerly Nominal of Coexistence
remaineth. Locke thought in this later our knowlege
was little or nothing whereas in this onely real knowlege
seemeth to be found.

PM   We must wth the Mob place certainty in the senses.   740

+   Tis a mans duty, tis the fruit of friendship, to speak well   741
of his friend, wonder not therefore that I do w^t I do.

I   A Man of slow Parts may overtake Truth &c Introd: 742
Even my shortsightedness might perhaps be aiding to me
in this Matter, twill make me bring the object nearer to
my thoughts. A Purblind Person etc Introd:

S   Locke to Limborch etc Talk of Judicium Intellectus   743
preceding the Volition   I think Judicium includes
Volition I can by no means distinguish these Judicium,
Intellectus, indifferentia, Uneasiness so many things
accompanying or preceding every Volition as e.g. the
motion of my hand.

S   Qu: w^t mean you by My perceptions, my Volitions?   744
Res, all the perceptions I perceive or conceive etc are
mine, all the Volitions I am Conscious to are mine.

S   Homo est agens liberum. w^t mean they by Homo &   745
     agens in this place?

E   Will any man say that Brutes have ye ideas, unity & Exis-   746
     tence? I believe not. yet if they are suggested by all the
     ways of sensation, tis strange they should want them.

I   It is a strange thing & deserves our attention, that the   747
     more time & pains men have consum'd in the study of
     Philosophy by so much the more they look upon them-
     selves to be ignorant & weak Creatures, they discover
     flaws & imperfections in their Faculties wch Other Men
     never spy out. they find themselves under a Necessity of
     admitting many inconsistent irreconcilable opinions for
     true. There is nothing they touch with their hand or
     behold with their eyes but has its dark sides much larger
     & more numerous than w^t is perceiv'd. & at length turn
     scepticks at least in most things etc I imagine all this
     proceeds from etc   Exord: Introd:

I   These men with a supercilious Pride disdain the common   748
     single informations of sense. they grasp at Knowlege by
     sheaves & bundles ('tis well if catching at two much at
     once they hold nothing but emptyness & air). they in y^e
     depths of their understanding Contemplate Abstract Ideas.
     etc Introduction

¹×² It seems not improbable that the most comprehensive &   749
     sublime Intellects see more M.V.s at once i.e. that their
     Visual spheres are the largest.

×   Words (by them meaning all sorts of signs) are so neces-   750
     sary that instead of being (w^n duly us'd or in their own
     Nature) prejudicial to the Advancement of knowlege,
     or an hindrance to knowlege that w^thout them there could
     in Mathematiques themselves be no demonstration.

     Mem: To be eternally banishing Metaphisics &c   751
     & recalling Men to Common Sense.

S   We cannot Conceive other Minds besides our own but as   752
     so many selves. We suppose ourselves affected wth such
     & such thoughts & such & such sensations.

S.I. Qu: whether Composition of Ideas be not that faculty   753
      which chiefly serves to discriminate us from Brutes. I
      question whether a Brute does or can imagine a Blue
      Horse or Chimera.

N   Naturalists do not distinguish betwixt Cause & occasion.   754
      Useful to enquire after coexisting Ideas or occasions.

Mo.   Morality may be Demonstrated as mixt Mathematics.   755

S   Perception is passive but this not distinct from Idea   756
      therefore there can be no Idea of volition.

M   Why I use not the Word thing instead of Idea? Introd.   757

×   Algebraic Species or letters are denominations   758
      of Denominations, therefore Arithmetic to be treated of
      before Algebra.

×   2 Crowns are called ten shillings hence may appear the   759
      nature of Numbers.

×   Complex Ideas are the Creatures of the Mind. hence may   760
      appear the Nature of Numbers. this to be deeply dis-
      cuss'd.

×   I am better inform'd & shall know more by telling me   761
      there are 10000 men than by shewing me them all drawn
      up. I shall better be able to judge of the Bargain you'd
      have me make w^n you tell me how much (i.e. the name
      of y^e) mony lies on ye Table than by offering & shewing
      it without naming. In short I regard not the Idea the
      looks but the names. hence may appear the Nature of
      Numbers.

×   Children are unacquainted with Numbers till they have   762
      made some Progress in language. This could not be if
      they were Ideas suggested by all the senses.

×   Numbers are nothing but Names, meer Words.   763

×   Mem: Imaginary roots to unravel that Mystery.   764

×   Ideas of Utility are annexed to Numbers.   765

×   In Arithmetical Problems Men seek not any Idea   766
      of Number. they onely seek a Denomination. this is all
      can be of use to them.

×   Take away the signs from Arithmetic & Algebra, & pray   767
      w^t remains?

×   These are sciences purely Verbal, & entirely useless but   768 for Practise in Societys of Men. No speculative knowlege, no comparing of Ideas in them.

Mo.   **Sensual Pleasure is the Summum Bonum. This the**   769
               Great Principle of Morality. This once rightly under-
               stood all the Doctrines even the severest of the Gospels
               may cleerly be Demonstrated.

×   Qu: whether Geometry may not be properly reckon'd,   770
               among the Mixt Mathematics. Arithmetic and Algebra
               being the only abstracted pure i.e. entirely Nominal.
               Geometry being an application of these to Points.

× Mo   Locke of Trifling Propositions. Mem: well to observe &   771
               con over that chapter.

E. ×   Existence, Extension etc are abstract i.e. no ideas. they   772
               are words unknown & useless to the Vulgar.

Mo.   **Sensual Pleasure qua Pleasure is Good & desirable by a**   773
               Wise Man. but if it be Contemptible tis not quâ pleasure
               but qua pain or Cause of pain. or (wch is the same thing)
               of loss of greater pleasure.

I   W^n I consider the more objects we see at once the more   774
               distant they are, & that Eye wch beholds a great many
               things can see none of them near.

I.M.   By Idea I mean any sensible or imaginable thing.   775

S   Agreeable to my Doctrine of Certainty. He that acts not   776
               in order to the obtaining of eternal Happyness must be an
               infidel at least he is not certain of a future Judgement.

S   To be sure or certain of w^t we do not actually perceive   777
               (I say perceive not imagine) We must not be altogether
               Passive, there must be a disposition to act, there must be
               assent, wch is active, nay w^t do I talk There must be
               Actual Volition:

×   W^t do we demonstrate in Geometry but that lines are   778
               equal or unequal i.e. may or may not be called by the
               same name?

I.M.   I approve of this axiom of the Schoolemen nihil est in   779
               intellectu quod non prius fuit in sensu. I wish they had
               stuck to it. it had never taught them the Doctrine of
               Abstract Ideas.

S.G.   Nihil dat quod non habet or the effect is contained in   780
ye Cause is an axiom I do not Understand or believe to
be true.

E   Whoever shall cast his eyes on the writings of Old or New   781
Philosophers & see the Noise is made about formal &
objective Being Will etc.

G   Absurd to Argue the Existence of God from his Idea.   782
we have no Idea of God. tis impossible!

M.E.   Cause of much errour & Confusion that Men Knew not.   783
w^t was meant by Reality.

I   Descartes in Med: 2. say's the Notion of this particular   784
wax is less clear than that of Wax in General. & in the
same Med: a little before he forbears to Consider Bodies
in general because (says he) these General Conceptions
are usually confused.

M.S.   Descartes in Med: 3 Calls himself a thinking substance   785
& a stone an extended substance. & adds that they both
agree in this that they are substances. & in the next
paragraph he Calls extension a Mode of substance.

S   Tis commonly said by the Philosophers that if the soul   786
of Man were self existent it would have given it self all
possible perfection. this I do not understand.

Mo   Mem. to excite men to the pleasures of the Eye & the   787
Ear wch surfeit not, nor bring those evils after them as
others.

S   We see no variety or difference betwixt the Volitions, only   788
between their effects. Tis One Will one Act distinguish'd
by the effects. This will, this Act is the Spirit, operative
Principle, Soul etc.

     No mention of fears & jealousies, nothing like a party.   789

M.   Locke in his 4th book & Descartes in Med. 6. use the same   790
argument for the Existence of objects viz. that sometimes
we see feel etc against our will.

S   While I exist or have any Idea I am eternally, constantly   791
willing, my acquiescing in the present State is willing.

E The Existence of any thing imaginable is nothing different 792
from Imagination or perception. Volition or Will wch is
not imaginable regard must not be had to its' existence at
least in the first Book.

Mo. There are four sorts of Propositions. Gold is a Metall, 793
Gold is yellow; Gold is fixt, ∧ Gold is not a stone. of
wch ye 1st 2nd & 3d are only Nominal & have no mental
propositions answering them.

Also of non-coexistence as Gold is not blue. 793a

M Mem. in vindication of the senses effectually to confute 794
w^t Descartes saith in ye last par. of the last Med: viz.
that the senses oftener inform him falsly than truely.
That sense of pain tells me not my foot is bruised or
broken but I having frequently observed these two Ideas
viz of that peculiar pain & bruised foot go together do
erroneously take them to be inseparable by a necessity of
Nature as if Nature were any thing but the Ordinance
of the free Will of God.

M.S. Descartes owns we know not a substance immediately 795
by it self but by this alone that it is the subject of several
acts. Answer to 2d objection of Hobbs.

S Hobbs in some degree falls in wth Locke saying thought 796
is to the Mind or him self as dancing to the Dancer.
object:

S Hobbs in his object. 3. ridicules those expressions of the 797
Scholastiques the Will wills etc so does Locke. I am
of another Mind.

S Descartes in answer to Object: 3. of Hobbs owns he is 798
distinct from thought as a thing from its modus or manner.

E.S. Opinion that existence was distinct from perception of 799
Horrible Consequence it is the foundation of Hobbs's
doctrine. etc.

M.P.E. Malbranch in his Illustration differs widely from me He 800
doubts of the existence of Bodies I doubt not in the least
of this.

P I differ from the Cartesians in that I make extension, 801

Colour etc to exist really in Bodies & independent of Our
Mind. All ye carefully & lucidly to be set forth.

M.P. Not to mention the Combinations of Powers but to say   802
the things the effects themselves to really exist even w^n not
actually perceiv'd but still with relation to perception.

× The great use of the Indian figures above the Roman   803
shews Arithmetic to be about Signs not Ideas, or not
Ideas different from the Characters themselves.

Mo.× Reasoning there may be about things or Ideas Actions   804
N but Demonstration can be only Verbal. I question, no
matter etc

G Quoth Descartes the Idea of God is not made by me   805
for I can neither add to nor subtract from it. No more
can he add to or take from any other Idea even of his
own making.

S The not distinguishing twixt Will & Ideas is a Grand   806
Mistake wth Hobbs. He takes those things for nothing
wch are not Ideas.

M. Say you, at this rate all's nothing but Idea meer   807
phantasm. I answer every thing as real as ever. I hope
to call a thing Idea makes it not the less real. truly I
should perhaps have stuck to ye word thing and not mention'd the Word Idea were it not for a Reason & I think
a good one too wch I shall give in ye Second Book.

I.S. Idea is ye object or Subject of thought; y^t I think on   808
w^{t}ever it be, I call Idea. thought it self, or Thinking is no
Idea tis an act i.e. Volition i.e. as contradistinguish'd to
effect, the Will.

I.Mo. Locke in B.4.c.5. assigns not ye right cause why Mental   809
Propositions are so difficult. it is not because of Complex
but because of abstract Ideas. ye Idea of a Horse is as
Complex as that of Fortitude. yet in saying ye Horse is
White I form a Mental Proposition with ease but w^n I
say Fortitude is a Vertue I shall find a Mental proposition
hardly or not at all to be come at.

S Pure Intellect I understand not.   810

Locke is in ye right in those things wherein He differs   811
from ye Cartesians & they cannot but allow of his

opinions if they stick to their own principles or cant of
Existence & other abstract Ideas.

G.S. The propertys of all things are in God i.e. there is in the   812
Deity Understanding as well as Will. He is no Blind
agent & in truth a blind Agent is a Contradiction.

G I am certain there is a God, tho I do not perceive him   813
have no intuition of him. this not difficult if we rightly
understand w^t is meant by certainty.

S It seems that the Soul taken for the Will is immortal,   814
Incorruptible

S Qu: whether perception must of necessity precede volition?   815

S.Mo. Errour is not in the Understanding but in ye Will. w^t I   816
understand or perceive, that I understand there can be no
Errour in this.

Mo. Mem: to take notice of Lockes Woman afraid of a   817
N. wetting in ye Introd: to shew there may be reasoning
about Ideas or things.

M. Says Descartes & Malbranch God hath given us strong   818
inclinations to think our Ideas proceed from Bodies. or
that Bodies do exist. Pray w^t mean they by this.
Would they have it that the Ideas of imagination are
images of & proceed from the Ideas of Sense. this is true
but cannot be their meaning for they speak of Ideas of
sense themselves as proceeding from being like unto I
know not w^t.

M.S. Cartesius per Ideam Vult omne id quod habet esse ob-   819
jectivum in Intellectu. V. Tract: de Methodo.

S Qu: may not there be an Understanding without a Will.   820

S Understanding is in some sort an Action.   821

S Silly of Hobbs etc to speak of ye Will as if it were Motion   822
wth wch it has no likeness.

M. Ideas of Sense are the Real things or Archetypes. Ideas of   823
Imagination, Dreams etc. are copies, images of those.

M. My Doctrines rightly understood all that Philosophy of   824
    Epicurus, Hobbs, Spinoza etc wch has been a Declared
    Enemy of Religion Comes to ye Ground.

G. Hobbs & Spinosa make God Extended. Locke also   825
    seems to do the same.

I.E. Ens, res, aliquid dicuntur termini transcendentales.   826
    Spinosa p. 76.prop.40.Eth.part.2.gives an odd account
    of their original. also of the original of all Universals
    Homo, Canis etc:

G. Spinosa (vid:Pref.oper:Posthum:) will Have God to be   827
    Omnium Rerum Causa immanens & to countenance this
    produces that of St. Paul, in him we live etc. Now this
    of St. Paul may be explain'd by my Doctrine as well as
    Spinosa's or Locke's or Hobbs' or Raphson's etc.

S   The Will is purus actus or rather pure Spirit not   828
    imaginable, not sensible, not intelligible, in no wise the
    object of ye Understanding, no wise perceivable.

S. Substance of a Spirit is that it acts, causes, wills,   829
    operates, or if you please (to avoid the quibble y^t may
    be made on ye word it) to act, cause, will, operate it's
    substance is not knowable not being an Idea.

G. Why may we not conceive it possible for God to create   830
    things out of Nothing. certainly we our selves create in
    some wise whenever we imagine.

G.N. Ex nihilo nihil fit. this (saith Spinoza op:posth:p 464) & ye 831
    like are called veritates aeternae because nullam fidem
    habent extra mentem. to make this axiom have a positive
    signification, one should express it thus. Every Idea has a
    Cause i.e. is produced. by a Will.

P. The Philosophers Talk much of a distinction twixt   832
    absolute & relative things, or twixt things consider'd in
    their own nature & the same things considered with
    respect to us. I know not w^t they mean by things con-
    sider'd in themselves. This is nonsense, Jargon.

S   It seems there can be no perception, no Idea without   833
    Will, being there are no Ideas so indifferent but one
    had rather Have them than annihilation, or annihilation
    than them. or if there be such an equall Ballance there

must be an equal mixture of pleasure & pain to Cause
it. there being No Ideas perfectly void of all pain &
uneasiness But w^t are preferable to annihilation.

×   Recipe in animum tuum per cogitationem vehementem   834
rerum ipsarum non literarum aut sonorum imagines.
Hobbs against Wallis.

×   Tis a perfection we may imagine in superior spirits that   835
they can see a great deal at once with the Utmost
Clearness & distinction whereas we can only see a point.

M.   Treating of Matter I had better say the proportion   836
& Beauty of Things than their species (wch Locke hath
proved already) are the Workmanship of the Mind.

×   Mem: w^n I treat of Mathematiques to enquire into   837
ye Controversy twixt Hobbes & Wallis.

G.   Every sensation of mine wch happens in Consequence   838
of the general, known Laws of nature & is from without
i.e. independent of my Will demonstrates the Being of a
God. i.e. of an unextended incorporeal Spirit wch is
omniscient, omnipotent etc.

Mo.   One great Cause of Miscarriage in Men's affairs is that   839
they too much regard the Present.

M.   I say not with J.S. that we see solids I reject his Solid   840
Philosophy. Solidity being only perceived by touch.

S   It seems to me that Will & understanding Volitions   841
& ideas cannot be severed, that either cannot be possibly
without the other.

E.S.   Some Ideas or other I must have so long as I exist or Will.   842
But no one Idea or sort of Ideas is essential.

M.   The distinction between Idea & Ideatum I cannot   843
otherwise conceive than by making one the effect or
consequence of Dream, rêverie, Imagination the other
of sense & the Constant laws of Nature.

P.   Dico quod Extensio non concipitur in se & per se contra   844
quam dicit Spinoza in ep: 1^a ad Oldenburgium.

G.   My Definition of ye Word God I think Much clearer   845

than that of Descartes & Spinoza viz. ens summè per-
fectum, & absolute Infinitum or ens constans infinitis
attributis quorum unumquodque est infinitum.

× . Tis chiefly the Connexion betwixt Tangible & Visible   846
     Ideas that deceives & not the visible Ideas themselves.

S.   But the Grand Mistake is that we know not w^t we   847
     mean by we oûr selves, our mind etc. tis most sure &
     certain that our Ideas are distinct from the Mind i.e. the
     Will, the Spirit.

S.   I must not Mention the Understanding as a faculty or   848
     part of the Mind, I must include Understanding &
     Will etc in the word Spirit by wch I mean all that is
     active. I must not say that the Understanding differs
     not from the particular Ideas, or the Will from particular
     Volitions.

S   The Spirit, the Mind, is neither a Volition nor an Idea. 849

N.S. I say there are no Causes (properly speaking) but   850
     Spiritual, nothing active but Spirit. Say you, this is
     only Verbal, tis only annexing a new sort of signification
     to the word Cause, & why may not others as well retain
     the old one, & call one Idea the Cause of another w^{ch}
     always follows it. I answer, if you do so, I shall drive you
     into many absuritys. I say you cannot avoid running
     into opinions you'll be glad to disown if you stick firmly
     to that signification of the Word Cause.

Mo. In Valuing Good we reckon too much on ye present   851
     & our own.

Mo. There be two sorts of Pleasure the one is ordain'd as a   852
     spur or incitement to somewhat else & has a visible
     relation & subordination thereto, the other is not. Thus
     the pleasure of eating is of the former sort, of Musick is
     ye later sort. These may be used for recreation, those
     not but in order to their End.

Mo. Three sorts of usefull knowlege, that of coexistence to be 853
N.   treated of in our Principles of Natural Philosophy,
×   that of Relation in Mathematiques, that of definition, or
     inclusion, or Words (wch perhaps differs not from that of
     Relation) in Morality.

S   Will, Understanding, desire, Hatred etc so far forth as   854
        they are acts or active differ not, all their difference
        consists in their objects, circumstances etc.

N.   We must carefully distinguish betwixt two sorts of Causes   855
        Physical & Spirituall;

N.   Those may more properly be Called occasions yet (to   856
        comply) we may term them Causes. but then we must
        mean Causes y^t do nothing.

S   According to Locke we must be in an Eternal uneasyness   857
        so long as we live, bating the time of sleep or Trance etc.
        for He will have even the Continuance of an action to be
        in his sense an action & so requirs a volition & this an
        uneasiness.

I   I must not pretend to promise much of Demonstration,   858
        I must cancell all passages that look like that sort of
        Pride, that raising of Expectation in my Readers.

I.   If this be the Case, surely a Man had better not Philo-   859
        sophize at all, No more than a Deform'd Person Ought
        to covet to behold himself by the Reflex light of a Mirrour.

I.   Or thus, like Deformed Persons who having beheld   860
        themselves by the reflex light of a Mirrour are displeas'd
        with their Discovery.

M.[1]   What can an Idea be like but another Idea, we can   861
        compare it with Nothing else, a Sound like a Sound, a
        Colour like a Colour.

M.[1]   Is it not nonsense to say a Smell is like a thing wch cannot 862
        be smelt, a Colour is like a thing which cannot be seen.

M.S.   Bodies exist without the Mind i.e. are not the Mind, but   863
        distinct from it. This I allow, the Mind being altogether
        different therefrom.

P.   Certainly we should not see Motion if there was no   864
        diversity of Colours.

P.   Motion is an abstract Idea i.e. there is no such Idea that   865
        Can be conceived by it self.

I   Contradictions cannot be both true. Men are oblig'd to   866
        answer Objections drawn from Consequences. Introd.

S.   The Will & Volition are words not used by the Vulgar, the   867
        Learned are banter'd by their meaning abstract Ideas.

×   Speculative Math: as if a Man was all day making hard   868
        knots on purpose to unty them again.

×¹³²   Tho it might have been otherwise yet it is convenient   869
        the same thing wch is M.V. should be also M.T. or very
        near it.

S   I must not give the Soul or Mind the Scholastique Name   870
        pure act, but rather pure Spirit or active Being.

S   I must not say the Will & Understanding are all one but   871
        that they are both Abstract Ideas i.e. none at all. they
        not being even ratione different from the Spirit, Qua
        faculties, or Active.

S   Dangerous to make Idea & thing terms Convertible, that   872
        were the Way to prove spirits are Nothing.

Mo.×   Qu: whether Veritas stands not for an Abstract Idea.   873

M   Tis plain the Moderns must by their own Principles own   874
        there are no Bodies i.e. no sort of Bodies without the Mind
        i.e. unperceived.

S.G.   Qu: whether the Will can be the object of Prescience or   875
        any knowlege.

P   If there were only one Ball in the World it Could not be   876
        moved. there could be no variety of Appearance.

×   According to the Doctrine of Infinite Divisibility there   877
        must be some smell of a Rose v.g. at an infinite distance
        from it.

M.   Extension tho it exist only in the Mind, yet is no   878
        Property of the Mind, The Mind can exist without it
        tho it cannot without the Mind. But in Book 2 I shall
        at large shew the difference there is betwixt the Soul &
        Body or Extended being:

S   Tis an absurd Question wch Locke puts whether Man be   879
        free to Will?

×   Mem. to enquire into the reason of the Rule for Deter-   880
        mining Questions in Algebra.

×   It has already been observ'd by others that names are no   881
        where of more necessary use than in Numbering.

M.P.*   I will grant you that extension, Colour etc may be said   882
        to be without the Mind in a double respect i.e. as
        independent of our Will & as distinct from the Mind.

MoN×   Certainly it is not impossible but a man may arrive at the   883
        knowlege of all real truth as well without as with Signs
        had he a Memory & imagination most strong &
        capacious. therefore reasoning & science doth not alto-
        gether depend upon Words or Names.

N   I think not that things fall out of necessity, the connexion   884
        of no two Ideas is necessary. 'tis all the result of freedom
        i.e tis all Voluntary.

M.1.   One simple Idea can be the pattern or resemblance only   885
        of another. So far as they differ one cannot resemble
        the other.

M.S.   If a man with his Eyes shut Imagines to Himself the Sun   886
        & firmament you will not say he or his Mind is the Sun or
        Extended. tho Neither sun or firmament be without his
        Mind.

S   Tis strange to find Philosophers doubting & disputing   887
        whether they have Ideas of spiritual things or no. Surely
        tis easy to know. Vid. De Vries de id:In.p.64

S   De Vries will have it that we know the Mind as we do   888
        Hunger not by Idea but sense or Conscientia So will
        Malbranch. This is a vain distinction

Philosophical Correspondence between Berkeley and Samuel Johnson

1729–30
First printed 1929

Samuel Johnson (1696–1772), the 'father of American philosophy', was to become first President of King's College, New York (now Columbia University). The correspondence took place between Stratford, Connecticut, and Newport, Rhode Island.

I JOHNSON TO BERKELEY

Stratford, Sept. 10, 1729

Rev'd Sir:

The kind invitation you gave me to lay before you any difficulties that should occur to me in reading those excellent books which you was pleased to order into my hands, is all the apology I shall offer for the trouble I now presume to give you. But nothing could encourage me to expose to your view my low and mean way of thinking and writing, but my hopes of an interest in that candour and tenderness which are so conspicuous both in your writings and conversation.

These books (for which I stand humbly obliged to you) contain speculations the most surprisingly ingenious I have ever met with; and I must confess that the reading of them has almost convinced me that matter as it has been commonly defined for an unknown Quiddity is but a mere non-entity. That it is a strong presumption against the existence of it, that there never could be conceived any manner of connexion between it and our ideas. That the *esse* of things is only their *percipi*; and that the rescuing us from the absurdities of abstract ideas and the gross notion of matter that have so much obtained, deserves well of the learned world, in that it clears away very many difficulties and perplexities in the sciences.

And I am of opinion that this way of thinking can't fail of prevailing in the world, because it is likely to prevail very much among us in these parts, several ingenious men having entirely come in to it. But there are many others on the other hand that cannot be reconciled to it; tho' of these there are some who have a very good opinion of it and plainly see many happy consequences attending it, on account of which they are well inclined to embrace it, but think they find some difficulties in their way which they can't get over, and some objections not sufficiently answered to their satisfaction. And since you have condescended to give me leave to do so, I will make bold to lay before you sundry things, which yet remain in the dark either to myself or to others, and which I can't account for either to my own, or at least to their satisfaction.

1 The great prejudice that lies against it with some is its repugnancy to and subversion of Sir I. Newton's philosophy in sundry points; to which they have been so much attached that they can't suffer themselves in the

least to call it in question in any instance, but indeed it does not appear to
me so inconsistent therewith as at first blush it did, for the laws of nature
which he so happily explains are the same whether matter be supposed or
not. However, let Sir Isaac Newton, or any other man, be heard only so
far as his opinion is supported by reason:—but after all I confess I have
so great a regard for the philosophy of that great man, that I would gladly
see as much of it as may be, to obtain in this ideal scheme.

2 The objection, that it takes away all subordinate natural causes, and
accounts for all appearances merely by the immediate will of the supreme
spirit, does not seem to many to be answered to their satisfaction. It is
readily granted that our ideas are inert, and can't cause one another, and
are truly only signs one of another. For instance my idea of fire is not the
cause of my idea of burning and of ashes. But inasmuch as these ideas are
so connected as that they seem necessarily to point out to us the relations
of cause and effect, we can't help thinking that our ideas are pictures of
things without our minds at least, tho' not without the Great Mind, and
which are their archetypes, between which these relations do obtain. I
kindle a fire and leave it, no created mind beholds it; I return again and
find a great alteration in the fuel; has there not been in my absence all the
while that gradual alteration making in the archetype of my idea of wood
which I should have had the idea of if I had been present? And is there
not some archetype of my idea of the fire, which under the agency of the
Divine Will has gradually caused this alteration? And so in all other
instances, our ideas are so connected, that they seem necessarily to refer
our minds to some originals which are properly (tho' subordinate) causes
and effects one of another; insomuch that unless they be so, we can't help
thinking ourselves under a perpetual delusion.

3 That all the phenomena of nature, must ultimately be referred to the
will of the Infinite Spirit, is what must be allowed; but to suppose his
immediate energy in the production of every effect, does not seem to
impress so lively and great a sense of his power and wisdom upon our
minds, as to suppose a subordination of causes and effects among the
archetypes of our ideas, as he that should make a watch or clock of ever so
beautiful an appearance and that should measure the time ever so exactly
yet if he should be obliged to stand by it and influence and direct all its
motions, he would seem but very deficient in both his ability and skill in
comparison with him who should be able to make one that would regularly
keep on its motion and measure the time for a considerable while without
the intervention of any immediate force of its author or anyone else impressed upon it.

4 And as this tenet seems thus to abate our sense of the wisdom and
power of God, so there are some that cannot be persuaded that it is
sufficiently cleared from bearing hard on his holiness; those who suppose
that the corrupt affections of our souls and evil practices consequent to
them, are occasioned by certain irregular mechanical motions of our bodies,
and that these motions come to have an habitual irregular bias and tendency by means of our own voluntary indulgence to them, which we might

have governed to better purpose, do in this way of thinking, sufficiently bring the guilt of those ill habits and actions upon ourselves; but if in an habitual sinner, every object and motion be but an idea, and every wicked appetite the effect of such a set of ideas, and these ideas, the immediate effect of the Almighty upon his mind; it seems to follow, that the immediate cause of such ideas must be the cause of those immoral appetites and actions; because he is borne down before them seemingly, even in spite of himself. At first indeed they were only occasions, which might be withstood, and so, proper means of trial, but now they become causes of his immoralities. When therefore a person is under the power of a vicious habit, and it can't but be foreseen that the suggestion of such and such ideas will unavoidably produce those immoralities, how can it consist with the holiness of God to suggest them?

5 It is, after all that has been said on that head, still something shocking to many to think that there should be nothing but a mere show in all the art and contrivance appearing in the structure (for instance) of a human body, particularly of the organs of sense. The curious structure of the eye, what can it be more than merely a fine show, if there be no connection more than you admit of, between that and vision? It seems from the make of it to be designed for an instrument or means of conveying the images of external things to the perceptive faculty within; and if it be not so, if it be really of no use in conveying visible objects to our minds, and if our visible ideas are immediately created in them by the will of the Almighty, why should it be made to seem to be an instrument or medium as much as if indeed it really were so? It is evident, from the conveying of images into a dark room thro' a lens, that the eye is a lens, and that the images of things are painted on the bottom of it. But to what purpose is all this, if there be no connection between this fine apparatus and the act of vision; can it be thought a sufficient argument that there is no connection between them because we can't discover it, or conceive how it should be?

6 There are some who say, that if our sensations don't depend on any bodily organs—they don't see how death can be supposed to make any alteration in the manner of our perception, or indeed how there should be (properly speaking) any separate state of the soul at all. For if our bodies are nothing but ideas, and if our having ideas in this present state does not depend on what are thought to be the organs of sense, and lastly, if we are supposed (as doubtless we must) to have ideas in that state; it should seem that immediately upon our remove from our present situation, we should still be attended with the same ideas of bodies as we have now, and consequently with the same bodies or at least with bodies however different, and if so, what room is there left for any resurrection, properly so-called? So that while this tenet delivers us from the embarrassments that attend the doctrine of a material resurrection, it seems to have no place for any resurrection at all, at least in the sense that word seems to bear in St. John 5; 28, 29.

7 Some of us are at a loss to understand your meaning when you speak of archetypes. You say the being of things consists in their being perceived.

And that things are nothing but ideas, that our ideas have no unperceived archetypes, but yet you allow archetypes to our ideas when things are not perceived by our minds; they exist in, *i.e.* are perceived by, some other mind. Now I understand you, that there is a two-fold existence of things or ideas, one in the divine mind, and the other in created minds; the one archetypal, and the other ectypal; that, therefore, the real original and permanent existence of things is archetypal, being ideas in *mente Divinâ*, and that our ideas are copies of them, and so far forth real things as they are correspondent to their archetypes and exhibited to us, or begotten in us by the will of the Almighty, in such measure and degrees and by such stated laws and rules as He is pleased to observe; that, therefore, there is no unperceived substance intervening between the divine ideas and ours as a medium, occasion or instrument by which He begets our ideas in us, but that which was thought to be the material existence of things is in truth only ideal in the divine mind. Do I understand you right? Is it not therefore your meaning, that the existence of our ideas (*i.e.* the ectypal things) depends upon our perceiving them, yet there are external to any created mind, in the all-comprehending Spirit, real and permanent archetypes (as stable and permanent as ever matter was thought to be), to which these ideas of ours are correspondent, and so that (tho' our visible and tangible ideas are *toto coelo* different and distinct things, yet) there may be said to be external to my mind, in the divine mind, an archetype (for instance of the candle that is before me) in which the originals of both my visible and tangible ideas, light, heat, whiteness, softness, etc., under such a particular cylindrical figure, are united, so that it may be properly said to be the same thing that I both see and feel?

8 If this, or something like it might be understood to be your meaning, it would seem less shocking to say that we don't see and feel the same thing, because we can't dispossess our minds of the notion of an external world, and would be allowed to conceive that, tho' there were no intelligent creature before Adam to be a spectator of it, yet the world was really six days in *archetypo*, gradually proceeding from an informal chaotic state into that beautiful show wherein it first appeared to his mind, and that the comet that appeared in 1680 (for instance) has now, tho' no created mind beholds it, a real existence in the all-comprehending spirit, and is making its prodigious tour through the vast fields of ether, and lastly that the whole vast congeries of heaven and earth, the mighty systems of worlds with all their furniture, have a real being in the eternal mind antecedent to and independent on the perception of created spirit, and that when we see and feel, etc., that that almighty mind, by his immediate *fiat*, begets in our minds (*pro nostro modulo*) ideas correspondent to them, and which may be imagined in some degree resemblances of them.

9 But if there be archetypes to our ideas, will it not follow that there is external space, extension, figure and motion, as being archetypes of our ideas, to which we give these names. And indeed for my part I cannot disengage my mind from the persuasion that there is external space; when I have been trying ever so much to conceive of space as being nothing but

an idea in my mind, it will return upon me even in spite of my utmost efforts, certainly there must be, there can't but be, external space. The length, breadth, and thickness of any idea, it's true, are but ideas; the distance between two trees in my mind is but an idea, but if there are archetypes to the ideas of the trees, there must be an archetype to the idea of the distance between them. Nor can I see how it follows that there is no external absolute height, bigness, or distance of things, because they appear greater or less to us according as we are nearer or remote from them, or see them with our naked eyes, or with glasses; any more than it follows that a man, for instance, is not really absolutely six foot high measured by a two foot rule applied to his body, because divers pictures of him may be drawn some six, some four, some two foot long according to the same measure. Nobody ever imagined that the idea of distance is without the mind, but does it therefore follow that there is no external distance to which the idea is correspondent, for instance, between Rhode Island and Stratford? Truly I wish it were not so great, that I might be so happy as to have a more easy access to you, and more nearly enjoy the advantages of your instructions.

10 You allow spirits to have a real existence external to one another. Methinks, if so, there must be distance between them, and space wherein they exist, or else they must all exist in one individual spot or point, and as it were coincide one with another. I can't see how external space and duration are any more abstract ideas than spirits. As we have (properly speaking) no ideas of spirits, so, indeed, neither have we of external space and duration. But it seems to me that the existence of these must unavoidably follow from the existence of those, insomuch that I can no more conceive of their not being, than I can conceive of the non-existence of the infinite and eternal mind. They seem as necessarily existent independent of any created mind as the Deity Himself. Or must we say there is nothing in Dr. Clarke's argument *a priori*, in his demonstration of the being and attributes of God, or in what Sir Isaac Newton says about the infinity and eternity of God in his *Scholium Generale* to his *Principia*? I should be glad to know your sense of what those two authors say upon this subject.

11 You will forgive the confusedness of my thoughts and not wonder at my writing like a man something bewildered, since I am, as it were, got into a new world amazed at everything about me. These ideas of ours, what are they? Is the substance of the mind the *substratum* to its ideas? Is it proper to call them modifications of our minds? Or impressions upon them? Or what? Truly I can't tell what to make of them, any more than of matter itself. What is the *esse* of spirits?—you seem to think it impossible to abstract their existence from their thinking. *Princ*. p. 143. sec. 98. Is then the *esse* of minds nothing else but *percipere*, as the *esse* of ideas is *percipi*? Certainly, methinks there must be an unknown somewhat that thinks and acts, as difficult to be conceived of as matter, and the creation of which, as much beyond us as the creation of matter. Can actions be the *esse* of anything? Can they exist or be exerted without some being who is the agent? And may not that being be easily imagined to exist without

acting, *e.g.* without thinking? And consequently (for you are there speaking of duration) may he not be said *durare, etsi non cogitet,* to persist in being, tho' thinking were intermitted for a while? And is not this sometimes fact? The duration of the eternal mind, must certainly imply something besides an eternal succession of ideas. May I not then conceive that, tho' I get my idea of duration by observing the succession of ideas in my mind, yet there is a *perseverare in existendo,* a duration of my being, and of the being of other spirits distinct from, and independent of, this succession of ideas.

But, Sir, I doubt I have more than tired your patience with so many (and I fear you will think them impertinent) questions; for tho' they are difficulties with me, or at least with some in my neighbourhood, for whose sake, in part, I write, yet I don't imagine they can appear such to you, who have so perfectly digested your thoughts upon this subject. And perhaps they may vanish before me upon a more mature consideration of it. However, I should be very thankful for your assistance, if it were not a pity you should waste your time (which would be employed to much better purposes) in writing to a person so obscure and so unworthy of such a favour as I am. But I shall live with some impatience till I see the second part of your design accomplished, wherein I hope to see these (if they can be thought such) or any other objections, that may have occurred to you since your writing the first part, obviated; and the usefulness of this doctrine more particularly displayed in the further application of it to the arts and sciences. May we not hope to see logic, mathematics, and natural philosophy, pneumatology, theology and morality, all in their order, appearing with a new lustre under the advantages they may receive from it? You have at least given us to hope for a geometry cleared of many perplexities that render that sort of study troublesome, which I shall be very glad of, who have found that science more irksome to me than any other, tho', indeed, I am but very little versed in any of them. But I will not trespass any further upon your patience. My very humble service to Mr. James and Mr. Dalton, and I am with the greatest veneration,

> Rev'd Sir,
> your most obliged
> and most obedient
> humble servant
> Samuel Johnson

II BERKELEY TO JOHNSON

[Nov. 25, 1729]

Reverend Sir,

The ingenious letter you favoured me with found me very much indisposed with a gathering or imposthumation in my head, which confined me several weeks, and is now, I thank God, relieved. The objections of a candid thinking man to what I have written will always be welcome, and

I shall not fail to give all the satisfaction I am able, not without hopes of convincing or being convinced. It is a common fault for men to hate opposition, and be too much wedded to their own opinions. I am so sensible of this in others that I could not pardon it to myself if I considered mine any further than they seem to me to be true; which I shall the better be able to judge of when they have passed the scrutiny of persons so well qualified to examine them as you and your friends appear to be, to whom my illness must be an apology for not sending this answer sooner.

1 The true use and end of Natural Philosophy is to explain the pheno- mena of nature; which is done by discovering the laws of nature, and reducing particular appearances to them. This is Sir Isaac Newton's method; and such method or design is not in the least inconsistent with the principles I lay down. This mechanical philosophy doth not assign or suppose any one natural efficient cause in the strict and proper sense; nor is it, as to its use, concerned about matter; nor is matter connected there- with; nor doth it infer the being of matter. It must be owned, indeed, that the mechanical philosophers do suppose (though unnecessarily) the being of matter. They do even pretend to demonstrate that matter is proportional to gravity, which, if they could, this indeed would furnish an unanswerable objection. But let us examine their demonstration. It is laid down in the first place, that the momentum of any body is the product of its quantity by its velocity, *moles in celeritatem ducta*. If, therefore, the velocity is given, the momentum will be as its quantity. But it is observed that bodies of all kinds descend in vacuo with the same velocity; therefore the momen- tum of descending bodies is as the quantity or moles, *i.e.* gravity is as matter. But this argument concludes nothing, and is a mere circle. For, I ask, when it is premised that the momentum is equal to the *moles in celeritatem ducta*, how the moles or quantity of matter is estimated? If you say, by extent, the proposition is not true; if by weight, then you suppose that the quantity of matter is proportional to matter; *i.e.* the conclusion is taken for granted in one of the premises. As for absolute space and motion, which are also supposed without any necessity or use, I refer you to what I have already published; particularly in a Latin treatise, *De Motu*, which I shall take care to send to you.

2 Cause is taken in different senses. A proper active efficient cause I can conceive none but Spirit; nor any action, strictly speaking, but where there is Will. But this doth not hinder the allowing occasional causes (which are in truth but signs); and more is not requisite in the best physics, *i.e.* the mechanical philosophy. Neither doth it hinder the admitting other causes besides God; such as spirits of different orders, which may be termed active causes, as acting indeed, though by limited and derivative powers. But as for an unthinking agent, no point of physics is explained by it, nor is it conceivable.

3 Those who have all along contended for a material world have yet acknowledged that *natura naturans* (to use the language of the Schoolmen) is God; and that the divine conservation of things is equipollent to, and in fact the same thing with, a continued repeated creation: in a word, that

conservation and creation differ only in the *terminus a quo*. These are the
common opinions of the Schoolmen; and Durandus,[1] who held the world
to be a machine like a clock, made and put in motion by God, but afterwards continuing to go of itself, was therein particular, and had few
followers. The very poets teach a doctrine not unlike the schools—*Mens
agitat molem* (Virg. *Aeneid* VI). The Stoics and Platonists are everywhere
full of the same notion. I am not therefore singular in this point itself, so
much as in my way of proving it. Further, it seems to me that the power
and wisdom of God are as worthily set forth by supposing Him to act
immediately as an omnipresent infinitely active Spirit, as by supposing
Him to act by the mediation of subordinate causes, in preserving and
governing the natural world. A clock may indeed go independent of its
maker or artificer, inasmuch as the gravitation of its pendulum proceeds
from another cause, and that the artificer is not the adequate cause of the
clock; so that the analogy would not be just to suppose a clock is in
respect of its artist what the world is in respect of its Creator. For aught
I can see, it is no disparagement to the perfections of God to say that all
things necessarily depend on Him as their Conservator as well as Creator,
and that all nature would shrink to nothing, if not upheld and preserved in
being by the same force that first created it. This I am sure is agreeable
to Holy Scripture, as well as to the writings of the most esteemed philosophers; and if it is to be considered that men make use of tools and
machines to supply defect of power in themselves, we shall think it no
honour to the Divinity to attribute such things to Him.

4 As to guilt, it is the same thing whether I kill a man with my hands or
an instrument; whether I do it myself or make use of a ruffian. The
imputation therefore upon the sanctity of God is equal, whether we suppose our sensations to be produced immediately by God, or by the mediation of instruments and subordinate causes, all which are His creatures,
and moved by His laws. This theological consideration, therefore, may be
waved, as leading beside the question; for such I hold all points to be
which bear equally hard on both sides of it. Difficulties about the principle
of moral actions will cease, if we consider that all guilt is in the will, and
that our ideas, from whatever cause they are produced, are alike inert.

5 As to the art and contrivance in the parts of animals, &c., I have
considered that matter in the *Principles of Human Knowledge*, and, if I
mistake not, sufficiently shewn the wisdom and use thereof, considered
as signs and means of information. I do not indeed wonder that on first
reading what I have written, men are not thoroughly convinced. On the
contrary, I should very much wonder if prejudices, which have been many
years taking root, should be extirpated in a few hours' reading. I had no
inclination to trouble the world with large volumes. What I have done was
rather with a view of giving hints to thinking men, who have leisure and
curiosity to go to the bottom of things, and pursue them in their own minds.
Two or three times reading these small tracts, and making what is read the

---

[1] [The reference seems to be to Durand de St. Pourçain (died 1332).—Jessop.]

occasion of thinking, would, I believe, render the whole familiar and easy to the mind, and take off that shocking appearance which hath often been observed to attend speculative truths.

6 I see no difficulty in conceiving a change of state, such as is vulgarly called Death, as well without as with material substance. It is sufficient for that purpose that we allow sensible bodies, *i.e.* such as are immediately perceived by sight and touch; the existence of which I am so far from questioning (as philosophers are used to do), that I establish it, I think, upon evident principles. Now, it seems very easy to conceive the soul to exist in a separate state (*i.e.* divested from those limits and laws of motion and perception with which she is embarrassed here), and to exercise herself on new ideas, without the intervention of these tangible things we call bodies. It is even very possible to apprehend how the soul may have ideas of colour without an eye, or of sounds without an ear.

And now, Sir, I submit these hints (which I have hastily thrown together as soon as my illness gave me leave) to your own maturer thoughts, which after all you will find the best instructors. What you have seen of mine was published when I was very young, and without doubt hath many defects. For though the notions should be true (as I verily think they are), yet it is difficult to express them clearly and consistently, language being framed to common use and received prejudices. I do not therefore pretend that my books can teach truth. All I hope for is, that they may be an occasion to inquisitive men of discovering truth, by consulting their own minds, and looking into their own thoughts. As to the Second Part of my treatise concerning the *Principles of Human Knowledge*, the fact is that I had made a considerable progress in it; but the manuscript was lost about fourteen years ago, during my travels in Italy, and I never had leisure since to do so disagreeable a thing as writing twice on the same subject.

Objections passing through your hands have their full force and clearness. I like them the better. This intercourse with a man of parts and philosophic genius is very agreeable. I sincerely wish we were nearer neighbours. In the meantime, whenever either you or your friends favour me with their thoughts, you may be sure of a punctual correspondence on my part. Before I have done I will venture to recommend these points: (1) To consider well the answers I have already given in my books to several objections. (2) To consider whether any new objection that shall occur doth not suppose the doctrine of abstract general ideas. (3) Whether the difficulties proposed in objection to my scheme can be solved by the contrary; for if they cannot, it is plain they can be no objections to mine.

I know not whether you have got my treatise concerning the *Principles of Human Knowledge*. I intend to send it to you with my tract *De Motu*. My humble service to your friends, to whom I understand I am indebted for some part of your letter.

> I am your faithful humble servant,
> George Berkeley.

III JOHNSON TO BERKELEY

Rev'd Sir:—

Yours of November 25th, I received not till January 17th, and this being the first convenient opportunity I now return you my humblest thanks for it.

I am very sorry to understand that you have laboured under the illness you mention, but am exceeding glad and thankful for your recovery; I pray God preserve your life and health, that you may have opportunity to perfect these great and good designs for the advancement of learning and religion wherewith your mind labours.

I am very much obliged to you for the favourable opinion you are pleased to express at what I made bold to write to you and that you have so kindly vouchsafed so large and particular an answer to it. But you have done me too great an honour in putting any value on my judgment; for it is impossible my thoughts on this subject should be of any consequence, who have been bred up under the greatest disadvantages, and have had so little ability and opportunity to be instructed in things of this nature. And therefore I should be very vain to pretend anything else but to be a learner; 'tis merely with this view that I give you this trouble.

I am sensible that the greatest part of what I wrote was owing to not sufficiently attending to those three important considerations you suggest at the end of your letter: and I hope a little more time and a more careful attention to and application of them, will clear up what difficulties yet lie in the way of our entirely coming into your sentiments. Indeed I had not had opportunity sufficiently to digest your books; for no sooner had I just read them over, but they were greedily demanded by my friends, who live much scattered up and down, and who expected I would bring them home with me, because I had told them before that if the books were to be had in Boston, I intended to purchase a set of them; and indeed they have not yet quite finished their tour. The *Theory of Vision* is still at New York and the *Dialogues* just gone to Long Island. But I am the better content to want them because I know they are doing good.

For my part I am content to give up the cause of matter, glad to get rid of the absurdities thereon depending; if it be defensible, I am sure, at least, it is not in my power to defend it. And being spoiled of that sandy foundation, I only want now to be thoroughly taught how and where to set down my foot again and make out a clear and consistent scheme without it. And of all the particulars I troubled you with before, there remain only these that I have any difficulty about, *viz.*, archetypes, space and duration, and the *esse* of spirits. And indeed these were the chief of my difficulties before. Most of the rest were such objections as I found by conversation among my acquaintance, did not appear to them sufficiently answered. But I believe upon a more mature consideration of the matter, and especially of this kind reply, they will see reason to be better satisfied. They that have seen it (especially my friend Mr. Wetmore) join with me in thankfully acknowledging your kindness, and return their very humble service to you.

1 As to those difficulties that yet remain with me, I believe all my hesitation about the first of them (and very likely the rest) is owing to my dulness and want of attention so as not rightly to apprehend your meaning. I believe I expressed myself uncouthly about archetypes in my 7th and 8th articles, but upon looking back upon your *Dialogues*, and comparing again three or four passages, I can't think I meant anything different from what you intended.

You allow, *Dial*. p. 74, 'That things have an existence distinct from being perceived by us' (*i.e.*, any created spirits), 'and that they exist in, *i.e.* are perceived by, the infinite and omnipresent mind who contains and supports this sensible world as being perceived by him.' And p. 109, 'That things have an existence exterior to our minds, and that during the intervals of their being perceived by us, they exist in another (*i.e.* the infinite) mind'; from whence you justly and excellently infer the certainty of his existence, 'who knows and comprehends all things and exhibits them to our view in such manner and according to such rules as he himself has ordained.' And p. 113, 'That, *e.g.* a tree, when we don't perceive it, exists without our minds in the infinite mind of God.' And this exterior existence of things (if I understand you right) is what you call the archetypal state of things, p. 150.

From those and the like expressions, I gathered what I said about the archetypes of our ideas, and thence inferred that there is exterior to us, in the divine mind, a system of universal nature, whereof the ideas we have are in such a degree resemblances as the Almighty is pleased to communicate to us. And I cannot yet see but my inference was just; because according to you, the ideas we see are not in the divine mind, but in our own. When, therefore, you say sensible things exist in, as being perceived by, the infinite mind I humbly conceive you must be understood that the originals or archetypes of our sensible things or ideas exist independent of us in the infinite mind, or that sensible things exist *in archetypo* in the divine mind. The divine idea, therefore, of a tree I suppose (or a tree in the divine mind), must be the original or archetype of ours, and ours a copy or image of His (our ideas images of His, in the same sense as our souls are images of Him) of which there may be several, in several created minds, like so many several pictures of the same original to which they are all to be referred.

When therefore, several people are said to see the same tree or star, etc., whether at the same or at so many several distances from it, it is (if I understand you) *unum et idem in archetypo*, tho' *multiplex et diversum in ectypo*, for it is as evident that your idea is not mine nor mine yours when we say we both look on the same tree, as that you are not I, nor I you. But in having each our idea, we being dependent upon and impressed upon by the same almighty mind, wherein you say this tree exists, while we shut our eyes (and doubtless you mean the same also, while they are open), our several trees must, I think be so many pictures (if I may so call them) of the one original, the tree in the infinite mind, and so of all other things. Thus I understand you—not indeed that our ideas are in any measure adequate resemblances of the system in the divine mind, but however that they are just and true resemblances or copies of it, so far as He is pleased to communicate His mind to us.

2 As to space and duration, I do not pretend to have any other notion of their exterior existence than what is necessarily implied in the notion we have of God; I do not suppose they are anything distinct from, or exterior to, the infinite and eternal mind; for I conclude with you that there is nothing exterior to my mind but God and other spirits with the attributes or properties belonging to them and ideas contained in them.

External space and duration therefore I take to be those properties or attributes in God, to which our ideas, which we signify by those names, are correspondent, and of which they are the faint shadows. This I take to be Sir Isaac Newton's meaning when he says, *Schol. General. Deus—durat semper et adest ubique et existendo semper et ubique, durationem et spacium, æternitatem et infinitatem constituit.* And in his *Optics* calls space *as it were God's boundless sensorium,* nor can I think you have a different notion of these attributes from that great philosopher, tho' you may differ in your ways of expressing or explaining yourselves. However, it be, when you call the Deity infinite and eternal, and in that most beautiful and charming description, *Dial.* p. 71, etc., when you speak of the *abyss of space and boundless extent* beyond thought and imagination, I don't know how to understand you any otherwise than I understood Sir Isaac, when he uses the like expressions. The truth is we have no proper ideas of God or His attributes, and conceive of them only by analogy from what we find in ourselves; and so, I think we conceive His immensity and eternity to be what in Him are correspondent to our space and duration.

As for the *punctum stans* of the Schools, and the τὸ νῦν of the Platonists, they are notions too fine for my gross thoughts; I can't tell what to make of those words, they don't seem to convey any ideas or notions to my mind, and whatever the matter is, the longer I think of them, the more they disappear, and seem to dwindle away into nothing. Indeed they seem to me very much like abstract ideas, but I doubt the reason is because I never rightly understood them. I don't see why the term *punctum stans* may not as well, at least, be applied to the immensity as the eternity of God; for the word *punctum* is more commonly used in relation to extension or space than duration; and to say that a being is immense, and yet that it is but a point, and that its duration is perpetual without beginning or end, and yet that it is but a τὸ νῦν, looks to me like a contradiction.

I can't therefore understand the term τὸ νῦν unless it be designed to adumbrate the divine omnisciency or the perfection of the divine knowledge, by the more perfect notion we have of things present than of things past; and in this sense it would imply that all things past, present and to come are always at every point of duration equally perfectly known or present to God's mind (tho' in a manner infinitely more perfect), as the things that are known to us are present to our minds at any point of our duration which we call *now.* So that with respect to His equally perfect knowledge of things past, present or to come, it is in effect always now with Him. To this purpose it seems well applied and intelligible enough, but His duration I take to be a different thing from this, as that point of our duration which we call *now*, is a different thing from our actual knowledge of things, as distinguished from our remembrance. And it may as well be said that God's immensity consists in His knowing at once what is, and is transacted in all places (*e.g.* China, Jupiter, Saturn, all the systems of the fixed stars, etc.) everywhere, however so remote from us (tho' in a manner infinitely more perfect), as we know what is, and is transacted in us and about us just at hand; as that His eternity consists in this τὸ νῦν as above explained, *i.e.* in His knowing things present, past and to come, however so remote, all at once or equally perfectly, as we know the things that are present to us *now*.

In short our ideas expressed by the terms immensity and eternity are only space and duration considered as boundless or with the negation of any limits, and I can't help thinking there is something analogous to them without us, being in and belonging to, or attributes of, that glorious mind, whom for that reason we call immense and eternal, in whom we and all other spirits, *live, move and have our being*, not all in a point, but in so many different points places or *alicubis*, and variously situated with respect one to another, or else as I said before, it seems as if we should all coincide one with another.

I conclude, if I am wrong in my notion of external space, and duration, it is owing to the rivetted prejudices of abstract ideas; but really when I have thought it over and over again in my feeble way of thinking, I can't see any connection between them (as I understand them) and that doctrine. They don't seem to be any more abstract ideas than spirits, for, as I said, I take them to be attributes of the necessarily existing spirit; and consequently the same reasons that convince me of his existence, bring with them the existence of these attributes. So that of the ways of coming to the knowledge of things that you mention, it is that of inference or deduction by which I seem to know that there is external infinite space and duration because there is without me a mind infinite and eternal.

3 As to the *esse* of spirits, I know Descartes held the soul always thinks, but I thought Mr. Locke had sufficiently confuted this notion, which he seems to have entertained only to serve an hypothesis. The Schoolmen, it is true, call the soul *actus* and God *Actus purus*; but I confess I never could well understand their meaning, perhaps because I never had opportunity to be much versed in their writings. I should have thought the Schoolmen to be of all sorts of writers the most unlikely to have had recourse to for the understanding of your sentiments, because they of all others, deal the most in abstract ideas; tho' to place the very being of spirits in the mere act of thinking, seems to me very much like making abstract ideas of them.

There is certainly something passive in our souls, we are purely passive in the reception of our ideas; and reasoning and willing are actions of something that reasons and wills, and therefore must be only modalities of that something. Nor does it seem to me that when I say (something) I mean an abstract idea. It is true I have no idea of it, but I feel it; I feel that it is, because I feel or am conscious of the exertions of it; but the exertions of it are not the thing but the modalities of it, distinguished from it as actions from an agent, which seem to me distinguishable without having recourse to abstract ideas.

And therefore when I suppose the existence of a spirit while it does not actually think, it does not appear to me that I do it by supposing an abstract idea of existence, and another of absolute time. The existence of John asleep by me, without so much as a dream is not an abstract idea, nor is the time passing the while an abstract idea, they are only partial considerations of him. *Perseverare in existendo* in general, without reflecting on any particular thing existing, I take to be what is called an abstract idea of time or duration; but the *perseverare in existendo* of John is, if I mistake not, a partial consideration of him. And I think it is as easy to conceive of him as continuing to exist without thinking as without seeing.

Has a child no soul till it actually perceives? And is there not such a thing as sleeping without dreaming, or being in a *deliquium* without a thought? If there be, and yet at the same time the *esse* of a spirit be nothing else but its actual thinking, the soul must be dead during those intervals; and if ceasing or intermitting to think be the ceasing to be, or death of the soul, it is many times and easily put to death. According to this tenet, it seems to me the soul may sleep on to the resurrection, or rather may wake up in the resurrection state, the next moment after death. Nay I don't see upon what we can build any natural argument for the soul's immortality. I think I once heard you allow a principle of perception and spontaneous motion in beasts. Now if their *esse* as well as ours consists in perceiving, upon what is the natural immortality of our souls founded that will not equally conclude in favour of them? I mention this last consideration because I am at a loss to understand how you state the argument for the soul's natural immortality; for the argument from thinking to immaterial and from thence to indiscerptible, and from thence to immortal don't seem to obtain in your way of thinking.

If *esse* be only *percipere,* upon what is our consciousness founded? I perceived yesterday, and I perceive now, but last night between my yesterday's and today's perception there has been an intermission when I perceived nothing. It seems to me there must be some principle common to these perceptions, whose *esse* don't depend upon them, but in which they are, as it were, connected, and on which they depend, whereby I am and continue conscious of them.

Lastly, Mr. Locke's argument (B. 2. Ch. 19. Sec. 4.) from the intention and remission of thought, appears to me very considerable; according to which, upon this supposition, the soul must exist more or have a greater degree of being at one time than at another, according as it thinks more intensely or more remissly.

I own I said very wrong when I said I did not know what to make of ideas more than of matter. My meaning was, in effect, the same as I expressed afterwards about the substance of the soul's being a somewhat as unknown as matter. And what I intended by those questions was whether our ideas are not the substance of the soul itself, under so many various modifications, according to that saying (if I understand it right) *Intellectus intelligendo fit omnia*? It is true, those expressions (modifications, impressions, etc.) are metaphorical, and it seems to me to be no less so, to say that ideas exist in the mind, and I am under some doubt whether this last way of speaking don't carry us further from the thing, than to say ideas are the mind variously modified; but as you observe, it is scarce possible to speak of the mind without a metaphor.

Thus Sir, your goodness has tempted me to presume again to trouble you once more; and I submit the whole to your correction; but I can't conclude without saying that I am so much persuaded that your books teach truth, indeed the most excellent truths, and that in the most excellent manner, that I can't but express myself again very solicitously desirous that the noble design you have begun may be yet further pursued in the second part. And everybody that has seen the first is earnestly with me in this request. In hopes of which I will not desire you to waste your time in writing to me (tho' otherwise I should esteem it the greatest favour), at least till I have endeavoured further to gain satisfaction by another perusal of the books I have, with the other pieces you are so kind as to offer, which I will thankfully accept, for I had not *The Principles* of my own, it was a borrowed one I used.

The bearer hereof, Capt. Gorham, is a coaster bound now to Boston, which trade he constantly uses (except that it has been now long interrupted by the winter). But he always touches at Newport, and will wait on the Rev'd Mr. Honyman both going and returning, by whom you will have opportunity to send those books.

> I am, Rev'd Sir,
> with the greatest gratitude,
> your most devoted humble servant,
> S. Johnson

Stratford, Feb. 5, 1729/30 [*i.e.* 1730]

IV BERKELEY TO JOHNSON

Reverend Sir,

Yours of Feb. 5th came not to my hands before yesterday; and this afternoon, being informed that a sloop is ready to sail towards your town, I would not let slip the opportunity of returning you an answer, though wrote in a hurry.

1 I have no objection against calling the ideas in the mind of God archetypes of ours. But I object against those archetypes by philosophers supposed to be real things, and to have an absolute rational existence distinct from their being perceived by any mind whatsoever; it being the

opinion of all materialists that an ideal existence in the Divine Mind is one thing, and the real existence of material things another.

2 As to Space. I have no notion of any but that which is relative. I know some late philosophers have attributed extension to God, particularly mathematicians, one of whom,[1] in a treatise, *De Spatio Reali*, pretends to find out fifteen of the incommunicable attributes of God in Space. But it seems to me that, they being all negative, he might as well have found them in Nothing; and that it would have been as justly inferred from Space being impassive, increated, indivisible, etc., that it was Nothing as that it was God.

Sir Isaac Newton supposeth an absolute Space, different from relative, and consequent thereto; absolute Motion different from relative motion; and with all other mathematicians he supposeth the infinite divisibility of the finite parts of this absolute space; he also supposeth material bodies to drift therein. Now, though I do acknowledge Sir Isaac to have been an extraordinary man, and most profound mathematician, yet I cannot agree with him in these particulars. I make no scruple to use the word Space, as well as all other words in common use; but I do not thereby mean a distinct absolute being. For my meaning I refer you to what I have published.

By the τὸ νῦν I suppose to be implied that all things, past and to come, are actually present to the mind of God, and that there is in Him no change, variation, or succession. A succession of ideas I take to *constitute* Time, and not to be only the sensible measure thereof, as Mr. Locke and others think. But in these matters every man is to think for himself, and speak as he finds. One of my earliest inquiries was about Time, which led me into several paradoxes that I did not think fit or necessary to publish; particularly the notion that the Resurrection follows the next moment to death. We are confounded and perplexed about time. (1) Supposing a succession in God. (2) Conceiving that we have an *abstract idea* of Time. (3) Supposing that the Time in one mind is to be measured by the succession of ideas in another. (4) Not considering the true use and end of words, which as often terminate in the will as in the understanding, being employed rather to excite, influence, and direct action, than to produce clear and distinct ideas.

3 That the soul of man is passive as well as active, I make no doubt. Abstract general ideas was a notion that Mr. Locke held in common with the Schoolmen, and I think all other philosophers; it runs through his whole book of Human Understanding. He holds an abstract idea of existence; exclusive of perceiving and being perceived. I cannot find I have any such idea, and this is my reason against it. Descartes proceeds upon other principles. One square foot of snow is as white as a thousand yards; one single perception is as truly a perception as one hundred. Now, any degree of perception being sufficient to Existence, it will not follow that we should say one *existed more* at one time than another, any more

[1] [Joseph Raphson.]

than we should say a thousand yards of snow are whiter than one yard. But, after all, this comes to a verbal dispute. I think it might prevent a good deal of obscurity and dispute to examine well what I have said about abstraction, and about the true sense and significance of words, in several parts of these things that I have published, though much remains to be said on that subject.

You say you agree with me that there is nothing within [*sic*;? without] your mind but God and other spirits, with the attributes or properties belonging to them, and the ideas contained in them.

This is a principle or main point, from which, and from what I had laid down about abstract ideas, much may be deduced. But if in every inference we should not agree, so long as the main points are settled and well understood, I should be less solicitous about particular conjectures. I could wish that all the things I have published on these philosophical subjects were read in the order wherein I published them; once, to take in the design and connexion of them, and a second time with a critical eye, adding your own thought and observation upon every part as you went along.

I send you herewith the bound books and one unbound. You will take yourself what you have not already. You will give the *Principles*, the *Theory*, and the *Dialogues*, one of each, with my service, to the gentleman who is Fellow of Newhaven College, whose compliments you brought to me. What remains you will give as you please.

If at any time your affairs should draw you into these parts, you shall be very welcome to pass as many days as you can spend at my house. Four or five days' conversation would set several things in a fuller and clearer light than writing could do in as many months. In the meantime, I shall be glad to hear from you or your friends, whenever you please to favour,

Reverend Sir,
Your very humble servant,
George Berkeley.

Pray let me know whether they would admit the writings of Hooker and Chillingworth into the library of the College in Newhaven.

Rhode Island, March 24, 1730.

Index